HOPE CHURCH
HOLLAND, MICHIGAN

The First 150 Years
1862—2012

HOPE CHURCH
HOLLAND, MICHIGAN

The First 150 Years
1862—2012

Judy Tanis Parr

Dickinson Press Inc.
Grand Rapids, Michigan

© 2012 by Judy Tanis Parr

All rights reserved. No part of this book may be reproduced, stored in a retrieval system, or transmitted in any form or by any means without prior written permission, except by a reviewer who may quote brief passages in a review.

First printing

Cover design: Christopher Wiers
Cover photo: Dan Joldersma
Author photo: Elizabeth De Bruyn

Hope Church
77 West Eleventh St.
Holland, MI 49423

http://www.hopechurchrca.org

office@hopechurchrca.org

Printed in the United States of America

ISBN: 978-0-615-62553-9

Contents

Illustrations...vii
Preface.. xiii
Acknowledgments... xiv
Introduction: Lost and Found............................. xv

Chapters:
1 The Beginning 1
2 Building and Rebuilding 39
3 Steadily Growing....................................... 87
4 Thriving into the Twentieth Century 131
5 Facing Challenges from 1925 to 1960 177
Insert: Windows and Woodcarving 239
6 Engaging in Social Justice Actions 247
7 Expanding Inclusion.................................. 309

Appendices:
A Consistory Members................................. 383
B Early Members.. 391
C Descendants of Albertus C. and Christina J. De Moen Van Raalte Who Became Members of Hope Church 409
D Music and Administrative Staff................... 417
E Members Who Became RCA Ministers or Missionaries 422
F Hope College – Hope Church Connections................ 430
G Ministers.. 438
H A Historical Digest of Hope Church Cookbooks 444
I Missionaries Supported by Hope Church................ 453
J A Doggie Story....................................... 455
K Chronology... 458

Bibliography... 464
Index 477

Illustrations

All photographs and illustrations are courtesy of the Joint Archives of Holland, Michigan, unless otherwise noted.

Philip Phelps Jr. as a young man 7
Bernardus Ledeboer *(http://www2.cityofholland.com/mayors/2.htm)* 13
Bernardus Grotenhuis 17
Margaret Anna Jordan Phelps as a young woman 19
Frances F. C. Phelps in 1882 21
Frances Phelps Otte celebrating 90 years (Hope Church News) 21
Van Vleck Hall in the nineteenth century 22
Margaret Anna Jordan Phelps in her mature years 24
Five Japanese students gathered for a memorial service in Japan 25
William Brokaw Gilmore 26
Henry Denison Post *(courtesy of the Archives of the
    Holland Historical Trust and Randall P. Vande Water's
    Holland Happenings, Heroes & Hot Shots, vol. 2)* 29
Anna Coatsworth Post *(courtesy of the Archives of the
    Holland Historical Trust)* 33
Mid-nineteenth-century melodeon
    (http://www.oldandsold.com/articles01/article542.shtml) 40
Hope Church's historic chandelier *(photo by Dan Joldersma,
    used by permission of the Holland Historical Trust)* 42
Middle Dutch Church of New York City in the eighteenth century
    (Arie R. Brouwer, Reformed Church Roots*)* 43
Philip Phelps Jr., first president of Hope College 45
Hope Church seal *(Hope Church directory of 1974)* 47
Abel T. Stewart 53
Hope Church's first parsonage *(Dan Joldersma, 2011)* 64
Area burned by the Holland fire of 1871 *(courtesy of Lumir Inc.)* 69
Hope College's first chapel/gymnasium 71
Hope Church of 1874 75
Interior of the 1874 church at 1882 Hope College Commencement 78

Interior of the 1874 church as it appeared in 1942 as a meeting room 79
Drawing of Holland, 1875 *(drawing by D. D. Morse, courtesy of the Archives of the Holland Historical Trust; Reprinted in "Progress '89," Holland Sentinel, 31 January 1989)*................................ 80
Hope Church environs, 1875 *(drawing by D. D. Morse, courtesy of the Archives of the Holland Historical Trust; Reprinted in "Progress '89," Holland Sentinel, 31 January 1989)*................................ 81
Daniel Van Pelt 89
Marietta Schuler Van Olinda 102
Thomas Walker Jones 107
Sketch of Hope College in about 1870.. 109
Phelps's study in Van Vleck Hall..110
Phelps's handwriting of a portion of *Consistorial Minutes*, vol. 1 111
John Tallmadge Bergen..117
Post Block in about 1898 *(Marie Zingle, Woman's Literary Society)*.......118
Gerrit J. Diekema *(http://www2.cityofholland. com/mayors/15.htm)* 120
Oscar Yates *(http://www2.cityofholland.com/mayors/13.htm)*...................... 121
Gerrit J. Kollen... 122
Henry G. Birchby 123
Philip Phelps Jr. in his mature years... 130
John Walter Beardslee.. 135
New York City's West End Collegiate Church, built in 1893 *(http://www.nytimes.com/2009/02/01/realestate/01scape.html)* 136
Vleeshal of Grote Markt, Haarlem, the Netherlands *(http://en.wikipedia.org/wiki/File:Vleeshal_Haarlem.jpg)*...................... 136
Front of Hope Church under construction in about 1900 136
Hope Church in the early twentieth century 137
Interior of Hope Church, 1901... 138
John M. Van der Meulen 146
Willis J. Hoekje, missionary to Japan 147
Edward Niles *(Second Presbyterian Church, Baltimore, Maryland)*............ 149
August F. Bruske 151
Peter P. Cheff... 153
Willard G. Leenhouts *(http://www.hollandmichpost6.org/content.php?id=2)*............................ 161

Holland women march for the right to vote in civil elections
(http://www.hollandsentinel.com/news/x89699615/90-years-of-women-s-right-to-vote, contributed by the Holland Museum) 164

Christina Van Raalte Gilmore 168

Thomas W. Davidson 178

Paul E. Hinkamp 189

Marion (Mert) de Velder early in his ministry 192

Hope Church choir, 1940 (Intelligencer-Leader) 194–95

James Hinkamp (Intelligencer-Leader) 196

Esther Snow, choir director (Intelligencer-Leader) 196

Lois Hinkamp Boersma (Intelligencer-Leader) 196

Paul Fried in 1942 (*Hope College* Milestone) 197

Paul Fried in 2006 (News from Hope College) 197

Statue honoring Dr. John A. Otte *(William Brown,
http://www.amoymagic.com/johnotte.htm)* 200

John P. and Virginia Muilenburg and children, missionaries to
China and the Philippines 206

Hope Church sanctuary in 1945 *(Vern and Lois Boersma)* 208

Last Supper woodcarving by Alois Lang *(http://www.hopechurchrca.org/carving.html from photograph by John Fleming)* 210

Alois Lang on *Time* magazine cover *(http://www.time.com/time/covers/0,16641,19300512,00.html)* 211

Alois Lang at work *(http://en/wikipedia.org/wiki/File:Alois_Lang.jpg)* 212

Elsie B. Stryker (Hope Church News) 215

James Wayer (Hope Church News) 221

Harold A. Colenbrander (Fiftieth Anniversary 1912–1962:
First Reformed Church of Hudsonville, Michigan) 226

Church School leaders honored in 1955: Edward J. Yeomans,
Eva Pelgrim, Milton Hinga, and Carol Van Putten
(Hope Church News) 227

Carollers choir in 1957 (Hope Church News) 230–31

Cherubs choir in 1957 (Hope Church News) 232–33

Chancel in the late 1950s 234

Marion de Velder in about 2000 (Person to Person:
Humorous Insights to Make Living Worthwhile) 237

One of three rose windows in the sanctuary
  (http://www.hopechurchrca.org/windows.html) 239
East windows in the church sanctuary
  (http://www.hopechurchrca.org/windows.html) 240
West windows in the church sanctuary
  (http://www.hopechurchrca.org/windows.html) 241
Last Supper woodcarving by Alois Lang in the chancel
  (Dan Joldersma) 242
Nicodemus Bosch memorial rose window (Dan Joldersma) 243
Gertrude Vander Broek memorial windows: Advent, Christmas,
  Epiphany (http://www.hopechurchrca.org/windows2.html) 244
Gertrude Vander Broek memorial windows: Lent, Easter,
  Pentecost (http://www.hopechurchrca.org/windows2.html) 245
Praise God from Whom All Blessings Flow cut-glass window
  by Eleanor DePree Van Haitsma 246
William C. Hillegonds 248
Dr. Vern Boersma (Vern Boersma) 253
1962 education wing from the courtyard (Rejoicing in Hope:
  Hope Church 1862 - 1962) 257
1962 education wing, north side 258
John R. Walchenbach (Archives of the Reformed Church in America) 259
Arthur H. Jentz Jr. 260
Children in Hope Church's Day Care Center 264
Sacred Dancers: Jane Den Herder (Park), Jo Anne Brooks,
  Shirley Bosch, and Maxine De Bruyn 265
Glen O. Peterman (Hope Church photo directory, 1974) 268
Char and Earl Laman transport items from Hope Church to the
  Community Kitchen (Hope Church photo directory, 2009) 272
James I. Cook (Jean Cook) 277
Walter and Betsy Martiny in the Family-to-Family task force
  (Church Herald) 278
John De Haan as Big Brother (Church Herald) 279
Marlin Vander Wilt 281
Karen and Larry Mulder at Chiapas, Mexico (Karen and Larry Mulder) 284
Ian and Jim McKnight at Water Missions International
  (Karen and Larry Mulder) 284

Luom and Ahn Vu Pham (1989 directory of Hope Church) 288
Paul R. Fries 293
Parish hall in mid-twentieth century 295
East view of church and parish hall before Parish Life Center
   was built (Hope Church Historical Booklet 1982:
   Our Time for Rededication) 297
East view of church after Parish Life Center was built
   (Hope Church Historical Booklet 1982:
   Our Time for Rededication) 297
Rooster weathervane *(Dan Joldersma)* 299
Sanctuary after 1984 renovations 301
Elsie Lamb *(Bill Lamb)* 304
Helen and Millard De Weerd (1994 church directory) 312
David Myers *(www.davidmyers.org)* 314
Hermina (Mickie) Lamb (Van Eyl) *(Jean Cook)* 316
Drs. John J. and Bernadine S. De Valois (Autobiography of
   John James De Valois Agricultural Missionary,
   Church of South India) 317
Carol Myers *(Carol Myers)* 318
Jean Cook *(Jean Cook)* 319
Trudy Vander Haar *(Trudy Vander Haar)* 319
Eloise Van Heest (1989 church directory) 320
Janet (Jenny) Everts
   (http://www.hope.edu/academic/religion/fac_staff/everts.html) 321
Lynn Japinga
   (http://www.hope.edu/academic/religion/fac_staff/japinga.html) 321
Carol Bechtel *(http://www.westernsem.edu/faculty/bechtel)* 321
Leanne Van Dyk *(http://www.westernsem.edu/faculty/vandyk)* 321
Marchiene Rienstra 324
Dennis L. TeBeest (1989 church directory) 326
Ann Piet Anderson leading Children in Worship
   (2009 Hope Church Directory) 328
RCA crest in needlepoint created by James Ward *(Dan Joldersma)* 333
Hope Church in needlepoint created by Kristine Bradfield
   (1989 church directory) 334

Needlepoint symbols in collection plates *(Dan Joldersma)* 334
Toni L. Macon (Church Herald) 340
Baptismal font and processional cross created by Todd Engle
    (Dan Joldersma) 341
Hope Church's peace pole *(Dan Joldersma)* 342
Mary T. Van Andel (1994 church directory) 343
Historical marker facing east *(Dan Joldersma)* 344
Historical marker facing west *(Dan Joldersma)* 345
Ruth Zwald Staal (1994 church directory) 346
Delbert Vander Haar *(Trudy Vander Haar)* 347
East view of Hope Church in 2011 *(Dan Joldersma)* 349
Doug Abell and David Van Heest (1994 church directory) 353
Arthur (Bud) Van Eck *(Archives of the Reformed Church in America)* 356
Evelyn De Jong Diephouse *(Evelyn Diephouse)* 356
Kathryn Davelaar *(Kathryn Davelaar)* 358
Gordon S. Wiersma *(Kevin Russell)* 360
Barbara Borr Veurink, organist (1994 church directory) 363
Jill R. Russell *(Kevin Russell)* 369
Multicultural diversity banner *(Christopher Wiers)* 374
Clark MacLean and Jon Jerow prepare to paint window frames
    at the Greenpoint Reformed Church *(Anne Duinkerken)* 380
Bethany Wiersma paints at the Greenpoint Reformed Church
    (Anne Duinkerken) 380
Some of the Van Raalte family in about 1911
    (courtesy of Helena Winter) 410–11
First graduating class of Hope College, 1866
    (Willard Wichers, ed., Hope Milestone of 1930) 431
First women graduates of Hope College 432
Rexall dyspepsia tablets advertisement 446
Detroit Jewel range advertisement 447

Preface

Recorded in hand-written minutes
    carefully penned in leather-bound volumes,
Preserved in rolls of microfilmed issues
    of the *De Grondwet, De Hope, Holland City News,*
    and *Holland Sentinel,*
Bound in tall tomes of *Christian Intelligencer*s,
Printed in pages of *Intelligencer-Leader*s and *Church Herald*s,
Written on pages about meetings and plans and visions,
Are the words, the voices, the stories of people long forgotten.

And when I open the books,
    unroll the microfilm,
    disturb the resting tomes,
    and read the pages,
The words speak volumes, the voices cry out,
    and the people come alive again.
This is what it is like to research and write the history of
    a place,
    a people,
    a congregation called Hope Church.
Within the pages of this book are the stories of some of those people.

Remember Thornton Wilder's *Our Town*?
Emily Webb, who died in childbirth, is granted a wish.
She returns to her family on the day of her twelfth birthday.
She sees them, but they don't really see her.
"Oh Mama," she pleads,
    "just look at me one minute
    as though you really saw me."
Emily doesn't stay long.
    "I can't. I can't go on," she cries out. "It goes so fast.
    We don't have time to look at one another."

So take your time, really look at one another, and look after each other.
Take up this book.
Look, read, see, learn,
And be grateful for those who, for more than a century and a half,
With God's help, became the congregation known as Hope Church.

Acknowledgments

Thanks to all who have helped me to find and transform the rich resources of Hope Church's history into the words and pictures in this book:

Paul E. Hinkamp, who researched and wrote a Hope Church historical booklet in 1942, and those who built on his work in historical booklets published in 1962, 1982, and 1987;

Elton Bruins, who encouraged me to write this book, suggested resources to pursue, shared information from his files, edited the first draft, and served as mentor;

Geoffrey Reynolds and Lori Tretheway, who assisted me in providing, copying, and scanning materials at the Joint Archives of Holland in the Theil Research Center;

Dan Joldersma, who took dozens of photographs for the book, including the one on the cover;

Christopher Wiers, who designed and produced the cover;

Brad MacLean, who assisted with file conversions;

William and Althea Buursma and Phil Van Eyl, who translated Dutch to English;

Russell L. Gasero, who provided photographs from the Archives of the Reformed Church in America;

Paul Smith and Glenda McKinley, who provided access to materials in the Beardslee Library of Western Theological Seminary;

Catherine Jung, who provided access to documents, photographs, and objects at the Holland Historical Trust Archives;

Bill Van Dyke, Lois Boersma, and Trudy Vander Haar of the History subcommittee of Hope Church's Sesquicentennial committee, who edited the first draft;

Lynn Japinga, Carol Myers, Bill Parr, and Marlin Vander Wilt, who edited the second draft; and

Laurie Baron, final editor.

Introduction: Lost and Found

Hope Church has celebrated its past by the publication of historical booklets in 1942, 1962, 1982, and 1987. The Reverend Paul E. Hinkamp[1] ferreted out the earliest history in his 1942 booklet, providing the foundation for all that followed. He and others reported that records of the first four decades of the history of Hope Church were incomplete.

It's understandable that the Holland fire of 1871 could have consumed earlier records, but the earliest book of church membership records has been preserved, along with many other documents now in the Joint Archives of Holland at the Theil Research Center. The second volume of *Consistorial Minutes* begins not in 1871 or 1872, as one would expect if fire had destroyed the earlier volume, but in January 1897.

The first volume of consistory records, missing for nearly one hundred years, likely buried in a box of old books resting in someone's attic, surfaced in January 1995. Its existence came to light when Larry Wagenaar, then director of the Joint Archives of Holland, received a phone call from a man claiming to have Hope Church's first record book containing consistory minutes through 1896. "Would the Archives give me $400 for it?" the man asked.

Wagenaar told the man the Archives had no funds for purchasing such materials but that he would call Lois Boersma, archivist for

---

[1] Hinkamp received his AB degree from Hope College in 1907. After completing studies at McCormick and Princeton Theological Seminaries and serving as pastor for three years at First Presbyterian Church in Sheboygan, Wisconsin, he became professor of Bible and philosophy at Hope College and joined Hope Church in 1918. He became registrar for Hope College in 1945 and retired in 1957. At Hope Church he was installed as elder in 1940 and was an active member until his death in 1971.

Hope Church,[2] to see whether Hope Church would be interested in buying it. Boersma, daughter of church historian Hinkamp, called the book-seller in an effort to persuade him to give the book to Hope Church for a tax deduction receipt. He refused, claiming that he "needed the money."

Boersma asked him how he came to possess the book. He replied that he frequently attended sales and didn't remember where he had purchased it. The book appealed to him because it was leather-bound. She asked him to hold the book until after the January 16th consistory meeting, and he agreed to do so.[3]

Soon after that, Carol Myers, senior elder of Hope Church, received a phone call from Elton Bruins,[4] founding director of the A. C. Van Raalte Institute. He told her about an advertisement in the *Flashes*, a local advertising newspaper, that he thought she and others in Hope Church would want to know about. In an auction notice, listed among the miscellaneous antiques and collectibles—between a brass inkwell and a 1914 cigar cutter—was a "leather bound 429 page ledger organization of the Second Ref. Church of Holland (Hope Church) July 20, 1862." The auction date was January 14 at the Port Sheldon Township Hall.

This latest news started a flurry of phone calls. Myers and Boersma discussed what each had learned and planned how best

---

[2] In 1990 Hope Church had appointed Lois Boersma its archivist. She and Wagenaar selected documents, photographs, and volumes of minutes and newsletters that filled more than ten banker boxes. *Consistorial Minutes*, 49:4 June 1990.

In 1984 Paul Fried had become Hope Church's first archivist. *Consistorial Minutes*, 44:10 December 1984. Bill Van Dyke became archivist after Boersma resigned in 2005. Minutes 2005\Consistory 03.doc, 14 March 2005.

[3] Lois Boersma, "Hope Church History," 2007. W91-1034, box 12, Hope Church, Holland, Michigan, Joint Archives of Holland.

[4] The Reverend Elton J. Bruins had inventoried the church's records in 1967 and recommended how best to preserve them. "Hope Church has had a significant history, and it has been a pace setter in the midwestern Reformed Church," he wrote, adding that a "definitive history should be written of the congregation" (*Consistorial Minutes*, 26:2 November 1967 insert).

to rescue the volume. "The book could have been pulled from the auction if we challenged the legality of ownership of the person with the book," recalled Myers. "Clearly no one would ever be able to prove that Hope Church had given up ownership of its own minutes book.... We were afraid that if we challenged it the book could be destroyed. So, we decided to swallow hard and redeem the book, if possible."[5]

Calling Judy Elenbaas, the auctioneer for Tulip City Appraisers, Myers learned that Hope Church could submit a proxy bid without having to attend the auction. Four families of the church each contributed to make a bid for $300.[6]

At the auction three bidders drove the price of the volume up to $100. After that the two remaining bidders were the auction's secretary (representing Hope Church's proxy vote) and the son of the owner of the book.[7]

The auctioneer, realizing that what the owner was doing was unethical, stopped the bidding at about $300.[8] "When I went to get the book," recalled Myers, "Judy Elenbaas ... said she felt terrible, that things happened fast and she got caught. It was the man's son who bid the book up. She also said that she would ban the family from any of her future auctions."[9] So it came to pass that Hope Church redeemed the record book that was lost and found.

The pages of that volume, several written by the hand of the Reverend Philip Phelps Jr. and others by various clerks of the consistory, contribute many details that help flesh out the early history of Hope Church. They record the inclusion into membership of individuals from various church denominations. They contain a letter by the Reverend Albertus Christiaan Van Raalte

---

[5] Notes from Carol Myers, November 2011. W91-1034, box 12, Hope Church, Holland, Michigan, Joint Archives of Holland.
[6] Boersma, "Hope Church History"; notes from interview of Myers on 5 Jul 2010; and notes from Myers, November 2011.
[7] Boersma, "Hope Church History"; and notes from Myers, November 2011.
[8] Boersma, "Hope Church History."
[9] Notes from Myers, November 2011.

that sheds some light on his and his congregation's responses to Freemasonry as early as January 1867. They tell of the consistory's invitation to women and men to vote to call a minister in 1878 and to vote for deacons and elders beginning in 1879.

This history, now encompassing 150 years, deserves a fuller telling. Of Hope Church, the acclaimed Dutch historian and author of *Nederlanders in Amerika*, Jacob Van Hinte, wrote in his *American Diary*, "*This church is a piece of history.*"[10] This book attempts to tell some of that history.

—Judy Tanis Parr

---

[10] Peter Ester, Nella Kennedy, and Earl Wm. Kennedy, eds., *The American Diary of Jacob Van Hinte: Author of the Classic Immigrant Study Nederlanders in Amerika*, Historical Series of the Reformed Church in America, no. 69 (Holland/Grand Rapids: Van Raalte Press/Eerdmans, 2010), 73.

1 ... The Beginning

Hope Church is the offspring of the desires of the Reformed Protestant Dutch Church in North America and of the Reverend Albertus Christiaan Van Raalte's colony of Dutch immigrants. The former traces its roots back to 1628 in New Netherland (New York) as "the oldest Protestant Church in the new world with a continuous ministry."[1] The latter traces its origin to 1847, the year Van Raalte and his followers arrived in what came to be Holland, Michigan. From one parent Hope Church inherited many of her earliest ministers, some of her members, and most of her early financial support; from the other she received a home. Common to both parents was the desire for an English-speaking Reformed church in Holland.

As early as 1848, two of the denomination's missionaries to the West recommended that their Board of Missions "give especial attention to the wants of the Protestant Hollanders, with a view to bringing them into connection with our own Church."[2] The chair of the Committee on Missions in his report to General Synod in 1848 viewed the recent immigration of Hollanders not only as a welcome bulwark to sustain a struggling English-speaking congregation in Grand Rapids but also as a potential victim to the predations of other denominations:

> Other denominations are using active measures to bring them under their influence while we, who are of the same origin, springing from the same branch of the Reformation, and adopting the same standards, are doing nothing but exposing them to be swallowed up by men of every name and every creed. These settlers are for the

---

[1] Howard G. Hageman, *Lily Among the Thorns*, 30th Anniversary ed. (New York: Reformed Church Press, 1983), 59.
[2] John Gosman, "Missions, Western Department," *Acts and Proceedings of the General Synod of the Ref. Prot. Dutch Church in North America, Convened at Brooklyn, L. I., September, 1848* (New York: John Gray, 1848), 427. The two missionaries are unnamed.

most part men of property and of the highest moral and religious character, and have come over with strong preferences for the Reformed Dutch Church.[3]

The chair likely overestimated the wealth and underestimated the separatist passions of the immigrants to Holland.

English Speaking, Teaching, and Preaching

Van Raalte realized how important the ability to communicate in English would be for the colonists. If they could understand and speak English, they could avoid being swindled and become more employable.[4] He saw in colonist Bernardus Grotenhuis an aptitude for learning English, urged him to learn English as fast as he could,[5] and sent him ahead of the others to prepare the way for colonists to travel their last stretch from Allegan to the Old Wing Mission, and from there to what would become the village of Holland.[6]

To learn to communicate in English, the Hollanders needed teachers, especially those who would honor the religious convictions of the colony. The first schoolmaster, Ira Hoyt, during the

---

[3] Gosman, "Missions, Western Department," *Acts and Proceedings of the General Synod ... 1848*, 425.

[4] Jacob Van Hinte, *Netherlanders in America: A Study of Emigration and Settlement in the Nineteenth and Twentieth Centuries in the United States of America*, vols. 1 and 2, ed. Robert P. Swierenga, trans. Adriaan de Wit (Grand Rapids: Baker, 1985), 133.

[5] Albert Hyma, *Albertus C. Van Raalte and His Dutch Settlements in the United States* (Grand Rapids: Eerdmans, 1947), 92. Sometimes the last name of Bernardus Grotenhuis was spelled Grootenhuis. Many of the older children of the early settlers learned English by working for Americans in neighboring places such as Allegan and Kalamazoo.

[6] Henry S. Lucas, *Netherlanders in America: Dutch Immigration to the United States and Canada, 1789–1950* (Grand Rapids: Eerdmans, 1989), 88–89.

The Old Wing Mission, located in northern Allegan County, east of Waverly Road and west of Black River's North Branch on the south side of 147th Avenue, was established in 1838 by the Reverend George N. Smith and Arvilla, his wife, Congregational missionary teachers to the Native Americans in Western Michigan.

winter of 1847–48 taught English to some children and adults. In 1848 Van Raalte donated some lots for a schoolhouse at the present location of Hope College's Van Zoeren Hall. A public meeting of taxable citizens voted some money for a public school, but the schoolhouse was not built until several years later.[7]

In 1849 Henry Denison Post, secretary for the school district, hired Miss Elvira Langdon from Allegan.[8] In addition to teaching for the school district, Miss Langdon organized the first Sunday School in Holland. After the Reverend Isaac N. Wyckoff of Albany, New York, visited the colony in 1849, Langdon reported, "he called on me in my little school and on his return sent me quite a Sunday School library which helped me a great deal as my little people began very soon to read English." After six months, the Sunday School was discontinued, however, because of the contagion of cholera and other sicknesses.[9]

Van Raalte and others saw the need not only for English teaching but also for English preaching. Soon after his arrival with the first colonists, they set about building a log church in what became Pilgrim Home Cemetery on 16th Street. Nearly all sermons there were in Dutch.

According to Anna Coatsworth Post, an early non-Dutch settler of Holland, the "first sermon in English was preached by Elder Nappen of Kalamazoo Co., in the summer of 1848."[10] After the arrival of

---

[7] Wynand Wichers, *A Century of Hope* (Grand Rapids: Eerdmans, 1968), 27–28.
[8] Wichers, *Century of Hope*, 29.
[9] Elvira Langdon Cooper, "Elvira Langdon's School Reminiscences," in *Dutch Immigrant Memoirs and Related Writings*, ed. Henry S. Lucas, 2nd ed. (Grand Rapids: Eerdmans, 1997), 1:395–96.
[10] "Hope Church Past and Present," *Ottawa County Times*, n. d. T88-0160. Post Family. Papers, 1848–1976, "Post, Margaret—Scrapbook 3 (1935–36)" folder. Archives of the Holland Historical Trust.
  Nappen is one of three credited with being the first to preach in English in Holland. Citing Anna C. Post's "Reminiscences," *De Grondwet*, 21 March 1919, Aleida J. Pieters credits another with being the first: "In the summer of 1848 the Reverend Mr. Payson of Galesburgh, Michigan, came to the Holland settlement and preached the first English sermon there." *A Dutch Settlement in*

a large English-speaking family from Geneva, New York, Van Raalte, according to Post, "felt we needed English services so much" that he "once preached in English, but it was like clipping the wings of the eagle and then telling it to fly."[11]

Americans in the general expansion of the population from the Eastern seaboard to the West were moving into Michigan, which achieved statehood in 1838, and into Holland. The forests of Allegan, Ottawa, and Kent Counties first drew lumbermen and traders to the area. After them came farmers and shop-keepers. When Van Raalte arrived in the area, American settlements were already established in Allegan, Hamilton, Douglas, Saugatuck, and Singapore (a village north of Saugatuck) to the south; Port Sheldon, Grand Haven, Ferrysburg, Spring Lake (Mill Point), Allendale, and Coopersville to the north; and Hudsonville, Forest Grove, Jamestown, Jenison, Grandville, and Grand Rapids to the east.[12]

Minutes of a meeting of the Classis of Holland[13] in April 1854 noted the "increasing number of the American population of the village of Holland," the influence of those people on the young people of the colony, and the need for a gradual transition from Dutch to English church services. The classis requested that the denominational Board of Education and Board of Domestic Missions work together to send "a faithful servant of Christ," who could both

---

Michigan (Grand Rapids: Reformed Press, 1923), 93. A newspaper summary of the early history of Hope Church credits Holland Academy teacher the Reverend Fred P. Beidler with the "first preaching in the English language" in 1854. "Hope Church," *Holland City News*, 16 May 1874:1.
[11] "Hope Church Past and Present."
[12] Lucas, *Netherlanders in America*, 92–93, 261, 272–76, 295.
[13] Elders and pastors of Dutch Reformed congregations in Holland, Zeeland, Vriesland, and Graafschap formed the Classis of Holland on 23 April 1848. *In Christ's Service: The Classis of Holland, Michigan, and Its Congregations 1847–1997* (Holland, MI: Classis of Holland), 1997, 2.

instruct their children in an English-speaking, church-supported academy and "preach among the American population."[14]

In 1855, the Reverend Fred P. Beidler, a missionary transferred from Constantine, Michigan, to Holland by the denomination, reported "a Sabbath School of sixty five attendants"[15] and "a fine opening for our church here. The young Hollanders already form a kind of nucleus for an English enterprise. All the members of our church seem to encourage English preaching very much." Yet, he conceded, "it will be some time before we can organize an English congregation."[16]

In the summer of 1855, the Reverend John Van Vleck, who had earlier that year graduated from New Brunswick Theological Seminary, was commissioned by the denomination to serve as missionary preacher in Holland. He became principal of Holland Academy, the name given to the church-supported college-preparatory school, and he occasionally conducted worship services in English in the district schoolhouse.[17] In 1856 the colonists moved

---

[14] *Classis Holland Minutes 1848–1858*, trans. Joint Committee of the Christian Reformed Church and the Reformed Church in America, 2nd ed. (Grand Rapids: Eerdmans, 1950), 155.

At the 1854 General Synod the chair of the Committee on Missions, George H. Fisher, in presenting the request from Holland Classis could not resist adding his own critique of the denomination's delay in moving from Dutch to English: "English preaching, the want of which in our early history has so irremediably injured and afflicted us, is asserted by the Classis of Holland as necessary to the religious education of their young people, the gradual preparation for American service, and their safety (as to sound doctrine) in hearing American preaching." *Acts and Proceedings of the General Synod ... 1854* (New York: Printed for the General Synod by John A. Gray, 1854), 472, 477–78.

[15] Philip Phelps Jr., "Historical Sketch of the Second Reformed Dutch Church at Holland in Michigan," *Consistorial Minutes*, 1:1–2. This is the volume that was lost for a century and purchased at an auction in 1995.

[16] *The Twenty-Third Annual Report of the Board of Domestic Missions of the Ref. Protestant Dutch Church: Presented to the General Synod at their Annual Meeting in New Brunswick, N. J., June 6, 1855 with Reports from Churches and Missionary Stations Aided by the Board* (New York: Board of Publication of the Reformed Protestant Dutch Church, 1855), 92.

[17] *Consistorial Minutes*, 1:2.

their worship services from the log church to a newly built First Church at Ninth Street and Cedar (now College) Avenue.[18] At its dedication on 29 June, Van Raalte conducted the morning service in Dutch, and Van Vleck conducted the evening service in English.[19]

Beginning in 1858, the Reverend Giles Vande Wall, born in the Netherlands and a recent graduate of New Brunswick Theological Seminary, assisted Van Vleck in teaching and in preaching Sabbath services in English. During the later 1850s there was "one English service on the Sabbath, which was attended almost exclusively by the younger Hollanders, there being as yet very few Americans in the place."[20]

Because of health problems, Van Vleck resigned in the spring of 1859. When Van Raalte first learned of Van Vleck's plans to resign, he immediately considered a man he had first met on one of his fund-raising trips to the East, Philip Phelps Jr., minister of the Reformed church in Hastings-on-Hudson, New York.[21] Phelps and his wife, Margaret Anna Jordan Phelps, had later visited Van Raalte's family

---

[18] This church has been known by various names: "Van Raalte's Church," "Old First Church," the "People's Church," the "Church of Holland," "First Reformed Church in Holland," and "Pillar Church." After the congregation joined the Christian Reformed Church, it was named "Ninth Street Christian Reformed Church," and since 1984 "Pillar Christian Reformed Church." Michael De Vries and Harry Boonstra, *Pillar Church in the Van Raalte Era* (Holland, MI: Pillar Christian Reformed Church, 2003), 2.

[19] *Minutes of the Ninth Street CRC [First Reformed Church] of Holland, Michigan*, trans. William and Althea Buursma, 2000:141. The typescript is among Elton J. Bruins's files at the Theil Research Center.

[20] *Consistorial Minutes*, 1:3. The number of Americans, though small, was increasing.

[21] Russell L. Gasero, *Historical Directory of the Reformed Church in America 1628–2000*. Historical Series of the Reformed Church in America, no. 37 (Grand Rapids: Eerdmans, 2011), 306. Hastings-on-Hudson was Phelps's second congregation. Before entering New Brunswick Theological Seminary, Phelps had taught for two years at Mansion Hall, Greenburgh, New York. Ordained in 1848, he served Greenburgh Church for two years before serving at Hastings-on-Hudson. According to Gasero, 530, the Greenburgh Church is also known as the Elmsford Church.

and the Holland colony in the autumn of 1856. He had preached in First Church on September 28.²² Van Raalte wrote to Phelps:

> Being very anxious over a successor, I take the liberty to suggest your coming in his place because I believe you are the man for it, not only as a teacher but also as a laborer to gather the Americans and the young Americanized people.... Your dear companion, I hope, has a heart for it, and the fact that she is able to converse with the Dutch would be a blessing to this community and could have a precious influence over the female portion. I hope her heart is willing.²³

Philip Phelps Jr. as a young man

Because the hearts of both were willing, they left the congregation which Phelps had organized in 1850²⁴ to come to Holland in October 1859. The denomination's Board of Education commissioned Phelps as principal of the Holland Academy, and its Board of Domestic Missions commissioned him as missionary preacher.²⁵

After Phelps's arrival, Vande Wall served various Holland Classis churches which had no pastors.²⁶ Beginning in the spring of 1860, Phelps and Vande Wall supplemented the Sabbath morning English service in the district schoolhouse with an evening English service in First Church, "which was well attended."²⁷

---

[22] Wichers, *Century of Hope*, 53.
[23] Van Raalte Papers, quoted in Wichers, *Century of Hope*, 52.
[24] Gasero, *Historical Directory*, 552.
[25] *Consistorial Minutes*, 1:3.
[26] *Consistorial Minutes*, 1:3.
[27] *Consistorial Minutes*, 1:3.

Four years after the dedication of First Church's new sanctuary on Ninth Street, people met in the Holland Academy chapel within Van Vleck Hall on 2 March 1860 to plan a second Reformed church in Holland.[28] They appointed Phelps, Vande Wall, and Henry Denison Post as a committee to obtain subscriptions for a church building. At this meeting Van Raalte promised to donate four lots, one acre, for the location of this second church. The committee secured promises of cash, lumber, shingles, other materials, and labor for a total value of about $700 from nearly fifty individuals who signed their promises to the following statement:

> We, the undersigned, feeling the importance of having a regular and comfortable place of worship, in which the service in the English language may be conducted and believing that the time has come for the establishment of a second church in the village of Holland, in connection with the General Synod of the Reformed Protestant Dutch Church in North America, do hereby agree to pay the sums respectively offered to our names, for the promotion of such object.[29]

---

[28] In its earliest days Van Vleck Hall served as a dwelling for the principal of the Holland Academy, a dormitory for students, classrooms, a library, a chapel, and a dining area—all in one. The chapel was then located in the northeast part of the basement of Van Vleck Hall. The money for constructing the building was collected mainly from Reformed Protestant Dutch Church donors of the East by Van Raalte, who made at least two trips for that purpose. See Wichers, *Century of Hope*, 44–46; Henry Boers, in Corwin, *Manual of the Reformed Church in America*, 4th ed., 194; and Paul E. Hinkamp, "Hope Church, Reformed Church in America, Holland Michigan: 1862–1942," 5.

[29] A copy of the three-page manuscript proposing the second church and containing the signatures and promises of donors is in W91-1034, box 12, Hope Church, Holland, Michigan, Joint Archives of Holland. The original is in the Archives of the Holland Historical Trust, Holland Museum.

As a result of the proposal for a second church, minutes of the January 1861 consistory meeting of First Church contain a request for "some competent members of our congregation to join so that there will be sufficient male members who can represent a congregation." *Minutes of the Ninth Street CRC [First Reformed Church] of Holland, Michigan*, trans. Buursma, 154.

The support from Van Raalte and the other signers, many of whom were members of Van Raalte's congregation, leads one to question Jacob Van Hinte's and Henry E. Dosker's assessment of the atmosphere preceding the genesis of Hope Church: "Van Raalte wanted to split the congregation

But, as Phelps commented in his "Historical Sketch," "various circumstances occasioned delays both in the organization of a church and the erection of a building."[30]

Vande Wall accepted a call to South Africa in 1861, leaving Phelps alone to do the work of two. Phelps discontinued the evening English service at First Church because of demands on this time and energy by the Holland Academy and "because the second service was not contributing to the upbuilding of an American Dutch Church."[31]

In 1861 the Methodist Episcopal Church was founded in Holland, becoming, as its Michigan historical marker proclaims, "the first English-speaking church organized in the Holland community." Its first pastors, the Reverends W. C. H. Bliss (1861) and A. J.

---

but his consistory would not yield. In 1862 during a new controversy, an English-speaking church, the 'Second Reformed' or 'Hope Church,' was organized, while those that lived on the 'town line' bordering the community also requested an independent organization. Then in 1866, a third congregation, *Ebenhaezer* [Ebenezer] was founded. Bitter jealousy developed among the sister congregations." Van Hinte, *Netherlanders in America*, 363; citing Henry E. Dosker, *Levensschets van Rev. A. C. v. Raalte* (Nijkerk: 1893), 281–82.

From my reading of Hope Church's *Consistorial Minutes*, and the translation of the minutes of First Reformed Church by the Buursmas, I detect no evidence of any such jealousy. For a volume of evidence for the close friendship between the founders of First and Second churches, see Elton Bruins and Karen G. Schakel, *Envisioning Hope College: Letters Written by Albertus C. Van Raalte to Philip Phelps Jr.*, Historical Series of the Reformed Church in America in Cooperation with the Van Raalte Institute, no. 71 (Holland/Grand Rapids: Van Raalte Press/Eerdmans, 2011). I have not read minutes of the Ebenezer church consistory but believe that, given its three-plus-miles distance southeast from First Church, it would be natural to start a church there.

If there was any jealousy among sister congregations, it was likely caused by the breaking away of the Graafschap, Noordeloos, Grand Rapids [Second], and Polkton congregations from the Classis of Holland in 1857. These seceding congregations became the nucleus of what then was called the True Dutch Reformed Church, later known as the Christian Reformed Church.

[30] *Consistorial Minutes*, 1:3. This may be a subtle reference to a decline in manpower owing to the enlistments of men into the Union Army during the Civil War.

[31] *Consistorial Minutes*, 1:4.

Van Wyck (1861–62), were circuit-riding preachers[32] appointed to serve congregations in Holland, Hamilton, Fillmore, and Ventura.[33]

Hope Church Is Organized on 20 July 1862

In the spring of 1862 Phelps sent a letter to the Classis of Michigan requesting the formation of a second church in Holland.[34] On 20 July 1862 the Second Reformed Protestant Dutch Church of Holland, Michigan, was organized as Hope Church.[35] At services held in the First Church, addresses were delivered in the English language by the Reverends Joseph H. Kershaw (pastor of the church of Centreville, Michigan), William Bailey (pastor of the church of Constantine, Michigan), and Philip Phelps Jr., and in the "Hollandish language" by Albertus C. Van Raalte.

---

[32] *150 Years Celebrating Our Ministry in Holland 1861–2011 First United Methodist Church*, 2011. The name Van Wyck suggests that he was of Dutch heritage; perhaps he could communicate with both Dutch and American settlers.

[33] *Holland City News*, 1 April 1937:4–5. Ventura is north of Holland, near the intersection of New Holland Street and Lakeshore Drive. Fred T. Miles in his 1961 "Historical Sketch" of the First Methodist congregation observed that the first two churches in Holland to use English "started within two years of each other, and have been good neighbors ever since," 3.

[34] Michigan Classis, formed in 1841, conducted its meetings in English and hence was the natural classis to which an English-speaking church in Holland should belong. According to *Minutes of the Particular Synod of Chicago; convened in Chicago, September 3, 1856, and April 22, 1857* (Chicago: Democratic Press Book Printing House, 1857), 3, the General Synod in 1856 grouped the classes of Illinois, Michigan, Holland, and Wisconsin into a new Particular Synod of Chicago. According to *Minutes of the Particular Synod of Chicago; convened ... May 13, 1863* (Grand Rapids: Stoompost Office, 1863), 18, other churches already belonging to the Classis of Michigan in 1862 were Battle Creek, Centreville (near Three Rivers), Constantine, Grand Rapids [First], Jefferson and Pittsford (near Hillsdale), Macon (near Ann Arbor), Mottville, Porter (near Constantine), Ridgeway (near Ann Arbor), and South Bend, Indiana.

[35] Perhaps the first reference to Holland's Second Reformed Church as Hope Church occurs under the topic, "Organization," written by Phelps in *Consistorial Minutes*, 1:13.

As Phelps described the service, "the usual devotional exercises were observed, in the offering of prayer, the reading of Scripture and the singing of hymns."[36] This singing of hymns, especially in First Church, must have raised a few eyebrows because for a long time the Reformed Churches in Holland confined their singing to Psalms (under the assumption that the Psalms were inspired by God but that hymns were the products of men and women).[37]

Charter members received into Hope Church were Dr. Bernardus Ledeboer, Allida Goetschuis Ledeboer, Bernardus Grotenhuis, Margaret Anna Jordan Phelps, William Brokaw Gilmore, Henry Denison Post, Anna Coatsworth Post, Charles Francis Post, Sarah Broadmore, and Elizabeth Welcher Sipp. The Ledeboers, Grotenhuis, Phelps, and Gilmore were received by transfer from other churches. The Posts, Broadmore, and Sipp were received on confession of faith.[38]

After the members were received, in the words of Phelps, the "male members retired and elected Bernardus Ledeboer and Bernardus Grotenhuis as elders and William B. Gilmore as deacon, who were thereupon ordained to their respective offices, and the church was declared duly constituted. The audience was large, and the occasion deeply interesting."[39]

Reporting on the meeting, Kershaw and Bailey wrote to the denominational newspaper, the *Christian Intelligencer*:

---

[36] *Consistorial Minutes*, 1:13.
[37] Elton J. Bruins in his history of Holland's Third Reformed Church, *The Americanization of a Congregation*, 2nd ed. (Grand Rapids: Eerdmans, 1995), 22–23, credits the minister of Third Church, the Reverend Henry Utterwick, with urging Holland Classis in 1874 to approve the singing of hymns in worship within churches. Bruins notes that Van Raalte agreed with this action in 1874, but his successor in the First Reformed Church, the Reverend Roelof Pieters, did not. Holland's Methodist Episcopal Church, immediately north of Hope Church, was singing hymns in English, of course, since its founding in 1861.
[38] *Records Hope Reformed Church Holland, Mich.* [Membership, Marriages and Baptisms list 1862–1878, during A. T. Stewart's ministry] (W91-1034, box 10, Hope Church, Holland, Michigan, Joint Archives of Holland).
[39] *Consistorial Minutes*, 1:13, 14.

> For several months past, the organization of a new Dutch Church, to be conducted according to our American usages, has been felt to be a growing necessity. The number of American families resident in the community has greatly increased of late. For their accommodation and spiritual profit as well as for that of several of the Hollanders themselves, who now are quite conversant with the English language, and desire to become more thoroughly Americanized, Dominie Van Raalte and Phelps, and others who have the welfare of the Church and community at heart, felt that the time had come to raise the standard of a new society there in the name of Christ....
>
> The occasion throughout was interesting and joyous. And we trust much good with respect to the Church of Christ, and the salvation of souls, will grow out of it.[40]

Five days later, the first meeting of the consistory of "the Second Reformed Protestant Dutch Church of Holland" was held in Phelps's study. "In accordance with the requirements of the constitution, the terms of office were decided by lot." Elder Ledeboer drew for two years and elder Grotenhuis drew for one. Deacon Gilmore's term was two years. Phelps was requested to act as secretary for the consistory.[41]

The Charter Members

Of the ten charter members joining Hope Church, only one, Bernardus Grotenhuis, was from the group of Van Raalte's colonists, and only one, Margaret Anna Jordan Phelps, was related in some way to Hope College. Only Dr. Bernardus Ledeboer and Bernardus Grotenhuis had been born in the Netherlands. The others, insofar as can be discovered from research, were likely born in America. The group comprised five men and five women. Four (or five, if

---

[40] Wm. Bailey and J. H. Kershaw, "Holland Academy—New Church Organized," *Christian Intelligencer*, 21 August 1862.
[41] *Consistorial Minutes*, 1:15. Appendix A lists all consistory members of Hope Church.

we count the missionary preacher as a member of Hope Church) were married couples. The backgrounds of the charter members provide insight into the diversity which was embodied in Hope Church from the very beginning.[42]

Charter Members Bernardus and Allida Goetschuis Ledeboer

Bernardus Ledeboer

Bernardus Ledeboer was born in the parsonage of Oud Beijerland, South Holland, Netherlands, on 24 February 1812.[43] After completing his medical education at the University of Groningen, he immigrated to New York City in 1834, married Allida Goetschuis[44] within the following decade, and moved to Grand Rapids in 1857.[45]

His reputation was such that after Holland's prominent physician Dr. C. P. Marsh left town, a public meeting was held in the old

---

[42] Appendix B lists information about the fifty-four members who joined Hope Church during her first five years.
[43] Philip Phelps Jr., "Bernardus Ledeboer," *Anchor*, Dec. 1892, 46.
[44] In Pilgrim Home Cemetery, Bernardus Ledeboer and his wife are buried side by side. Her tombstone reads "Allida Goetschuis wife of Bernardus Ledeboer" and indicates place and date of her birth as "Ramapo, New Jersey" and "October 21, 1822." These facts, carved in stone, refute statements made by Edward Prins in his *Grootenhuis Families of Gelderland Netherlands* that Bernardus Ledeboer married Bernardus Grootenhuis's sister Alida, born in 1823 in Gelderland, the Netherlands.
[45] Jan Peter Verhave, "Disease and Death among the Early Settlers in Holland, Michigan." Van Raalte Visiting Lecture Series lecture no. 4, 9 November 2006, published privately by the Van Raalte Institute, 2007:41. Retrieved from http://www.hope.edu/vri/JP_Verhave_Disease_and_Health_2007_7_19.pdf

log store of Mr. Plugger and a committee consisting of Messrs. Pfanstiehl, Plugger, and Trimpe was instructed to take the necessary steps to secure a competent physician. The result of their discussion was that, much as if Dr. Ledeboer were a dominie called by a consistory, he was "extended a call backed with a pledge guaranteeing a stipulated income for at least two years."[46]

Ledeboer and his family arrived in Holland during the summer of 1859. Not only did he serve as physician, but he also took on a number of responsibilities in service to his community and church. He soon became a trustee of the district school and later also served on the Holland Academy Council and its Executive Committee. Supervisor of Holland Township from 1861 to 1866, he served as Holland's second mayor, from 1868 to 1872.[47] After the Holland fire of 1871 destroyed more than four hundred structures, he chaired the local relief committee.[48] He was president of the local board of the American Bible Society and of the Democratic club.[49] At his death in 1879 he was president of the Board of Education of Holland.[50]

Having transferred his membership from the Congregational Church of Grand Rapids,[51] he served as one of Hope Church's first

---

[46] "Calling a Doctor," *Holland City News*, 28 April 1909:1. Pfanstiehl was an old acquaintance of Ledeboer. They had met in New York, where Pfanstiehl worked as a shoemaker for eight months before moving with his family to Van Raalte's colony in 1848. "Pieter Frederick Pfanstiehl," *Holland City News*, 16 July 1892:4.
[47] From Hope Church have come thirteen of Holland's forty-one mayors: Bernardus Ledeboer, 1868–72; Edward J. Harrington, 1872–74 and 1892–93; Henry Kremers, 1889–90; Oscar Yates, 1890–92; Gerrit J. Diekema, 1895–96; William Brusse, 1900–02; Henry Geerlings, 1904–06 and 1936–44; Jacob G. Van Putten, 1906–08; Nicodemus Bosch, 1912–16, 1918–20, and 1932–36; Earnest Brooks, 1928–32; Robert Visscher, 1955–61; Lawrence W. (Bill) Lamb Jr., 1971–73; and Philip A. Tanis, 1987–89 (though Tanis joined Hope Church after serving as mayor). http://www2.cityofholland.com/mayors/
[48] Phelps, "Bernardus Ledeboer," 47.
[49] *Holland City News*, 18 October 1879:4.
[50] Phelps, "Bernardus Ledeboer," 47.
[51] Although Hope Church records indicate his transfer from the Congregational Church of Grand Rapids, minutes of the consistory of the First Reformed Church in Holland indicate that Ledeboer had inquired about and

two elders from 1862 to 1872. "At one critical period in the history of Hope Church," wrote Phelps, Dr. Ledeboer "delayed for a very long time the purchase of carpets for his household, that he might have the means of giving a hundred dollars to the church."

> In such spirit his excellent wife shared: and it was my intimate acquaintance with the family that led to a knowledge of the fact. How often it was my privilege, sometimes for days or weeks in succession, to sit at his bountiful table. The only spice lacking was our failure to disagree on any topic.[52]

Ledeboer was "ever ready to devote himself freely to the general welfare," and, added Phelps, "in everything that he undertook, he was enthusiastic and self-sacrificing." For health reasons, he and his wife moved to Paterson, New Jersey, for a time in the late 1870s, seeking relief by means of salt-water baths there,[53] but they soon returned to Holland and to Hope Church. At his death in 1879 at age 67, a dozen physicians "united in public expression of their esteem for him as a citizen and as a physician.... His widow, whose membership with that of her husband had been transferred from the Congregational Church in Grand Rapids to Hope Church in 1862, did not long survive him; she died in 1882."[54]

In addition to all that Bernardus Ledeboer accomplished as a physician, city leader, and churchman, he and his wife parented at least five sons and three daughters. William G. Ledeboer, born

---

perhaps requested transfer to that church in 1860. Objections by that consistory were resolved and it was "decided that Dr. Ledeboer and his family, because previously they belonged to our denomination and left it temporarily in Grand Rapids, joining the Congregationalists, because there was no congregation of our own conducting services in their language, will be received as members." "Consistory Meeting of June 15, 1860," *Minutes of the Ninth Street CRC [First Reformed Church] of Holland, Michigan*, trans. Buursma, 140–41. Implied by the minutes is a questioning of whether the faith of a Congregationalist would meet the standards of the Reformed Confessions.

[52] Phelps, "Bernardus Ledeboer," 47.
[53] *Holland City News*, 25 April 1874:4.
[54] Phelps, "Bernardus Ledeboer," 48.

30 September 1844, enlisted in the 25th Michigan Infantry, Co I, on 14 August 1862, for three years. He became ill with dysentery and measles and died in Bowling Green, Kentucky, on 11 May 1863 at age 18. His body was sent home to Holland, Michigan, and buried in Pilgrim Home Cemetery.[55] F. S. Ledeboer, who never joined Hope Church, became a physician in Holland. Buried near William G. are his parents and a brother, Peter G. Ledeboer (1858–1919), who never joined Hope Church. Rachel Bogert Ledeboer and Katharine Ledeboer joined Hope Church by confession of faith in 1866, and Sarah Louisa Chatman Ledeboer, baptized by Phelps in 1862, did likewise in 1877. Katharine (Kate) Ledeboer married Dirk Blikman Kikkert Van Raalte, son of Albertus C. and Christina Van Raalte.[56]

Hope Church's first recorded baptism, on 3 August 1862, was for two-year-old John Trimpe Ledeboer.[57] On 15 January 1865, William Ledeboer (namesake of his deceased elder brother), born 18 May 1864, was the first baby baptized in the newly built Hope Church building. By all accounts, Bernardus and Allida Ledeboer were fruitful in children and in good works.

---

[55] http://ottawa.migenweb.net/obits/k-r/ledeboerWm.html
A letter written by Civil War soldier Johannes Van Lente to his brother Hendrikus on 27 April 1863 from Louisville, Kentucky, mentions his surprise at seeing and visiting with Dr. Ledeboer on his way to Bowling Green to visit his very ill son. Johannes Van Lente, *The Civil War Letters of Johannes Van Lente*, ed. Janice Van Lente Catlin (Okemos, MI: Yankee Girl Publications, 1992), 46.
[56] Appendix C provides information about the Van Raalte descendants who became members of Hope Church.
[57] Note that the child's middle name, Trimpe, is the same as the last name of one of the three men who delivered to Ledeboer the "call" to Holland. John Trimpe Ledeboer was the first of six children baptized by Phelps "in connection with the English service; and the place of baptism was the District School House, which was the place of worship" before the Hope Church building was constructed. Others baptized on 3 August 1862 were Sarah Louisa Chatman Ledeboer, John Coatsworth Post, Mary Post, Thomas Martin Sipp, and Margaret Jane Sipp.
  Phelps also baptized two dying babies of non-members, proceeding "in the principle that outside of his Denomination he has a sphere of duty with reference to the Kingdom of Heaven." *Membership Records of the Hope Reformed Church of Holland Michigan Book 2*, 334–35. W91-1034, box 11, Hope Church, Holland, Michigan, Joint Archives of Holland.

Charter Member Bernardus Grotenhuis

Bernardus Grotenhuis

Born 1814 in Ommen in the Netherlands, Bernardus Grotenhuis was a member of Van Raalte's congregation there and followed him to Arnhem, where he served as deacon and then elder. He and his wife, Janna Hogewind (sometimes spelled Hoogewind), immigrated to Holland with Van Raalte's first group of colonists on the *Southerner*.[58] He was helpful as an advance man, making contact with Americans and clearing the way toward the place that would become Holland. Though a painter by trade, Bernardus Grotenhuis assisted in the platting and surveying of Holland and some surrounding areas. After the village of Holland was platted, Bernardus Grotenhuis with Albertus C. Van Raalte and three other men served as a board of trustees which sold lots to the settlers.[59]

At the request of Van Raalte, Grotenhuis was one of several who traveled to New York during late 1847 to purchase large amounts of supplies to be resold to the colonists. He was put in charge of the resulting colony store in 1848, which soon failed because of "too much competition from newly developed private enterprise."[60]

In 1852, Grotenhuis and his wife and family of at least two sons—Johannes and Jacobus—moved to Detroit, then to Grand Rapids, and in 1862 back to Holland.[61] His wife, whose desire to learn English did not match her husband's, never joined Hope Church.

---

[58] Lucas, *Netherlanders in America*, 506.
[59] "Bernardus Grootenhuis," *Holland City News*, 11 March 1893.
[60] Van Hinte, *Netherlanders in America*, 227–28.
[61] "Bernardus Grootenhuis," *Holland City News*, 11 March 1893.

Nor did any of the Grotenhuis children.[62] Like Albertus C. and Christina Van Raalte, the Grotenhuises sent two sons to fight in the Civil War. Like Bernardus and Allida Ledeboer, the Grotenhuises lost a son to war. Jacobus (James), age 18, enlisted on 29 February 1864 in Grand Rapids in Company D of the Ninth Michigan Infantry. Less than three months later, he was wounded in the Battle of the Wilderness and died from amputation of the right leg in the field hospital at Fredericksburg on 18 May 1864.[63]

Early records from the First and Second Reformed churches in Grand Rapids indicate that the Bernardus Grotenhuis family was one of four which left the Second (Dutch-speaking) Reformed church to revive the languishing First Reformed Church in December 1859. Listed as the reason for their transfer: they "desired the English language for the sake of their children."[64] Hope Church records

---

[62] "Bernardus Grootenhuis," *Holland City News*, 11 March 1893. In addition to the two sons who immigrated with the Grotenhuises, a son Henry was born in 1862 and died in 1888, his funeral taking place at Third Reformed Church, according to his obituary, "Henry Grootenhuis," *Holland City News*, 17 March 1888:1. Retrieved from http://ottawa.migenweb.net/obits/a-j/grootenhuisHenry.html. Listed among the survivors of Bernardus Grotenhuis in 1893 were his wife, their son John and two daughters, Mrs. J. Kerkhof and Mrs. L. Ter Beek—none of whom ever joined Hope Church.

[63] http://ottawa.migenweb.net/obits/a-j/grootenhuisJas.html

Many families from all churches in Holland sent their sons to fight for the Union in the Civil War. Hope Church consistory minutes reveal little reference to the war and no expressions of condolence to those whose relatives were killed in the war.

[64] Daniel L. Ballast, *Then Now Always 1840-2004 Jesus Is Lord: The History of Central Reformed Church: 1840-2004* (Grand Rapids, MI, n.d.), 66.

Records from the short-lived South Holland Presbyterian Church of Holland, Michigan, indicate, however, that Bernardus, Janna, and sons Johannes and Jakobus transferred there "from First Holland RCA in 1860." "South Holland (Michigan) Presbyterian Church Family Records, 1849–1867, compiled by Richard H. Harms. Retrieved from http://www.calvin.edu/hh/family_history_resources/soholland_church.htm. To complicate matters further, consistory records of Van Raalte's First Church as of 3 January 1862, indicate that Bernardus Grotenhuis and his wife transferred there "from Grand Rapids." *Minutes of the Ninth Street CRC [First Reformed Church] of Holland, Michigan*, trans. Buursma, 170.

indicate that Bernardus Grotenhuis transferred to Hope Church in 1862 by certificate from the First Reformed Church in Grand Rapids, Michigan.[65]

After joining Hope Church, he stayed. With fellow charter member Ledeboer, Bernardus Grotenhuis served as one of Hope Church's first two elders, his term of service being 1862 through 1875. Elected supervisor of Holland Township in 1867, he served for three years. Later he was appointed county drain commissioner for four years.[66] He died 3 March 1893 in Holland at age 79.[67]

Charter Member Margaret Anna Jordan Phelps

Margaret Anna Jordan Phelps as a young woman

Margaret Anna Jordan Phelps was born in New York City in 1828, and graduated from Albany Academy in 1842, where Philip Phelps Jr. received his primary and secondary education; they likely were classmates. After graduating, she taught in the Rensselaer Street Mission School.[68] A member of the First Presbyterian Church of Albany, which she joined by confession of faith in 1842, she organized a women's prayer meeting there.[69] She also learned some Dutch and practiced it when she assisted Hollanders stopping in Albany on their way westward. She and Philip Phelps Jr. were married in 1853.[70]

---

[65] *Consistorial Minutes*, 1:13.
[66] "Bernardus Grotenhuis," *Holland City News*, 11 March 1893.
[67] "Bernardus Grotenhuis," *Holland City News*, 11 March 1893.
[68] Wichers, *Century of Hope*, 53.
[69] Ame Vennema, "Margaret A. Phelps," *Christian Intelligencer*, 1 May 1907.
[70] Wichers, *Century of Hope*, 53.

After moving to Holland in 1859, they lived in an apartment within Van Vleck Hall. There they raised their four surviving children: Francis Few Chrystie, Philip III (Tertius), Eliza Tephi, and Theodore Seth,[71] each of whom joined Hope Church by confession of faith.[72]

Frances Few Chrystie Phelps, whose first and middle names pay tribute to a philanthropic couple in Phelps's Hastings-on-Hudson church,[73] was one of the first two women to graduate from Hope College.[74] After graduating in 1882, she married John A. Otte, also a Hope College graduate, who went on to complete medical studies at the University of Michigan and the University of Utrecht and became the denomination's first medical missionary to China.[75]

Together they went to serve in Amoy (Xiamen), China, in 1887. Dr. Otte caught pneumonic plague from one of his patients and died in Amoy in 1910.[76] After living in Grand Rapids and later with her brother, Philip Tertius Phelps, in New Jersey, Frances Phelps Otte returned to the city of her childhood, transferring her membership to Hope Church from the First Reformed Church of New

---

[71] According to a note among the papers in a folder titled "biography" in H88-0122, box 1, Phelps, Philip, Jr., Joint Archives of Holland, in addition to the surviving children, the Phelpses had a son John, who was born and died on the same day in August 1854. They also had a son, Edward J. H., who was born in 1866 and died the following year. The note states that his body "was packed in ice pending his father's return" from the East.

[72] *Record of Hope Church Holland Michigan 1862–1916.*

[73] According to a letter from George B. Scholten in a folder titled "Biography" in H88-0116, box 1, Otte, Frances Phelps, Joint Archives of Holland, "a Mr. Chrystie ... had married a Frances Few" and the Phelps's first daughter was named for this couple. Wichers, *Century of Hope*, 56, states that Mrs. Few Christie [sic] from Phelps's Hastings-on-Hudson congregation helped pay for construction of the chapel-gymnasium on the campus of what would become Hope College.

[74] Wichers, *Century of Hope*, 89.

[75] Julie Van Wyk [Clough], "'Unto the Least of These': Hope Science Graduates Abroad," in *Into All the World: Hope College and International Affairs: Essays in Honor of Paul G. Fried,* ed. Robert J. Donia and John M. Mulder (Holland, MI: Hope College, 1985), 42.

[76] Wichers, *Century of Hope*, 180.

Brunswick, New Jersey, in October 1941.[77] When she died on 22 October 1956 at the age of 96, she was the oldest alumna of Hope College[78] and the oldest member of Hope Church.

Frances F. C. Phelps in 1882

Frances Phelps Otte celebrating 90 years

Philip Tertius Phelps, who graduated from Hope College with his sister in 1882,[79] never married. After receiving an M.A. degree from Hope College in 1885 and graduating from New Brunswick Theological Seminary in 1889, he was ordained. From then until 1922, he served Reformed churches in six New York cities. He died in 1944.[80]

---

[77] *Consistorial Minutes,* 5:2 October 1941.
[78] "Oldest Hope Graduate Dies In City at 96," *Holland Evening Sentinel,* 22 October 1956:1.
[79] Wichers, *Century of Hope,* 106.
[80] Gasero, *Historical Directory,* 306.

Eliza Tephi Phelps, who graduated from Hope College in 1885, moved to Antes Fort, Pennsylvania, where she taught. The same heavy rains that broke a dam and caused flooding that devastated Johnstown in 1889 also caused the drowning of many in Antes Fort, including in its toll Eliza Tephi Phelps.[81]

Theodore Seth Phelps, born in 1865, did not graduate from Hope College. He died in 1924.[82]

Not only did the Phelpses raise their own family in Van Vleck Hall, Margaret Phelps literally was the *alma mater* to the young men who lived on its upper two floors. Motoitero Oghimi, one of several young men from Japan who came to the Hope Preparatory School in 1868,[83] lived in Van Vleck Hall during his first six years in Holland. Oghimi wrote years later that he and the four other

Van Vleck Hall in the nineteenth century

---

[81] Wichers, *Century of Hope*, 106.
[82] Typed page numbered 119 and handwritten note among the papers in a folder titled "biography" in H88-0122, box 1, Phelps, Philip, Jr., Joint Archives of Holland.
[83] Wichers, *Century of Hope*, 104.

Japanese students who lived for a time in Van Vleck Hall called Mrs. Phelps their "American mother," for "every time we were sick in bed she made some suitable food and brought it to us herself as a loving mother attends to her child."[84]

Oghimi's recollection of the Holland fire of 1871 and the responses of Margaret Phelps to it speak to the depth of her character and faith:

> She, [Mrs. Phelps] taught me however as much with her silent example of piety and faith during six days as with the earnest talk on the Sabbath. One Autumn morning soon after the College opened a great forest fire broke out in the neighboring woods when the wind was violently blowing. And after some hours the fire became so general that Holland was surrounded by it almost on every side. It was fast approaching the City. Soon some houses in the City were burnt down, and the people thus left homeless and those otherwise all fleeing from the angry fire came for refuge into the College Chapel; some weeping were carrying their crying babes, or taking their sobbing children by the hand. At this moment she, as if she had forgotten all her domestic affairs, went out to meet them, and did all she could to comfort and sustain them. The wind meanwhile became more furious, and Van Vleck Hall itself seemed almost lost, some trees and bushes on the College ground catching fire, though the President and the students tried hard to extinguish it. Some students already began to let down their trunks out of the windows by ropes, and dig the ground to burry [sic] them. Some asked her if they could do the same for her, and she corteously [sic] but positively declined, saying, "If it is the Lord's will that we be deprived of what we have, all our efforts to save them are useless; but if He means otherwise, however dangerous it may appear, all is safe. His sovereign will be done."
>
> After a while the wind subsided, and blew in the contrary direction, and all was safe, as she had said.[85]

---

[84] Letter in folder "Phelps, Philip, Jr., Margaret Phelps" in H88-0122, box 1, Philip Phelps, Jr., Joint Archives of Holland.
[85] Letter in folder "Phelps, Philip, Jr., Margaret Phelps" in H88-0122, Philip Phelps Jr., box 1, Joint Archives of Holland. For more information about Hope College's first students from Japan, their joining Hope Church, their ordination as ministers in the Reformed Church in America, and their ministry as educators and pastors in Japan, see Neal Sobania, "Hope and Japan: Early Ties," *News from Hope College*, December 1998:11.

Seven months after the fire, Japanese students Motoitero Oghimi, Kumaje Kimura, and Rio Zon Tsugawa with their teacher-interpreter, Margaret Phelps, went to the meeting of the "Spiritual Consistory," the elders of Hope Church, which held their meeting in the church parsonage. There the students professed their faith and responded to the elders' questions. The elders, finding the students "well acquainted with the main truths of the Bible," welcomed the Hope College students from Japan into the membership of Hope Church.[86]

Phelps accepted a call in 1886 to serve a pair of Reformed churches in Blenheim and Breakabeen, New York. Margaret moved with him there, where he served for nine years. He died in 1896.[87] She died on 3 April 1907, at the home of her son, the Reverend Philip Tertius Phelps, at Gansevoort, New York. In an obituary notice for her in the denominational newspaper, Ame Vennema, who would become the fourth president of Hope College, recalled the following:

Margaret Anna Jordan Phelps in her mature years

> [The students living in Van Vleck Hall] were in a sense members of her family, and shared in her motherly prayers and counsels. My eye fell recently upon a photograph of five Japanese, taken in Tokyo, all of whom were students at Hope, and learned from the lips of Mrs. Phelps not only the alphabet of the English language, but that of the Christian religion.

---

[86] *Elders' Minutes of Second Reformed Protestant Dutch Church of Holland, Michigan*, 1 June 1872:27–28. W91-1034, box 5, Hope Church, Holland, Michigan, Joint Archives of Holland.
[87] Gasero, *Historical Directory*, 306.

[As a charter member of Hope Church,] ... she helped to give tone to church life and stimulus to its activities, and made herself useful in advancing the work of the Master in that community, and in the wider sphere of home and foreign missionary enterprise.... She was always a welcome caller in the homes of the people. A foreign language was no effectual barrier—her thought was understood, her motives appreciated, her example was an inspiration for good always.[88]

Five Japanese students gathered for a memorial service in Japan after learning of the death of Phelps. A framed photograph of Phelps is on the table. Motoitero Oghimi (Hope College class of 1879) is on the far right.

---

[88] Vennema, "Margaret A. Phelps," *Christian Intelligencer*, 1 May 1907.

Charter Member William Brokaw Gilmore

Born in White House, New Jersey, in 1834,[89] William Brokaw Gilmore later moved with his family to Fairview, Illinois, about thirty miles west of Peoria. He became a teacher before entering Holland Academy in 1861 as a student preparing to become a minister. While a student, he served as tutor of music at the academy.[90] He joined Hope Church by letter of transfer from the Reformed Church of Fairview.[91] Organized in 1837, this church is the "oldest [still active] Reformed congregation west of the Allegheny Mountains."[92] It was formed by a Reformed Protestant Dutch Church group, the Gilmore family among them,[93] who had migrated from the vicinity of New Brunswick, New Jersey, to Fairview.[94]

William Brokaw Gilmore

Phelps in his "Historical Sketch" of Hope Church notes that Gilmore was both the first deacon and the first chorister for the congregation:

---

[89] Elton J. Bruins, Karen G. Schakel, et al., *Albertus and Christina: The Van Raalte Family, Home and Roots* (Grand Rapids: Eerdmans, 2004), 147.
[90] Philip Phelps Jr., "Historical Sketch [of Hope College]." Typescript in H88-0122, Philip Phelps Jr., box 1, Joint Archives of Holland, 30.
[91] *Consistorial Minutes*, 1:13.
[92] Retrieved from http://churches.rca.org/fairviewreformed/History.html.
[93] Retrieved from http://churches.rca.org/fairviewreformed/History.html.
[94] Preston J. Stegenga, *Anchor of Hope: The History of an American Denominational Institution Hope College* (Grand Rapids: Eerdmans, 1954), 45–46. At about the same time, other Reformed Church people from New Jersey and New York were settling in Lenawee, Hillsdale, St. Joseph, Calhoun, Allegan, and Kent Counties in Michigan. The expansion into these areas, according to Stegenga, encouraged the General Synod to create the Classis of Michigan in 1841.

Since 1858, the devotional singing had been conducted by a choir, but with many interruptions and changes. In 1862, deacon William B. Gilmore began his labor of training an efficient choir, which he afterward continued with great interest and success. His services as chorister [leader of the choir] were rendered gratuitously for a term of years.[95]

Gilmore was a member of the first class to graduate from Hope College. After graduating in 1866, he continued his studies in the Theological Department, forerunner to Western Theological Seminary. From 1867 through 1869, he served as elder and secretary of consistory.[96] In 1869, he completed his theological studies, and in the following year he was licensed and ordained by the Classis of Michigan,[97] the first member of Hope Church to enter the ministry.

Soon after graduating from the Theological Department, he moved to Amelia Court House, Virginia, site of Van Raalte's venture to establish a new Dutch colony about fifty miles southwest of Richmond. On 14 July 1869, he, age thirty-four, and Christina Van Raalte, age twenty-three, were married by Van Raalte at Amelia Court House.[98]

Van Raalte, his wife, and daughters Mary and Anna moved back to Holland from Amelia Court House in August 1869,[99] leaving the small congregation there to the leadership of Gilmore, who also became the principal of Amelia Institute, a school modeled on

---

[95] *Consistorial Minutes*, 1:5. Appendix D lists choristers, choir directors, organists, and other supportive staff of Hope Church.
[96] "Elders," in *Record of Hope Church Holland Michigan 1862–1916*, a typed alphabetical listing of members with lists of elders and deacons; pages are unnumbered. W91-1034, box 10, Hope Church, Holland, Michigan, Joint Archives of Holland.
[97] Gasero, *Historical Directory*, 146. Appendix E lists Hope Church members who entered ordained ministry or full-time missionary service.
[98] Bruins, Schakel, et al., *Albertus and Christina*, 147.
[99] Bruins, Schakel, et al., *Albertus and Christina*, 149–50.

the successful Holland Academy. But the school "failed to prosper" and the congregation "disintegrated."[100]

The Reverend William B. Gilmore, his wife, and their son, Albertus (Raalte), returned to Holland in 1872.[101] For one year Gilmore taught with Marietta Van Olinda in a combined department of primary and female education below the grammar school level, an "experiment in primary education for both sexes in connection with the college."[102]

In 1873 the family moved to Spring Lake, Illinois, where Gilmore served as pastor of its Reformed Church for nine years. In 1882 he accepted a call to the Reformed Church in Havana, Illinois, where he served until his sudden death in 1884.[103]

The *Holland City News* provided details of Gilmore's death, funeral, and burial:

> The remains of Rev. William B. Gilmore, who died at his late home in Havana, Ill., on Friday, April 25, arrived in this city last Tuesday accompanied by his widow and young son, and were taken to the home of his sister, Mrs. [Sarah Gilmore] Alcott. On Wednesday afternoon at 1 o'clock brief services were conducted at the house by Rev. Thomas Walker Jones after which the remains were taken to Hope Church followed by relatives and friends in large number. The services at the church were of a very impressive character being conducted by Revs. Drs. Phelps, Scott, and Beck, who were his instructors during life at Hope College. The sermon, which was delivered by Rev. P. Phelps, D. D., was an able one, the speaker exhibited much feeling, and spoke of the years that had been passed by the diseased [sic] under his tutorship while connected with the college, saying that he had looked upon him more as a co-laborer than as a student.... A quartette of voices, with the church organist conducting, rendered some very appropriate music, among which was a hymn selected by the diseased before his death in which the

---

[100] Lucas, *Netherlanders in America*, 311–12.
[101] Bruins, Schakel, et al., *Albertus and Christina*, 151, 156.
[102] Wichers, *Century of Hope*, 89. Appendix F lists all Hope Church members who were also members of the faculty or staff of Hope College.
[103] Gasero, *Historical Directory*, 146.

whole congregation were requested to join, entitled, 'Asleep in Jesus.' At the close, the large congregation viewed the remains which were very natural in expression of countenance and impressed all who viewed them that it was indeed a sleep in Jesus. The funeral cortege was large. The floral offerings were numerous. The remains were interred in the Van Raalte lot in our [Pilgrim Home] cemetery by the side of his three children who had gone before.[104]

Charter Members Henry Denison and Anna Coatsworth Post

Born in 1824 in Rutland, Vermont, Henry Denison Post came to Michigan in 1832.[105] By 1848 he was a teacher in Mason, Michigan.[106] He first met Van Raalte in 1847 in Kalamazoo, soon after the first band of colonists had arrived in Holland.[107] Post described the impression that Van Raalte made on him:

Henry Denison Post

> In the year 1847 my first visit of curiosity was made to the new colony at Black Lake; on my return [to Kalamazoo] from there, never expecting to see the place again, much less of making the camping ground of the Dutch settlers at the head of Black Lake my home, and the field of my life labor, I casually met Van Raalte and was introduced to him by a friend. Very naturally, my recent visit to the colony was mentioned, and the project became the subject of our conversation. After listening to his glowing prophesies of the future

---

[104] *Holland City News*, 3 May 1884:6. The words for the hymn "Asleep in Jesus" were written by Margaret Mackay.
[105] Peter Moerdyk[e], "Chicago Letter," *Christian Intelligencer*, 28 July 1897.
[106] Marie Zingle, *The Story of the Woman's Literary Club: 1898–1989* (Holland, MI: Woman's Literary Club, 1989), 1.
[107] "The Late Henry D. Post," *Holland City News*, 24 July 1897:4.

city of the eastern shore, based upon his deep judgment of its great advantages of position and future resources, I caught the infection of his enthusiasm, and when he asked me to come and help lay the foundations of the future commonwealth, I enlisted with him, heart and hand, in the service.[108]

In much the way that Van Raalte had relied on Bernardus Grotenhuis to communicate with Americans on the way to Holland, he now came to rely on Post while in Holland.[109] A letter containing a donation from First Church to the treasurer of the Board of Domestic Missions as early as 1851 bears the signature and local pride of H. D. Post, an early indication of his affiliation with the Reformed Dutch Church:

> DEAR SIR: --Inclosed [sic] is *thirteen* dollars from "the missionary box" of the First Reformed Dutch church of Holland. The amount is small, but it has *cost* more than *ten thousand* would have cost some of your old rich New York churches. It is in more respects than one like the poor widow's two mites. It is also the *first fruits* from a people struggling with privations in the wilderness. May it do much good to the cause to which it is given.
>
> With much respect,
> Yours in Christian bonds,
> H. D. POST.[110]

Post not only assisted Van Raalte in his English correspondence but also taught him how to govern "in accordance with the custom of the country."[111] In 1848, when the first school district was

---

[108] Henry D. Post, *Holland City News*, 1 August 1896.
[109] Hyma, *Van Raalte and His Dutch Settlements*, 241.
[110] J. G., "A Blossom from the Wilderness," *Christian Intelligencer*, 20 March 1851.
[111] Albertus C. Van Raalte, "Commemoration Address, 1872," in *Dutch Immigrant Memoirs and Related Writings*, ed. Henry S. Lucas, 2nd ed. (Grand Rapids: Eerdmans), 2:489.

formed, he was elected its director.[112] When the ten persons who had the right to vote met in Van Raalte's home in 1849, they organized Holland Township, electing him as supervisor.[113] He started a township library and became Holland's first librarian in the early 1850s.[114] In 1873 the Board of Education appointed him librarian for the city.[115]

Post also became Holland's first postmaster, serving from 1848 to 1861. Because there was already a post office named Holland in Michigan, the post office for the colony took the name Black River, changing it later to Holland.[116] He also served for a time as justice of the peace.[117]

In the summer of 1848 he married Anna Coatsworth in Mason, Michigan.[118] She was born in 1822 in Dunham, Ontario, Canada, and attended Dunham Academy. After moving to Michigan in 1846, she taught school in Mason.[119]

After the wedding, the couple traveled to Holland by way of Singapore, near the mouth of the Kalamazoo River, where they were delayed a week, awaiting favorable sailing weather. The first thing attracting her attention on the morning of their arrival via

---

[112] Van Hinte, *Netherlanders in America,* 257.
[113] "In the first two or three years Post wrote Van Raalte's letters to important personages in the United States," wrote Hyma, *Van Raalte and His Dutch Settlements,* 249.
[114] *Holland Sentinel,* 17 July 1926:1. According to Holland library historian Dora Schermer, who wrote the *Sentinel* account, the library was first housed in the city clerk's office on the second floor on the Fire Engine house on East Eighth Street. Later it was located on the second floor of the building then known as the YMCA building in the Post block of Eighth Street. In 1911 the library was moved to the second floor of City Hall on River Avenue.
It was moved in 1960 to its current location south of City Hall on River Avenue and is now known as the Herrick District Library.
[115] *Holland City News,* 23 May 1873:4.
[116] Hyma, *Van Raalte and His Dutch Settlements,* 185.
[117] Engbertus van der Veen, "Life Reminiscences," in *Dutch Immigrant Memoirs and Related Writings,* 1:511.
[118] "The Late Henry D. Post," *Holland City News,* 24 July 1897:4.
[119] "Anna C. Post," *Holland City News,* 27 December 1906.

boat in Holland was "the singing in all the little houses near us. I soon learned," she added, that "my neighbors sang the psalms after every meal."[120]

Her first days in Holland were filled with surprises. When her husband and his brother Hoyt were taking a walk, Anna was alone in their new home. "I heard a slight noise and at once went downstairs," she stated. "An Indian stood just over the threshold, holding in his extended hand a strip of raw meat. He advanced toward me and I receded. He then laid the meat on the table and departed." As Hoyt Post explained to her upon returning, "the Indian was a friend of his who was about to leave the place and ... had brought the tenderloin of a deer as a parting gift."[121]

Upon first meeting Van Raalte, Anna confessed being "struck with his youthful appearance.... In those early years," she continued, [the Van Raaltes] were our most intimate acquaintances; and the pleasant visits with them are among the brightest recollections of those times. Mr. Van Raalte possessed rare conversational powers and every sentence he uttered was worth remembering. His noble wife was a lady of culture and refinement."[122]

With Van Raalte, Henry D. Post started an ash factory to make black salt or potash, an ingredient used to make soap, for the Chicago market.[123] He also became an agent for the Scottish Commercial Insurance Company and the Fire and Marine Insurance Company.[124]

---

[120] "Anna C. Post's Remembrances," in *Dutch Immigrant Memoirs and Related Writings*, 1:398.
[121] "Anna C. Post's Remembrances," in *Dutch Immigrant Memoirs and Related Writings*, 1:398-99.
[122] "Anna C. Post's Remembrances," in *Dutch Immigrant Memoirs and Related Writings*, 1:399.
[123] Engbertus van der Veen, "Life Reminiscences," in *Dutch Immigrant Memoirs and Related Writings*, 1:500.
[124] Typed notes in "Post family papers inventory," Archives of the Holland Historical Trust.

His other business ventures included a pharmacy and store, both of which burned along with his home in the Holland fire of 1871.[125] He served in Bernardus Ledeboer's local relief committee after the fire,[126] was appointed librarian by the Holland Board of Education in 1874,[127] and was also president of the Waverly Stone Company.[128]

The Posts learned some Dutch from their neighbors,[129] and Anna assisted her husband in sorting mail. At Hope Church she became active in the Ladies' Aid Society and the Missionary Society. She also became active in the Woman's Christian Temperance Union and founded the Bay View Reading Circle, which became the Woman's Literary Club in 1898.[130]

In 1862 both joined Hope Church by reconfirmation because each had been too long

Anna Coatsworth Post

---

[125] "A Contemporary Account of the Holland Fire," in *Dutch Immigrant Memoirs and Related Writings*, 2:495.
[126] Gerrit Van Schelven, "The Burning of Holland," in *Dutch Immigrant Memoirs and Related Writings*, 2:5.
[127] *Holland City News*, 23 May 1874:5.
[128] "The Late Henry D. Post," *Holland City News*, 24 July 1897:4.
[129] "Anna C. Post's Remembrances," in *Dutch Immigrant Memoirs and Related Writings*, 1:400.
[130] Zingle, *Woman's Literary Club*, 2.

absent from their prior churches to receive a certificate of transfer. On 3 August 1862 their children, John Coatsworth Post and Mary Post, were baptized by Phelps.[131] Though Henry D. never served as deacon or elder, both he and his wife remained life-long members of Hope Church.

Henry D. Post died in July 1897, and his funeral took place at Hope Church, the Reverends Henry G. Birchby and John T. Bergen and Dr. G. J. Kollen officiating.[132] The Reverend Peter Moerdyke, a member of Hope Church during his Hope College years, eulogized H. D. Post in the *Christian Intelligencer*:

> Henry D. Post ... accepted the invitation of the Rev. A. C. Van Raalte in 1847 to cast in his lot with the Holland colonists as a business man. He became thoroughly identified with them and served them with marked ability in many capacities.... He was a well informed, widely read man, fond of scientific study, a practical naturalist, and exceptionally familiar with all the questions of our day. Living deliberately to him [meant] life was process, growth and achievement. In spite of his marked modesty he filled a very large place in the community, and found unbounded satisfaction in the healthful development of the 'colony' and of his beloved city. He delighted in the success of good causes and good men.[133]

---

[131] *Hope Church Membership Records 1862–1901*, 334-35, W91-1034, box 11, Hope Church, Holland, Michigan, Joint Archives of Holland. According to text on the Moses memorial window in Hope Church, John Coatsworth Post was the "first child baptized in Hope Church." Born in 1854, he would have been eight or nine years old at baptism. The *Hope Church Membership Records* state, however, that the "first child baptized in connection with the English service" was John Trimpe Ledeboer. See note 57 in this chapter for the names of the six children baptized at the first baptismal service on 3 August 1862.

[132] "The Late Henry D. Post," *Holland City News*, 24 July 1897:4.

[133] Peter Moerdyk[e], "Chicago Letter," *Christian Intelligencer*, 28 July 1897. The allusion to "Living deliberately" suggests that Moerdyke may have caught the phrase from reading Henry David Thoreau: "I went to the woods because I wished to live deliberately, to front only the essential facts of life ... and not, when I came to die, discover that I had not lived." "What I Lived For," *Walden*, which was first published in 1854. It's likely that Post, a librarian and a "widely read man," also may have read *Walden*.

Anna Coatsworth Post died in 1907. Not only did the children of Henry D. and Anna Coatsworth Post join Hope Church but so also did their grandchildren.[134]

Charter Member Charles Francis Post

In addition to his brother Hoyt, Henry D. Post had a brother, Charles F., who was born on 2 March 2 1834 in London, Michigan. In 1854 Charles moved to Holland, Michigan, where he helped Henry D. Post run his drug store.[135] He joined Hope Church with Henry D. and Anna Coatsworth Post in July 1862, and a month later he enlisted in Co. I of the 25th Michigan Infantry.

After serving nearly two and a half years, he returned to Holland. On 2 February 1865, he married Charlotte D. Taylor of Geneva, New York. (Walter T. Taylor, from Geneva, New York, was the first principal of Holland's Pioneer School—forerunner of Holland Academy—serving 1851–1854;[136] perhaps she was related to him.) She joined Hope Church by confession of faith in August 1865.

Charles F. and Charlotte D. Post had five children. Frances Caroline Post, born 17 January 1866 and baptized 10 June 1866, was

---

[134] *Record of Hope Church Holland Michigan 1862-1916*. Mary joined by confession of faith in 1869 and married fellow member Charles S. Dutton, who became a minister in the Reformed Church, serving churches in Michigan and Illinois from 1884 to 1888. Mary reunited with Hope Church in 1889, and the Dutton children joined by confession of faith as follows: Henry P., 1901; Charles Llewellyn, 1901; John C., 1901; Robert Denison, 1911. John Coatsworth Post and his wife, Kate Garrod, joined by confession in 1892. Their children joined by confession of faith as follows: Richard Henry, 1897; Hoyt Garrod, 1899; Katherine C., 1901; Ruth Coatsworth, no date cited; and John Coatsworth Jr., 1912.
[135] "Charles F. Post," *Holland City News*, 6 May 1915.
[136] Wichers, *Century of Hope*, 35–40.

the first child baptized by the Reverend Abel T. Stewart in Hope Church.[137] Walter Teller Post joined by confession of faith in 1886 and transferred in 1890 to the House of Hope Church in St. Paul, Minnesota. Charlotte Margaret Post joined by confession of faith in 1887 and transferred to a church in South Bend, Indiana, in 1903. Charles F. Post joined by confession of faith in 1890. Edward H. Post joined by confession of faith in 1891.[138]

Charles F. Post served as an elder at Hope Church from 1869 to 1883. He maintained his membership for twenty years, even after leaving his farm near Holland and moving to South Bend, Indiana. At the time of his death on 30 April 1915 at age 81, he was the only surviving charter member of Hope Church. Gerrit J. Kollen and the Reverend Charles S. Dutton officiated at funeral services held several days later at the home of Mrs. J. C. [Kate Garrod] Post. He was buried in Pilgrim Home Cemetery.[139]

Charter Member Sarah Broadmore

Sarah Broadmore was the widow of Francis Broadmore. Records of children baptized by Phelps include two unnamed children of "Widow Broadmore" on 15 January 1865.[140] In 1869 Annie E. Broadmore, who later became the wife of Walter Hinman, joined Hope Church by confession of faith. In 1870, Martha Harriet Broadmore, who later became the wife of George Young, joined Hope Church by confession of faith.[141]

---

[137] "Record of Members of Hope Church made out by me Abel T. Stewart Aug 1874," *Records Hope Reformed Church Holland Mich*. W91-1034, box 10, Hope Church, Holland, Michigan, Joint Archives of Holland.
[138] *Record of Hope Church Holland Michigan 1862-1916*.
[139] "Charles F. Post," *Holland City News*, 6 May 1915.
[140] *Membership Records of the Hope Reformed Church of Holland, Michigan*, Book 2, 334. W91-1034, box 11, Hope Church, Holland, Michigan, Joint Archives of Holland.
[141] *Record of Hope Church Holland Michigan 1862–1916*.

In 1876 Sarah Broadmore's membership and that of daughter Martha Harriet were transferred to the Congregational Church of Grand Ledge, Michigan.[142] Sarah Broadmore died in February 1887, and the Reverend Charles Scott, who at that time was president of Hope College, officiated at her funeral in Grand Ledge.[143]

Charter Member Elizabeth Welcher Sipp

Elizabeth Welcher Sipp, wife of James Sipp, joined by transfer from an unnamed church.[144] James, who joined three days after his wife, was the only adult baptized by Phelps under his missionary pastorate at Hope Church.[145] On 3 August 1862, Phelps baptized two Sipp children: Thomas Martin, born in 1860; and Margaret Jane, born in 1862.[146] Elizabeth Welcher Sipp died in 1866. In 1870 James Sipp (and presumably his children) transferred to a Presbyterian Church in Oakland, Nebraska.[147]

---

[142] *Record of Hope Church Holland Michigan 1862–1916.*
[143] *Holland City News*, 26 February, 1887.
[144] *Consistorial Minutes*, 1:13.
[145] *Membership Records of the Hope Reformed Church of Holland, Michigan, Book 2*, W91-1034, box 11, Hope Church, Holland, Michigan, Joint Archives of Holland, 32.
[146] *Membership Records of the Hope Reformed Church of Holland, Michigan, Book 2*, 334–35.
[147] *Membership Records of the Hope Reformed Church of Holland, Michigan, Book 2*, 32.

2 ... Building and Rebuilding

Hope Church grew quickly. Within a year of organizing, she reported thirty families attending, fifteen communicant members, five infants baptized, one adult baptized, thirty-five in biblical instruction, seventy as average Sabbath School attendance, and $58.63 in benevolent contributions.[1]

In 1863 Phelps, having successfully developed Holland Academy into the beginnings of Hope College and having established a congregation of English-speaking Reformed Christians as Hope Church, asked the Board of Domestic Missions to appoint another minister to take over his Hope Church ministry. From then on, he was supported only by the Board of Education, though he continued both callings until another man became minister of Hope Church.[2]

The First Church Building

After money and materials had been secured through the subscriptions solicited in 1860 and collected by elder Bernardus Ledeboer, the congregation met on 28 July 1862 to select a Building Committee of five men, the majority of whom were not members of Hope Church. The Building Committee resolved that the dimensions of the new church would be about 35 by 60 feet. Phelps, secretary of the consistory, noted, however, that "No action was ever taken by the Building Committee; and at length in [the fall of] the following year, a church edifice was begun and completed under direction of the Consistory and [himself]."[3] The 30-by-50-foot sanctuary, built

---

[1] *Minutes of the Particular Synod of Chicago, Convened ... May 13th, 1863* (Grand Rapids: Stoompost Office, 1863), 18.
[2] Philip Phelps Jr., "Historical Sketch of the Second Reformed Dutch Church at Holland in Michigan," *Consistorial Minutes*, 1:5.
[3] *Consistorial Minutes*, 28 July 1862, 1:16-17.

principally by A. Meerman and P. Nagelkerke,[4] faced Tenth Street and was located closer to that street than to Eleventh Street.[5]

Elder Ledeboer presented the church with a Communion set, and the ladies of the congregation donated a melodeon.[6] The ladies likely raised the money for their donation by the work of their Sewing Society.[7] The melodeon did not last long, however. In February 1868 the consistory authorized William Brokaw Gilmore to dispose of the church melodeon for $125 and replace it with an organ valued at $300.[8]

Mid-nineteenth-century melodeon

In 1864, the Classis of Michigan held its regular fall session in the partially constructed wooden frame-structure building. This was the first meeting of an American classis in the bounds of the colony.[9] Also that year, Phelps became president of the General Synod.[10] In

---

[4] "Hope Church," *Holland City News*, 16 May 1874, 1.
[5] "Hope Congregation Bids Farewell to Old Church," *Holland City News*, 9 July 1901.
[6] *Consistorial Minutes*, 1:6.
[7] First mention of a Sewing Society occurred in *Consistorial Minutes*, 25 September 1868, 1:54.
[8] *Consistorial Minutes*, 27 February 1868, 1:51.
[9] *Consistorial Minutes*, 1:6. The first Michigan Classis meeting attended by representatives of Hope Church was in the spring of 1864. Details from Phelps's account of his travel with elder Grotenhuis to that meeting give some idea of the difficulties posed by a distance of about seventy-five miles as the crow flies: "Leaving Holland at 7 o'clock in the morning, we rode in special conveyance to Kalamazoo, arriving there at about one o'clock the following morning. The rest of the night was spent at a hotel, and all the next day was consumed in reaching Constantine by the regular stage. The expenses were not paid either by the Church or the Classis, and each one met his own outlay. That of ... [Phelps] alone was about twenty dollars." *Consistorial Minutes*, 1:32–33.
[10] Gasero, *Historical Directory*, 306.

his summary of the year, Phelps referred to the increasingly American character of the congregation:

> The changes incident to a new community and especially the increase of the American element had been continually modifying the character of the congregation. Among the growing American population, there were very few who had had a previous acquaintance with the American Reformed Dutch Church. On the contrary they were composed of all Denominations—and many of them without special religious training. The enlistment into the army during the civil war drew away many young men who had been in the habit of attending the English service once on the Sabbath until at length in 1864, the congregation had become mainly Americans, that term being used to denote those not belonging to the Holland colonists.[11]

Phelps's summary indicates that some Dutch colonists were worshiping each Sunday both at the First Reformed Church and (perhaps to aid their learning English) at the Second Reformed Church. Because many of these colonists were young men who enlisted as soldiers in the Civil War, he noted the resulting loss in Reformed Dutch influence caused by their departure.

On the final Sunday morning of 1864, Christmas Day, the congregation moved from the school house to their newly constructed church building. In the morning Phelps preached in the district school house. His text was "For he cometh," from Psalm 96:13. In the evening dedication service at the new church, he preached to a large crowd a sermon on the text from Romans 14:17, "For the kingdom of God is not meat and drink but righteousness and peace and joy in the Holy Ghost."[12]

Phelps considered the sixty-fourth year significant. In 1664 the Dutch in America transferred New Netherland to the English crown to become the states of New York, New Jersey, Delaware, and Connecticut. In 1764 ministers in America's Reformed Protestant

---

[11] *Consistorial Minutes*, 1:6.
[12] *Consistorial Minutes*, 1:25.

Dutch Church began to preach sermons in English. To celebrate the symbolic continuity of Hope Church with her denominational tradition, a chandelier, which in 1764 had hung in New York City's Middle Dutch Church and which Phelps purchased and brought with him to Holland, was suspended from the ceiling of the new church.[13]

Hope Church's historic chandelier

---

[13] *Consistorial Minutes*, 1:25. Information about this chandelier, acquisition number 1941.23.21 in the Holland Museum, indicates that the "chandelier was made in the Netherlands about the year 1714. It hung for many years in the old Middle Dutch Church in New York, then located on Nassau St., between Liberty and Cedar Streets, lighting the evening devotions of two or three generations.... When this site was abandoned in 1844, the old building becoming the Post Office, the chandelier passed into the possession of Rev. Philip Phelps, D.D., and hung for several years in [his] church at Hastings-on-the-Hudson. It then went west with him to Michigan.... There it was first lighted for the commencement exercises of the Holland Academy, June 27, 1861, and subsequently shed its light upon other Commencement stages of Academy and College, hanging during the intervals for many years in Dr. Phelps [sic] study in Van Vleck Hall, Hope College. It was also used on Sunday evening, Dec. 25, 1864" for the dedication of Hope Church. File 1941.23.21_info.pdf from Holland Museum Collections Manager Stacey Tvedten to the author on 20 May 2011.

Middle Dutch Church of New York City in the eighteenth century

Phelps reported that interest in the 1865 week of prayer "was so great that a meeting was held every evening from January 1st to January 15th inclusive. The condition of the Church and Sabbath School," he added, "seemed highly encouraging." And deacon Gilmore "was exceedingly able and faithful" in his "superintendence of the Sunday School."[14]

---

[14] *Consistorial Minutes*, 1:7.

Phelps As Influential Speaker and Beloved Pastor

In June 1865 Phelps preached before the General Synod, meeting in New Brunswick, New Jersey, a revised version of the first sermon preached in the new Hope Church sanctuary. The main point conveyed by Phelps in that sermon was that the Apostle Paul "is reproving professed Christians for their contentions about non-essentials, for their uncharitable judgments in matters which were really of no consequence in the sight of God."[15] In this sermon Phelps expressed a theme that set the irenic tone of Hope Church consistory meetings and set Hope Church apart from the family quarrels characteristic of many of the Dutch-speaking churches of Holland Classis.[16] He preached that the essence of the Christian Church consists not in "national distinctions," not in "rites and ceremonies," and not in "its outward organization or mode of human supervision." Instead, preached Phelps, the Church of Christ is characterized by *"righteousness,* and *peace,* and *joy in the Holy Ghost."*[17]

The need to release the tie to the Dutch language and embrace Americanization were themes that Phelps developed two years later in his inaugural address to the first graduating class of Hope College. Speaking shortly after his investiture[18] as president of

---

[15] Philip Phelps Jr., "Synodical Sermon," *Christian Intelligencer,* 15 June 1865, vol. 36, no. 24, 1–2.
[16] For evidence, see *Minutes of the Ninth Street CRC [First Reformed Church] of Holland, Michigan,* Buursma. Also see *Classis Holland – Minutes 1848–1858,* 2nd ed. (Grand Rapids: Eerdmans, 1950) and De Vries and Boonstra, *Pillar Church in the Van Raalte Era,* especially its chapter "Eavesdropping on the Consistory Meeting." For an analysis of the contentious spirits and causes of the breaking away of the Christian Reformed Church from the Reformed Church in America, see Robert P. Swierenga and Elton J. Bruins, *Family Quarrels in the Dutch Reformed Churches of the Nineteenth Century,* Historical Series of the Reformed Church in America, no. 32 (Grand Rapids: Eerdmans, 1999).
[17] Phelps, "Synodical Sermon," 1–2.
[18] According to Wichers, *Century of Hope,* 68, "the new President was invested with the academic regalia presented by the women in the community." Undoubtedly among those women were those from Hope Church and other women who were grateful for Phelps's attempts to include girls in the primary

*Philip Phelps Jr.,
first president of Hope College*

Hope College by the Reverend Isaac N. Wyckoff, the pastor to whom he had confessed his faith at age sixteen and by whom he had received his ordination at age twenty-four,[19] Phelps criticized the denomination, the "Reformed Protestant Dutch Church of North America," for waiting so long before it endorsed worship in English, and he advocated dropping "Dutch" from the name:

> We are retaining a national distinction in our name, which, so far as the progress of our church in this land is concerned, is a very millstone around its neck. Our Church, instead of marching under its historic banner, as the Reformed Protestant Church in America, or the American Reformed Church, clings to a nickname put upon it

---

department in connection with Hope College. Given the whiteness of his hair and beard, this photograph was likely taken several decades later, perhaps in 1894, when (like Elijah passing his mantle to Elisha) he presented his cap and gown to Gerrit J. Kollen, the third president of Hope College.
[19] "In Memoriam, *Anchor*, October 1896, 10.

by others; and instead of going simply to preach the gospel of Christ, would make all men submit to Dutch circumcision.[20]

Phelps criticized the Reformed churches in the East, which had held on to their Dutch language and ways long after New Amsterdam became New York City—to the detriment of their growth in an English-speaking America. Just as the early Christian church quickly came to realize that one need not come under the Jewish knife of circumcision to become Christian, so, Phelps declared, one need not learn and become Dutch before becoming a Reformed Christian. In contrast to his chiding of the congregations of the East, Phelps praised the colonists of Holland, Michigan, for their willingness to wean themselves from the Dutch language to English more quickly:

> Those of you in my audience who are Holland colonists here ... are pursuing a different course. You are using the language of the land, and are educating your sons to preach to yourselves in Dutch, while you need it, and to your children in English.[21]

Because of his growing responsibilities with the development of the Holland Academy into Hope College, as early as November 1864 Phelps encouraged the consistory to call a full-time pastor. Worship services in 1865 and 1866 were conducted by Phelps, the Reverends Theodoric Romeyn Beck and Pieter J. Oggel from Hope College, and Samuel J. Rogers from Battle Creek.[22]

The consistory, however, desiring to keep Phelps as their missionary pastor, delayed making any decision to call a new pastor. In January 1865, without telling Phelps, its secretary, the consistory

---

[20] Philip Phelps Jr., *Hope College Remembrancer: First Inauguration and First Commencement*, 1867, 16.
[21] Phelps, *Hope College Remembrancer: First Inauguration and First Commencement*, 16.
[22] *Consistorial Minutes*, 17 November 1864, 1:7, 20. Professor Beck taught Latin and Greek languages and literature, and professor Oggel taught sacred literature.

met to tender a call to him. Stating that "though he was bound by very special ties to this church," Phelps declined the call.²³

Within a week of Phelps's declining the call, a congregational meeting was held to rent the pews of the new church and issue a call to a different pastor. As an expression of their appreciation to Phelps, the congregation gave him free use of a pew, furnishing it "with carpet and cushion." Thanking the congregation, Phelps nevertheless "claimed the privilege of paying full pew rental." Pew renting began in 1865 and in the first year brought in $195.75.²⁴ The congregation directed the consistory to send a call to the corresponding secretary of the Board of Domestic Missions, the Reverend Goyn Talmadge.²⁵

After Talmadge declined the call, the male members of Hope Church met and unanimously voted to call the Reverend Abel T. Stewart, pastor of the First Reformed Church in Tarrytown, New York. In late May 1865 Phelps personally delivered that call to Stewart, who accepted it with the understanding that he would begin his ministry at Hope Church in July of 1866.²⁶

In 1866, the "Second Reformed Protestant Church of Holland, Michigan" was officially incorporated as "Hope Church." In the following year, a seal bearing that name was established.²⁷

Hope Church seal

---

²³ *Consistorial Minutes*, 17 November 1864, 1:20; 20 December 1864, 1:22; 13 January 1865, 1:24.
²⁴ *Consistorial Minutes*, 1:39.
²⁵ *Consistorial Minutes*, 16 January 1865, 1:26; 7 May 1865, 1:27.
²⁶ *Consistorial Minutes*, 29 and 30 May 1865, 1:28–29.
²⁷ *Consistorial Minutes*, 1:13, 33.

Responses to the Revival Brought by Elder Clapper

Several months before Stewart's arrival in Holland in the summer of 1866, the churches of Holland experienced a revival, the result in large part of the efforts of a Methodist exhorter named Michael J. Clapper. The youngest of eleven offspring of John Clapper and Elizabeth Murphy, he was born in New York in 1808. He was baptized in the Reformed Dutch Church in Kinderhook, New York,[28] and that may have had a part in his feeling "called of God to save Holland."[29] By 1850, Michael J. Clapper, with a wife and seven children, had moved to Genesee County, Michigan, northwest of Flint. In 1860 he moved to Holland Township and owned land in the northwest corner near where Lakeshore Drive and Ransom Street now intersect.[30] His attempts to save Holland elicited a variety of changing responses from young and old, from the Dutch and the non-Dutch.

Through his cautious and indirect style, Phelps in his "Historical Sketch" reveals his response to this phenomenon and describes the responses of Hope Church:

> About this time, it pleased the Lord for excellent and wise reasons which the reflecting Christian could discern to introduce the instrumentality of a Methodist Exhorter named Clapper, a mason by occupation, in order to commence a work of revival. He opened a meeting above one of the saloons of the place which became so crowded that they adjourned to the town hall, though an

---

[28] Robert C. Mahaney, "MICHAEL J. CLAPPER," a page in the "Clapper, Elder Michael" folder in "Van Raalte's Contemporaries" file cabinet at the Joint Archives of Holland in the Theil Research Center. According to *History of Ottawa County, Michigan, with Illustrations and Biographical Sketches of Some of Its Prominent Men and Pioneers* (Chicago: H. R. Page, 1882), 92, Michael J. Clapper was born in Columbia County, New York, and learned the skills of carpentry and herbal medicine.
[29] "Fragment of Our History," trans. Nella Kennedy, *De Hope*, December 22, 1886. In "Clapper, Elder Michael" folder in "Van Raalte's Contemporaries" file cabinet, Joint Archives of Holland.
[30] Mahaney, "MICHAEL J. CLAPPER."

inconvenient place. Application was made for the use of the Second Church [Hope Church], but the Consistory recognizing the presence of the Spirit of God, preferred to commence special services under their own auspices; and accordingly devotional exercises were maintained in the Church for upwards of two months. In these exercises, aid was rendered chiefly by Rev. T. Romeyn Beck. Rev. Henry E. Decker, at that time Pastor of the First Reformed Church of Grand Rapids Michigan, and a member of the Council of Hope College, was present one week, and presided in the Day of Prayer for Colleges. Rev. Abel T. Stewart, the Pastor-elect spent two Sabbaths with the intervening week at Holland.

Meanwhile Mr. Clapper's adherents who numbered many of the Hollanders had obtained the use of the First [Dutch] Reformed Church, where they held evening meetings for a number of weeks. A number of souls were hopefully converted, most of whom were gathered into the First Dutch [Reformed] Church. In the end, it added to the formation of a [Wesleyan] Methodist Church in the community.[31]

In contrast to Hope Church, which co-opted the spirit of revival coming from outside its denomination by attempting to conduct its own revival with familiar Reformed preachers,[32] First Church was of a mixed mind. When Elder Clapper asked the consistory of First Church for permission to use the sanctuary for his revival meetings, the first response of its consistory, like that of Hope Church, was to deny the request. "Clapper was a Methodist

---

[31] *Consistorial Minutes*, 1:7–8. The "Methodist Church" referred to is not the Methodist Episcopal Church, which had already formed, but rather what is now known as Central Wesleyan Church, which credits Clapper's revival as influencing its birth. http://www.centralwesleyan.org/history/history/menu-id-25.html
Other accounts of the Clapper revival are based in large part on "*Fragment uit onze Geschiedenis*," *De Hope*, 22 December 1886 and Gerrit Van Schelven, "*De Tweede Revival*," *De Grondwet*, 23 December 1913, 14; and 30 December 1913, 11.
[32] "*De 'Revivals'*," *De Grondwet*, 20 February 1877, reported the start of a "prayer meeting for youth" in Hope Church.

whose theology was tainted with Arminian theology, and the settlers were bitterly opposed to Arminianism."[33]

But Van Raalte saw things differently. Intervening on Elder Clapper's behalf, he rebuked the consistory:

> Are you blind to what is happening around us? Do you not see the hand of God in it? That he [Clapper] has something to tell us all, consistory, congregation, people? Shall we resist the Spirit of God? When will the consistory of Holland learn to understand its duty! I should have had another consistory long ago![34]

As a result of Elder Clapper's revival meetings at First Church during the winter of 1865–66, the congregation grew by sixty-two people who declared their professions of faith.[35] Before his congregation Van Raalte proclaimed:

> Twenty years I have worked among this people; but where were the fruits? And now, God sends to us a Methodist to mow where we have sown; and such a Methodist! But I lay my hand on my mouth and worship![36]

---

[33] Michael De Vries and Harry Boonstra, *Pillar Church in the Van Raalte Era* (Holland, MI: Pillar Christian Reformed Church, 2003), 91.
Arminianism, which took its name from Jacob Arminius and his followers, is the label attached to a set of doctrines to which the Canons of Dordt were opposed. Whereas the Canons of Dordt state that in the work of salvation "God and God alone acts," the followers of Arminius believed that in the work of salvation "man is in some sense a co-worker with God." Howard G. Hageman, *Lily Among the Thorns*, 53–54.
[34] De Vries and Boonstra, *Pillar Church in the Van Raalte Era*, 92. Van Raalte's words as translated by De Vries and Boonstra are from "De Tweede Revival," *De Grondwet*, 13 December 1913. About this quotation a note on page 147 of the book states, "Henry Dosker claims that Van Raalte uttered these words at a *secret* consistory meeting, in *Levensschets van Rev. A. C. Van Raalte* (Nijkerk: Callenback, 1893), 159. This would explain the absence of these remarks in the official 'Consistory Minutes.'"
[35] De Vries and Boonstra, *Pillar Church in the Van Raalte Era*, 91–92.
[36] De Vries and Boonstra, *Pillar Church in the Van Raalte Era*, 92; translating a quotation of Van Raalte from Gerrit Van Schelven, "De Tweede Revival," *De Grondwet*, 23 December 1913.

On 8 March 1866 Van Raalte confided in a letter to Phelps his views about the revival, giving credit to "God's work" rather than Exhorter Clapper's efforts. The letter also mentions the coming of Stewart to Hope Church and the qualities he should have to succeed:

Rev[d] P. Phelps D.D.

Dear Brother....
About the gracious reviving of God's work, the Conversion of Sinners among us, the means thereto and the Conflicting views about matters, you are I understand informed. A eternitij will tell of its great value. Satan was to work but did not succeed. At the present, the Methodists have another preacher in their house: The first church keeps up evening meeting.—
The Second Dutch gets her pastor verij late but nobodij wonders at it.—Br. Stuart must find all his delight in Saving Souls and must have quite a deal warm earnestness, bot be pleased with moulding of the future and, guiding the currents here....
A. C. Van Raalte[37]

Though Phelps and Van Raalte responded quite differently to Elder Clapper's revival,[38] they did not allow these differences to interfere with their friendship as leaders in the Holland colony.

Abel T. Stewart, Hope Church's First Full-Time Minister

When Stewart accepted the call from Hope Church in 1865, he had been serving Tarrytown's First Reformed Church for thirteen

---

[37] Bruins and Schakel, *Envisioning Hope College: Letters Written by Albertus C. Van Raalte to Philip Phelps Jr., 1857 to 1875*, 139–40. The spelling and punctuation are faithful to Van Raalte's handwritten text.
[38] According to Mahaney, "MICHAEL J. CLAPPER," the revival leader married Elizabeth Perrin after the death of his first wife, Mary. He died in December 1886 of a stroke and is buried in Lakeshore Cemetery, resting between his two wives.

years.³⁹ The church in Tarrytown had a history going back to 1685.⁴⁰ What would move a man to accept a call from a church so new that it had neither a full-time pastor nor a parsonage?

The Chronicles of Tarrytown and Sleepy Hollow tells of an incident in 1863 related to Civil War draft riots occurring that year in New York City. Repercussions from those riots reached Tarrytown and likely increased Stewart's receptivity to the call from Hope Church.

In New York City, groups of white men opposed to the likelihood of being drafted by the Union Army staged several riots in 1863. News reached Tarrytown that "a band of several hundred rioters was reported to be on the road to Tarrytown" in pursuit of "a long line of negroes [who had] fled to the woods to escape a threatened massacre."⁴¹

> The rioters were within a short distance of the town, and no man in the community dared put himself in their way till [sic] Abel T. Stewart, minister of God's Word, accompanied by one faithful companion, Captain Oscar Jones, a soldier home on furlough, marched out with splendid audacity to meet them....
>
> Mr. Stewart met the rioters and reasoned with them. He told them that their reception would be warm; that a gunboat, which had just arrived in the river, would shell the houses of their sympathizers without mercy if they persisted; he used cogent reasoning, convincing even to such a bloodthirsty mob of anarchists; and in the end he succeeded in turning them back. Then he went quietly home.⁴²

Because all too often no good deed goes unpunished, Stewart's brave defense of the African-Americans and of the peace of

---

³⁹ Gasero, *Historical Directory*, 376. For information about his education and where he served before Hope Church and for similar information about other Hope Church ministers, see Appendix G.
⁴⁰ Gasero, *Historical Directory*, 486.
⁴¹ Edgar Mayhew Bacon, *Chronicles of Tarrytown and Sleepy Hollow* (New York: Putnam, 1905), 62–63. On 1 January 1863, President Abraham Lincoln signed and issued the Emancipation Proclamation, which freed all slaves, and many began moving to the North. As this incident indicates, not all places in the North were safe or hospitable toward the former slaves.
⁴² Bacon, *Chronicles of Tarrytown and Sleepy Hollow*, 63–64.

Tarrytown met with faint praise. The people of Tarrytown were indignant with Stewart because in his reasoning with the rioters he had addressed them as "my friends." According to *The Chronicles of Tarrytown and Sleepy Hollow*, "Partisan animosity and misunderstanding were so strong that the usefulness of the minister of the First Reformed Church was greatly curtailed, and at last it seemed wise for him to seek new fields of usefulness, and to labor in some town that he had never saved."[43] Tarrytown's loss became Holland's gain.

When he was installed as the first pastor of Hope Church in May 1866,[44] he found a congregation of thirty families, among which were twenty-five members. They were meeting in their first church, a work in progress, and a parsonage was still in the planning stages. Because there was not enough money for Hope Church to support its pastor, most of his support came from the Board of Domestic Missions.[45]

Abel T. Stewart

During the twelve years Stewart served Hope Church, he also reached out to unchurched people in the community and built cordial relations with the Methodist Episcopal Church across the street. On at least one Thanksgiving, the Reverend William Coplin of the

---

[43] Bacon, *Chronicles of Tarrytown and Sleepy Hollow*, 65.
[44] "Hope Church," *Holland City News*, 16 May 1874, 1.
[45] Charles Scott, "Sermon," in *Memorial of the Rev. Abel T. Stewart, D. D., First Pastor of Hope Church, Holland, Michigan. Who died at Watkins, N. Y. May 24th, 1878. AET, 55*, ed. Charles Scott, Thomas E. Annis, and Henry Baum (New York: Board of Publications, Reformed Church in America, 1878), 26. W88-1106, box 1, Stewart, Abel T. (1822–1878), Joint Archives of Holland.

Methodist Episcopal Church preached the sermon at Hope Church, followed by Stewart's "earnest exhortation to the people."[46]

Stewart also performed valued services for Hope College. Filling occasional teaching vacancies, he taught mental and moral philosophy and sacred rhetoric.[47] He served for twelve years on the Hope College Council, predecessor to the Board of Trustees, and for many of those years he was its secretary. "The students had reason to appreciate his regard for their welfare, and especially did the strangers from Japan find in him a warm friend and a kind counselor."[48]

He also guided Hope Church through two important challenges: one to their understanding of qualifications for church membership and the other to their perseverance in the face of a fiercely destructive fire.

Testing

Within his first year at Hope Church, Stewart and the consistory of Hope Church received a challenge from the consistory of First Reformed Church. Their response helped spare Hope Church from many of the divisive tensions that led years later to the expulsion of First Reformed Church from its beloved pillared sanctuary.

Minutes of the consistory meeting of 13 March 1867 record receiving and reading the following letter from the consistory of First Church, Holland:

>Holland, Mich., Jan 1867.
>The Rev'd Consistory of the 2nd Ref. Dutch Church of Holland.
>Beloved Brethren:__
>   Please bear with us in addressing you on the subject of the Secret Society of the Free Masons, and allow us to bring our objections

---

[46] William M. Coplin, "Address," in *Memorial of the Rev. Abel T. Stewart*, 34.
[47] P. D. Van Cleef, "Abel T. Stewart, D. D.," *Christian Intelligencer*, 6 June 1878, 4.
[48] Charles Scott, "Sermon," in *Memorial of the Rev. Abel T. Stewart*, 28.

before you against the connection of Church members with that Society.

We know every one of the Asiatic churches[49] did receive her own epistle of Jesus, and was held responsible for her own peculiar field of action. Yet allow us, on account of our close connection and the mutual influence on one another and duties towards one another. We believe this connection to be unworthy [of] the Church of Christ, especially on account of the abuse of the Oath.

The oath belongs to the public adoration of God to his divine service: Deut. VI:13.__Thou shalt fear the the [sic] Lord thy God, and serve him, and shalt swear by his name.

Therefore we believe the oath to be allowed when the magistrates demand it of subjects; or when necessity requires us thereby to confirm fidelity and truth, to the glory of God, and the safety of our neighbor.

Then the sacred oath ought not to be used for light-abhorring ends. It is said that the Society is harmless and innocent; that the oath is only used to bring about attraction, a certain reverence, and to make the Society more efficient for works of love. This refuge of strength for heathen idolatry is below the light-giving and light-spreading character of Christendom.

Then, we deem it unmanly and unchristianlike to swear away to man our sacred privilege to be a witness for truth: our high calling of giving testimony must remain free, and only subject to God and conscience.

This Society requires the oath of secrecy, even before the nature and working of the Society is known. And, even if it was known, how can a Christian swear secrecy to a body of men, even if that body was as holy as the Church of God, where the constant change of persons and circumstances at any moment may reveal to him facts which he may be obliged for God's glory and men's welfare to uncover?

Dear Brethren, may the Lord give us harmony on this subject, for Jesus' sake.

With love and best wishes,
Your Brother in Christ,
A. C. Van Raalte

---

[49] "Asiatic churches" alludes to the seven churches in Asia Minor to which John is instructed to write. The first three chapters of the book of Revelation contain messages to the angels of seven churches in Asia Minor.

Per order of the Consistory of the 1st Reformed Dutch Church of Holland.[50]

The consistory of Hope Church authorized Stewart to draft a reply. At an informal meeting on 18 April, the consistory adopted a resolution and read and approved the reply written by Stewart. The resolution admonished Free Masons who were members of Hope Church to withdraw from the lodge, and the letter provided reasons why Hope Church would accept the membership of Free Masons who met the criteria set for all seeking membership:

> Resolved, That the Consistory admonish these brethren belonging to the Order of Free Masons to cease their connection with that body, in order that peace and harmony may prevail

---

[50] *Consistorial Minutes*, 13 March 1867, 1:42–43. As early as 1853, minutes of the Holland Classis indicate a discussion about Freemasonry. In response to a First Church member's question "whether or not it is lawful for a member of the church to be a Freemason," the response of Holland Classis was "All look upon it as works of darkness, and thus unlawful for a (church) member." *Classis Holland Minutes 1848–1858*, 144. According to the 6 March 1866 consistory minutes of First Church, there was "general agreement that members of the Masonic Lodge should not be admitted to the Lord's table," and a month later that consistory added theater attendance as an additional prohibition for those partaking of Communion. Minutes of the 22 October 1866 consistory of First Church stated the plan: "Since the English, or Second Church locally, seems to have no objection to receiving members of the Masonic Lodge into the fellowship of their congregation and admit them to the table of the Lord, it was decided that it is our calling in a Christian protest to witness against this, following the church order." The following month's minutes indicate that in response to a question raised by elder [Teunis] Keppel, "the pastor replied that he has prepared a protest to the local Second church concerning their acceptance of members of their congregation who are Masons." *Minutes of the Ninth Street CRC [First Reformed Church] of Holland, Michigan*, Buursma, 259a–59b, 263a, 271–72.

This contrasts somewhat with Harry Boonstra's statement in his monograph, "The Dutch Equation in the RCA Freemason Controversy, 1867–1885," that during Van Raalte's ministry, the Freemasonry "issue did not become problematic." Lecture Series of the Van Raalte Institute, Visiting Research Fellows Program, no. 6 (Holland, MI: Van Raalte Press, 2008), 26. By 1867, Freemasonry had become problematic enough for Van Raalte to sign his name to a friendly admonition from First Church to Second (Hope) Church.

among us and others of our brethren who deem such connection contrary to the Word of God.[51]

Holland, Mich. Apr. 9th 1867
To the Consistory of the 1st Refd Prot. Dutch Church of Holland.
Dear Brethren:__

Your letter [of January], sent to us the last week in February, containing "objections against the connection of our Church members with the Society of Free Masons" has been carefully considered.

The majority of us do not see the subject in the light that you do. To us, Free Masonry seems like some other things, a matter about which Christians do and may conscientiously differ.

The persons of that Order admitted to our Church answered the requirements of the 81. question of the [Heidelberg] Catechism, and we could not refuse to receive them.

They do not belong to the character described under the 82. question, and we cannot exclude them.

We appreciate your letter, and the kind spirit in which it is written; and, for the sake of harmony, we will endeavor to persuade these brethren to withdraw from their society. And we desire you to ask yourselves whether, on a view of the whole subject, it would not be better for you, as well as for us, to receive these people into the Church on their giving evidence of conversion; and then teach them a better way.

With great respect and Christian love, we remain your Brethren in Christ

Abel. T. Stewart, Pastor[52]

The nuanced combination of the recommendation and the letter, which at first reading might sound contradictory, served several purposes. The recommendation showed critics in First Church that Hope Church was making efforts to convince Free Masons among its membership to leave the lodge in order to preserve peace between the Second and First churches. The letter, on the other hand, defended the presence of Free Masons among the membership of

---

[51] *Consistorial Minutes*, 18 April 1867, 1:44.
[52] *Consistorial Minutes*, 1:44–45.

Hope Church because these members had met requirements of the Heidelberg Catechism. Questions and answers 81 and 82 of the catechism concern qualifications for those receiving the Lord's Supper; these received into Hope Church had confessed their faith that Christ forgave their sins, and they were not by their words and actions infidels and ungodly. Regarding membership criteria, Stewart appealed to the Heidelberg Catechism, thus conveying that his response was grounded in the Reformed tradition. Rather than concede to the admonition from First Church, however, Stewart responded with what he and Hope Church considered "a better way," a way that First Church chose not to take and later suffered the consequences.

Consistory minutes of the First Reformed Church reveal its response to the letter from Hope Church: Van Raalte "reports that an answer to the protest sent to the Second church about membership in the Masonic order has been received. In a very irenic manner they have given their reasons why they are of a different opinion than we. It was decided to bring the matter to classis and afterward to synod."[53]

Influenced by the Christian Reformed Church's decision in 1867 to ban by synodical order membership in lodges such as the Masons and Odd Fellows, Wisconsin Classis and Holland Classis in the following year asked the General Synod to declare membership in the lodge and in the church incompatible and to condemn freemasonry.[54] In contrast, the churches of the East, whose votes prevailed, viewed lodge membership as compatible with Christianity and left membership in lodges up to individual consciences.[55]

Unwilling to accept the General Synod's vote, the Wisconsin and Holland Classes in 1869 presented overtures to reverse the decision of the previous year, and the synod referred the matter to a committee. The response of that committee in 1870 was that

---

[53] "Consistory Meeting of April 12, 1867," *Minutes of the Ninth Street CRC [First Reformed Church] of Holland, Michigan*, Buursma, 288.
[54] Swierenga and Bruins, *Family Quarrels*, 114.
[55] Swierenga and Bruins, *Family Quarrels*, 113.

the 1868 decision would not be overturned for two reasons: to do so would have set up a new (in other words, unbiblical) test of membership, and it would have interfered with the right of the consistory of each congregation to decide who could and could not be church members.[56]

Hope Church, which belonged to the Classis of Michigan, was somewhat removed from the controversy. If the consistory had any requests for membership from members of lodges, it was not about to deny membership on that basis alone. In fact, it even allowed the Oddfellows Lodge to conduct in Hope Church the funeral service of John Aling, a member of the Oddfellows Lodge. Adding diversity to the hospitality extended by Hope Church, the funeral sermon at that service was preached in Dutch by the Reverend Henry Utterwick of Holland's Third Reformed Church.[57]

A Christmas Interlude

After slogging through pages of consistory minutes, General Synod proceedings, and a funeral, it is high time for an interlude, a look back to Christmastide 1866. In January 1867, William A. Shields, a deacon, sent two letters to the *Christian Intelligencer* relating recent developments among churches in Holland and describing Christmas festivities at Hope Church.

By early 1867, the city of Holland had four churches and was about to gain a fifth. "Besides the First Dutch" church, wrote Shields, "there are several other churches in this place. One is composed in

---

[56] Swierenga and Bruins, *Family Quarrels*, 115.
[57] *Holland City News*, 10 June 1876, 5. "Pillar Church Families by Head of Household" lists Jan Aaling, a likely alternate spelling of John Aling, as a member of First Church. Retrieved from http://www.calvin.edu/hh/family_history_resources/Pillar Families.pdf. He was not likely a member of that congregation and of the Oddfellows Lodge at the same time. Members of Hope Church who were active in the local Unity Lodge of Freemasons included Jacob O. Doesburg, Gerrit Van Schelven, [Ernst] Herold, [Edwin Jerome] Harrington, and others. Retrieved from http://ottawa.migenweb.net/holland/history/1882history.html#SOCIETIES.

part of persons who have left the First Church and are called by them seceders, but by themselves the 'True Reformed Protestant Dutch Church'[58].... There is also here a Methodist church." A "Second Reformed Dutch" church, known as the English Church or Hope Church, "has lately been completed and much improved in appearance and comfort at an expense of $530, all raised by subscription in the place. It has a flourishing Sabbath-school and an encouraging attendance upon the Sabbath services, and the weekly meeting for lecture and prayer. It is still small in membership, but evidently growing in numbers and influence."[59] The fifth church emerging in Holland would be the Third Reformed Dutch Church at the corner of Twelfth Street and Pine Avenue, comprising mainly members of the First Church who lived on the west side of town; Van Raalte had recommended splitting First Church into "two manageable congregations."[60]

Here, Shields digresses, "we must ... go and see the Christmas-tree which the ladies of the Second Dutch Church are getting up for the children."[61]

> The Christmas-tree in the Second Church of Holland ... was not so large as those that appeared in some of our larger churches at the East, nor did it cost so much. It was about eighteen feet high, reaching from the pulpit platform nearly to the ceiling.... It was

---

[58] The True Reformed Protestant Dutch Church, later called Market Street Church, and now Central Avenue Christian Reformed Church, was organized 8 November 1865. Mary Van Heuvelen, *Our Story: Central Avenue Christian Reformed Church*, esp. chapters 1 and 2, n.d. (http://www.centralavecrc.org/ History of Central Avenue.htm).

Its first members were the Dutch who found it too inconvenient to travel to Graafschap, more than three miles away, and too untrue to their beliefs to join First Church, less than two blocks away.

[59] [William] A. [Shields], "Letter from the West," *Christian Intelligencer*, 3 January 1867.

[60] *Minutes of the Ninth Street CRC [First Reformed Church] of Holland, Michigan*, Buursma, 26 July 1867, 292.

[61] [Shields], "Letter from the West," *Christian Intelligencer*, 3 January 1867. Hope Church is called the "Second Dutch Church" because the denomination did not drop "Dutch" from its name until after June 1867.

tastefully hung with useful and fancy articles gotten up by the ladies. The whole was lighted up in the presence of one hundred and fifty children belonging to the school or schools under the care of the Consistory, and an interested and observing congregation.

The services were opened with prayer and reading of the Scriptural accounts of the birth of Jesus. Suitable addresses were made by Rev. Dr. Phelps, Profs. Crispell and Scott, and the pastor, and the whole was interspersed with excellent singing by the school.

Much of the success of this school is doubtless owing to the labors and musical training of its superintendent, Mr. William Gilmore. On this occasion extravagance and fooleries were carefully avoided, and the effort made, we believe with success, to combine edification with pleasure.[62]

Notice that in mentioning the size of the Christmas tree, Shields was comparing Hope Church with churches in the East, not with First Church, which likely had no Christmas tree in its sanctuary. His reference to the ladies and children revealed that the life of Hope Church included more than what occurred in consistory meetings and worship services. The large number of children likely included children from the primary department connected with Hope College as well as children from Hope Church's Sunday School; Gilmore was music tutor in the first and superintendent of the second. That "extravagance and fooleries were carefully avoided" implies that on other occasions the congregation did experience times of fun and play, and these times often included the ladies and children.

Stewart Preaches to Michigan Classis

In 1867, at the request of Michigan Classis, the *Christian Intelligencer* published the sermon that Abel T. Stewart preached to classis that year. Based on Isaiah 54:2, "Enlarge the place of thy tent, and let them stretch forth the curtains of thine habitations; spare not, lengthen thy cords, and strengthen thy stakes," Stewart's sermon

---

[62] [Shields], "Letter from the West," *Christian Intelligencer*, 10 January, 1867.

urged four actions: 1. Faithful support for all of the denomination's benevolent boards, 2. Establishment in the West of depositories of books of the Board of Education, 3. Removal of "Dutch" from the name of the denomination, and 4. Establishment of a theological seminary in the West.

In developing his second point, Stewart identified inadequate access to Reformed publications as a major reason for misunderstandings about the Eastern congregations by some congregations in the West:

> We have among the Hollanders, as some of you are aware, a body of seceders. They seceded in this country several years after the Holland churches united with our denomination. They think and teach that we, the Reformed Protestant Dutch Church in North America, do not believe the Canons ratified by the Synod of Dordrecht. This on their part is simply ignorance. Why, if they had come and told us that the sun of our day does not shine, when he shines so fully that we cannot look at him in his dazzling splendor, we could not be more surprised than we were when we first heard this objection. Let them with equal truth tell us that we do not believe the Bible, but let us pour upon their minds the light of our publications. Let there be no abuse, not the first word of it, but the steady light of the truth until they feel it. Let us circulate our books, containing sometimes the exact words of the Canons, and always their thoughts, and give to the younger part of these people who read English an opportunity to see for themselves the great mistake under which their fathers labor as to our doctrinal views, and while the fathers may be lost to our fold, their children may yet return.[63]

Supporting his third point, Stewart added that "Dutch" was added to the denominational name to distinguish it from the English Episcopal Church. Long after Dutch ceased to be the language preached from Eastern American pulpits, it lingered in the denominational name. "The name is a great hindrance to our growth," declared Stewart, "It has misled and thus prevented

---

[63] Abel T. Stewart, "Church Extension," *Christian Intelligencer*, 23 May 1867.

thousands from entering our fold."[64] In 1867 the General Synod voted to change the name of the denomination from the Reformed Protestant Dutch Church in North America to the Reformed Church in America (RCA).[65]

Like Philip Phelps Jr., Abel T. Stewart saw the need for a Western theological seminary, one more accessible than New Brunswick in New Jersey, for preparing Hope College graduates to become ministers and missionaries. Hope's addition of a Theological Department and Phelps's aspirations toward making Hope College into Hope Haven University,[66] when added to the differences between Western and Eastern congregations on the issue of freemasonry, created tensions within the denomination that lasted for many years.

In 1868, Stewart noted in a report to the *Christian Intelligencer*: "Hope Church is holding on her way, with more to encourage than discourage her.... She has paid off about $1100 of debt, and added to her property $700 in improvements. She is now striving for a parsonage, with a reasonable hope of succeeding. In the meantime, she makes and steadily increases the amount of regular collections for our Boards."[67]

In the years 1868-71 Hope Church received a silver baptismal bowl and pulpit Bible from Henry O. Dubois of Hudson, New York; $200 from Simon Shindler of New York; $250 from the estate of J. B. Stewart and $100 from the First Reformed Church of Brooklyn, New York.[68]

---

[64] Stewart, "Church Extension," *Christian Intelligencer*, 23 May 1867.
[65] *The Acts and Proceedings of the General Synod of the Reformed Church in America, Convened in Extra Session in the City of Albany, in November, 1867* (New York: Board of Publication of the Reformed Church in America, 1867), 334. This document is contained within *Acts and Proceedings of the General Synod of the Reformed Church in America*, vol. 11 (New York: Board of Publication of the Reformed Church in America, 1869).
[66] Wichers, *Century of Hope*, esp. "The University Idea," 82-93.
[67] "Holland City," *Christian Intelligencer*, 12 March 1868.
[68] *Consistorial Minutes*, 18 January 1868, 1:49; 8 December 1869, 1:59; 6 May 1870, 1:62; 15 March 1871, 1:64; 12 April 1871, 1:65.

The parsonage was built in 1869 at a cost of $3,000.[69] At its May 1870 meeting, the consistory voted to insure the church for $1,200 and the parsonage for $1,500.[70] Surprisingly, the parsonage survived the fire of 1871 and still exists, though not at its original location and no longer serving as a parsonage. In about 1909 it was moved to its current location at 195 West Tenth Street.[71]

Hope Church's first parsonage

---

[69] "Hope Church," *Holland City News*, 16 May 1874, 1.
[70] *Consistorial Minutes*, 6 May 1870, 1:62.
[71] "Hope Church Highlights: An Historical Chronology of Events and Persons 1854 to 1987 Published on the Occasion of the One Hundred Twenty Fifth Anniversary of Hope Church, Holland, Michigan," 1987, 3.

The Holland Fire of 8 and 9 October 1871

The steady progress of Hope Church—as well as of the Third Reformed, Methodist Episcopal, Wesleyan,[72] and Grace Episcopal[73] churches—was severely challenged by the great fire of 1871. All five churches were destroyed, leaving only the First Reformed Church, and the True Dutch Reformed Churches.[74] After an exceedingly dry summer and autumn, fires broke out on 8 October 1871 in many places, including Peshtigo, Wisconsin; Chicago, Illinois; and Holland, Michigan. Firsthand accounts of Motoitero Oghimi (see page 23), Hope Church charter member Charles Francis Post, and Stewart supplement others readily available.[75]

Charles Francis Post's Account of the Fire

Post's account of the Holland fire became widely known after his daughter Margaret discovered among her deceased father's papers a letter that he had written on 20 December 1871 to a woman in Deedham, Massachusetts. He wrote his account of the fire to this woman in response to a request that she had pinned to a bed quilt that she and her neighbors had sent with "some twelve or fifteen

---

[72] The Wesleyan Church traces its origin to the revivals of Elder Michael Clapper in 1866. http://www.centralwesleyan.org/history/history/menu-id-25.html
[73] Grace Episcopal Church was organized in 1868. Charles A. Huttar, "The History of Grace Episcopal Church of Holland," *Joint Archives Quarterly*, 12, no. 1 (spring 2002), 1.
[74] "A Contemporary Account of the Holland Fire," in *Dutch Immigrant Memoirs and Related Writings*, ed. Henry S. Lucas, vol. 2 (Grand Rapids: Eerdmans, 1997), 496–97.
[75] Among published accounts of the Holland Fire of 1871 are Gerrit Van Schelven, "The Burning of Holland, 9 October 1871," and anon., "A Contemporary Account of the Holland Fire." Both are in *Dutch Immigrant Memoirs and Related Writings*, ed. Henry S. Lucas—2:1–7, and 2:492–97, respectively. Other accounts are summarized or quoted in Elton J. Bruins, "Holocaust in Holland: 1871," *Michigan History*, vol. 55, no. 4 (Winter 1971), 289-304.

barrels and three large cases of clothing for distribution among the sufferers."[76] The woman sent the letter to the editor of her local newspaper in 1871 so that those who had contributed relief could learn more about the fire and those who received the aid. In 1939 Margaret, who was living in South Bend, Indiana, sent the letter to the *Holland City News*, which published the story shortly before the sixty-eighth anniversary of the fire. Following is the account of Charles F. Post:

> The fire that swept away two-thirds of our young city was, in respect to description, like a great battle-field, each one engaged in battle can tell what he saw, but cannot give an account of the whole scene. Thus I can only tell what I saw, which will be but a small part of the whole scene in detail, though it may apply as a general view.
>
> Imagine, then, our town lying lengthwise East and West. On the south were cultivated farms, pieces of woodland, fields of fallen timber, piles of old logs, treetops and stumps, bordering on the southern limits of the city, all in the process of being cleared up and improved. Several weeks before the fire, some farmer, south-west of the city, had, in the process of clearing his land, set some fire. No rain falling, the fire had remained in the stumps and old roots, smoldering all these weeks. At last the fearful wind of Oct. 8th fanned these sparks into flames, and catching fences on fire, was carried on the wings of the wind; buildings were soon on fire[;] some low, swampy ground, ordinarily fire-proof, now dry as tinder, next came in the way. The heavy smoke enveloped the city; the people went out to see if there was any danger to the city. With any ordinary wind there was no danger but what could be met and overcome at a moment's notice. At the speed that the fire was then making it would not reach the city's limits before Monday evening. So many returned to their houses; I returned to mine, but I could not rest easy, so I got all the pails, wash-tubs, etc. that we had, and filled them with water. I then took a large sprinkler, and carried water upon the house-roof and wet it thoroughly. As the sun went down the wind increased instead of decreased, as is usual, and soon the tolling of the church bells told of danger. People hurried to the 'front', and fought the flames inch

---

[76] "Man's Personal Experience in Fire of 1871," *Holland City News*, 8 October 1939, 1.

by inch, yet still it advanced. The wind blew a fearful gale, carrying coals far over the heads of those who fought. Flesh and blood could not longer stand the heat and smoke. Buildings were already on fire, so each one fled for their home to save, if possible, something. I had returned to my house before the unequal contest was given up, and was on my house top when the flames from the south-west swept in. My house is in the southern part of the city, about midway East and West [immediately south of the Market Square, now Centennial Park]. As I stood on my roof the fire swept nearly all west of me, moving from south-west to north-[east], so that it passed me by. It seemed as though the fire leaped from roof to roof, from house to house, faster than a person could run. The truth was it rained coals of fire and huge fire brands clear through the city after the first buildings were on fire; from these the fire sprang up at every point, so people had to flee for their lives, there being no time to save anything. My wife, with her little ones, had fled to the north-east part of the city to her sister's; she soon returned to me to know where next to go, as that place did not seem safe. I directed her to go to a place farther east. No building had burned there as yet, and I thought we were safe, though the heat and smoke were so great as to be unbearable almost. As I still carried water upon my roof, I turned my eyes South. I saw a large field of timber, hitherto untouched by fire, but now just caught; the flames leaped from tree to tree and rolled in vast sheets over the dry timber of the ground; soon, two houses and a barn were on fire, and the flames flowing directly from them to where I was. I saw no chance to save my house now; I was almost blinded with smoke, so I gave up and went in search of my wife and little ones. I found they had reached the place I directed, which proved to be a place of safety, though it had been a hard struggle. Baby [Margaret] was about eighteen months old; she had been ill during the summer; my wife carried her, though the wind was so strong that several times she had to throw herself on the ground until the fury of the wind had passed, and then struggle on. Walter is a manly little fellow of five years. His uncle had given him a nice little wheelbarrow but a few weeks before; this he would not leave behind, but kept it till he came back home. Once the wind took both the boy and his wheelbarrow clear from the ground, and carried them some little distance; still, Walter would not let go the handles, though his hat was gone and his eyes full of sand. Here with my family I waited for a while, when, hearing from one who had fled later, that my house still remained, I tried to go back, but found so much fire burning old stumps and fences between where I was and my house, and the heat and smoke so great, that I could not get through. I waited again for a while, then taking another route, I reached my house and found it safe, although my barn, a little southwest on the same quarter acre lot was burned, and the fence burned to within forty feet of the house. The house had been on fire, but some who had no families to look after, had stayed and extinguished the flames, as the thorough wetting I had given the roof made it slow to burn. My forethought in wetting the roof and leaving plenty of water standing ready for use, saved my house, and not mine only, but at least two-thirds of the one-third of the unburned of the city, as my house was the key to the greater part of the rest of the town.

Still not until the next day could I bring my family back, so great was the heat and smoke. This was my personal experience, others had a still more trying one. One old lady carried out of her house some things, and returning for more, was caught in the flames and burned....

Many, when they saw the danger, buried their beds, clothes and other valuables in the light sand of which the soil is composed, but the wind blew the sand off, and the goods were burned. Clothes and beds put in wells were even burned down to the water. It does not seem possible that fire could have sought out and burned as it did in so many apparently safe places.

After the smoke and heat of the fire had cleared away, what a scene of desolation and sorrow was present. Where was food and clothing to come from? Our sister city of Grand Haven answered the first question by sending a car load of cooked provisions. Other towns near were but a little behind her. Never did plump loaves of bread, and pans of baked pork and beans look more tempting. The hungry were hardly fed before boxes of clothing began to arrive, and from week to week came until our wants were supplied. We organized, and began a systematic distribution of clothing and bedding. For nearly sixty days I worked in the committee room of the clothing department.

Our fire was a great and terrible one, but the great and noble response to our city for help, from all parts of our country was equal to the emergency. When I was a boy, and for the first time unfurled the 'Stars and Stripes' for a Fourth of July celebration I felt proud of being an American; when, in later years, at my country's call I enlisted in the army, I was proud of my nation. Now, when I see the prompt and noble response of a whole nation when suffering people cry, I feel a higher, deeper and holier pride in my nation and my people.[77]

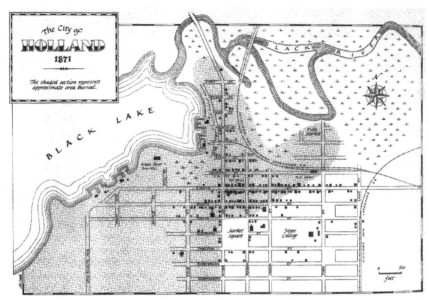

Area burned by the Holland fire of 1871

Abel T. Stewart's Account of the Fire

Stewart's account of the great fire is in an article he wrote to the editor of the *Christian Intelligencer* soon after the fire:

> Our last public service in Hope church was held in the morning, and the sermon on Proverbs 30:1-5 inclusive, bore reference to the dangers with which we were surrounded. In the afternoon we shortened the exercises of the Sabbath-school and left the house, then filled with smoke from approaching fires in the country, and went out to ward them off, if possible, at a distance. They had been beaten back on the previous Wednesday night, when they reached to Prof. Crispell's

---

[77] "Man's Personal Experience In Fire Of 1871," *Holland City News*," 8 October 1939, 1, 4.

garden, in the southeast portion of the city; but they continued to thicken out on the southern and southwestern border until about __ [sic] A.M., on Sabbath night, when they kindled upon the Third Reformed church in the rear, and spread rapidly in the direction of the wind to the northeast, taking Hope church, the Methodist Episcopal church, and everything that would burn, to the Fish-Market on the river. Earlier in the night, the fire had burned northeast, along the lake, to Eighth-street, and now it burned eastwardly and northeastwardly; also destroying almost every building in its track. The parsonage of Hope church,[78] the college buildings, residences of Prof. Crispell and Beck, and Dr. Ledeboer, and the parsonage and church edifice of the First Reformed church, are spared, but more than two-thirds of the city, including almost all of the business portion, are swept away.

Heavy is the loss of Prof. Scott, for it consists not merely of house and household comforts, but of his entire library and all his papers. As teacher in the Academic and Theological departments, he cannot go on with advantage without receiving immediate help in the way of suitable books. The Church pays nothing to Prof. Scott and his associates for theological instruction, and when their libraries are burned up, she ought at once to see that the loss is made up so far as not to permit the students to suffer loss.

Some of our citizens hastily buried a few things, and where they succeeded in getting them three or four inches under the sand, preserved them, but most of those burned out buried little or nothing. After the fire really took hold of the city, there was not opportunity. The wind was so strong that one could scarce stand up against it, the sparks and cinders so thick upon the earth that there was scarcely a bare inch on which to tread, and the smoke was yet more terrible than the fire. From two to four o'clock A.M., I saw no living thing on an area of four acres, but a cat which was often under my feet.

Some who had opportunity to view the desolating flames say the scene was grand beyond what they had ever seen. In one sense, I believe it was so, but to me and in my district, during a portion of the night, the fire was simply a terrible monster, an awful thing of

---

[78] According to "Hope Church Highlights: An Historical Chronology of Events and Persons 1854 to 1987 Published on the Occasion of the One Hundredth Twenty Fifty Anniversary of Hope Church, Holland, Michigan," 1987, this parsonage was moved from its location then (presumably not far from Hope Church) to its present location at 195 West 10th Street in about 1909.

life, that leaped and ran over roof and turret and ground and tree, shrieking and roaring, and licking up every material thing in its track. A brick building was no more than a frame one. The very earth burned and threw sparks for several hours. In a few instances, human effort was marked by signal success; in others, neglect had its terrible reward, while in others, no care, no labor, no preparation on that terrible night could have availed. The visitation seemed almost direct from God.

Why this calamity has overtaken us, let me not now undertake to say, God's "judgments are a great deep."

On last Sabbath, what could be gathered of Hope church congregation went to and worshipped in Hope College chapel. We were an humble and yet, I trust, a grateful people. Did we think of our house just freed from debt, and lamps and pulpit-cushion and library from Tarrytown, our beautiful Bible, just given by Henry Dubois, of Hudson, new organ, communion service, swinging-lamp chain from First church, New-Brunswick. Oh! yes, we did, and we were able to think that, severe as was the loss, the Church itself, the body of Christ as represented here in His members, was not destroyed.

Hope church had become nearly half sustaining. It is not so now. But God permitted her loss.... Surely He doeth all things well, and we know that all things work together for good to them that love God, to them who are called according to His purpose.[79]

Hope College's first chapel/gymnasium, built by Phelps and his students in 1862

---

[79] "Correspondence, Holland City, Mich., Oct 17th, 1871," *Christian Intelligencer*, 26 October 1871.

Despite all of the material losses, Hope Church's historic chandelier from New York City's Middle Dutch Church was rescued before the fire consumed the building. In 1885 the chandelier was returned to New York. After being stored for several years in the parsonage of the First Reformed Church in Ghent, New York, it was lighted on Christmas Eve of 1895 in that church, where Philip Tertius Phelps was the minister.[80] Philip Tertius Phelps never married, and for several years his widowed sister, Frances Phelps Otte, lived with him. He died in 1944 in East Northfield, Massachusetts.[81] The Phelps family donated the chandelier to the Hope College Museum, and the Holland Museum now owns the chandelier.[82]

After the fire, the Hope Church congregation worshipped for many months in the Hope College building that served as gymnasium and chapel. Elders' meeting minutes for 19 January 1872 contain a succinct, sad understatement: "the regular time for communion season had been postponed and the place of meeting changed in consequence of the burning of our church edifice, communion service, and everything used in our worship."[83]

Rebuilding Hope Church and Holland

Stories about the Holland fire stirred the hearts and opened the purses of many. The Board of Education of the RCA collected and sent about $40,000 for assistance to Holland. The funds came

---

[80] Typed pages about "THE CHANDELIER" in the "biography" folder, H88-0122, box 1, Phelps, Philip Jr., (1826–1896), Joint Archives of Holland. See also 1941.23.21_info.pdf file from Holland Museum Collections Manager, Stacey Tvedten, to the author.
[81] Gasero, *Historical Directory*, 306.
[82] 1941.23.21_info.pdf file from Holland Museum Collections Manager, Stacey Tvedten, to the author. The chandelier, once having been in a New York Post Office, is now in a building that once was Holland's Post Office. The Hope College Museum at one time occupied the top floor of Van Raalte Hall, a landmark that was consumed by fire in April 1980. Had the chandelier not been transferred to the Holland Museum, it likely would have perished.
[83] *Elders' Minutes*, 19 January 1872:26.

"mainly from friends of the Holland Colony" in the East, but also from Pella, Iowa, and the Netherlands.[84] The *Consistorial Minutes* of Hope Church recorded more than fifty-five contributions received for rebuilding and furnishing the sanctuary. They range from $2 from Sing Sing (perhaps from a prisoner?) to $1,000 each from a Mrs. Dinison from Brooklyn and from a Mrs. Mary Lee Stewart. At least thirty churches, twelve Sabbath School classes, and ten individuals sent contributions totaling about $8,300.[85] There is no record of funds received from insurance; many insurance companies failed because of the extensive fires in 1871.

Carl Pfeiffer of New York City was hired as architect under the supervision of J. Masterton of Bronxville, New York. Building superintendents were first W. G. Robinson of Grand Rapids and then J. R. Kleyn of Holland. The builder was J. W. Minderhout, a member of Hope Church. Painters were charter member Bernardus Grotenhuis and son. The Building Committee comprised Bernardus Grotenhuis, Dr. Thomas E. Annis, Henry D. Post, and Prof. Charles Scott.[86] By the end of October 1872, the *Holland City News* reported: "Ground is being broken preparatory to laying the foundation walls of the Second Reformed Church in this city. It is to be re-built upon the grounds of the former church edifice; it will cost about $10,000."[87] The first church had faced Tenth Street, but the new church faced Eleventh. Unconfirmed hearsay passed

---

[84] *Holland City News*, 10 October 1891, 8. The funds were likely distributed by the local relief committee chaired by Dr. Bernardus Ledeboer. Members of this committee included Henry D. Post, secretary; K. Schaddelee, treasurer; Albertus C. Van Raalte, Philip Phelps Jr., Charles Scott, Abel T. Stewart, Gerrit Van Schelven, and others.

[85] *Consistorial Minutes*, 1:76–82.

[86] "Hope Church," *Holland City News*, 16 May 1874, 1. Architect Carl Pfeiffer, born in Germany in 1834, came to the United States in his teens. Among buildings in New York City that he designed were the Church of the Messiah, the 1871 Roosevelt Hospital, and the Fifth Avenue Presbyterian Church. http://en.wikipedia.org/wiki/Carl_Pfeiffer_%28architect%29

[87] *Holland City News*, 31 October 1872, 3. Including the furnace, the cost came to $11,000, as reported in "Hope Church," *Holland City News*, 16 May 1874, 1.

down for several generations reckoned that the new church "was built near 11th Street to escape the far-reaching voice of the pastor in a neighboring church on 10th Street."[88]

Shortly before the formal dedication of the new church on 4 May 1874, Stewart announced "an outstanding indebtedness of $600." Of that amount "over $500 was immediately assumed by the congregation present," and about $100 was assumed by Stewart. He conducted the dedication service, assisted by Philip Phelps Jr., Cornelius E. Crispell, Charles Scott, and Theodoric Romeyn Beck—all of Hope College—Henry Utterwick of Third Reformed Church, and the Reverend John H. Karsten of Alto, Wisconsin. At that time the total adult membership of Hope Church was sixty-one.[89]

The 1874 "Rural Gothic" church,[90] set back eighty feet from Eleventh Street,[91] was fifty-five feet across the front and seventy-five feet deep. At the rear were three classrooms, totaling forty-four by thirty-one feet. Stone for the foundation and basement walls came from the Waverly quarry of John Roost. The church tower, which remains into the twenty-first century, is eighty feet tall. Topping it are an open bracketed belfry and a thirty-one-foot spire.[92]

---

[88] "50 Years Ago Today February 17, 1942," a news clipping likely from the *Holland Sentinel*, among a file of clippings in W91-1034, box 10, Hope Church, Holland, Michigan, Joint Archives of Holland. A check of *Holland City News* and *Holland Sentinel* of February 1892 failed to substantiate the clipping.
[89] "Hope Church," *Holland City News*, 16 May 1874, 1.
[90] "Hope Church," *Holland City News*, 16 May 1874, 1.
[91] "Losing a bit of history: Hope Church project to eliminate building," *Holland Sentinel*, 21 February 1981, 8.
[92] "Hope Church," *Holland City News*, 16 May 1874, 1.

Hope Church of 1874

The fencing around the church, likely added after 1874, served a useful purpose. According to an old story, on a sultry August evening a village cow had wandered over to graze on the grass surrounding Hope Church. The cow's bell provided antiphonal accompaniment to Stewart's sermon. He interrupted his sermon to ask sexton William Deming to drive the cow away. The sexton left the worship service, found the cow, and made sure the cow circled the church, the bell jingling all the way, until the sermon was completed.[93]

The forty-two by seventy-three-foot sanctuary of the church contained ninety-two pews and could seat five hundred people. The interior walls were "plastered with a sand finish, painted a pink color, and paneled off with ornamented borders." Its stained glass windows were created by George Misch and Brothers of Chicago, Illinois.[94]

The newspaper account of the dedication praised Stewart for his "incessant labors in obtaining the funds required for this costly and beautiful edifice," especially from his friends in the East. As of 1874, the "present value of the property of Hope Church, including the real estate, church building and parsonage" was "$16,000."[95] The corresponding secretary's report to the *Christian Intelligencer* in October 1875 stated:

> Hope church has everything desirable in the way of attractive church accommodations and a very intelligent audience and is steadily growing. Its position and usefulness here will be better understood and appreciated when God shall have broken the barriers down and melted away the lines formed by languages, customs, and nationalities by an abundant effusion of the quickening Spirit.[96]

In 1875, the consistory appointed Miss Bessie Pfanstiehl and Miss Laura Heald to head a committee of ladies to solicit subscriptions to procure matting for the aisles of the church. Within a month, they had raised the necessary $47. Three years

---

[93] "The Village Cow Bell," *Holland City News*, 18 May 1939, 1.
[94] "Hope Church," *Holland City News*, 16 May 1874, 1.
[95] "Hope Church," *Holland City News*, 16 May 1874, 1. One of those friends from the East, the Reverend Anson Du Bois, for example, presented some lamps from his Flatlands, New York, congregation to Hope Church. *Holland City News*, 22 August 1874, 4.
[96] "Domestic Missions.—Holland Hope College and Seminary," *Christian Intelligencer*, 7 October 1875.

later money contributed by the Ladies' Society was used to purchase a carpet for the pulpit and a large lamp outside the church.[97]

In 1882, as in several other years, Hope Church was the setting for the Commencement exercises of Hope College. Frances Phelps Otte, commenting on the photograph of the church interior, stated that the draperies, flower-covered fountains, anchor symbol, and class motto, "Step By Step, Lifting Better Up to Best," were additions for the Commencement.[98] She and Sarah Gertrude Alcott, the first two women to graduate from Hope College, were among eight comprising the class of 1882.

---

[97] *Consistorial Minutes*, 1:85, 107, 108.
[98] Photograph. W91-1034, box 11, Hope Church, Holland, Michigan, Joint Archives of Holland.

*Interior of the 1874 church at
1882 Hope College Commencement*

Interior of the 1874 church as it appeared in 1942 as a meeting room

The sketch below (a portion of a larger drawing) shows the extent to which Holland rebuilt itself by 1875. Van Vleck Hall (2), First Reformed Church (3), and the True Dutch Reformed Church (6) at the site where Central Avenue Christian Reformed Church is located were untouched by the fire, but much else in the sketch was constructed after the fire.[99]

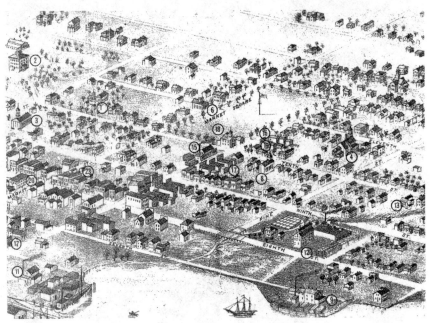

Drawing of Holland 1875

1: Public School, 2: Van Vleck Hall, 3: First Reformed Church, 4: Second Reformed (Hope) Church, 6: True Dutch Reformed Church, 8: Methodist Church, 9: Plugger Lumber & Flour Mills, 11: Stave Factory, 12: Cappon & Bertsch Lumber Co., 13: City Brewery, 15: Phoenix Planing Mill, 16: Sash, Door & Agricultural Shops, 17: Carriage Factory, 18: Engine Rooms, 20: City Hotel, 23: Post Office. (Several numbered buildings are not shown in this portion of the drawing.)

---

[99] Gerrit Van Schelven, "The Burning of Holland, 9 October 1871," in *Dutch Immigrant Memoirs and Related Writings*, 2:3.

A view of the environs of Hope Church shows other churches that also were rebuilt after the fire: Third Reformed Church, Grace Episcopal Church, and the Methodist Episcopal Church.

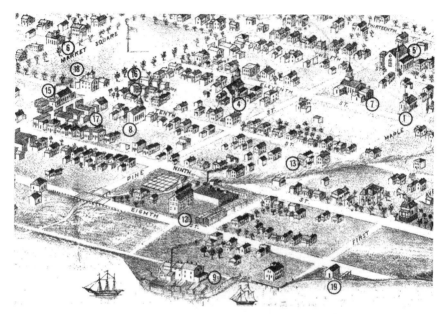

Hope Church environs 1875

1: Public School, 4: Second Reformed (Hope) Church, 5: Third Reformed Church, 6: True Dutch Reformed Church, 7: Grace Episcopal Church, 8: Methodist Episcopal Church, 9: Plugger Lumber & Flour Mills, 11: Stave Factory, 12: Cappon & Bertsch Lumber Co., 13: City Brewery, 15: Phoenix Planing Mill, 16: Sash, Door & Agricultural Shops, 17: Carriage Factory, 18: Engine Rooms, 19: Ship Yard. (Several numbered buildings are not shown in this portion of the drawing.)

The new Hope Church drew new members. At one service in the spring of 1876 Stewart baptized eleven babies and children.[100] The Sunday School picnic that summer was a day-long outing:

> Hope Church Sabbath-school had a very fine picnic on Thursday last. It was quite well attended and was not marred by the slightest accident. The tug Twilight had a barge handsomely fitted up with awnings and evergreens, on which they embarked in the morning and were towed down to the mouth, and after roaming and frolicking over the romantic hills near Black Lake harbor, returned in the evening perfectly satisfied and weary.[101]

In 1877 the belfry tower received its bell. Measuring forty-one inches across its mouth, the bell in the church's tower weighed more than fifteen hundred pounds. Stationary, it was rung by a 250-pound hammer. Because the bell, purchased from a closing Battle Creek church, was costlier than anticipated, the entire community was invited to contribute to its purchase, and many responded.[102]

Hope Church in its 1877 annual report to the Particular Synod of Chicago commented on "the prosperity of her Sunday School, the attendance upon the word, her growth in spiritual life and large increase of membership."[103] In addition to the regular morning and evening Sabbath services and Sunday School, three groups met weekly: a young people's group, a regular prayer meeting, and a Sunday School teachers' meeting. As a result of missionary work at Ventura in the Lake Shore area, virtually in Elder Clapper's

---

[100] News item from 17 June 1876, quoted by Gary Pulano, *Holland Sentinel*, 17 June 2001, A14.
[101] *Holland City News*, 15 July 1876.
[102] "Losing a bit of history: Hope Church project to eliminate building," *Holland Sentinel*, 21 February 1981, 8. The Battle Creek church that closed could well have been its Reformed Church. According to Gasaro, the Battle Creek Reformed Church ended in 1877, and Christ Community Reformed Church in Battle Creek was started in 1947, *Historical Directory*, 491.
[103] *Reformed Church in America. Minutes of the Particular Synod of Chicago.* vol. 3, (Constantine, MI: L. T. Hull, 1876–1885), 41.

backyard, nineteen members were received on confession and six by letter of transfer in 1877.

Looking Outward

The attractive new church sanctuary did not cause Hope Church to focus inward. As a delegate of the Reformed Church, Stewart in 1874 visited the General Assembly of the Southern Presbyterian Church in Columbus, Mississippi. Addressing that body, he alluded to a "plan of co-operation" between that assembly and the Reformed General Synod. "The general outlook to me," said Stewart, "is that all barriers will be removed, and the churches will become one."[104]

> We can wait for this union. It is too good and glorious to be spoiled by haste. Our standard and yours emanated from the same source, the word of God. The union will be the outgrowth of love, founded on truth.[105]

The next year he reported on his visit as a delegate to the Union Committees of the Southern Presbyterian Church and RCA meeting in New York City. His report was similar to reports of comparable interdenominational meetings a century later. Said Stewart about the meeting:

> Union between us can only be the work of time and patient effort, and as long as there is a growth in this respect we should be thankful. When our delegate to the next General Assembly shall meet the Southern brethren, hear them preach, observe their purity of doctrine and fervent desire to extend the gospel kingdom, he will wish more than ever that [we] were one.[106]

---

[104] *Holland City News*, 30 May 1874, 4.
[105] *Holland City News*, 30 May 1874, 4.
[106] "Holland City, Michigan," *Christian Intelligencer*, 11 March 1875.

Reporting on recent visits by missionaries to Holland, Stewart described in glowing terms the enthusiasm of local Reformed churches in learning about and supporting foreign missions:

> We lately had a great treat in hearing Rev. Jacob Chamberlain, M.D. [missionary to India], speak on missions. In the morning he spoke an hour and a half in Hope church, and in the evening nearly two hours in the First church. The attendance was very large, and no one seemed to tire. He told us of the settlement and work of our dear Brother [Enne J.] Heeren [missionary to India]. Hope Church seemed to see again her son, and the Holland churches who are supporting him to see their encouragement. We shall not forget Dr. Chamberlain and his story of the preaching of the gospel among the Telugus. We were reminded of [Elihu] Doty [missionary to Batavia, Borneo, and China] and [William Henry] Steele [missionary to Java and Borneo] and [John Van Nest] Talmage [missionary to China] and [John] Scudder [missionary to India] and others coming back to their native lands to regain strength to prosecute their work. How grand it is.[107]

Abel T. Stewart's Legacy

Late in 1877, Stewart was "prostrated by a tedious illness," and for the first three months of 1878 he was absent for medical treatment in the East. In his absence, professors of Hope College conducted worship services.[108]

In May 1878, the consistory received a letter from Stewart, who was convalescing at the home of his sister in Watkins, New York:

> After an absence of nearly five months in quest of health, I find my recovery so slow and so doubtful that I think it my duty to resign my Pastorate.
>
> When this relation was formed twelve years ago, you numbered between twenty and twenty-five members, owned a house of worship

---

[107] "Holland City, Michigan," *Christian Intelligencer*, 11 March 1875.
[108] *Consistorial Minutes*, 20 March 1878, 1:107.

which, exclusive of its indebtedness, was valued at fifteen hundred dollars, and was entirely dependent on the Board for the Pastor's salary. Now it numbers one hundred and fourteen members, has new and ample accommodations in the way of Church building and Parsonage, at a cost of many thousands of dollars, entirely out of debt and is—considering its benevolence, given mostly to the Boards and direct interests of the denomination—half self-sustaining.[109]

He instructed the consistory to read the letter as his farewell to Hope Church. Days later, a telegram informed the consistory of the death of Stewart.[110]

That ties between Hope Church and the Methodist Episcopal Church were close is evident from the cancellation of worship services on 2 June 1878 so that its pastor and congregation could attend Stewart's memorial service at Hope Church.[111] The Reverend Paul D. Van Cleef's eulogy of Stewart gives him major credit for the rebuilding of Hope Church after the fire:

> The great fire consumed their house of worship, and the little church staggered under the fearful calamity that fell upon the young city of Holland. But the pastor, nothing daunted, went to work immediately to erect another and a larger building. By his personal efforts, and by dint of wise business management he succeeded in an undertaking which at that time seemed almost helpless, and a large and beautiful sanctuary erected at a surprisingly small cost, stands a monument to his zeal, his self-sacrifice, and his judicious management.[112]

The most impressive memorial of all came by letter to Professor Charles Scott from Motoitero Oghimi, one of the Japanese students whom Stewart had baptized into the Christian faith:

---

[109] *Consistorial Minutes*, 22 May 1878, 1:109.
[110] *Consistorial Minutes*, 22 May 1878, 1:110. He was fifty-six years old.
[111] *Holland City News*, 1 June 1878, 5.
[112] P. D. Van Cleef, "Abel T. Stewart, D. D.," *Christian Intelligencer*, 6 June 1878, 4.

The Japanese members of Hope Church desire to express their deep sense of the loss of our esteemed pastor, Dr. Stewart.... It is true that our minister sometimes felt discouraged, because he did not see the good results which he had anticipated from his labor; but perhaps he did not realize what he had been doing. In his flock were gathered four of those who came from a heathen country, and who had never known the way of life; but here they learned with joy to love 'the sweet name of Jesus.' It was not through him alone that we became converted, yet he was one of the chief instrumentalities which God used to bring our souls 'out of the darkness into light.' We are, therefore, conscious that when we shall have returned to Japan, imparting what we have received to others, our deceased pastor's work for Christ will bear fruit, even on the other side of the Pacific.[113]

---

[113] *Memorial of the Rev. Abel T. Stewart*, ed. Charles Scott, Thomas E. Annis, and Henry Baum.

3 ... Steadily Growing

Upon the death of the Reverend Abel T. Stewart, the consistory sought advice from the male members of the congregation and those who contributed to the support of the pastor. It then proceeded to call the Reverend Abraham Thompson, a missionary pastor in Pella, Iowa,[1] who declined. The consistory then sought advice from the Board of Domestic Missions, which sent the Reverend Daniel Van Pelt "to occupy the pulpit three Sabbaths and make the acquaintance of the congregation."[2]

In June 1878, the consistory invited "members of the church, both male and female, and others who contribute to the support of the church" to vote by ballot whether to call Van Pelt of Spring Valley, New York. Based on the outcome of the vote, a call was sent to Van Pelt.[3] He declined. The consistory then called him again. The terms of the call were the same except the term was shortened to a year.

Van Pelt's response to this second call was bold. He refused a one-year term, which "would necessarily lessen the heartiness of my labor." Instead, he made a counter-proposal, asking for a commitment from Hope Church to take steps to become a self-supporting congregation. His own words convey his persuasive voice:

---

[1] Gasero, *Historical Directory*, 395.
[2] *Consistorial Minutes*, 10 October 1878, 1:119.
[3] *Consistorial Minutes*, 2 November 1878, 1:120–21. Technically, consistory rather than the congregation calls a minister; a consistory acting without support of the congregation can find itself in trouble.

In the following year, "members both male and female" were invited to a meeting for the election of church officers." *Consistorial Minutes*, 5 December 1879, 1:136.

Voting by women in most Reformed churches, especially those in the Midwest, was not permitted until many decades later. In the denomination, decisions on who were allowed to participate in congregational votes were left to each congregation.

I must see one great obstacle removed. I cannot agree to accept your call unless all my salary comes from the people. <u>Upon this point I am not to be shaken</u>. But you will say that you can not possibly raise nine hundred dollars. I know that; and I would not do you the injustice of insisting upon this point, if I wished this to remain the amount of my salary. But I have a proposition to make. Your portion of the sum stipulated in the present call is four hundred dollars. Now, make me out another call and promise to give me six hundred dollars without any aid from the Board. Thus I alone personally, if the way should be clear to my acceptance of it, would sacrifice three hundred dollars, asking the people to bear united only an additional two hundred. Propose this to the people, and see if they have spirit enough to unite heart and hand in accomplishing this thing. An opportunity is afforded them to become a self-supporting church at once. The very sense of being such would give you an impulse towards a glorious prosperity. You and I both would enjoy this satisfaction of being independent and not objects of charity. No doubt this very feeling would have such a salutary effect that in another year you could give me an adequate salary such as you yourself would be proud to give the Pastor of Hope Church.... I am confident the Lord has guided me in making the present proposal.[4]

In response to this letter, the consistory appointed a committee to solicit additional subscriptions to the pew rents in order to raise $600 and comply with conditions of Van Pelt's proposal. They so informed Van Pelt, and he then accepted the call.[5]

Daniel Van Pelt's Ministry

After completing his theological studies at New Brunswick Theological Seminary and serving fewer than two years in his first pastorate in Spring Valley, New York—a church organized in 1863—Van Pelt came to Hope Church in early 1879.

His powers of persuasion soon led to his marriage to Gertrude F. Scott, a member of Hope Church who was the daughter of the

---

[4] *Consistorial Minutes*, 6 December 1878, 1:124–25.
[5] *Consistorial Minutes*, 6 December 1878, 1:125–26.

Reverend Charles Scott, the second president of Hope College. Daniel Van Pelt, age 26, and Gertrude Scott, age 24, were married 21 July 1879 by the bride's father.[6]

His powers of persuasion were not effective, however, in preventing the loss of a considerable number of church members. In 1880, the twenty-five members received in 1877 as a result of missionary work at Ventura were "by their own request dismissed to form a Separate [Reformed] Church organization; provided committee of classis deem such organization advisable."[7] The members were dismissed, but Michigan Classis apparently did not give its blessing to creation of a Reformed Church in Ventura. Reports of Michigan Classis to the Particular Synod of Chicago make no mention of a proposed church in Ventura. The potential church plant was likely plucked by a church of another denomination, perhaps the Wesleyan Methodists at Ventura led by exhorter Michael J. Clapper.[8]

Daniel Van Pelt

Nor were Van Pelt's powers of persuasion effective in a rare attempt to exercise church discipline on a church member. *Elders' Minutes* of the summer of 1881 reveal the saga of the attempts of the consistory and pastor to change the behavior of Peter F. Pfanstiehl,

---

[6] *Membership Records of the Hope Reformed Church of Holland, Michigan*, Book 2, 278. W01-1034, box 11, Hope Church, Holland, Michigan, Joint Archives of Holland. See also "Record of Hope Church Holland Michigan 1862–1916." W91-1034, box 10, Hope Church, Holland, Michigan, Joint Archives of Holland.
[7] *Elders' Minutes*, 13 September 1880:51–52.
[8] The former Wesleyan Methodist Church of Ventura is now the residence of Hope Church members Jean McFadden and Ben Picciuca.

who with his wife Helena had joined Hope Church in 1878.[9] The consistory sent the following letter to Pfanstiehl:

> It became known, to us, after having been publicly talked about & made the occasion of much scandal to this church, that Mr. Peter Pfanstiehl, member of this church & captain of a steam-tug-boat, had been running excursion parties up & down Black Lake on Sabbaths June 5 & June 29 & others. On ascertaining this to be the fact the pastor made several attempts to see the brother personally: after failing once or twice he sent a note, requesting him to mention a time when he could be seen. Mr. Pfanstiehl did not appoint a time but left word with his family to tell the pastor that it was of no use seeing him, as he was not going to stop this thing for the church or anybody. At a meeting of the consistory, on July 1st the pastor brought the matter before them. This being a case of general rumor, ... preliminary steps (except such as pastor had voluntarily taken already) were unnecessary, neither were witnesses required at whose instance the member was to be cited. A citation was therefore drawn up, specifying charges, & summoning the brother to appear before consistory on Friday 22nd July inst., giving him more than the required 10 days to put in an appearance & answer.[10]

To this summons the pastor received a reply from Pfanstiehl:

---

[9] *Hope Church Membership Records 1862–1910*, 54. W91-1034, box 11, Hope Church, Holland, Michigan, Joint Archives of Holland. This Peter Pfanstiehl, husband of Helena Meulenbroek, with whom he had seventeen children ("Pieter Frederick Pfanstiehl," *Holland City News*, July 16, 1892, 4), is not to be confused with the Peter Pfanstiehl married to Cornelia Dykema, who with his wife joined Hope Church by transfer from the Third Reformed Church in 1875 and whose daughter Christina married Albertus (Allie) C. Van Raalte, grandson of Holland's founder.

[10] *Elders' Minutes*, 53–54. This sensitivity to desecration of the Sabbath was not unique to Hope Church. In 1879, the Particular Synod of Chicago passed a resolution to urge upon all Churches and Church members within its bounds, the duty ... to abate or remove the violation of the holy Sabbath by Sunday railroad trains, steamers, mails, etc., and to refrain from all complicity with and encouragement of such, or other Sabbath desecration." *Reformed Church in America. Minutes of the Particular Synod of Chicago, Convened in Holland, Michigan, May 7, 1879.* vol. 3 (Constantine, MI: L. T. Hull, 1879), 112–13.

I am ready for my discharge from Hope Church, so don't count me member any more.[11]

Elders' Minutes tell how Hope Church leaders responded:

To this pastor replied by letter (as more than half-a-dozen attempts to meet the brother had met with the same failure) that a member could not be thus summarily discharged, explaining to the brother the constitutional steps necessary, telling him the consequence of his not appearing at the time & place specified by summons.[12]

After Pfanstiehl twice more refused to appear before consistory to answer its charges, the consistory "resolved to suspend Mr. Peter Pfanstiehl from the privilege of communion for an indefinite period."[13]

Less than two years later, however, with no evidence in the minutes of any repentance by Pfanstiehl or of a reconciliation between him and consistory, the tide of disapproval inexplicably turned. Van Pelt's successor, the Reverend Thomas Walker Jones, "delivered a very eloquent and feeling address in behalf of the guests present" at the golden anniversary celebration of Peter and Helena Pfanstiehl, and Philip Phelps Jr. praised Pfanstiehl for the "prominent part" he had played in developing businesses in Holland.[14] After Pfanstiehl's death in 1892, his funeral was held in Hope Church with the Reverend Henry E. Dosker of Third Reformed Church preaching in English and the Reverend Jacob Van Houte of First Reformed Church preaching in Dutch.[15]

---

[11] *Elders' Minutes*, 54.
[12] *Elders' Minutes*, 54.
[13] *Elders' Minutes*, 55.
[14] "Golden Wedding," *Holland City News*, 9 June 1883:4. It's possible that Pfanstiehl, though denied Communion, received praises from Jones and Phelps to keep the good will of his family, which included his son, the Reverend Albert A. Pfanstiehl, and to keep a door open to repentance.
[15] "Pieter Frederick Pfanstiehl," *Holland City News*, 16 July 1892, 4. Pfanstiehl died after the Reverend John T. Bergen had resigned to care for his aged parents and before the Reverend Henry G. Birchby was called, so Dosker preached.

Despite difficulties in trying to discipline a recalcitrant member and some "agitations" over Freemasonry in Holland Classis, Van Pelt in his annual report for 1880 indicated that Hope Church was running on an even keel:

> We have nothing special to record as regards the state of religion in our church during the present year. God sees the hearts of men and he alone can rightly judge them. What we have seen of the evidence of the Christian life among our people would lead us to think that they are thoughtful, attentive to the preached Word, and careful in attending the ordinances of Grace. The agitations round about us find little sympathy in our midst; and, while desirous of remaining true to Christ, we hesitate to do injustice to our Christian brethren. Our experiment of self-support has succeeded during the first year, though we need still strain to place it upon a firmer and more permanent basis.[16]

In 1881 the consistory instituted a new plan for pew rentals. Instead of an assessment per pew, there would be an auction of pews to raise money for the pastor's salary.[17] The auction of pews proved so successful that consistory raised the pastor's salary to $700 for 1882.

Though the increase in salary might have sweetened his sojourn in Holland, Van Pelt had little sympathy for its anti-Freemasonry climate. In January and February 1880 the *Holland City News* had published the heated debate between Van Pelt and First Church elder Teunis Keppel over Freemasonry. In his front-page sermon upon the assassination of President James A. Garfield in 1881, Van Pelt could not resist defending Garfield's membership in the Order of Free Masons:

> I am aware that by the standard of many in this community, there is one circumstance about Mr. Garfield's life, on account of which they would have us forbear to pronounce him a Christian. Thank God

---

[16] *Consistorial Minutes*, March 1880, 1:142.
[17] *Consistorial Minutes*, 20 September 1881, 1:155.

that the standard of judgment on the great Day of Final Account will be God's own and Christ's own, and not that of some people![18]

These skirmishes in the newspaper were building up to a momentous congregational meeting in February 1882 in First Church.

Freemasonry Controversy Splits First Church

The story about the controversy over Freemasonry in Holland Classis, a contest that pitted the Western classes against the Eastern classes of the Reformed Church in America, has been told and analyzed many times. It is recounted here so that some less strident voices can be heard, those of Philip Phelps Jr. and of Geesje Vander Haar Visscher.

As early as 1874, *Holland City News* editor Gerrit Van Schelven[19] predicted serious troubles to come:

> Judging from the history of the past years, this opposition to secret societies on the part of the Hollanders in the West is evidently the greatest difficulty for the Reformed Church to overcome, in Americanizing the Hollanders within their ranks. Call it what name you may please, highly cultured intelligence or ignorant prejudice, a pious zeal, or heresy-hunting, (and far be it from us, to impugn anybody's motives,) we think that this is the beginning of an unpleasant controversy, and may lead to a serious quarrel, and perhaps rupture, within the denomination with which the Holland emigration of the past twenty-five years has formally united and identified itself.[20]

---

[18] "The Death of President Garfield: A Sermon Preached in Hope Church, Sunday Evening, September 25, 1881," *Holland City News*, 8 October 1881, 1.
[19] Gerrit Van Schelven and his wife, Priscilla, joined Hope Church by confession of faith in June 1879. They remained members until their deaths; he died in 1927 and she died in 1931. *Membership Records of the Hope Reformed Church of Holland, Michigan, Book 2*, 56. W91-1034, box 11, Hope Church, Holland, Michigan, Joint Archives of Holland.
[20] *Holland City News*, 23 May 1874, 4.

Several years after the death of Albertus C. Van Raalte on 7 November 1876, the Freemasonry controversy among churches in the Holland Classis came to a full boil.[21] The event that was most destructive to the stability of Holland's Reformed churches occurred on the evening of 27 February 1882. First Church had been without a minister since 1880, when Van Raalte's successor, the Reverend Roelof Pieters, died after serving there for eleven years. Leadership was in the hands of consistory president Teunis Keppel. The consistory called a congregational meeting for that evening "to discuss the question of leaving or staying within the Reformed Church of America."[22]

The church was filled to capacity. Though the Reverend Nicholas M. Steffens of Zeeland,[23] president of the classis committee supervising vacant congregations, was present—as were the Reverends Henry Utterwick of Grand Rapids,[24] Derk Broek of the Third Church in Holland, and Philip Phelps Jr.—president of consistory Teunis Keppel yielded to no one in carrying out the agenda at hand.[25]

---

[21] Swierenga and Bruins, *Family Quarrels*, 116.
[22] "Report of the First Church of Holland meeting on 27 February," *De Grondwet*, 28 February 1882. Trans. Simone Kennedy, 1. A copy of this typescript is in the "Masonry" folder in the Van Raalte Contemporaries cabinet of the Joint Archives of Holland at the Theil Center. Page numbers in this and subsequent references are to the typed translation.
[23] Steffens was the pastor of Zeeland's First Reformed Church 1878-82. He served as pastor of Holland's First Reformed Church 1883-84. Gasero, *Historical Directory*, 374.
[24] According to Gasero, *Historical Directory*, 402, Utterwick, who had served the Third Reformed Church of Holland 1872-80, was dismissed to serve the Congregational denomination in 1880.
[25] "Report of the First Church of Holland meeting on 27 February," 1. Henry Utterwick, also spelled Uiterwijk, had been pastor of the Third Reformed Church of Holland from 1872 to 1880. Derk Broek followed Utterwick, serving there until 1888. Philip Phelps Jr., though forced by the General Synod to resign from his presidency of Hope College in 1878 on charges of failing to maintain financial solvency for the college and attempting to develop a Theological Department into a Western seminary, was still living with his family in Van Vleck Hall. Preston J. Stegenga, *Anchor of Hope: The History of an American Denominational Institution Hope College*

After reading the list of grievances against the Reformed Church in America, elder Keppel prepared to call for a vote on whether to "break our community with the Reformed Church in America because of existing grievances."[26]

Steffens objected: these church members "have no right to vote on the proposed resolutions, neither yes nor no."[27]

Elder Keppel replied that because Steffens was not a member of the congregation he had no right to speak. Keppel wondered aloud "who gave the Rev. Steffens the order to cause such turmoil in this congregation?" and proceeded with the vote. The majority voted to leave the Reformed Church in America.[28]

Steffens stated that Keppel was no longer an elder and no longer presiding officer of the meeting. Now that Keppel's work was over, Steffens then announced that the minority voters would like to hold a meeting. Elder Keppel claimed that the "consistory has more rights in this church than the Rev. Steffens from Zeeland" and attempted unsuccessfully to quell the agitation of the crowd.[29]

Phelps intervened. According to a report of the meeting,

> [Phelps affirmed] that he has enjoyed close ties with First Church for the last 22 years and that he still highly respects and loves this church. That is why he comes forward as a friend. But he wants to let them know that the majority has made a mistake this night. They meant to do good and promote the kingdom of God, but they are wrong. Their separation will encourage Freemasonry and injure the Kingdom. Moreover, their actions were unlawful. Those who declared in favor of separation are only a small minority if you also

---

(Grand Rapids: Eerdmans, 1954), 101–6. See also Wichers, *Century of Hope*, 100–107.

[26] "Report of the First Church of Holland meeting on 27 February," *De Grondwet*, 28 February 1882, 5. Prominent in the list of grievances was the General Synod's refusal to recognize membership in the Order of Free Masons and other secret oath-taking organizations as sinful to the extent of denying members of such organizations church membership.

[27] "Report of the First Church of Holland meeting on 27 February," 3.

[28] "Report of the First Church of Holland meeting on 27 February," 4–5.

[29] "Report of the First Church of Holland meeting on 27 February," 6.

count the women[30] and children in church.... Phelps declared that he agreed with the minority, but wanted to advise them to return quietly to their homes, so that they would not violate the house of God.... When the tumult was at its highest level, the Rev. Steffens declared his willingness to leave with Dr. Phelps, and so he did.[31]

One of the women whose views likely were known by Phelps was Geesje Vander Haar Visscher.[32] About the congregational meeting on 27 February 1882, she wrote in her diary:

[I]n First Church there is much dissension and strife, primarily about free-masonry. Monday evening they had a congregational meeting and 85 members seceded from the Ref. church.[33] An elder was the ringleader and there was much confusion because the consistory would not permit the members to vote and so organize a new consistory. The elder demanded that the seceding group

---

[30] Unlike women in Hope Church, the women in First Church had not yet been granted the privilege to vote in congregational elections. Had the women been included in the voting at First Church, the outcome of the vote might well have been different.
  Women members of Ninth Street (Pillar) Christian Reformed Church were not allowed to vote in elections for elders and deacons until 1960, according to church historian Dawn Bredeweg (conversation with the author 23 June 2012).
[31] "Report of the First Church of Holland meeting on 27 February," 7, 9.
[32] She was a member of First Church at least until 1872 but by 1880 was regularly attending and likely a member of Third Reformed Church. The Visschers' oldest son, William, had studied under Philip Phelps Jr. for eight years in the Holland Academy and in the class of 1868 of Hope College. After Holland Classis denied William acceptance after completion of his theological studies in 1870, Phelps encouraged his moving to Albany to study medicine in preparation for becoming a medical missionary. Six months after his move to Albany, William died suddenly of smallpox. Phelps and an elder of First Church together delivered the sad news to the Visschers. When Phelps preached a sermon at First Church in memory of William Visscher, the church was filled. *Diary of Mrs. Geesje Vander Haar Visscher 1820–1901*, trans. C. L. Jalving (Holland, Michigan, 1954), 26–32, 66–67. Joint Archives of Holland. The original is held by the Archives of the Holland Historical Trust (Holland Museum).
[33] Swierenga and Bruins, *Family Quarrels*, 128, citing *Classis of Holland Minutes*, 1 March 1882, 545–548, state that the vote was 86 men for breaking away from the Reformed Church in America and 18 against.

should retain possession of the church properties, and those who didn't agree with them would have to find a place elsewhere. Oh, what will be the end of such dissension and strife? Many prayers had been offered that God might prevent the break and that those who were acting with misguided zeal might see the error of their ways but now that break had come. It gives the people of the world occasion to revile God's name and to point at God's people with a finger of scornful disdain. Oh, that God might enlighten the minds of those misguided leaders that they may see how wrong it is to secede from the Reformed Church merely because there are sinners in it when our Master, Jesus, was such a friend of sinners and tried to bring them all to Him. Oh that we might exhibit a greater spirit of tolerance and feel more of Jesus' love in our own hearts and show it in our deeds, that sinners might feel that we love them.

Yesterday we had a meeting of our mission society and prayer meeting but most of them were so depressed because of what had happened that prayer was almost impossible. Later I felt ashamed because to Whom else shall we go but to God who has said that even the portals of hell will not prevail against His church? God give us more of the spirit of prayer and a trusting reliance upon Him![34]

Several months later Van Pelt was elected as one of two temporary clerks of the 1882 General Synod. Reporting to the *Holland City News*, Van Pelt included the following details about the synod's responses to the latest overtures on the Freemasonry issue:

The Holland and Wisconsin [Classes'] memorials were read and patiently listened to. The three resolutions recommended by the committee were then adopted one by one. The sum and substance of these was, that every consistory has the inalienable right and power to discipline in the way of censure, suspension, and excommunication, any member of the church, for any cause judged adequate to condemn. If throughout any part of the Church, East or West, any consistory choose to sever a man from its church-communion, on the ground of his connection with Free Masonry, or any other oath bound secret society, there is nothing to interfere with such action of consistory. Thus Synod does not protect Free Masonry,

---

[34] *Diary of Mrs. Geesje Vander Haar Visscher 1820–1901*, 72.

nor pretend to say that Free Masonry may not be touched by the discipline of the Church.... It is felt in Synod that Synod has gone as far as it can go, and can be reasonably asked to go in this matter. If any wish to go further, the only open and manly thing to do, is to bring accusations against the persons who are well known to be Free Masons; and thus to cease flinging away energy and argument upon mere abstractions. It will therefore be seen that it is a most unjust and unwarrantable slander against the Reformed Church, that it protects Free Masonry. As long as men refuse to bring the matter up before Synod in a way that it can *act*, it is unfair to charge it with cowardice and unfaithfulness in this matter.[35]

The congregational meeting of 27 February 1882 split First Church, its majority voters staying to become a True Dutch Reformed (later Christian Reformed) congregation, and its minority leaving to build a new First Reformed Church at the southeast corner of Ninth Street and Central Avenue.[36] The synod's stand that Freemasonry be left for consistories to deal with on an individual basis rather than become a denominational test of church membership remained unchanged.[37]

---

[35] *Holland City News*, 17 June 1882.
It is significant to note that German Evangelical and Reformed Church congregations were not caught up in condemning Freemasonry. See David Dunn, Paul N. Curios, et al., *A History of the Evangelical and Reformed Church* (New York: Pilgrim Press, 1990), which makes little, if any, reference to Freemasonry. Perhaps the difference between the Dutch and German Reformed Churches is that the former had greater differences between the settlers in the East—who had been becoming Americanized for two centuries—and the nineteenth-century settlers in the Midwest, many of whom resisted Americanization as too much resembling the shortcomings of the state church of the Netherlands.
[36] The First Reformed Church moved from that site to its current location at 630 State Street in 1962. Swierenga and Bruins, *Family Quarrels*, devote a full chapter, "1882 Secession Yet Again: The Masonic Controversy," to a detailed exploration of the causes and results of this troubling time for the Dutch-speaking churches of Holland, Michigan.
[37] As the Reverend Donald J. Bruggink perceptively pointed out in his essay "Extra-Canonical Tests for Church Membership and Ministry," the Freemasonry issue of the nineteenth century presents comparisons readily applicable to the homosexuality issues of our day. Both were attempts to

Membership of active communicants in the First Reformed Church in Holland dropped from 324 in 1880 to 80 in 1881–82.[38] The Third Reformed Church, less severely affected by the split, reported 250 members in 1880 and 206 in 1885.[39] As a member of Michigan Classis, Hope Church, relatively immune from the turmoil of Holland Classis and of First Church in particular, also lost members between 1880 and 1885. Its *Consistorial Minutes* reported 119 members in 1880 and 105 in 1885.[40]

After the agitations in Holland over the issue of Freemasonry, Van Pelt was ready to move back to New York. By September 1882, the consistory and Van Pelt were taking steps mutually to dissolve the pastoral relationship, and the membership of Mrs. Van Pelt was transferred to the Reformed Church of East New York City.[41]

Before he left, however, he could not resist penning a letter to the editor of the *Holland City News*. Selected quotations from the letter, which took up nearly two full columns on the front page, tell why he was ready to shake the dust of Holland from his feet:

---

impose extra-canonical tests for church membership and ministry. The way that the denomination handled the Freemasonry controversy offers instruction to our day: "Classes and consistories should be allowed to fulfill their historic Reformed roles to exercise discipline within their proper spheres. The church should avoid the use of extra-canonical tests to address issues of disputed biblical interpretation and complex social issues. It is sincerely hoped," concludes Bruggink, "that the precedent set by the Synods of 1870 and 1889 will continue to provide a guide to right action in the present." "Extra-Canonical Tests for Church Membership and Ministry," in *A Goodly Heritage: Essays in Honor of the Reverend Dr. Elton J. Bruins at Eighty*, ed. Jacob E. Nyenhuis, Historical Series of the Reformed Church in America, no. 56 (Grand Rapids: Eerdmans, 2007), 63.

[38] *150th Anniversary First Reformed Church* (Grand Rapids: West Michigan Printing), 1997, 62.

[39] Bruins, *Americanization of a Congregation*, 2nd ed., 178.

Bruins notes the long-term ripple effects of the Freemasonry conflict into the twentieth century. In 1928 when community leader Henry Geerlings was elected elder of Third Church, "certain members asked him not to accept the position because he was a Mason." He "graciously declined to serve and later [in 1939] transferred his membership to Hope Church" (*Americanization*, 93).

[40] *Consistorial Minutes*, March 1880, 1:141; March 1885, 1:203.

[41] *Consistorial Minutes*, 4 September 1882, 1:163.

A Sad State of Affairs in the holy City of Holland.
MR. EDITOR:....

Much of the christian [sic] sentiment of this city, which makes itself so conspicuous for its piety in other matters, is in support of saloons, practices the thing which keeps saloons in our midst, and looks upon total abstinence as folly and fanaticism....

This is a bad and a sad state of affairs for a city of such pronounced and obstreperous piety as ours. It can not tolerate some evils which are prevalent a thousand miles away, and which our most influential citizens have moved heaven and earth to eradicate as there existing. It would be well if this closer evil obtained a little attention....

We have read the description of the Last Judgment as given in Christ's own words in the 25th Chapter of Matthew. He asks several questions about prisons, and poverty, and sickness, all relating to the miseries of men, whether they have been relieved. But I have not as yet been able to find out whether he put in any questions about the Canons of Dort, or the five points of Calvinism, or the Heidelberg Catechism....

Yours respectfully
Sept. 14, 1882   D. VAN PELT[42]

After he with his wife and son left Holland, Van Pelt served as minister to the East New York Church and later the Astoria Reformed Church in New York. In his later years, he pursued his interests in historical research and writing. His two-volume *History of Greater New York* was published in 1898.[43] His sudden death in 1900 at age forty-seven, as described by E. T. Corwin, seems quite out of character for this man who stood so firmly for his convictions: "Bathing, before retiring, in the East River, a little above Astoria, he was, in some way, swept out into the current, and was drowned."[44]

---

[42] *Holland City News*, 16 September 1882, 1.
[43] *Acts and Proceedings of the General Synod of the Reformed Church in America*, vol. 19 (New York: Board of Publication of the Reformed Church in America, 1901), 1248-49.
[44] *A Manual of the Reformed Church in America (Formerly Ref. Prot. Dutch Church), 1628-1902*, 4th ed. (New York: Board of Publication of the Reformed Church in America, 1902), 841.

Beginnings of Holland's Temperance Movement

The national Women's Christian Temperance Union (WCTU) was founded in Cleveland, Ohio, in 1874. Through education and example the WCTU promoted total abstinence first from alcohol and later also tobacco and other drugs. Within a short time the WCTU became the largest women's organization in the United States. Though women lacked the power to vote in civic elections, they could organize protests and exercise moral persuasion.[45]

In 1877 the WCTU of Holland was founded, and Sarah J. Annis of Hope Church was its first president.[46] In that year Hope Church also began to host meetings of the local WCTU.[47] Minutes of a consistory meeting in 1878 show the appointment of Dr. Thomas Annis to "procure unfermented wine for use at the Communion."[48]

Ministers of the Methodist Episcopal Church and Hope Church addressed the local Convention of the Woman's Christian Temperance Union in 1880. Van Pelt in a speech to the women at that convention issued a challenge to the men:

> The question remains, while the women have thus been true to their standard, where have the men been, and what are they going to do? There was such a thing as a Red Ribbon Club in Holland once. Has

---

[45] Retrieved from http://www.wctu.org/earlyhistory.html.
[46] *Holland City News,* 12 May 1877.
[47] *Consistorial Minutes,* 23 May 1877, 1:100.
[48] *Consistorial Minutes,* 30 December 1878, 1:129–30. Dr. Thomas Annis was the husband of Sarah J. A decade later, consistory unanimously reaffirmed use of "unfermented wine for Communion." *Consistorial Minutes,* 23 March 1888:265. Contrast this with a mid-nineteenth-century dispute that Van Raalte had with a Mr. Post, likely Henry D. Post, who "refused to make communion wine available, asserting that the alcohol law forbids this." Van Raalte viewed this action as an interference with religious freedom and was quite indignant with Post. Van Raalte thus took steps "to purchase communion wine in another community." *Minutes of the Ninth Street CRC [First Reformed Church] of Holland, Michigan, November 5, 1850–May 24, 1855,* trans. William and Althea Buursma, 2000, 82–83. The Temperance movement and later the Prohibition movement were American led, not rising from groups recently emigrating from Europe.

it evaporated? or have they 'fused' with the WCTU, allowing the ladies to do the rough work, and keeping modestly back for fear of being seen.[49]

In 1885 the consistory of Hope Church adopted the following resolution and directed that it be read from the pulpit and published in the local newspapers:

> In view of the evils of intemperance and Sabbath desecration in our midst, and as the season is again opening when the saloons are taking a new license and Sunday excursions usually begin, the Consistory feel that it is their duty to request and advise the membership and these attendants of this church to discourage these evils in all practicable ways, as being inconsistent with the interests and advancement of the cause of Christ.[50]

Hope Church in 1887 granted the WCTU use of the church for its County Convention.[51] In 1924 and 1929 Hope Church opened its rooms for use by the State Convention of the WCTU.[52]

Marietta Shuler (Mrs. Owen) Van Olinda, a member of Hope Church from 1864 until her death at age ninety in 1907, was a leader in the causes of temperance and missions. She received her education in Albany, New York, and moved to Grand Haven, Michigan, to

Marietta Schuler Van Olinda

---

[49] *Holland City News,* 27 November 1880.
[50] *Consistorial Minutes,* 23 April 1885, 1:205.
[51] *Consistorial Minutes,* 21 August 1887, 1:243.
[52] *Consistorial Minutes,* 5 September 1924, 3:162; 14 June 1929, 3:307–8.

teach in the public school there in 1857. The following year she moved to Holland, where she taught at Holland Union School. In 1872, she taught for several years in the female and primary departments of Hope College—its first woman instructor. She chaired the foreign work committee of the national WCTU and wrote tracts for this organization, translating them into various languages for distribution overseas and among the immigrants in this country.[53] Among titles and tracts written and/or translated by Mrs. Van Olinda are "What Are We Doing About It?" "The Danger of Social and Moderate Drinking," "Honor or Dishonor? Life or Death?" "Am I My Brother's Keeper?" "The Home of the Foreigner," and "The Mother's Opportunity and Duty."[54]

Women's Participation in Church Activities

Not only did Hope Church women vote with the men of the congregation in calling Van Pelt to become their minister in 1878, but as early as 1879 they also began to vote in elections for deacons and elders.[55] Hope Church was likely a forerunner church among Reformed congregations in Holland in extending this privilege to women.

In March 1880, the consistory of Hope Church enlisted its women to become the nineteenth-century version of Welcome Wagon for the church. "Resolved, that a committee of ladies be appointed to visit strangers in the city. As such a committee, ... [Maria Scott

---

[53] "Deaths," *Holland City News*, 28 November 1907.
[54] M. S. Van Olinda, "Holland Department," *Reports of Department Superintendents: Foreign Work*. National Woman's Christian Temperance Union. Annual Meeting (Chicago: Woman's Temperance Publication Association, 1893), 244. Retrieved from http://asp6new.alexanderstreet.com/wam2/wam2.object.details.aspx?dorpid=1000689037
[55] *Consistorial Minutes*, 5 December 1879, 1:136.

and Marietta Van Olinda] were appointed for the East part of town and ... [Susanna Herold and Alice Bangs] for the West part."[56]

Also in March 1880, in response to an appeal from the Women's Board of Foreign Missions, several women organized the Holland Women's Foreign Missionary Society. Its president, Margaret Anna Jordan Phelps, spoke English, and its secretary, Mrs. Wykhuizen, wrote the minutes in Dutch. Meetings were conducted in both English and Dutch.[57]

The *Annual Report of the Woman's Board of Foreign Missions* in 1880 praised the work of Marietta Van Olinda in directing a union of First, Second (Hope), and Third Reformed Churches in Holland to form a Foreign Missions Auxiliary. It comprised a group for "married ladies," another for "young ladies," and a Mission Band and Circle for the children and youth.[58] In the mid-1880s, First Church and Hope Church each also established a Women's Missionary Society, and Hope Church member Christine Van Raalte Gilmore for many years wrote the minutes of both societies.[59]

The Ladies' Aid Society of Hope Church was organized 8 May 1883. "All the ladies of the congregation" were considered members of this society, the purpose of which was "to develop the social and benevolent activities of those who compose its membership." Detailed descriptions of the work of the society's committees indicate that they performed some of the tasks typically performed

---

[56] *Consistorial Minutes*, 17 March 1880, 1:143. The names of the women in the minutes were listed as Mrs. Scott, Mrs. Van Olinda, Mrs. Herold, and Mrs. Bangs.
[57] Eloise Van Heest, "Women's Societies in Holland Classis," in *In Christ's Service: The Classis of Holland and Its Congregations 1847–1997*, ed. Gordon G. Beld (Holland: Classis of Holland, 1997), 6.
[58] *Annual Report of the Woman's Board of Foreign Missions*, 1880, 19. For more about the participation of women in support of missionary activities, see Mary L. Kansfield, *Letters to Hazel: Ministry within the Woman's Board of Foreign Missions of the Reformed Church in America*, Historical Series of the Reformed Church in America, no. 46 (Grand Rapids: Eerdmans, 2004).
[59] Van Heest, "Women's Societies in Holland Classis," in *In Christ's Service*, 6–7. Christina was also called Christine.

by Community and World and Congregational Care ministries a century later:

> Two Committees shall be annually chosen by the Society: A Visiting Committee and a Social Committee. The Visiting Committee shall consist of two ladies for each of the three districts into which the congregation shall be divided, whose duties shall be to call upon families not in attendance upon any Church, invite them to our Church and endeavor to make them feel at home amongst us; also to call upon families in sickness or sorrow and extend to them, in the name of the Church, Christian sympathy and attention. The Social Committee shall be composed of five ladies, whose duties shall be to have charge of whatever social gatherings may be arranged by the Society. Special Committees for special purposes may be appointed at any meeting of the society.[60]

A summary of the Reformed Church General Synod of 1883 praised the work of women across the denomination for their support of home and foreign missions:

> The women are rousing the churches of our country on the great question of evangelizing the world and how to do it. The results of their labors during the few years that the Women's Boards of Mission have been in existence are really surprising. Latest at the cross, and earliest at the tomb, they are now taking a leading part in spreading the knowledge of a risen Saviour.[61]

---

[60] "Constitution of the Ladies' Aid Society of Hope Reformed Church, Holland, Mich.," 1883. W91-1034, box 5, Hope Church, Holland, Michigan, Joint Archives of Holland at the Theil Center. First officers of the society were Mrs. Thomas Walker (Kittie) Jones (the minister's wife), president; Mrs. Charles A. (Martha) Dutton, Mrs. Ben (Julia Gilmore) Van Raalte, and Mrs. Owen (Marietta Schuler) Van Olinda, vice-presidents; Miss Gertrude Alcott, secretary; and Miss Frances Phelps, treasurer. The Visiting Committee for District No. 1 was headed by Mrs. Cornelius (Mary) Doesburg and Mrs. Gerrit (Priscilla) Van Schelven; for District No. 2, by Mrs. Gerrit J. (Maria Van Raalte) Kollen, and Mrs. Theodoric Romeyn (Irene) Beck; and for District No. 3, by Mrs. Wilson (Lucy) Harrington and Miss Emeline Dutton.

[61] P. D. Van Cleef, "The Reformed Church Synod," *Holland City News*, 30 June 1883.

In January 1886, the consistory received a report from the Ladies' Aid Society stating that from $77 collected by subscriptions and at socials, the society was able to make some repairs and improvements to the parsonage. The consistory thanked them for their efforts.[62] A similar vote of thanks was extended to the Ladies' Aid Society in 1886 for raising money by means of a strawberry festival and other fund-raising events for purchasing carpets and pulpit furniture for the church.[63]

Participation of women in organizations such as the Woman's Christian Temperance Union, Missionary Societies, and the Ladies' Aid Society helped carry out the ministry of the church in the community and worldwide. Women in these organizations not only learned about the dangers of intemperate drinking of alcoholic beverages but also about the lives and needs of people in countries where missionaries served and about ways to address poverty and hardships in Holland. Church-related organizations met the social needs of women and helped develop their leadership skills, preparing them and their daughters for enlarged roles they would have in the twentieth century.[64]

---

[62] *Consistorial Minutes,* January 1886, 1:213.
[63] *Consistorial Minutes,* 1 June 1886, 1:226; 7 December 1886, 1:229.
[64] For more information about the growth of women's organizations in the denomination, see John W. Coakley, "Women in the History of the Reformed Church in America," in *Patterns and Portraits: Women in the History of the Reformed Church in America,* ed. Renée House and John Coakley, Historical Series of the Reformed Church in America, no. 31 (Grand Rapids: Eerdmans, 1999), 1–15. For more information about organizations in which many Hope Church women participated in the early twentieth century, see Mary Kansfield, "Francis Davis Beardslee and the Leading Ladies of Holland, Michigan, 1912-1917," in *Tools for Understanding: Essays in Honor of Donald J. Bruggink,* ed. James Hart Brumm, Historical Series of the Reformed Church in America, no. 60 (Grand Rapids: Eerdmans, 2008), 67–109.

Thomas Walker Jones's Ministry

After the departure of Van Pelt in 1882, Hope Church called Thomas Walker Jones, minister of the Reformed Church in Fonda, New York. Completing twelve years of ministry in Fonda, he accepted the call from Hope Church and moved to Holland in January 1883.[65] After attending the first service led by Jones, the editor of the *Holland City News* predicted that Jones "will meet with abundant success in building up Hope Church.... The church will eventually be the leading English church in the Reformed denomination in the West."[66]

Thomas Walker Jones

Hope Church's report to Michigan Classis and the Particular Synod of Chicago in 1884 was encouraging:

> SECOND HOLLAND, HOPE, looks back with satisfaction over the year.... It has been marked by a large increase in the regular attendants and supporters of the church. The list of pew-holders has been about doubled. The finances of the church have been greatly developed. The quarterly pew-rents and weekly collections receive the generous support of the people. Special attention has been paid to the music of the church. The choir has been considerably enlarged. Hymn books have been purchased for the entire congregation, two books having been placed in each pew. Congregational singing is a prominent feature of Sabbath worship. The Sabbath School is

---

[65] *Elders' Minutes*, 1 March 1883:57.
[66] *Holland City News*, 13 January 1883.

increasing. The prayer meeting is marked by spiritual fervency. A special interest in missions extends throughout the church.[67]

Jones, on behalf of Hope College and Reformed churches in the community, invited delegates and guests of the General Synod meeting in June 1884 in Grand Rapids to come to Hope College. More than two hundred people arrived from Grand Rapids by train on Saturday, June 7. They were met at the depot by a reception committee and became a parade marching by twos from Eighth Street to the campus, where they approached Van Vleck Hall, viewed the campus buildings, and proceeded to the pine grove.

After the officers of the synod, Hope College president Charles Scott, faculty members, ministers of the Classis of Holland, and committee of arrangements were seated on the platform and the delegates were seated, Phelps prayed and the Hope Church choir, together with the students of the college, sang a song of welcome which had been composed for the occasion.[68]

President Scott delivered the welcoming address, harking back to the 1864 General Synod, when the idea of Hope College was "endorsed and its proposed endowment fully recommended." He described the arrival of Van Vleck, the development of Holland Academy, and the construction of Van Vleck Hall. But he saved his words of choicest praise for Phelps:

> Twenty-five years ago another principal came to carry on the work. Under his assiduous care and earnest toil the Academy became a College, and the goodly tree spread forth its branches in richer fruit. All the future will record the labors of Dr. Philip Phelps. You will visit a neat and appropriate chapel; this was built by the students in 1862. You will find six other buildings, plain to look upon and unadorned, and yet, to us, somewhat as Bethel was to Jacob; and all these are the erections of the nineteen years in which Dr. Phelps was

---

[67] *Reformed Church in America. Minutes of the Particular Synod of Chicago, Convened in Grand Haven, Wednesday, May 7th, 1884.* vol. 3. (Constantine, MI: L. T. Hull, 1884), 265.
[68] "The General Synod's Visit to Holland," *Holland City News*, 14 June 1884.

Principal and President. We have no sightly halls; no architectural adjuncts, with their cost of thousands of dollars; but we have just those things which God has brought to us, as hidden jewels, and which will grow up under His shaping hand into an educational palace.[69]

This school, said Scott, is "'the rock of hope' for the Hollanders in our land and the foremost 'anchor of hope' for the Reformed church in America."[70]

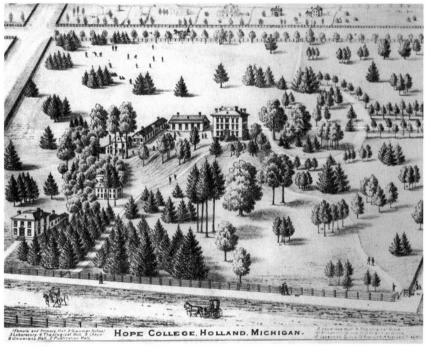

Sketch of Hope College in about 1870

---

[69] Charles Scott, "General Synod's Welcome to Hope College," *Christian Intelligencer*, 16 July 1884, 12.
[70] Scott, "General Synod's Welcome to Hope College," *Christian Intelligencer*, 16 July 1884, 12.

Rev. Phelps's Last Services to Hope Church

After his forced resignation by the General Synod in 1878,[71] Phelps continued to appeal to the synod and to all churches in the denomination to encourage financial support for the college, add a Theological Department, and restore him to presidency of the college. In 1884 General Synod passed a resolution asking Phelps to vacate his rent-free lodging in Van Vleck Hall.[72]

Phelps's study in Van Vleck Hall

---

[71] Though the reasons for the forced resignation are complex, Phelps was forced to resign mainly because the college could no longer pay its bills. His vision to turn Hope College into Hope Haven University exceeded the means to bring it about. Wichers, *Century of Hope*, 82–89. The 1871 Holland fire, 1873–79 national financial panic, and other matters beyond Phelps's control also contributed to the college's dire straits.
[72] Wichers, *Century of Hope*, 100–03.

In the fall of 1884 Phelps penned a "Historical Sketch" and the consistorial minutes from the earliest years of Hope Church into the record book that later was lost, found, and purchased at an auction. As an excerpt titled "The Records" indicates, though the ink has faded, the elegance of the handwriting remains.

Phelps's handwriting of a portion of Consistorial Minutes, *vol. 1*[73]

---

[73] "The Records," *Consistorial Minutes*, 1:33. "So many were the details of duty pressing on the Missionary arising from his relation to the Academy and the Church that the Minutes were not permanently recorded at the time, though they were regularly kept. But soon after the arrival of Pastor Stewart, the draft of the preceding history and minutes was read in the hearing of the members of Consistory, with reference to their being copied in the permanent books. This copying, however, was not done till the Fall of 1884; and the preceding minutes were then read by Rev Ph Phelps Jr. in his study in the college building, Monday evening Oct 6th 1884, in the hearing of the surviving members of Consistory, viz. Rev. Theodoric Romeyn Beck and Elder Bernardus Grotenhuis."

Another Christmas Interlude

While church leaders in the denomination and in Holland Classis were debating about Freemasonry and about supporting financially fragile Hope College in its growing role in preparing ministers, most church members were going about the ordinary practices of church life: attending worship services, visiting the sick, ministering to the needy, teaching Sabbath School, and attending Ladies' Aid and Women's Missionary Society meetings. One of the occasions that people of all ages looked forward to was the annual Christmas program.

In the nineteenth century there were no movies, television, or computers. Many looked to their church to be a source of entertainment as well as a community of worshipers. Instead of providing movie reviews, the *Holland City News* in 1884 provided detailed reviews of the Christmas programs in various churches. Churches vied with each other for large, appreciative audiences. Of the following three programs reviewed, guess which one is that of the Methodist Episcopal Church, that of the Ninth Street Christian Reformed Church, and that of Hope Church.

Singing, Marching, and Pails of Christmas Goodies

> On Tuesday evening the Christmas entertainment of the Sunday school took place. At an early hour the seats and aisles of the church were packed with people. The large and growing school was present in full force. The interior of the church was handsomely decorated. Two large trees beautifully ornamented and brilliantly lighted stood upon the pulpit platform, one on each side. A star shone out brightly above the pulpit recess. Evergreen festoons were hung about the room with pleasing effect.... The program ... consisted of responsive reading, prayer by the pastor, scripture recitations, speaking, address by the superintendent, singing in great abundance and pleasing variety, and offerings by 'Santa Claus.' The 'marching song' with which the exercises began was most inspiring. The whole school, over two hundred in numbers, marched in from the chapel

rooms. Banners handsomely inscribed with golden mottoes were carried by the scholars. All were singing as they marched led by the thrilling music of cornet and organ. The effect was grand.... We have not the space to make reference to the different parts taken by the speakers and singers.... Immediately after the superintendent's 'remarks' and a suggestive song by one of the younger members of the school, the doors in the rear of the platform were thrown open and the exclamation points of the printed program were explained. The vocal 'exclamations' of the scholars were enthusiastic as a large pyramid of 'Christmas pails' filled with 'Christmas goodies' greeted their sight. The demolishing of this 'work of art' and 'thing of beauty' by the giving of a pail to every member of the school was the closing scene. [The church], we think, excelled itself on this occasion. The two hours spent in the church were the shortest and happiest which any could wish.[74]

Eere zij God in de Hoogste

The usual Christmas services were held ... on the evening of the 24th.... The teachers and scholars assembled in the consistory room adjoining the church edifice, and at the appointed time marched in to the church and took the seats assigned to each class. Over the platform on the wall in letters of gold was the usual motto, 'Eere zij God in de Hoogste' ['Glory to God in the Highest'].[75] The exercises were opened with prayer by the assistant superintendent, ... which was followed by an address of welcome by the pastor; after which the ... program of exercises was carried out.... Distribution of S. S. cards and candies.... The dialog, 'Een Zamenspraak' ['A Speech Together'], by ... two little girls ... drew forth the applause of the audience, notwithstanding the request that no applause take place, and we feel warranted in adding that all did well. The carrying out of the program gave evidence of thorough preparation. In no case was any prompting necessary in the recitation of the pieces, and all, both children and parents, went home well pleased with the exercises of the evening.[76]

---

[74] "Christmas at Our Churches," *Holland City News*, December 27, 1884, 1.
[75] To an American ear, unlearned in Dutch, the clause might suggest "Here is God in the hog-sty."
[76] "Christmas at Our Churches," *Holland City News*, 27 December 1884, 1.

Jolly Old St. Nicholas Descends Down the Chimney

> At this church a "log cabin" took the place of the usual Christmas tree on Christmas Eve. The cabin was built on a large platform, and was tastefully relieved by evergreen trees in the "front yard." The snow on the roof and "logs" seemed as though it had just fallen. An owl had perched on the roof and seemed sternly wise as he looked down upon the people. About 7:30 o'clock the large audience which had assembled were cheered by an organ voluntary. Then followed declamations, dialogues and scripture readings, interspersed with well chosen Christmas carols and other songs. Then the organ strains heralded "Jolly Old St. Nicholas." He was first seen at the chimney of the cabin. Before he descended out of sight he made a spicy little speech to the children. Soon after he went down the chimney he came out of the cabin door bringing his wife with him. After being introduced she had a nice little talk with the children about the "geography of Christmas." She made a very favorable impression on the whole audience. Then Mr. and Mrs. "Santa Claus" brought out the presents—and it seemed their cabin was full of them.... The exercises were heartily applauded and enjoyed by all.[77]

"Singing, Marching, and Pails of Christmas Goodies" was about the Hope Church program, "Eere zij God in de Hoogste" was about the Ninth Street Christian Reformed Church program, and "Jolly Old Saint Nicholas Descends Down the Chimney" was about the Methodist Episcopal Church program. The program reviews suggest a combination of the characteristics of the reviewer (presumably one of the members of each respective church) and convey hints about the personalities of the congregations.

Jones Resigns

In January 1886, the *Holland City News* announced the organization of a "young people's meeting" at Hope Church. Meeting at 6:30 p.m., an hour before the preaching service, it would be "in charge

---

[77] "Christmas at Our Churches," *Holland City News*, 27 December 1884, 1.

of the young men of the church." On the same page, the topic of the sermon by the Reverend H. D. Jordan of Holland's Methodist Episcopal Church was announced: "Have women a right, under the gospel, to speak and pray in promiscuous assemblies, and to preach the gospel?"[78]

In its 1886 annual report to the Classis of Michigan, Hope Church remarked about increased Sunday School attendance, the zeal of the young people, and the vitality of the church ladies:

> Our Sunday School shows increasing prosperity in members, gifts and general interest. A large proportion of these welcomed within the fold of the Church, was from the Sunday School. Our young people are full of zeal. A young people's meeting...is very successful.... The Ladies of the Church have been full of their accustomed activity. A short time ago a Woman's Missionary Society was organized. It is auxiliary to both the Domestic and Foreign Boards, its funds being divided between these two important and related objects.[79]

In 1886 Sunday School enrollment was 275, more than double the number of confessing church members, and 11 people were received into membership by confession of faith.[80] A newspaper account of the Sunday School picnic that summer reported 300 people participating. All were conveyed by the steamer *Macatawa* to and from Macatawa Park.[81]

A hint of diminished prosperity, however, was evident in the necessity for a consistorial committee in 1887 to canvass the congregation for additional pledges beyond pew rentals. Pew rentals in 1884 were slightly more than $1,000, but by 1887 they had slipped

---

[78] *Holland City News*, 16 January 1886, 1. Page 4 of this newspaper indicated that Jordan's sermon would be about "Women's rights under the gospel." Also on page 4 was the topic of the Reverend E. Bos's sermon at First Reformed Church: "The cause of our corruption." Jones's sermon at Hope Church for the same Sunday morning would be "God's Interview with Abraham Respecting Sodom."
[79] *Consistorial Minutes*, April 1886, 1:221.
[80] *Consistorial Minutes*, April 1886, 1:222.
[81] *Holland City News*, 21 August 1886.

to $761 and the following year to $750.[82] So perhaps some were not greatly surprised when at the end of January 1888, Jones submitted his letter of resignation to the consistory:

> I take this step in the spirit of Christian love and good will. I cherish nothing but the kindest feelings toward the people of my charge. I trust the future of Hope Church will be increasingly bright and prosperous....
>
> During these five years of my pastorate I have officiated at twenty-six marriages and twenty-seven funerals. I have baptized twenty-two persons; sixteen infants and six adults. I have received into the membership of the church sixty-five individuals; twenty-nine by certificate and thirty-six by confession.
>
> A most hopeful feature of the church is the interest of the young people. A Sunday evening meeting has been sustained by them for the past two years with increasing life and power while the Sunday-school is in a most prosperous condition. The activity of the Ladies in the development of the social and missionary work of the church is most encouraging.[83]

Concluding his ministry at Hope Church, Jones, with his wife and son, moved to serve the Reformed Church in Bushnell, New York. After serving in that church for three years, he served in the Reformed Church in Bedminster, New Jersey, for fourteen years. He died in 1909 at the age of 66.[84]

---

[82] *Consistorial Minutes,* October 1887, 1:254–55.
[83] *Consistorial Minutes,* 30 January 1888, 1:257–61.
[84] *Consistorial Minutes,* 25 March 1888, 1:269. Also see Gasero, *Historical Directory,* 201. His previous two pastorates were three years at the Pottersville, New Jersey, Reformed Church and eight years in the Reformed Church in Fonda, New York; a five-year pastorate at Hope Church was not unusual in that context.

John Tallmadge Bergen's First Term of Ministry

After the departure of Jones, Hope Church called the Reverend John Tallmadge Bergen, minister of the Reformed churches in Shokan and Shandaken, New York. Completing three years of ministry there, he accepted the call from Hope Church and moved to Holland in 1889.[85]

John Tallmadge Bergen

Bergen helped Hope Church link with Christian Endeavor, an American ecumenical and evangelical organization for young people. Hope Church organized a Christian Endeavor society in 1890, and within the first year thirty people were attending its meetings.[86] In its report to the Michigan Classis and the Particular Synod of Chicago in 1891, Hope Church presented promising news:

> Hope Church has been greatly favored. The church building has been re-roofed, the interior tastefully decorated, and the pastor's salary substantially increased. They have enjoyed three weeks of union evangelistic services, and the Holy Spirit has brought many

---

[85] *Consistorial Minutes*, 25 March 1888, 1:269. Also see Gasero, *Historical Directory*, 26.

[86] *Consistorial Minutes*, 1 April 1890, 1:301. The Young People's Society of Christian Endeavor was an ecumenical, evangelical society founded in 1881 by the Reverend Francis Edward Clark in Portland, Maine. Among its purposes were to strengthen spiritual life and promote Christian activities among its members.

unto the confession of faith. The work still continues, and they hope and pray for a full outpouring of the Spirit in the year before them.[87]

To honor Bergen's support for another ecumenical organization, the Young Men's Christian Association, local YMCA members named its meeting place Bergen Hall.[88] Located on the north side of Eighth Street in what was then known as the Post block, it is

Post block (Eighth Street east of River Avenue) in about 1898

---

[87] *Reformed Church in America. Minutes of the Particular Synod of Chicago*, 1981 4:259.
[88] "Good-Bye," *Holland City News*, 12 March 1892, 4. The Young Men's Christian Association was formed by George Williams in London in 1844, and the first organization of the YMCA in America was in Boston in 1851. As early as 1872 a YMCA reading room was opened in Holland, but it soon closed. Attempts to revive the organization were made in 1873, 1875, and 1882. Bergen Hall was opened in early 1893. *Holland City News*, 28 December 1872, 4 January 1873, 7 February 1874, 16 January 1875, 23 January 1886, 23 October 1886; and *Ottawa County Times*, 23 December 1892.

the third building east from the corner at River.[89] The YMCA offered an alternative to taverns as a place for young men to read and socialize.

After three years, Bergen informed the consistory that as the eldest of several sons he wanted to move closer to his aging parents. This and an opportunity for a field "of wider scope and more enlarged demands" led to his accepting a call to South Reformed Church of Brooklyn, New York, to which he and his family moved in 1892. To his letter of resignation he added: "My relations with you, dear Brethren, and with 'Hope Church' have been of the most blessed character. All that you promised to do for me, as your Pastor, you have done and more."[90]

On the last Sunday before his departure, nineteen new members were added to the membership rolls—nine by confession of faith and ten by letter of transfer. At that evening service, so many came to hear his parting words to the young people that the church could not contain them all. The congregation held a farewell gathering the following evening, the description of which extended to four columns in the *Holland City News*.

---

[89] Zingle, *Woman's Literary Club*, 1, 2, 5. In 1898 the Woman's Literary Club, founded by Anna Coatsworth Post, held its first meeting in this building.
[90] *Consistorial Minutes*, 1 February 1892, 1:333.

Speaking on behalf of the young people, Gerrit J. Diekema,[91] in a cadenza of rhetorical eloquence, extolled Bergen's qualities as a teacher:

Gerrit J. Diekema

Your interest in the [S]unday [S]chool has inspired your fellow-teachers; and through your missionary spirit, you have gone into every part of our city and have added many new scholars to the roll.... Youth is impatient of precept, but willingly follows example, and by your example you have been our great teacher.... Following the example of your great Teacher, you have interpreted to us the language of the starry sky, the gathering cloud, the rumbling thunders, the lightning's flash, the lofty majestic mountain, the silent landscape, the waving fields of golden grain, the stately forests, the tumultuous ocean, the rushing torrent and the rippling brook; and henceforth all these shall speak to us of God. You have mingled the voices of nature and grace, and have pointed us upward to their common source.[92]

---

[91] Gerrit J. Diekema was arguably one of Hope Church's most famous members. After graduating from Hope College in 1881 and receiving his law degree from the University of Michigan in 1883, he moved back to Holland, began a law practice, and joined Hope Church in 1885. He was elected to the Michigan House of Representatives from 1885 to 1891, serving as its speaker in 1889 and 1890. He served as mayor of Holland from 1895 to 1896, and for the following two years he was president of the Michigan Sunday School Association. In 1908 he was elected to the U.S. House of Representatives for two years. In 1916 he ran for governor but was not elected. In 1929 Herbert Hoover appointed him United States Minister to the Netherlands. He died at The Hague in 1930. An estimated 8,500 paid their respects as he lay in state in the recently constructed Hope Memorial Chapel (later named Dimnent Memorial Chapel). The Reverend John M. Vander Meulen delivered the funeral sermon. http://www2.cityofholland.com/mayors/15.htm.
[92] *Holland City News*, 12 March 1892, 4.

Next, mayor Oscar Yates,[93] also a member of Hope Church, praised Bergen for his good citizenship within the community:

> He has met and mingled with all classes of our community to their lasting good. He has raised and sustained the fallen, strengthened the weak, cheered the sorrowing and inspired in all a thorough respect for a strong, fearless, tender, [C]hristian manhood.[94]

Oscar Yates

---

[93] Oscar Yates, Holland's thirteenth mayor, served from 1890 to 1892. Before settling in Holland in 1883, he attended Mayhew's Business College in Albion, Michigan, and Eclectic Medical Institute in Cincinnati, Ohio. After graduating from Michigan Agricultural College, he practiced medicine in Ottawa County. Before and after his term as mayor, Dr. Yates served as Ottawa County Coroner. Noted for working with the music community, he established Holland's Century Club. http://www2.cityofholland.com/mayors/13.htm

[94] *Holland City News*, 12 March 1892, 4.

Finally, speaking on behalf of Hope College, Gerrit J. Kollen, also a member of Hope Church,[95] praised Bergen for his breadth of vision:

> Your life, as it has reflected that of our Savior, has warmed ours, has given us a deeper sympathetic feeling for the world, and a higher appreciation of those outside of our own little communion. Our minds and hearts have been enlarged and our spiritual vision widened. We are also glad to say that we have seen in your life, as well, and even more, the spirit of energetics as that of apologetics; and in consequence thereof we have been somewhat lifted out of our little church ruts and obtained a greater interest in the Church universal.[96]

Gerrit J. Kollen

Who could leave for long after such a loving farewell? In February 1894 Bergen returned briefly to Holland to present the first of a series of YMCA lectures. To a large audience in the opera house he spoke on "Christian Laymen."[97] In 1895, after a three-year ministry in Brooklyn's South Reformed Church, he and his family would return for a longer stay.

---

[95] Born in the Netherlands, Gerrit J. Kollen immigrated to Overisel, Michigan, with his mother and four older siblings in 1851. He graduated from Holland Academy and Hope College. In 1871 he became professor of mathematics and later also taught political science and logic. In 1893, he became president of Hope College. A capable fundraiser, he put the college into sound financial condition. Under his administration (1893–1911), four major buildings—Graves Hall, Van Raalte Hall, Carnegie Gymnasium, and Voorhees Hall—were added to Hope's campus. Wichers, *Century of Hope*, 126–45.
[96] *Holland City News*, 12 March 1892, 4.
[97] *Ottawa County Times*, 2 February 1894, 1.

Henry G. Birchby's Ministry

In 1892 Hope Church called the Reverend Henry G. Birchby, who had been born in Euxton, England, and was currently serving a Presbyterian church in Smithfield, New York. He accepted and moved his extended family, which included his wife and, since 1888, also the wife and four sons of his deceased brother, William. It so happened that Mrs. Henry G. (Lillie) Birchby and Mrs. William (Clare) Birchby were sisters.[98]

Birchby found himself in the unenviable position of following a minister who was dearly adored. Problems soon developed.

Henry G. Birchby

Consistorial minutes of 1893 hint that all was not harmonious in the church's music program. Not long after chorister Dr. B. J. De Vries was appointed by consistory to ask William N. Birchby, a nephew of the pastor, to become church organist, chorister De Vries and all members of the choir tendered their resignations. Consistory then offered the position of chorister to John B. Nykerk, a music professor, who declined the offer, and William N. Birchby resigned as organist.[99] Six months later, the consistory resolved that "Dr. De Vries be placed in charge of the choir; and that they all take 10 lessons at the expense of the church and that Dr. De Vries offer Prof. Campbell $4.00 a lesson." Four months later, the consistory approved payment of $50.00

---

[98] *Holland City News*, 22 July 1898, 1.
[99] *Consistorial Minutes*, 16 March 1893 1:354, 361. Nykerk, a member of Hope Church, was appointed director of music at Hope College in 1891.

to Prof. Campbell. Over a year later, William N. Birchby, upon the recommendation of the Committee on Music, was appointed organist.[100]

These notes from the consistory minutes raise many questions: Were the resignations of the chorister and all of the choir members after William N. Birchby's becoming organist more than coincidental? Were the resignations in protest of nepotism or undue influence over the worship style by a nephew of the pastor? The result of displacement of a favorite organist? Consistory minutes reveal that between the call of Birchby and his arrival, organist Beca Boone and chorister Kittie M. Doesburg each became married and moved away.[101] So both chorister De Vries and organist Birchby were new and part of a natural succession. Perhaps they were not a good match for each other. But how to explain the need for music lessons for all choir members? Perhaps the congregation and consistory were raising expectations for performance beyond what they had accepted in previous years. It's all rather disconcerting.

In its report to Michigan Classis in 1893, Hope Church reported that a "Pastor's visitation-society of 25 elect ladies has been organized, which has canvassed the city, house by house—hence, we know our constituency." The report concluded: "all we need is the outpouring of the Holy Spirit, a Pentecostal blessing. May the Lord of the Harvest hear our cry!"[102] Whether this call for a Pentecostal blessing was a cause of or remedy for various tensions in the church is uncertain.

In his annual consistorial report for 1897, Birchby characterized the year as one of "hard work and 'hard times.' All the departments of church-life have been kept moving and we look up, take courage

---

[100] *Consistorial Minutes*, 6 November 1893, 1:372; 5 February 1894, 1:377; 14 May 1895, 1:409. The professional affiliations of Dr. Bernard J. De Vries, who was a Hope Church elder, and Prof. Campbell were not with Hope College.
[101] *Consistorial Minutes*, 19 September 1892, 1:348–49.
[102] *Consistorial Minutes*, 4 April 1893, 1:364–65.

and press on."[103] October 1897 minutes reveal a lack of unanimity, perhaps a hint of a deepening rift:

> A petition to the Postmaster General was laid before the Consistory, requesting that our City Post-Office be closed from Saturday evening to Monday morning. After some discussion, some members of the Consistory signed it.[104]

In March 1898 consistory minutes indicate that the "Pastor and Deacon Brusse were appointed a Committee to draw up a resolution by which the Consistory declared its opposition against card-playing, dancing, etc." Nine months later, consistory authorized Birchby to prepare and have printed a church directory that would contain the names and addresses of all of the members and a list of the officers of the various church organizations.[105] This collection of names and addresses would make it easier to mail letters to members.

In the spring of 1899 the General Synod condemned remarriage after divorce, the selling of liquor in army canteens, and the seating of a polygamist from Utah in the U.S. House of Representatives.[106] During that same spring, the *Holland City News* offered a reward for the arrest and conviction of the "evil inclined person actuated by race prejudice [who] threw a stone through the window of the Chinese Laundry on River street."[107] These were some of the social evils identified at the denominational, national, and local levels. This list makes all the more striking the list of sins highlighted in a letter that was sent "to each member of our Congregation":

---

[103] *Consistorial Minutes,* 1897, 2:7.
[104] *Consistorial Minutes,* 18 October 1897, 2:10.
[105] *Consistorial Minutes,* 2 March 1898, 2:25–26; 6 December 1898, 2:38–39.
[106] *Acts and Proceedings of the General Synod of the Reformed Church,* 1899 (New York: Board of Publication of the Reformed Church in America), 502–5.
[107] "City and Vicinity," *Holland City News,* 28 April 1899, 1.

HOPE CHURCH, HOLLAND, MICH.

May 15, 1899

Dear Brethren: - -

We feel constrained, as a Consistory to whom is entrusted the spiritual interests of the Church, to call your attention to certain matters, which seem to us to be detrimental to the church's best life and growth.

Many things, which may not be absolutely sinful in themselves, yet in their tendency, and because of their influence, become exceedingly harmful. It was in reference to such things, that Paul declared, - - I Cor. VIII, 13 - - "Wherefore if meat make my brother to offend, I will eat no meat while the world standeth.' This is the Royal Law of Liberty, which if all Christians should follow, how soon and how surely would the world be convinced of the reality of our religion.

Your Consistory believe that any thoughtful man will concede, that there is an alarming increase of Sabbath desecration in our city, and in view of this fact we ask you to consider, most earnestly and prayerfully, whether it is not our duty, as Christians, both by precept and by example, to stem this tide, which threatens to destroy our Sabbath, and also to deny ourselves, for the sake of our example and influence, what may seem to us harmless pleasure.

We would urge you further to consider, whether such amusements, as dancing, card-playing, etc., do not have a decided tendency to lower the standard of Christian living, and give occasion to the world to scoff at our religion? While these things may be harmless in themselves, yet should we not, as Christians, abstain from all appearances of evil, and deny ourselves indulgence in what may give "occasion of stumbling" to others?

Shall we, for whom Christ died, be so forgetful of His love, as willingly to cause a weak brother to fall, or bring reproach upon His Name? Is it not the duty of us, who are parents, to use our influence and authority with our children and cause them to refraim [sic] from these and other like questionable amusements?

We most earnestly and lovingly urge upon all our fellow-members the thought, that while we are "in the world" we should not be of it!

Praying that God may help us all to attain a purer and higher standard of Christian living, we remain,

> Your Fellow Workers,
> H. Gough Birchby, Pastor.
> G. J. Kollen, William Brusse,
> C. Doesburg, Henry Boers,
> D. B. K. Van Raalte, Geo. H. Souter,
> Chas. S. Dutton, Frank D. Haddock.[108]

One can readily notice the difference between what Phelps considered the essentials of Christian faith in his inaugural sermon at Hope Church in 1864 ("For the kingdom of God is not meat and drink but righteousness and peace and joy in the Holy Ghost," Romans 14:17) and the "amusements" Birchby and his consistory focused on in this letter. Did this letter help unite pastor, consistory and congregation around shared values and faith, or did it become a wedge that would soon separate the pastor from Hope Church?

Six months after the letter was sent, while Birchby and his wife were in the East "on account of his wife's ill health," the consistory requested elder Dutton to write a letter to Birchby, advising him of the "sentiments of the Consistory in regard to the present condition of 'Hope Church.'" The content of Dutton's letter is not in the minutes, but the letter received by elder Cornelius Doesburg from Birchby two weeks later is. His decision to resign, he wrote to Doesburg, "is in harmony with the manifest direction of the will of God, the great Shepherd of His Church; and it is my delight to obey. He leads in and <u>out</u>, and where He leads I will follow." To the rest of the consistory and to the members of Hope Church, he wrote another letter, which began, "Owing to reasons, which are plain and plain to all, I feel it my duty to resign and hereby do resign the pastorate of this church, which was committed to me more than seven years ago."[109]

But those reasons, which may have been plain to all in 1899, are a mystery to later readers, largely because at this point in the letter two pages are missing from the volume of *Consistorial Minutes*. Why were the two pages torn out? By whom? No clues are present

---

[108] *Consistorial Minutes*, 15 May 1899, 2:44–45.
[109] *Consistorial Minutes*, 19 November 1899, 2:48.

in the minutes. Nor are clues present in the minutes of the Ladies' Aid Society. Minutes of the Women's Missionary Society at the Joint Archives of Holland lack minutes for 1897–1904, and so we are left with little more than speculations.

Was the letter to the congregation concerning Sabbath desecration and questionable amusements a reason for the resignation? Or was the spiritual climate of the congregation, which influenced the letter to be sent, the cause? Was his wife's "ill health" somehow related not only to the need for trip to the East but also to the wish to leave Holland permanently?[110] Was the reason related to the pastor's extended family?[111] Was Birchby on the wrong side in the Boer War (favoring the British instead of the Dutch), or was trouble caused by his wife's sister's recipe for "Calf's Foot Jelly" in the Ladies' Aid Society's cookbook?[112] Was the cause something too embarrassing or shocking to reveal?

On the page after the missing two pages, the *Consistorial Minutes* continue: "After a quiet and thoughtful consideration" and time spent "in discussion concerning the condition of our congregation, etc.," consistory accepted Birchby's resignation and expressed its "appreciation of the ability and faithfulness with which he has preached the Gospel in its fullness and simplicity, during the years of his pastorate among us."[113]

Elders were directed to ask Hope College professor John Tallmadge Bergen to preach until another minister would accept a call

---

[110] Because of Birchby's trip to the East, consistory did not meet in October 1899; at its November meeting, consistory directed elder Dutton to write the letter about the "present condition of 'Hope Church.'"

[111] Another possible contributing cause for the resignation of Rev. Birchby could have been the sudden death of his fourteen-year-old nephew, Hubert, from appendicitis and the effect of that on the extended family. *Holland City News*, 22 July 1898, 1. The Junior Christian Endeavor Society donated to Hope Church a Communion table in memory of Hubert Birchby. *Consistorial Minutes*, 6 December 1898, 2:36.

[112] The Ladies' Aid Society published the first of several cookbooks in 1896. For this unusual recipe as well as a sampling of recipes from subsequently published cookbooks, see Appendix H.

[113] *Consistorial Minutes*, 19 November 1899, 2:51; 28 November 1899, 2:52.

to Hope Church. Bergen, who, after serving as pastor for three years at the South Reformed Church in Brooklyn, New York,[114] had returned in 1895 to teach at Hope College, readily accepted the expanded vocational scope of this request.

Relying on his Presbyterian connections, Birchby transferred in December 1899 to the Presbytery of Columbus, Ohio, and the membership certificates of his wife and several family members, including organist William N. Birchby, were transferred to the Presbyterian congregation in Westerville, Ohio.[115]

Honoring and Mourning Phelps

Before closing out accounts of Hope Church in the nineteenth century, it is fitting to recount what became of the founder of Hope College and Hope Church after his removal from the presidency of the college. In 1886, Phelps and his family left Van Vleck Hall after he accepted a call to serve a pair of Reformed churches, Blenheim and Breakabeen, in New York. Responding to the invitation of Hope College alumni, he returned briefly to Holland in 1890 for the college's quarter-centennial celebration during which he was "thrilled with the love and devotion of the students."[116] In 1894, he returned to Hope College to deliver the principal address at the presidential inauguration of one of his former students, Gerrit J. Kollen. Phelps passed along to him the cap and gown which had been presented to him by the ladies of Holland for his inauguration in 1866.[117]

In the summer of 1896 Phelps was invited to supply the vacant pulpit of his first charge, Hastings-on-Hudson. After the Sunday

---

[114] Gasero, *Historical Directory*, 26.
[115] *Consistorial Minutes*, 12 December 1899, 2:53–54.
[116] *Acts and Proceedings of the General Synod of the Reformed Church in America*, 1897, 759.
[117] Philip Tertius Phelps, *A Brief Biography of Rev. Philip Phelps, D.D., LL.D....*, 1941, 12. H88-0122, Phelps, Philip Jr., box 1, Joint Archives of Holland.

service in late July, he became ill from the "severe heat of the season." The illness left him considerably weakened, and on September 4 at the age of seventy he died at the home of his sister in Albany, New York.[118]

"It was a solemn time in Hope Church when the death of Dr. Phelps was announced," wrote charter member Anna Coatsworth Post to Mrs. Phelps, "for we can never forget that he laid the foundation stones for our church.... I shall ever cherish you and dear Dr. Phelps who labored so faithfully here amid so many discouragements."[119] In assessing the career of Phelps, Wynand Wichers deemed him "a man of integrity and intellectual ability who had given the best nineteen years of his life to an impossible task.... In spite of his treatment at the hands of the Synod, Phelps never lost his love for Hope College."[120]

Philip Phelps Jr. in his mature years

As the nineteenth century closed, Hope Church reflected four decades of fruitful ministry and faithful congregational life. Phelps, Stewart, and Van Pelt had helped build and rebuild the church; Jones and Bergen had helped infuse it with an evangelical spirit. The church, except for an occasional setback or two along the way, had been growing steadily, and Bergen was about to pick up and repair whatever pieces were broken during Birchby's ministry.

---

[118] Phelps, *A Brief Biography of Rev. Philip Phelps.*
[119] "Rev. Philip Phelps, D. D., LL. D.," [scrapbook], 133. H88-0122, Phelps, Philip Jr., box 1, Joint Archives of Holland.
[120] Wichers, *Century of Hope,* 104, 106.

4 ... Thriving into the Twentieth Century

Ushering Hope Church into the twentieth century was the returning Reverend Bergen. He was followed by the Reverends John M. Van der Meulen (1907–09), Edward Niles (1910–11), August F. Bruske (1911–16), and Peter Paul Cheff (1918–24). Early in the century, Hope Church built a new church sanctuary, blessed soldiers sent to fight in World War I, and encouraged the women's suffrage and prohibition movements.

Bergen Returns

Like Phelps, Bergen combined teaching at Hope College with ministering at Hope Church. Returning from Brooklyn to Holland in 1895, he organized and chaired the Department of Bible and Ethics at Hope College. He also taught courses in ethics, logic, oratory, Bible, and evidences of Christianity.[1] As an aid for the last course, he published the textbook, *Evidences of Christianity*. Sentences from the preface of that book give an idea of Bergen's stance in the classroom and likely also in the pulpit:

> A new Spinozism is to-day standing in the path of Christian progress and striking lusty blows at *miracles*. The materialism of our times is clothed and fed by this mechanical hypothesis of the universe. Christian evidences must be employed in the conquest of this foe.... That this little volume may prove to be one little dart that will find a joint in the enemy's armor, is the author's prayer.[2]

---

[1] Wichers, *Century of Hope*, 175. Also see *Holland City News*, 18 September 1903, 1.

[2] John Tallmadge Bergen, *Evidences of Christianity* (Holland, MI: Bingham, 1902), iv. Spinozism refers to the philosophy of Baruch de Spinoza, a seventeenth-century Dutch Jewish rationalist who among other things questioned whether God intervenes in human affairs.

In 1900, after the departure of Birchby, Bergen began a six-year ministry at Hope Church concurrent with his teaching at the college. He served the first three years as part-time stated supply and the next three years as Hope's full-time minister.

During Bergen's ministry, the consistory tried a variety of methods to generate enough money to support a full-time minister and sustain the congregation. Because the traditional pew rental system no longer brought in sufficient funding, the congregation voted early in 1900 to replace the pew rental system with pledges, and to allow people to sit anywhere they wished in Hope Church. Pledges would be taken on an annual basis and paid quarterly. That method began to raise more money than the pew rental system had produced.[3]

In May 1900, the consistory appointed a committee "to secure plans for a new church or for remodeling the present structure."[4] Six months later, the consistory approved a request by Hope Church's Christian Endeavor Society to allow three evangelists "belonging to the 'Moody Movement'" to use the church building for three evenings in January. The Moody Movement was related to the evangelistic enterprise of Dwight L. Moody of Chicago, founder of the Moody Bible Institute. In contrast to the consistory of 1866 under Phelps, which distanced itself from Michael J. Clapper's revival, the 1900 consistory was more open to allowing an evangelist outside the Reformed Church to speak during Hope Church's Week of Prayer.

In January 1901, at Bergen's request that the Week of Prayer of the previous week be continued, the consistory resolved unanimously to continue prayer meetings into a second week.[5] The Consistorial Report to Classis for 1901 witnesses the results of those prayer meetings:

---

[3] *Consistorial Minutes*, 4 January 1900, 2:58–60.
[4] *Consistorial Minutes*, 7 May 1900, 2:66.
[5] *Consistorial Minutes*, 19 November 1900, 2:77; 28 November 1900, 2:78; 13 January 1901, 2:80.

'Hope Church' reports a year of great spiritual and temporal blessings. The plans for a new Audience-room have matured, and the new Building is nearly ready for dedication. From the beginning of the Week of Prayer an unusual spiritual interest was manifest, which culminated in the special services during February under the management of Rev. C. C. Smith, formerly of the Moody Church, Chicago. As a result of the prayers of our people and the special services, we report large accessions. We give all glory to God, and trust him for still greater blessings.

While we, as a Consistory, give full credit to the work of Evangelist Smith, we also wish to bear witness to the faithful work done by Prof. Bergen, who has acted as Stated Supply for the church during the year.

His earnest gospel-preaching, his helpful conduct of the Prayer-meetings, his zealous work in catechizing the children have been no small elements in bringing out the results for which we thank God. Prof. Bergen has, as far is it lay in his power, done the full work of a pastor.[6]

Received on Confession	108	Communicants	338
Received by Certificate	11	Catechumens	60
Dismissed	4	Infants baptized	6
Suspended	1	Adults baptized	35
Died	3	Sunday School enrollment	250[7]

In 1901 the congregation called the Reverend John M. Van der Meulen, but he declined.[8] Meanwhile Bergen continued to serve Hope Church part time.

The Hope Church directory published in 1902 listed (in addition to Sunday morning and evening worship services and Wednesday

---

[6] *Consistorial Minutes*, May 1901, 2:89–90. Evangelist C. C. Smith became a Holland favorite. A front-page article in the *Holland Sentinel*, 4 April 1924, describes the return of C. C. Smith to conduct gospel meetings at the Methodist Episcopal Church: "Dr. Smith still possesses his old-time fire and enthusiasm and manifests the splendid vigor of a younger man.... Last night Dr. [Albertus (Raalte)] Gilmore, a long-time friend of the evangelist, who accompanied him for some time as his singer and chorus leader, was in the choir and sang with him a duet."
[7] *Consistorial Minutes*, May 1901, 2:90–91.
[8] *Consistorial Minutes*, May 1901, 2:95–96.

evening prayer meetings) seven regular meetings of organizations for women and children:

> Sunday School meeting at the close of the morning service, 12 o'clock
> Ladies' Missionary Society ... meeting first Wednesday of month at 3 p.m.
> Ladies' Aid Society meeting third Wednesday of month
> Young Ladies' Aid Society meeting second Wednesday of month at 2 p.m.
> Young People's Society of Christian Endeavor meeting every Sunday, at 6:15 p.m.
> Junior Christian Endeavor meeting every Thursday at 4 p.m....
> King's Daughters meeting on alternate Thursdays at 7:30 p.m.[9]

Though there was no specific organization for men, they were eligible by election to serve on consistory. Term limits for consistory members were briefly considered in 1901, but within two weeks of that discussion consistory resolved to "strike out whatever alludes to the rotation of offices of our church."[10]

Building a New Church

Because of the increase in new members arising from the work of evangelist Smith, pastor Bergen, and the Holy Spirit, the committee appointed in May 1900 focused not on remodeling the 1874 church but on building a new church sanctuary. Consistory appointed John Walter Beardslee, professor at Western Theological Seminary, to chair a building committee. The new sanctuary

---

[9] *Hope Church (Second Reformed) Holland, Michigan 1902 [Directory]*. W91-1034, Hope Church, Holland, Michigan, box 8, Joint Archives of Holland.
[10] *Consistorial Minutes*, 20 March 1901, 2:83, 84. According to Van Hinte, *Netherlanders in America,* Reformed churches in the Holland colony had a "bitter and continual fight" over whether elders and deacons "should relinquish their office after two years in accordance with the church order of Dordt" or whether "according to the Utrecht revision ... they could remain in office for the rest of their lives" (362–63).

would be constructed on the south side of the 1874 church, which was to be renovated for use by the Sunday School classes, prayer meetings, and society meetings.[11]

On an evening in October 1900, "large bonfires lighted up the yard and lent an air of cheerfulness to the solemn and impressive occasion" of the laying of the cornerstone. Among items put into the cornerstone box were copies of various local newspapers, a 1900 penny and nickel, and presidential campaign pins of William McKinley and William Jennings Bryan.[12]

Designed by the Bay City architectural firm of Dillon P. Clark and Alverton G. Munger,[13] the building of Flemish stepped-gable style was constructed of local materials. Foundation stones came from Holland's Waverly quarry, and orange-red bricks were supplied by the Veneklasen Brick Company of Zeeland.[14] In style the structure resembles the West End Collegiate Church in New York City, which was styled after the 1606 Vleeshal (meat-hall) of the Grote Markt of Haarlem, The Netherlands.[15]

John Walter Beardslee

---

[11] "Hope Congregation Bids Farewell to Old Church," *Holland City News*, 5 July 1901, 4. Later this structure was called the parish hall.
[12] "Corner Stone of Hope Church," *Holland City News*, 2 November 1900, 8.
[13] "Building—Structure Inventory Form," in "Hope Church Historical Marker" folder. W91-1034, Hope Church, Holland, Michigan, box 12.
[14] Michael J. Douma, *Veneklasen Brick: A Family, a Company, and a Unique Nineteenth-Century Dutch Architectural Movement in Michigan* (Grand Rapids: Eerdmans, 2005), 59.
[15] Retrieved from http://www.westendchurch.org/history-and-belief.

New York City's West End Collegiate Church, built in 1893

Vleeshal of Grote Markt, Haarlem, The Netherlands

Front of Hope Church under construction in about 1900

The new church was dedicated on 6 July 1902, forty years after Hope Church was first organized. Beardslee in his dedicatory sermon set forth three purposes for churches, highlighting in his second point the distinct mission for Hope Church:

> Three great thoughts are applicable to every church. There must be a place where [C]hristians can worship unitedly, and this place should be made as attractive as possible. Secondly this place should be designed to its original purpose, to be the center of all helpful influences of all classes of people. Hope church should be true to its mission, being the pioneer American church, to be a typical American church. It must appeal to the people, it must develop socially and civilly as well as spiritually. Is should minister to all the wants of the people. Thirdly, it must be ever true to the great gospel that points out but one way for sinful people to find rest and peace—Jesus Christ.[16]

Hope Church in the early twentieth century

Commenting on the attractiveness of Hope Church, an unnamed reporter for the *Holland City News* waxed rhapsodic:

---

[16] "Hope Church Dedicated," *Holland City News*, 11 July 1902, 4.

The exterior is severely plain and chaste in outline but is imposing. The interior is a marvel of good taste and beauty of design. Artistic simplicity is aimed at throughout. The walls and ceiling are finished in terra cotta touched here and there with a line of blue. The floors are covered with a green carpet. The windows of frosted glass admit the softened rays of the sun in the day time and at night electric lights set off the interior to good advantage. In appointments, beauty of design and purity of architectural tone the interior cannot be excelled and resembles a fairy palace. The whole is set off to excellent advantage by a handsome pipe organ, one of Kimball's best creations. The pipes are ornamented with pink and green trimmed in gilt and gold, and harmonizes with the simple but rich shades on the walls and ceiling.[17]

Interior of Hope Church, 1901

Women's groups, through sales of cookbooks and other money-raising efforts, contributed $418 for carpeting and matting for the new sanctuary and $38 for sodding and curbing, and the Young

---

[17] "The New Hope Church," *Holland City News*, 12 July 1901, 4.

Ladies' Aid Society contributed $80 for pulpit furniture.[18] During the dedicatory services, Bergen gave credit where it was due:

> Prof. Bergen praised the members of the Ladies' Aid Society ... for the bravery they exhibited in assuming the responsibility of raising $2,400 for the pipe organ. He extolled the ladies of the church for providing the carpets a feature which seemed hopeless of acquirement at first, but led by the Mesdames [Ida] McLean, [Frances] Browning, and [Mrs. Adolphus] King, the ladies had raised more than enough to purchase the carpet, and the male members of the congregation were advised to recognize the financiering ability of the ladies in the future.[19]

The congregation donated the pulpit furniture from the 1874 sanctuary to the Fourteenth Street Christian Reformed Church of Holland. It also gave pews to that church and to the Methodist Episcopal Church.[20]

Bergen concluded the Consistorial Report for 1902, "a year attended with God's blessing," by stating that he had supplied the church for the year, "and steps are now being taken to secure a prominent pastor."[21] However, after inviting a potential pastor from New York to preach, the consistory decided not to issue him a call. Instead, the congregation voted in 1903 to issue a call to their stated-supply pastor, Bergen, and he accepted. Though Hope College reduced his administrative and teaching load, he continued to teach English Bible study and oratory courses.[22]

---

[18] *Consistorial Minutes*, 9 January 1902, 2:110–11.
[19] "The New Hope Church," *Holland City News*, 12 July 1901, 4.
[20] *Consistorial Minutes*, February 1903, 2:138; 10 November 1903, 2:155. It is likely that the Fourteenth Street Christian Reformed Church did not accept this gift because, according page 210 of the *Consistorial Minutes*, the consistory voted to "donate our pulpit chairs which were used in the old church, to the Reformed Church of Harrison, S. Dakota on condition that they pay cost of freight and packing." The minutes do not indicate whether the church in Harrison accepted this offer.
[21] *Consistorial Minutes*, April 1902, 2:144.
[22] *Holland City News*, 18 September 1903, 1.

Changing How Communion Was Served

In May 1902 the consistory responded to a request to use individual Communion cups by laying "this matter indefinitely on the table in order to wait for further developments."[23] Within ten months, the Young Ladies' Aid Society presented the church with a Communion set of individual cups, and they were first used in the Communion service 1 March 1903. The following year, the Young Ladies' Aid Society gave the church a cabinet for the Communion service.[24] Each of these events was recorded in the minutes with no details of any discussions.

The transition from Communion by common cup to individual cups, which in many denominations and congregations was controversial, was smooth at Hope Church. While many ministers felt their authority and liturgical orthodoxy challenged by church members and physicians who were advocating individual cups on grounds of sanitation, this was not so at Hope Church.[25] Perhaps the transition was smooth because Bergen was a stated supply part-time pastor who did not feel threatened by new ideas from young women. Perhaps the members of the Young Ladies' Aid had sympathetic family members on consistory. The easy transition to individual Communion cups is evidence of an ethos at the church that was grounded in Phelps's inaugural sermon text, "For the kingdom of God is not meat and drink but righteousness and peace and joy in the Holy Ghost" (Romans 14:17), a focus on essential faith rather than peripheral matters. It also demonstrated the gratitude felt by the consistory toward the money-raising efforts of the young women on behalf of the church. Women were not allowed

---

[23] *Consistorial Minutes*, 6 May 1902, 2:121–22.
[24] *Consistorial Minutes*, 3 March 1903, 2:140; 8 June, 1904, 2:169.
[25] For a discussion of the controversy within various Protestant denominations regarding the move from common Communion cup to individual cups, see Daniel Sack, *Whitebread Protestants: Food and Religion in American Culture* (New York: St. Martin's, 2000), 31–58.

to serve on consistory, but by their generosity they changed how Communion would be served.

Supporting the Church through Apportionments

Despite the generosity of the young women and the addition of a large number of new members by the revival of 1901, Hope Church, like many churches, continued to experience difficulty in raising money to support itself and its benevolences. Having changed from the pew rental system to pledges as a means of sustaining the church, the consistory still found it necessary to prompt giving. In August 1902 consistory members divided among themselves the list of delinquent givers and visited each of them. In February 1904, members of the congregation were assigned to members of consistory "for the purpose of securing pledges for the support of the church for the year." Five months later, the consistory hired a Mrs. Vos to become the "church collector," visiting those in arrears with their giving; her annual salary was set at $50.[26]

In October 1904, the consistory began to use an apportionment system. It appointed an Apportionment Committee of six church members and six consistory members to develop a plan for "apportioning the amount to be contributed by each member for the support of the church for the ensuing year." Three months later, the consistory abolished the position of church collector, and consistory members resumed their practice of contacting members "delinquent in the payment of dues."[27] Whether the apportionment system was so successful that a church collector was no longer needed is perhaps too optimistic an interpretation, but the minutes reveal nothing about the congregation's response to the apportionment system.

---

[26] *Consistorial Minutes*, 12 August 1902, 2:126; 29 February 1904, 2:163; 25 June 1904 2:169, 8 July 1904, 2:170.
[27] *Consistorial Minutes*, 20 October 1904, 2:175; 3 January 1905, 2:179; 30 January 1907, 2:208.

Bergen Performs Some Missionary Work in Oklahoma

A month after Hope Church's new building was dedicated in 1902, Bergen announced that in September he "expected to be absent for a couple of weeks to do some mission work in Oklahoma."[28] He had made the acquaintance of the Reverend Frank Hall Wright, son of a Choctaw minister who had married a white missionary teacher among the Choctaw Indians;[29] later Bergen would invite Wright to conduct gospel meetings at Hope Church.[30]

In Oklahoma Bergen and Wright worked together at Ft. Sill for several weeks in 1902 and then again in 1903 to present evangelistic camp meetings to groups of Apaches and Comanches. In September 1902, Geronimo, a leader of the Apaches, arrived on Sunday, the last day of the camp meetings. He did not attend the morning service. In the afternoon, Wright and Bergen met with Geronimo in his tent and invited him to attend the evening meeting. Along with about two hundred Native Americans, Geronimo came to that service. In the words of Bergen:

> I preached on the Atonement—'Ye are bought with a price.' Geronimo came early, sat near me, and as I turned and looked into his face again and again during the sermon, and saw those gleaming eyes set like two stars amidst a wrinkle of clouds, I prayed as I preached, with all my soul that God would force some feeble thought of mine into that old, hard heart.
>
> Then Wright exhorted and invited, and they came—a throng of Indians to be prayed for. One of those deeply moving moments came over our meeting; one could feel the Power present, and Geronimo was stirred. Leaping to his feet be began to pour out an impassioned

---

[28] *Consistorial Minutes*, 12 August 1902, 2:126.
[29] LeRoy Koopman, *Taking the Jesus Road: The Ministry of the Reformed Church in America Among Native Americans*, Historical Series of the Reformed Church in America, no. 50 (Grand Rapids: Eerdmans, 2005), 76. Though Wright was neither ordained nor installed by the Reformed Church in America, he did graduate from Union College in Schenectady, New York, and from Union Seminary in New York City.
[30] *Consistorial Minutes*, 7 October 1902, 2:128.

speech to his people. Some one, an Apache, standing near, translated it at once into English, and a Comanche caught up the latter's words and rendered them in Comanche, all three talking at the same time, and all three distinctly understood by their respective peoples. The burden of Geronimo's address was that the 'Jesus road' was best and he would like all his people to travel in it. 'Now,' said he, 'we begin to think the Christian white people love us.'[31]

After the service, Wright and Bergen talked and prayed with Geronimo but sensed he was not ready to accept Jesus for himself. In months to follow, Bergen continued to pray "that God's spirit might enlighten and regenerate" Geronimo.[32]

In July 1903 Bergen and Wright resumed their camp meetings, and Geronimo listened to many sermons. After one of the services at which Bergen preached, Geronimo stayed and asked the pastors to pray that Jesus would give him "a new heart."[33]

A week later, when questioned about his faith, Geronimo's answers clearly provided evidence of his knowledge of the Christian faith. Baptized with six others, Geronimo became a member of the Reformed Church in America, and he attended worship services regularly at the Apache Mission in the Ft. Sill Military Reservation.[34]

To those who questioned the conversion of Geronimo, Bergen replied: "The same sovereign grace that has brought Geronimo to the light can keep him to the end. Some people say, 'Have you any faith in Geronimo?' and I answer, 'No! Our faith is in the power of Christ.'"[35]

Though Geronimo "had difficulty breaking with lifelong habits of gambling and drinking," there is "no evidence, either in the records of the Apache church or in any article published by

---

[31] "Geronimo's Conversion," *Historical Highlights*, no. 40, February 1994, 16–17. Reprinted from a tract, undated, published by the Chicago Tract Society.
[32] "Geronimo's Conversion," *Historical Highlights*, 17.
[33] "Geronimo's Conversion," *Historical Highlights*, 19.
[34] Koopman, *Taking the Jesus Road*, 117–18.
[35] "Interesting Discourse," *Ottawa County Times*, 31 July 1903, 1.

the Reformed Church, that Geronimo was ever suspended from membership."[36]

In March 1904 the Hope Church congregation was saddened by the death of Bergen's wife at the age of forty-three. Ella Dean Bergen had suffered for about six weeks after the birth of her sixth child before succumbing to Bright's disease, an illness affecting the kidneys.[37]

Two years later Bergen announced that he had received a call to the Presbyterian Church in Dubuque, Iowa. Despite pleas to remain at Hope Church, in August 1906 Bergen announced his acceptance of that call.[38]

Accompanying the petition to the classis for dissolution of the pastoral relations between Bergen and Hope Church is the affirmation of Bergen's ministry as written and signed by elders Henry Boers and Charles S. Dutton:

> While we write with him this request for a severance of the pleasant relations which have existed between us as pastor and people, we do so with great regret, feeling that there was never a time in the history of Hope Church when she so much needed the services of a faithful pastor, and never a time when this field gave such large promise of wide usefulness and abundant reward in the Master's service.[39]

Bergen remained with the Presbyterian church for the rest of his life. After his death in Minneapolis in 1948, Hope Church member

---

[36] Koopman, *Taking the Jesus Road*, 118–19. Koopman's assessment, based on close familiarity with the subject, does not agree with the statement in "A Timeline of RCA History (with related American and world history events)," compiled by Russell L. Gasero, that Geronimo "was later expelled for gambling." http://images.rca.org/docs/archives/rcatimeline.pdf
[37] "Death of Mrs. J. T. Bergen," *Holland City News*, 11 March 1904, 4.
[38] *Consistorial Minutes*, 13 March 1906, 2:194; 7 August 1906, 2:199. In this volume of *Consistorial Minutes*, the pages that would have been numbered 197 through 204 are torn at the top outer edge. Notes on pages 196 and 197 state the cause: "Beware the dog!"
[39] *Consistorial Minutes*, 7 August 1906, 2:200.

and Hope College administrator Paul E. Hinkamp wrote a tribute to him that said in part:

> Dr. Bergen ... [was] tall, straight, ruddy with iron gray hair and well-trimmed goatee. He spoke forcefully, without apparent effort, and was always interesting. No one ever dozed when Dr. Bergen spoke.
>
> He was a lover of nature and of nature's God. The great outdoors fascinated him. He loved to hunt. A peculiar deficiency in vision compelled him to wear thick-lensed glasses. While he could not see what naughty boys were doing in the back of the classroom, he could shoot a rabbit on the run. He was always bursting with enthusiasm and gave the impression of exuberant vitality....
>
> He preached with vigor and conviction. His sermons were evangelistic and thrilling. Of course he always preached a sermon on birds in the spring and on colored leaves in the fall, but such aberrations from Reformed Church sermon-topics only served to make his people love him the more. He had the courage to be different, but no one doubted his absolute sincerity. For under his leadership Hope Church had greatly increased its membership and built a new edifice to the glory of God....
>
> His students and parishioners all remember him as a colorful, earnest and effective servant of God. He made religion interesting, virile and strong. Like 'Teddy' Roosevelt he lived the strenuous life.[40]

John M. Van der Meulen's Ministry

In October 1906, the consistory arranged for the Reverend John M. Van der Meulen, professor of psychology and education at Hope College, to preach every other Sunday and take charge of the prayer meetings and Young People's meetings at Hope Church. His father, John, had been a minister of Ebenezer Reformed Church, east

---

[40] Paul E. Hinkamp, "Dr. John T. Bergen, a Tribute," *Alumni News*, Dec. 1948, 27–28.

John M. Van der Meulen

of Holland, and his grandfather, Cornelius, was the first minister of the Reformed Church of Zeeland. Before coming to teach at Hope College, John M. Van der Meulen had served for two years as a missionary in Oklahoma.[41]

In January 1907 Hope Church extended a call to Van der Meulen. He accepted, and four months later he became Hope Church's pastor.[42] Like Bergen, he combined ministry with teaching until he accepted a call to another church.

In 1907 Hope Church sought funds from the congregation to support a missionary to a foreign country. By election, the congregation chose to support the Reverend Willis G. Hoekje,[43] a 1904 graduate of Hope College and 1907 graduate of Western Theological Seminary, who would serve as missionary to Japan and to Japanese people from 1907 to 1949, the year of his death.[44] Treasurer's reports indicate ongoing annual support for Hoekje by Hope Church until 1932, when the Great Depression forced major reductions in funding. Regular support was picked up again in 1940 and continued through 1945.[45]

---

[41] Gasero, *Historical Directory*, 412.
[42] *Consistorial Minutes*, 22 January 1907, 2:207; 7 April 1907, 2:211.
[43] *Consistorial Minutes*, 31 July 1907, 2:214.
[44] Gasero, *Historical Directory*, 178. The *Hope Church Directory* for 1923 shows support later also provided to Mrs. B. D. Hakken (nee Elda Van Putten), a missionary in Arabia. W91-1034, Hope Church, Holland, Michigan, box 8, Joint Archives of Holland.
[45] *Consistorial Minutes*, 23 February 1910, 2:300; 10 January 1940, 5:216; 27 August 1945, 7:141. For a list of missionaries supported by Hope Church, see Appendix I.

In 1908, in response to "the numerous notices now required in our Sabbath services," the consistory began to consider publication of a "weekly bulletin of our church work, for general distribution."[46] By 1910 a "Bulletin" committee was added among the consistorial committees.[47]

The consistory also considered plans to build a new parsonage. At a congregational meeting the plan to build a parsonage was approved. A committee "of three gentlemen and two ladies to prepare plans and secure bids" for the construction of a parsonage was appointed: Charles M. McLean, Bastian D. Keppel, W. J. Garrod, Kate Garrod Post, and Mary Diekema.[48] Concluding his report of the congregational 1908 meeting, consistory secretary Henry Boers praised the Ladies' Aid: "There followed a social hour enjoyed by all. The parlors were beautifully decorated with lilacs, excellent refreshments were served, hearty welcome and good cheer [were] in evidence everywhere—all because the ladies of the Aid Society had done their part so kindly and willingly."[49]

Willis J. Hoekje, missionary to Japan, supported by Hope Church 1907–1945

In February 1909 Van der Meulen announced that he had received and declined a call from a church in New Jersey. Five months later, he announced that he had received and accepted a call

---

[46] *Consistorial Minutes*, 6 March 1908, 2:228; 16 April 1908, 2:230.
[47] *Consistorial Minutes*, 22 February 1910, 2:297.
[48] *Consistorial Minutes*, 22 May 1908, 2:236.
[49] *Consistorial Minutes*, 22 May 1908, 2:237.

to the Hamilton Grange Reformed Church of New York City.⁵⁰ Like Bergen, Van der Meulen was an eloquent preacher and beloved by the congregation.⁵¹ During July and August in the early 1920s, he returned to Hope Church in the late summer weeks to preach while its minister, the Reverend Peter P. Cheff, took vacation..⁵²

Edward Niles's Ministry

In April 1910, Hope Church extended a call to the Reverend Edward Niles, who for nine years had been pastor of the South Bushwick Reformed Church in Brooklyn, New York. He accepted, and the consistory explored various options for supplying him and his family housing because the former parsonage was no longer available and the parsonage under construction was not yet finished.⁵³ Bergen and Van der Meulen had purchased their

---

⁵⁰ *Consistorial Minutes*, 1 February 1909, 2:259; 7 July 1909, 2:275.
⁵¹ After ministering to the Hamilton Grange Reformed Church for three years, he was dismissed to the Presbyterian denomination. Gasero, *Historical Directory*, 412. After serving as pastor of the Second Presbyterian Church in Louisville, Kentucky (1912–17) and of the First Presbyterian Church in Oak Park, Illinois (1917–20), he served as president of the Louisville Presbyterian Theological Seminary (1920–30) and taught systematic theology courses there (1934–36). Rick Nutt, *Many Lamps One Light: Louisville Presbyterian Theological Seminary: A 150th Anniversary History* (Grand Rapids: Eerdmans, 2002), 70.
⁵² *Consistorial Minutes*, 21 September 1921, 3:90.
⁵³ *Consistorial Minutes*, 20 April 1910, 2:305; 1 May 1910, 2:306. According to information in Hope Church's Centennial booklet, this parsonage, located immediately west of Hope Church on Eleventh Street, housed ministers and their families until 1957, when it was used to supplement the Church School facilities, provide office space for the pastor and director of music, and furnish a place for the Hope Church Boy Scout Troop to meet. Known as the "West Church House," it was razed in 1962 to make room for the church's new Educational Unit.

own homes when they were professors at Hope College. Hope Church member Louise Martin (Mrs. Frank) Thurber agreed to rent a house at the corner of River and Thirteenth to Hope Church as a residence for the Niles family, and Niles was installed as minister in September of 1910.[54]

Twelve months later, at a meeting of the consistory, Niles presented in writing two resolutions and then left the room:

Edward Niles

I. That the President of Consistory is ex officio member of all Committees of Consistory and should be consulted by them before any new policy is recommended to Consistory.
II. That the Church Treasurer be requested to present at the monthly meetings of Consistory a statement of receipts and expenses during the previous month, and of balances in his hands, for information of members.[55]

If there were already a cordial and trusting relationship between pastor and consistory, such resolutions might have been presented in a different manner, favorably received, and acted upon, but their manner of presentation and their content caused the consistory to respond unfavorably. Speaking for the entire consistory, elders Charles S. Dutton and Henry Boer replied the following day by a letter with the following conclusion: "The present relations should, for the mutual good of both pastor and people, not continue longer than is necessary."[56]

---

[54] *Consistorial Minutes*, 12 May 1910, 2:308; 1 July 1910, 2:317; 22 September 1910, 2:323.
[55] *Consistorial Minutes*, 1 September 1911, 2:351.
[56] *Consistorial Minutes*, 2 September 1911, 2:353.

Three weeks later Niles announced to the congregation and wrote to the consistory that he was resigning "in order to accept a call to a new field in New York City," with his resignation to be effective the following week.[57] He did not move to New York City, but instead to the Second Presbyterian Church in Baltimore, Maryland, where he served eleven years before serving the First Newtown Reformed Church in Elmhurst, New York, where he served for sixteen years.[58] The short term of ministry at Hope Church in the context of these longer terms elsewhere can perhaps best be explained by housing problems and a power struggle between a consistory accustomed to a rather free rein and a pastor desiring firm control. Consistory minutes of Hope Church are generally discreet about negative details. Had there been a recording device in the consistory room before, during, and after meetings, we might know more about the reasons for Niles's brief ministry at Hope Church. Like Birchby's departure, the departure of Niles is an enigma.

August F. Bruske's Ministry

After Niles left, the consistory tentatively queried several ministers about whether they would consider receiving a call from Hope Church. Early in 1912 it sent a letter to the Reverend Abraham J. Muste, a Hope College graduate who held degrees from New Brunswick Theological Seminary and Union Theological Seminary and was then pastor of the recently organized Fort Washington Collegiate Church in New York City.[59] Muste, who became a prominent advocate for pacifism, replied that he was not willing to receive a call at this time.[60]

---

[57] *Consistorial Minutes*, 24 September 1911, 2:354.
[58] Gasero, *Historical Directory*, 287, 529.
[59] Gasero, *Historical Directory*, 281, 597.
[60] *Consistorial Minutes*, 8 February 1912, 2:369.

August F. Bruske

In August 1912, the consistory extended a call to retired Alma College president the Reverend August F. Bruske to serve as a stated supply pastor at Hope Church for a term of two years. He accepted the call and with the consistory's consent renewed the agreement for a second two-year commitment until his request for retirement in 1916.[61]

During the summer of 1913 Hope Church invited summer residents of Macatawa Park to worship services at Hope Church. Bruske and professor John B. Nykerk called on several families there and made sure that advance church bulletins were sent to those interested in attending church.[62] Hope Church was attempting to reach those affluent enough to afford summer homes near Lake Michigan. Results of these efforts are largely unknown.[63]

At the annual meeting of the congregation in 1916, the "Sunday School orchestra played two selections and a pleasing programme of readings and other music was rendered." The men served the refreshments and a social time was enjoyed by all.[64] Church business was combined with entertainment, refreshment, and socializing—evidence of affluence and leisure. Perhaps another sign of growing

---

[61] *Consistorial Minutes*, 3 August 1912, 2:384, 386; 7 March 1914, 2:420; 10 March 1916; 2:460–61.
[62] *Consistorial Minutes*, 31 July 1913, 2:408.
[63] John H. Parr, proprietor of the hotel at Castle Park, and his wife, Flora Pennell Parr, joined Hope Church in 1914. "Record of Hope Church Holland Michigan 1862–1916," W91-1034, box 10, Hope Church, Holland, Michigan, Joint Archives of Holland. *Michigan State Gazetteer and Business Directory* (Detroit, MI: R. L. Polk & Co., 1907), 529.
[64] *Consistorial Minutes*, 3 February 1916, 2:456–57.

affluence among members was the suggestion from deacon John Nykerk later that year that the church have a vested choir. The consistory referred the recommendation to the Music Committee and to the Ladies' Aid Society.

Later that year the consistory decided to try "the single envelope system of collecting church dues ... for the coming year."65 The apportionment of "church dues" initiated in 1904 continued for at least a decade.

Among collections received and disbursed in 1915 was $110 for the Arabian Mission. This was in addition to the $700 annually given to missionary Hoekje in Japan. In 1916, the middle of World War I, donations of $56 each were sent to Poland and to Serbia for the relief of those suffering there.66

In 1884, 1895, and 1904, delegates and guests of General Synods meeting in Grand Rapids had made brief visits to Holland, but in 1916, for the first time, the General Synod held its official sessions in Holland. Delegates and guests were housed in the Ottawa Beach Hotel on Lake Michigan, and the synod's official sessions were held in Hope Church. The Reverend Peter Moerdyke, a member of Hope College's first graduating class (1866) and a member of Hope Church during his college years, was elected president of the General Synod. John. M. Van der Meulen presented the Hope College alumni address, and Hope Church member the Honorable Gerrit J. Diekema, secretary of the Hope Council (predecessor to the Board of Trustees) since 1893, also addressed the synod.67

In 1917, the consistory recommended that in addition to the already existing Men's Bible Class a Men's Forum be organized. Meeting the same time as the Sunday School, it would focus discussion on topics of applied Christianity. The consistory recommended Dr. Abraham Leenhouts, a distinguished physician and elder, to be its first leader.68

---

65 *Consistorial Minutes*, 10 March 1916, 2:461; 11 October 1916, 2:471.
66 *Consistorial Minutes*, 28 February 1917, 2:485.
67 Wichers, *Century of Hope*, 151–52.
68 *Consistorial Minutes*, 14 May 1917, 3:2.

Peter P. Cheff's Ministry

After tentatively exploring whether various ministers would be open to receiving a call from Hope Church, the consistory in November 1917 extended a call to Peter P. Cheff, minister of the First Reformed Church in Zeeland and instructor of Bible at Hope College. There were many in the congregation who pressed for his selection, and the formal vote gave him 102 of the 111 votes cast. The affirmative reply from Cheff two weeks later was "enthusiastically received" by the consistory.[69]

Peter P. Cheff

Rallying Around the Flags

America entered World War I in 1917. The people of Holland and most of its churches were caught up in a wave of patriotism and a desire to engage in the "war to end all wars" and "make the world safe for democracy." The Memorial Day parade that year was "the greatest popular patriotic demonstration ever witnessed in this city."[70] Bergen came from Minneapolis to speak to a Memorial Day crowd in Centennial Park. Mingling patriotism with theology, he defended the honor of being conscripted into military service:

---

[69] *Consistorial Minutes*, 22 November 1917, 3:9–11; 14 December 1917, 3:14.
[70] "Demonstration Greatest in City's History," *Holland City News*, 7 June 1917, 6.

> You Hollanders ... ought to understand better than anyone else that enrolling in the nation's service through the selective conscription system is fully as honorable as through the volunteer system. When I was here twelve years ago, I used to hear a good deal about Armenianism [sic] and Calvanism [sic]. Now Armenianism corresponds to the volunteer plan while Calvanism is the selective conscription in religious [terms]. God, according to Calvinism, chooses his men. He chose Abraham and Moses, and even in the New Testament Jesus chose his disciples. And the only one among these disciples who stood out against the selective conscription was Judas Iscariot....
>
> God is today saying to America, Here is your great chance to help in the work of establishing a stable, world-wide democracy; will you answer the world call?[71]

The report that Hope Church provided to the Particular Synod of Chicago after the first few months of Cheff's ministry indicated that the church was prospering:

> Hope, Holland.—Tho without a leader during 1917, the church has prospered in every department. She is grateful for her new pastor, is ready to fulfill her God-given task, and is eager to do her share to help to win the war, and thus to promote the cause of peace. She is 100% loyal to the cause of God, the country and humanity. She feels the need of divine aid, and prays for spiritual guidance.[72]

In January 1918, the consistory appointed elders Abraham Leenhouts and Charles W. McLean, with the pastor, to be a committee to confer with Sunday School superintendent Gerrit J. Diekema and the superintendent of public schools, Egbert E. Fell, to secure a service flag for the church. Two months later, the committee reported to consistory that the flag would have at least forty-six stars—a star for each member of Hope Church serving in the armed

---

[71] "Conscription Is Like Calvinism," *Holland City News*, 7 June 1917, 6.
[72] *Reformed Church in America. Particular Synod of Chicago*, vol. 7 (1918), 31.

forces—and that it would be dedicated with a suitable program on Sunday evening March 17.[73]

In February, news of Bergen's attempt to enlist as a volunteer soldier appeared in the *Holland City News*. Though he was fifty-six years old, he attempted to join one of two regiments that former President Theodore Roosevelt was forming in Minnesota. Bergen had both volunteered to serve and been elected a captain, but his attempt to serve failed when Congress and President Wilson withdrew support for these Minnesota regiments.[74]

That both his attempt at volunteering and his being "elected" a captain (a combination of Bergen's versions of Arminian and Calvinist flavors of patriotism) failed to the meet the approval of Commander in Chief Wilson might have caused a crisis of faith in a lesser patriot. But this temporary setback did not prevent Bergen and others in the regiments from finding other ways to serve their country:

> Bergen, together with two hundred Minnesota sportsmen, all deer hunters who carried deer rifles, formed themselves into a volunteer company to do home guard duty. They were sworn in as deputy sheriffs and put on guard to protect the great grain elevators in Minneapolis,... the "bread-baskets of the world." Immediately at the outbreak of the war repeated attempts were made to burn these elevators and 300,000 bushels of wheat were burned.... Bergen declared there was proof that these attempts were financed from Germany. When this company of sportsmen went on home guard

---

[73] *Consistorial Minutes*, 18 January 1918, 3:17, 21.
[74] "Former Pastor Is Not a Pacifist," *Holland City News*, 14 February 1918, 2. In 1917, Theodore Roosevelt was eager to train regiments of "Rough Riders" at Ft. Sill, Oklahoma, and elsewhere. The secretary of war, Newton T. Baker, on behalf of President Woodrow Wilson, refused to support Roosevelt's plans. See Theodore Roosevelt, *The Foes of Our Own Household*, esp. Appendix G, "Correspondence with the President and the Secretary of War" (New York: George H. Doran Company, 1917), 304-47, for evidence of Roosevelt's persistent but futile petitions to change the minds of men then in power.

duty the attempts on the elevators ceased. The guards are all crack shots.⁷⁵

In mid-February, a service flag honoring fifty-one Hope College men then in active service—not counting alumni and former students—was unveiled in Winants Chapel. Praising this action, Gerrit J. Diekema stated, "If the flag stands for all that is pure and noble and good, it is worthy of being unfurled in any building on the face of the earth. The very portals of heaven would welcome such an emblem." Cheff closed that service with prayer.⁷⁶

Some of Diekema's comments were made in response to the Reverend Herman Hoeksema's refusal to admit the presence of an American flag or any service flag in the Fourteenth Street Christian Reformed Church during worship services.⁷⁷ Proudly displaying American flags and service banners in their church sanctuaries were First Reformed, Hope Church, Third Reformed, Grace Episcopal, Methodist Episcopal, and St. Francis de Sales Catholic, but not Fourteenth Street Christian Reformed, the first English-speaking congregation of that denomination in Holland.⁷⁸

In a debate carried on by way of the *Holland City News*, Cheff challenged Hoeksema's refusal to display the American flag in church:

> I do not care to argue the theological contention advanced, viz: that the church as the manifestation of the body of Christ is universal in character.... I fail to see the slightest connection. Does this universality exclude nationalism? Cannot a man love humanity and be a patriot just the same? Isn't it perfectly proper to show one's colors and not at all to clash with the universal character of the Church? If theology makes a man 'neutral' while in the house of prayer on the Sabbath, God deliver us from such theology!...

---

⁷⁵ "Former Pastor Is Not a Pacifist," 2.
⁷⁶ "Flag in Church, Controversy," *Holland City News*, 21 February 1918, 2.
⁷⁷ "Flag in Church, Controversy," 2.
⁷⁸ Robert Swierenga, "Disloyal Dutch? Herman Hoeksema and the Flag in Church Controversy during World War I," *Origins*, vol. 25, no. 2 (2007), 30, 33, 35. Swierenga cites *Holland City News*, 28 June 1917; 21 February 1918, 7 March 1918, 14 March 1918, 21 March 1918, and 30 May 1918.

> To exhibit the flag in a church could never be wrong; at the most it is a matter of indifference since no principle need be involved. But as a constant inspiration it might be the source of great good. And as to the singing of national hymns in church, not to do so in times like these is positively criminal and a reflection on an entire congregation if not the whole community.[79]

Hoeksema responded to Cheff in the style of a sermon with three points: first giving his personal views about America and the war, then describing his views on government, and concluding with his view of the nature of the church of Jesus Christ. He began by chiding his critics for questioning "the old truth, embodied in the laws of our own dear country":

> I refer of course to the truth of separation of church and state. Nevertheless, gentlemen whom I esteem highly, who know far more about Civil government than I do, and who also seem to have studied Theology, make the incomprehensible mistake of taking the stand that caused Luther to kindle the fire of the Reformation, and that drove our Pilgrim Fathers to these shores of Religious Liberty! Amusing indeed, if it were not for the fact, that these same gentlemen, that make this serious, and principally so dangerous mistake, a mistake thru which they stab unwittingly at the heart of all real liberty in the state, take occasion to bring the indictment against a really patriotic citizen, who truly loves his country, and who seeks the good of his country.[80]

Developing his second point, Hoeksema affirmed the need for citizens to pray for and support the government. He concluded by citing the dangers of not separating the spheres of church and state:

> In the church of Jesus Christ, we raise no flag, and sing no national anthems.... The church and state are separate, must be separate, and if you do not keep them separate, it is you who stab at the heart of true liberty. Then you will either come to the domination of church

---

[79] "Flag in Church? Sure! Why Not?" *Holland City News*, 21 February 1918, 2.
[80] "Answer Made by Pastor in Controversy," *Holland City News*, 21 February 1918, 2.

over state, as is the ideal of Roman Catholicism, or to the subjugation of the church to the state, as was the condition in Old England, at the time of our Pilgrim Fathers.[81]

Though Herman Hoeksema's view was not popular, his argument for the separation of church and state is compelling. He appealed more to reason than did the more passionate rhetoric of Diekema and Cheff, which roused their audiences to spirited applause. Had more of the post-World-War-I German churches and more American churches throughout its history been perceptive to and critical of the easy tendency to conflate Christianity with patriotism and conflate God's will with national interests, the world would have been spared much harm.

Undaunted by Hoeksema's critique, Cheff and Hope Church proceeded with plans to dedicate their service flag. On Sunday evening, 17 March, Hope Church was filled to capacity with many standing and scores of others turned away. While the congregation sang "Onward Christian Soldiers," the choir led the procession, followed by the veterans of the Grand Army of the Republic (Civil War) and the ladies of the War Relief Committee. After they were seated, the choir sang an anthem titled "Our Country and Our God." Then boys with flags of the allied nations stood at attention on either side of the aisle while Boy Scouts processed forward, presenting the service flag. The flag to be dedicated contained fifty-seven stars, one for each of the young men of the church serving in the armed forces.[82]

---

[81] "Answer Made by Pastor in Controversy," 3. Not afraid of controversy, Hoeksema criticized the principle of common grace, the idea that though God chose some to be "elect" and others to be "reprobate," God granted some goodness and favor to all of humankind—that God makes the sun to shine and the rain to fall not only on the good and just but also on the evil and unjust (Matthew 5:45). James D. Bratt, *Dutch Calvinism: A History of A Conservative Subculture* (Grand Rapids: Erdmans, 1984). 107–15. Hoeksema's views prompted his removal from the Christian Reformed Church, and he proceeded to create the Protestant Reformed denomination.
[82] "Hope's Flag Dedication Impressive," *Holland City News*, 21 March 1918, 12. Among those represented by a star were Gerrit John Diekema Jr., Simon

Then followed the orators of the evening: Cheff, Gerrit J. Diekema, Dr. Abraham Leenhouts, and the minister of the Methodist Episcopal Church, the Reverend J. F. Bowerman. They were followed by fifty-seven children, each carrying a carnation representing one of the young men in the service. A young woman representing a Red Cross nurse, who carried the America flag, concluded the procession.

"With much feeling, Dr. Leenhouts, in the name of the fathers, mothers, and friends of the men in service, presented the service flag to the church." Said Dr. Leenhouts, "'We bring this banner at the hands of the children of our homes, with flowers and banners which indicate that our homes are back of these boys.'" While Dr. Leenhouts read the names of the soldiers, the children placed their flowers on the altar. Cheff accepted the service flag and displayed it before the congregation. The Boy Scouts who had carried it in knelt for the dedicatory prayer by Cheff, who "implored life, courage, health and victory for the men who had consecrated their lives to the service of God and humanity."[83]

After the congregation sang "God Save Our Men," Cheff delivered a sermon "which in the opinion of many was the most thrilling he has yet delivered in Holland."[84] Said Cheff,

> It was two millenniums ago that God sent his Son into the territory of the enemy to suffer, to bleed, to die—and He also prepared a star.... That star of Bethlehem ... is leading us today. It leads us across the sea—to Belgium ... to France ... into Armenia ... [and] Poland. And they who are following that star are following Jesus Christ, suffering, bleeding, dying—Jesus Christ with the sword of militarism in his

---

Den Uyl, John Lewis Kleinheksel, Willard G. Leenhouts, Irwin Lubbers, and John J. Riemersma. Wichers, *Century of Hope*, 155, reported that by April 1918 sixty-four young men had left the college to serve in the war. The next month that number increased to eighty-one.

[83] "Hope's Flag Dedication Impressive," *Holland City News*, 12. These "Boy Scouts" were young boys, perhaps in some uniform, but not officially members of the Boy Scouts of America. Hope Church did not organize a Boy Scout troop until 1924. See *Consistorial Minutes*, 31 January 1924, 3:151–52.

[84] "Hope's Flag Dedication Impressive," *Holland City News*, 12.

side and the thorny crown of 'might is right' pressed down upon his head. And as the Father of us all symbolized his sacrifice in a star, so do we.[85]

After the choir sang "The Heavens Are Telling," Gerrit J. Diekema, the Sunday School superintendent, delivered a speech, which, "as usual, stirred his audience to a high pitch of patriotic enthusiasm." After chiding "slacker cowards," Diekema pleaded, "Give me a son with red, American blood in his veins. Far better a dead hero than a live coward in a great republic such as ours. We're going to add some more stars to that flag soon, and every last one of them will be a shooting star." A four-column article in the *Holland City News* claimed that this service flag dedication service was "without a doubt the most impressive ever held in Hope Church."[86]

World War I and Its Repercussions

Missing out on all of this celebration was Willard G. Leenhouts, son of Dr. Leenhouts. He had not waited until after high school graduation but enlisted 17 April 1917 and sailed for France on 19 September 1917.[87]

Elder Leenhouts, reporting for the Committee on the Soldier Boys, informed the consistory that its members were "getting in touch with our boys in the service and to each one had been sent a program of the dedicatory services of the Service Flag and a copy of the address delivered by Mr. Diekema on that occasion."[88]

In a letter written to his parents on 20 April 1918, Willard G. Leenhouts described his experiences in the war:

---

[85] "Hope's Flag Dedication Impressive," *Holland City News*, 12.
[86] "Hope's Flag Dedication Impressive," *Holland City News*, 12.
[87] Randy Vande Water, "Holland's First Soldier Killed in WW I Remembered," *Holland Sentinel*, 25 July 2010, C6. Willard G. Leenhouts had joined Hope Church in 1913, one of eight to profess their faith on May 28. *Consistorial Minutes*, 28 May 1913, 2:405.
[88] *Consistorial Minutes*, 8 April 1918, 3:23.

I have not received the fruit cake you said was sent and I am looking forward anxiously toward the day it comes....

I am writing under difficulties lying on my bunk, which happens to be an upper one two feet from the top in a two by four dugout. Our dugout has about five feet thickness of earth on top of it which makes it pretty safe.

I am not driving ambulance now on account of the Army having taken over all that line of work, but I am standing by for some other kind of motor job. Perhaps I will get a motorcycle and do dispatch riding. Hope so.

I wish I could speak of the war the way you do in your letters. It would make correspondence more interesting, but you can see that is impossible.

In your letter you had said that I had not mentioned guns, cannons, air raids, bombs, etc., but up to this date I can tell you I have experienced all of them ... which is all I had better say....

Willard G. Leenhouts

You had asked about my smoking. I am smoking quite a little but when you are out in the open all the time and live the way we live it does not hurt one compared to the pleasure it returns. It is about the only pleasure and pastime we have. I am waiting now for my pay which I don't expect to get for a month yet. When I do get it I will have enough to 'make a liberty' to some large city here in France.

I have not taken out any insurance although I had intended to and now the time has come when we can no longer do so. I surely am sorry about it but it's over now.

      Willard G. Leenhouts,
      Hdg. Co. 15th Reg. U.S.M.C.[89]

---

[89] "Last Letter Received from Willard Leenhouts...," *Holland City News*, 23 August 1918, 3.

The family of Willard G. Leenhouts did not receive this letter until the latter part of May. On August 15 former Congressman Gerrit J. Diekema delivered to the Leenhouts family a telegram that conveyed sad news.[90] Nineteen-year-old Willard, their oldest son, had died, "killed by shrapnel on the battlefield" in France. Thus did Hope Church and Holland receive the first gold star on its service flag.[91]

The memorial service in honor of Willard G. Leenhouts on August 18 "brought out one of the largest audiences that ever gathered in that church." Cheff presented the memorial sermon and Diekema delivered the memorial address. Both "emphasized the fact that the sacrifice of this young life should serve as a challenge to greater endeavor to free the world of the German menace."[92]

Although the telegram that the family received from the War Department indicated that Leenhouts's body was to be returned to the United States at the end of the war, his remains were permanently interred in France. A tombstone placed in the family plot in Pilgrim Home Cemetery reads: "Willard G. Leenhouts 1898-1918 Chateau Thierry France."[93]

Hope Church's report to the Particular Synod of Chicago for 1918 indicated its interest in reconstruction across the world after the war:

> All the departments of church work have prospered and the attendance at services has been gratifying. Interest in the prayer services is manifest by increased attendance. The patriotism and loyalty of the church during the war has been exemplary. Seventy of her sons have joined the colors, one of whom has been called to

---

[90] Vande Water, "Holland's First Soldier Killed in WW I Remembered," *Holland Sentinel*, C6.
[91] "Gives His Life Fighting on the Field of Honor," *Holland City News*, 23 August 1918, 3.
[92] "Say Holland Boy's Death Is a Challenge," *Holland City News*, 23 August 1918, 3.
[93] Vande Water, "Holland's First Soldier Killed in WW I Remembered," *Holland Sentinel*, C6.

give his life for the cause of his country. It is hoped that the soldiers on their return may occupy the places in the church made vacant by those who have been called to their reward. With trust in God the church hopes to do its part in the great reconstruction work of the Church of Christ for the world.[94]

The Prohibition of Alcoholic Beverages

Not long after the end of World War I, the United States approved Constitutional Amendments Eighteen and Nineteen, both attributable in large part to the advocacy of social issues by women. The Women's Christian Temperance Union and the Anti-Saloon League pushed hard for the Eighteenth Amendment, which prohibited the manufacturing, importing, and exporting of alcoholic beverages. That amendment was passed in 1919 and repealed in 1933 by the 21st Amendment.

Anticipating the prohibition of alcoholic beverages in Holland, elder Charles S. Dutton in a consistory meeting in March 1918 "brought up the subject that the saloons in Holland and all over the state would have to close in a short time and something should be done to devise some way of giving the men in our community suitable opportunity for recreation which is more uplifting and healthful." In response to his concern, consistory appointed a committee "to arrange for a meeting with representatives of all churches and organizations in Holland who might be interested."[95]

The Women's Suffrage Movement

Amendment Nineteen, which was passed in 1920, prohibited the federal government and the states from forbidding any citizen from voting on the basis of that citizen's sex. Passage of this amendment allowed women to vote in city, state, and federal elections. Since 1878, Hope Church women members could vote to call

---

[94] *Reformed Church in America. Particular Synod of Chicago*, vol. 7 (1919), 28.
[95] *Consistorial Minutes*, 8 March 1918, 3:21-22.

a minister and, since 1879, to elect deacons and elders. They, like all women in the denomination, had to wait many decades more before they could become deacons, elders, and ministers in the Reformed Church in America.

Holland women march for the right to vote in civil elections

At the denominational level, overtures to the General Synod in 1918 from the Particular Synod of Albany and the Classis of Montgomery introduced the issue of the ordination of women to the offices of deacon and elder. The overtures proposed removing "male" from the qualifications for those offices as indicated in the RCA Constitution.[96] The synod's review committee recommended, however, that the "overture be not entertained, believing that the submission of the proposed amendment to the Classes will work injury through friction and division out of all proportion to any

---

[96] Edwin G. Mulder, "Full Participation—A Long Time in Coming!" *Reformed Review*, vol. 42, no. 3 (Spring 1989), 227–28. Also see John W. Coakley, "Women in the History of the Reformed Church in America," in *Patterns and Portraits: Women in the History of the Reformed Church in America*, ed. Renée House and John Coakley, Historical Series of the Reformed Church in America no. 31 (Grand Rapids: Eerdmans, 1999), 1–15.

possible good that might accrue to any portion of our church."[97] Fuller implications of the decision were spelled out in the summary of synod actions published in the *Holland City News*: "Women members of the Reformed Church in America were refused a place on the governing boards and a voice in the church affairs."[98]

Locally, this attempt to maintain the status quo was challenged by a Hope Church consistory member. After one of the deacons resigned from consistory in 1920, deacon Gerrit Van Schelven made a motion to fill the vacancy by the election of a deaconess. The motion, however, was tabled.[99] That a consistory member would even propose election of a deaconess, especially given the denomination's stance, was a remarkable step.

In 1918 a proposed state equal suffrage amendment appeared on the November 5 ballot. Campaigning for that amendment, many women of Hope Church added their signatures among those of the 535 women who signed a petition to the voters of Ottawa County. Among the more than 35 Hope Church women signing the petition were Jane Boyd, Harriet Walker (Mrs. Peter P.) Cheff, Mary Diekema (Mrs. George) Kollen, Elizabeth De Kruif (Mrs. Abraham) Leenhouts, Kate Garrod (Mrs. John C.) Post, Christine Cornelia Van Raalte, Kate Ledeboer (Mrs. Dirk B. K.) Van Raalte, Amelia (Mrs. Henry) Winter, and Alice Kools (Mrs. William G.) Winter.[100]

Despite the petition, the amendment was voted down by a two-to-one majority in Holland and Ottawa County. Other voters

---

[97] *Minutes of General Synod*, 1918, 478.
[98] "Church Refuses Women Authority," *Holland City News*, 13 June 1918, 2.
[99] *Consistorial Minutes*, 4 June 1920, 3:56. Gerrit Van Schelven, editor of the *Holland City News* in the mid-1870s and Hope Church deacon from 1902 until his death in 1927, was a long-time advocate for women's suffrage. In an article, "Woman-Suffrage," Van Schelven concluded, "the wildest dreams of unity of races are being fullfilled [sic] in our day; thus doing away with destinction [sic], because of color. And we only await the day when, in matters of vital importance to life, liberty, and pursuit of happiness, there will be neither 'male nor female,' doing away with the destinction [sic] because of set [sic], on the broad battlefield of America." *Holland City News*, 30 May 1874, 1.
[100] *Holland City News*, 31 October 1918, 2.

across Michigan, however, approved the amendment. Within weeks of the granting of the right to vote to the women citizens of Michigan, approximately 900 of Holland's 2,500 women eligible to vote registered at city hall.[101] Though this may suggest that women's "suffrage was not a burning issue among most women of Holland,"[102] it was important to many of the women of Hope Church.

Evidence for this interest among Hope Church women is found in the composition of the first jury in Holland to contain women. Among the twelve jurors chosen for a trial in 1919 were six women—Anna C. Aldworth, Elizabeth Drew, Elizabeth Fell, Jeannette Mulder, Margaret Olive, and Helen Wing—each of whom were or would soon become Hope Church members.[103]

A large crowd gathered in the courtroom to witness what was informally called the "Chicken Case." It was a case about whether one woman had slandered another in accusing her of having stolen a chicken. Adding interest to the case was the testimony of a six-year-old boy, "who was supposed to have chased the chicken in dispute." The youngster refused to testify until the court gave him a penny.[104]

The unanimous decision of the jury after deliberating for some time was that the defendant was guilty of slander, and the judge

---

[101] Robert P. Swierenga, "Getting Political in Holland," paper presented to the Holland Historical Society, April 11, 2006. Retrieved from http://www.swierenga.com/PoliticsHHSpaper2006.html.
[102] Swierenga, "Getting Political in Holland," from http://www.swierenga.com/PoliticsHHSpaper2006.html.
[103] "Pioneer Woman [sic] Jury Chosen in Case Today, *Holland Sentinel*, 4 March 1919, 1. Anna Aldworth joined in 1921 by transfer from a church in Philadelphia, PA. Elizabeth (Mrs. Charles E.) Drew joined by confession of faith in 1913. Elizabeth (Mrs. Egbert E.) Fell joined by transfer in 1910 from a Presbyterian congregation. Jeannette Mulder joined by confession of faith in 1910. Margaret (Mrs. William J.) Olive joined by transfer from Grace Episcopal Church in 1918. Helen (Mrs. William H.) Wing joined Hope Church in 1891. Each of these women also were or would become members of Holland's Woman's Literary Club. Zingle, *Woman's Literary Club*, 31.
[104] "Pioneer Woman [sic] Jury Chosen in Case Today," 1.

fined her $50 and court costs.[105] Not satisfied with the verdict, the defendant appealed to the Circuit Court in Grand Haven. Twelve men were drawn for that jury. After hearing from ten witnesses and deliberating for nearly seven hours before they reached an agreement well past midnight, the all-male jury sustained the verdict of the earlier trial.[106]

By 1920 women in Holland had the right to vote in city, state, and federal elections, but they were not encouraged to take the reins of political power. Invited to speak at the local chapter of the Women's Christian Temperance Union on "Women and Politics," Cheff stated that he "was strongly for equal rights for women," but encouraged women to seek "to exercise influence" rather than "to wield power."[107] He supported his case with three reasons:

1. Woman's physical idiosyncrasy makes her unfit to cope with the strenuous duties of high officials.

2. Woman is the fountain-head of church, society and the nation. All nations depend upon their homes, good, solid and old-fashioned. A home is only a house without the homemaker. Remove her from the home and she loses much of her tremendous influence.

3. Women in their organizations do great work in civic improvement and in the slums, work that men could never do. Put women in legislature and other high offices, and communities would thus suffer. There are, however, political positions which women ought to fill, viz., on school and library boards, as police matrons and on various important committees."[108]

---

[105] "Holland's First Woman Jury Says 'Guilty,'" *Holland Sentinel*, 5 March 1919, 1.
[106] "Verdict of Woman Jury Is Sustained," *Holland Sentinel*, 3 April 1919, 1.
[107] "Gives Address on 'Women in Politics," *Holland City News*, 6 April 1922.
[108] "Gives Address on 'Women in Politics." (Spelling and grammar errors in the quoted text are corrected.)

Changing Attitudes about Women's Roles and Sabbath Rules

Despite Cheff's reverence for the old-fashioned value of women as homemakers, Hope Church members were changing their attitudes about the roles of women. Christina Van Raalte Gilmore, for example, who likely inherited a goodly portion of her father's spirit, combined motherhood with serving Hope Church, Hope College, the denomination, and the community. Returning to Holland after the death of her husband, she became the "Lady Principal" and then the

Christina Van Raalte Gilmore

dean of women at Hope College for nearly two decades.[109] She also was active in the Women's Board of Domestic Missions of the Reformed Church. Within that organization she became Vice-President of the Particular (regional) Synod of Chicago, serving in that office from 1887 to 1932. In addition to that, she served as president of the Women's Union Missionary Conference of Holland Classis for thirty consecutive years. In 1919 she organized a co-operative interchurch movement, Holland's Federation of Women's Societies, serving as its president for many years.[110] In response to contributions collected by the Federation and given to medical missions in Portuguese East Africa, a hospital in the

---

[109] Christina Catharina Van Raalte Gilmore was the sixth child of Albertus C. and Christina De Moen Van Raalte. After the death of her husband, the Reverend William Brokaw Gilmore, and the deaths of three of their four children, Christina Gilmore and their son Albertus (Raalte) returned from Havana, IL, to Holland, where she lived from 1884 to her death in 1933. Bruins et al., *Albertus and Christina*, 56–57, 152–53.

[110] *Holland City News*, 25 December 1919, 6; 13 April 1933, 1.

city of Inhambane was named in her honor as the Christine Van Raalte Gilmore Home for Lepers.[111]

Near the end of her many years of service, one of her colleagues praised her for having the "resoluteness, force of character and resourcefulness of the pioneer" in addition to "a deeply religious and devotional nature." Gilmore "was notable as an organizer in the days when women's work was new and less understood. She was a wonderful platform speaker, gifted in the use of both the English and Holland Languages. She was indefatigable in all Kingdom service."[112]

In addition to encouraging women to take up roles of leadership, albeit in women's church organizations rather than on consistory, Hope Church members were changing some of their attitudes in response to changing times. They were becoming less rigid in enforcing rules related to observance of the Sabbath, and they were increasingly attracted to values associated with material prosperity.

In contrast to the consistory which in 1899 sent to Hope Church members a letter decrying the "alarming increase of Sabbath desecration in our city,"[113] the consistory of 1921, when sent a petition for "signatures by a nameless Committee ... asking the Mayor and Common Council of Holland to close on Sunday all places of business not dealing in necessities," took no action.[114]

---

[111] Bruins et al., *Albertus and Christina*, 155. Portuguese East Africa is now Mozambique. The leprosy hospital in Inhambane ceased operation in the 1970s, according to Amanda Palomino, "The Leprosy Federation," *The Joint Archives Quarterly* 21, no. 4 (Winter 2012):6.

[112] Edith H. Allen, "A Tribute to Mrs. C. V. R. Gilmore," *Golden Years in Miniature: A History of the Women's Board of Domestic Missions of the Reformed Church in America from the Time of Its Organization in 1882 As the Women's Executive Committee of the Board of Domestic Missions to Its Present Golden Anniversary Year* (New York: The Women's Board of Domestic Missions, 1932), unnumbered page between pages 22 and 23.

[113] *Consistorial Minutes*, 15 May 1899, 2:44–45.

[114] *Consistorial Minutes*, 8 July 1921, 3:87.

Historian Jacob Van Hinte's Impressions of Hope Church

Dutch historian Jacob Van Hinte, author of the significant history of Dutch immigration titled *Nederlanders in Amerika*, visited Holland, Michigan, in August 1921 to gather information for that book. What impressed him about attending a worship service at Hope Church was its "typically American ... desire for 'pomp and splendor.'"[115]

> There is often no expression of spiritual meekness or humility. Indeed, the people coming to the service ... and leaving afterward made one think of a theater performance rather than of a religious service. It all seemed very mundane and worldly, due to the sumptuous automobiles and the fashionable clothes and modern coiffures of the ladies. [Hope Church] is the 'elite' church and many of the prominent families have their private and reserved pews, the Diekemas, the Keppels, the Van Schelvens, etc.[116]

Van Hinte's diary of his American travels reveals his observations and reflections in more detail and candor. His entry for 7 August 1921 begins with his description of the worship service at Hope Church:

> A church day. At ten-thirty in the morning to the aristocratic Hope Church, on West Eleventh Street, where I am seated in the Van Schelven pew between the old Mr. and Mrs. Van Schelven. <<*Hope Church was the first English language Reformed Church in Holland. Not only Dutch belong, but also, by attestation, members from Presbyterian, Congregational, Baptist, and Methodist churches. Every member has his own seat. This church is a piece of history.*>> I get a peculiar impression of this church: heavy green carpet, and in front of the pulpit—or should I say platform?—about three chairs, a table with flowers. The American flag next to it.
>
> A gracious public—especially the elegantly dressed women and girls—comes pouring in. A young man in a white robe seats himself at the organ, and then, to my great surprise, about eight young men

---

[115] Van Hinte, *Netherlanders in America*, 973. The work was translated to English by Adriaan de Wit, edited by Robert P. Swierenga, and published in 1985 by Baker Book House as *Netherlanders in America*.
[116] Van Hinte, *Netherlanders in America*, 973–74.

and about eleven young women enter through the side doors, while singing. I was reminded of a town theater!

The violin solo by Miss Ruth Keppel, however, made me think of a concert hall.... A short pithy sermon by Rev. [John M.] Van der Meulen from Louisville, Kentucky, gave the "reformed" stamp to this gathering, which was full of variety. No less for the hymn responses than for the modern sung psalms. After the service I met the pastor.

I thought of the theater again once outside of the church: numerous beautiful cars, busily talking women and men. Well dressed young people. Some of them introduced themselves to me. Two of them, a young man and his girl friend even knew some Dutch. Easy, smart young people.[117]

After attending Hope Church's morning service, Van Hinte attended the afternoon service at the Ninth Street Christian Reformed (Pillar) Church. His diary reveals impressions that contrasted considerably with his experiences of the morning:

In the afternoon to church again. This time to the Van Raalte church. It now belongs to the Christian Reformed Church, who "stole" it from the Reformed Church. Lots of thoughts welled up in me in seeing this wooden church, prominent with its ... columns on the front, reminiscent of so many Dutch churches in the nineteenth century. And what a peaceful setting. Beautiful trees. The church was to begin at three. I was there already at two o'clock. Slowly the worshippers appeared.

What simple people and faces. As if they had just arrived from the Netherlands this morning and this afternoon. What extremes, the worshippers of this morning and this afternoon. This morning not a buggy in sight, but several of them this afternoon. The little

---

[117] Ester, Kennedy, and Kennedy, *The American Diary of Jacob Van Hinte,* 73–75. Ester et al. note that after Ruth Keppel attended the Oberlin Conservatory of Music and graduated from Chicago Musical College, she returned to Holland to teach violin and to direct the Holland Junior and Senior High orchestras. On the Sunday of Van Hinte's visit, Cheff was on vacation. Van der Meulen, pastor of Hope Church 1907–1909, came to Holland from Louisville Presbyterian Seminary, where he was president, to preach on this and subsequent Sundays in August.

buggies look aged and often appear neglected.... Also cars drove up, on the other side, disgorging large families. In the meantime a woman chatted with me in Dutch. A lot of Dutch was heard here, again in contrast to the morning.

She began to speak about the Freemasons [who had come to Holland that weekend to celebrate the opening of the new Masonic Hall located about midway between Hope Church and Ninth Street Christian Reformed Church]. "No, you could tell that that movement was not biblical," she had told her husband immediately. "No, that could not be according to the Old Testament. People had never looked like that, that sword, that plumed three-cornered hat." And I had a glimpse of the atmosphere of the Seceders. It struck me again to see the many children, just as in other Christian Reformed churches. Entire families. Rev. Ghysels was not preaching, but I heard candidate Essenburg preach in rather good Dutch. How protracted the Psalms sounded compared to this morning's hymns. And the involuntary thought came to me that the development of these people was just as slow or as fast as their singing. After the service I looked at the Van Raalte memorial plaque, then went outside. The cars were already driving away, but several women were still busy harnessing the horses, in front of the buggies.[118]

After attending the two worship services, Van Hinte passed up returning to Hope Church for its evening service in which, according to the church "program," Van der Meulen's sermon was to be "An Impersonation of Judas Iscariot." The morning had been theatrical enough. Instead, Van Hinte took a walk to Lake Macatawa.[119]

---

[118] Ester, et al., *American Diary of Jacob Van Hinte*, 75–76. As Ester, et al. note, the "Van Raalte memorial plaque" was "dedicated in 1879, three years after his death. It is still attached in the same place, on the front wall of the sanctuary. The inscription, in Dutch, reads: *In Memoriam van Rev. A. C. Van Raalte, D. D., Eerste Leeraar dezer Gemeente en Vader onzer Nederzetting. Een Dienstknecht des Heeren, Krachtig in Woorden en Werken* (In memory of Rev. A. C. Van Raalte, D. D., first minister of this congregation and the father of our settlement. A servant of the Lord, mighty in words and deeds)," 76.
[119] Ester, et al., *American Diary of Jacob Van Hinte*, 77–78.

Enjoying Prosperity

Since its beginnings, Hope Church had been markedly different—in language and responses to social issues—from the predominantly Dutch immigrant congregations that found their homes in the First and Third Reformed churches. It was even more different from the True Dutch Reformed Churches, which became Central Avenue Christian Reformed Church and Ninth Street Christian Reformed Church. Yet Hope Church found among the congregations of Van Raalte's colony nourishment and collegiality to help sustain the early years of its own ministry.

When Hope Church was organized in 1862, it joined eleven other English-speaking Reformed churches already established by the denomination in the region: Battle Creek, Centreville, Constantine, Grand Rapids, Jefferson and Pittsford (near Hillsdale), Macon (near Ann Arbor), Mottville, Porter (near Constantine), Ridgeway (near Ann Arbor), and South Bend (in Indiana).[120] By 1923, only two of these congregations were still alive as Reformed churches.[121] One was the First Reformed (English-speaking) in Grand Rapids, which merged with Grand Rapids's Second (formerly Dutch-speaking) in 1918 to form Central Reformed Church. The other was Hope Church. How else can one explain the longevity of Hope Church in Holland and Central Reformed Church in Grand Rapids except by bonds to their neighboring Dutch-related congregations?

In 1923 the Michigan Classis was disbanded and classis boundaries were rearranged. As a result Hope Church, with American Hamilton, Third, and Trinity, were merged into the Holland

---

[120] *Minutes of the Particular Synod of Chicago; convened...May 13, 1863* (Grand Rapids: Stoompost Office, 1863), 18.
[121] Gasero, *Historical Directory*, 510, 519, 544, 546, 556–57, 564, 579, 589, 618, 624, 639–40, 641. According to *Acts and Proceedings of the General Synod of the Reformed Church in America, 1923* (New York: Board of Publication and Bible-School Work), 232, Michigan Classis comprised ten congregations in Grand Rapids, three in Holland, three in Kalamazoo, three in the Muskegon area, and one each in Allendale, Hamilton, Corinth, Grand Haven, and Detroit.

Classis,[122] joining not only Holland's First, Central Park, Fourth and Sixth Reformed churches but also Beaverdam, East Overisel, Hamilton First, Harlem, Hudsonville, Jamestown First and Second, North Blendon, North Holland, Ottawa, Overisel, South Blendon, Vriesland, and Zeeland First and Second Reformed churches.[123] Also in 1923, the Holland Classis "formally recognized the use of English—for ecclesiastical purposes."[124]

In the early 1920s, a time of relative prosperity for Holland and the entire country, Hope Church paid off to the Board of Domestic Missions a $600 mortgage on its 1864 church building, built an addition large enough to accommodate four Sunday School rooms west of and adjacent to the church parlors, replaced three "rose" windows with colored opalescent glass, and installed ten memorial windows in the church sanctuary.[125]

The first Sunday of August 1924 was designated "home-coming day," and Bergen, pastor of the First Presbyterian Church in Minneapolis, was invited back to dedicate the memorial windows. Assisting him were Cheff and the Reverend Edwin Paul McLean,

---

[122] *Reformed Church in America. Particular Synod of Chicago*, vol. 7 (1923), 17, 20. According to *Reformed Church in America. Particular Synod of Chicago*, vol. 7 (1922), 14, Holland Third moved for one year, 1922, from Classis Holland to Classis Michigan. According to Gasero, *Historical Directory*, 551, 557, American Hamilton, organized in 1913, merged with Hamilton First in 1944. Third Reformed Church was organized in 1867, and Trinity Reformed Church was organized in 1911.
[123] *The Acts and Proceedings of the General Synod of the Reformed Church in America 1924* (New York: Board of Publication and Bible-School Work), 635. See also *In Christ's Service: The Classis of Holland, Michigan, and Its Congregations 1847–1997* (Holland: Classis of Holland, 1997).
[124] Bruins, *Americanization of a Congregation*, 41.
[125] *Consistorial Minutes*, 14 December 1922, 3:121; March 1924, 3:155. Another sign of Holland's prosperity was the completion of the Warm Friend Tavern in 1925 (strangely named "Tavern" during the Prohibition era). Later named the Warm Friend Hotel, this landmark, now owned by Resthaven Care Community, was largely the creation of the Holland Furnace Company, which rose and fell between 1906 and 1966. P. T. Cheff, son of Hope Church's Peter P. Cheff, contributed toward its fall. See Donald L. Van Reken and Randall P. Vande Water, *Holland Furnace Company 1906–1966* (Holland: Donald L. Van Reken, 1993).

son of Mr. and Mrs. Charles M. McLean. Edwin Paul McLean is one of several Hope Church members who joined the ministry.[126]

In November 1924 Cheff accepted a call from the Westminster Presbyterian Church in Omaha, Nebraska, to become its minister. At a farewell gathering in December, the congregation presented him and his wife a "purse" of $1,400.[127]

---

[126] "Windows Are Dedicated at Hope Church," *Holland City News*, 7 August 1924, 3. For a complete list of Hope Church members who became ministers or missionaries, see Appendix E.
[127] *Consistorial Minutes*, 7 November 1924, 3:169; 5 December 1924, 3:172.

5 ... Facing Challenges from 1925 to 1960

After the Reverend Peter P. Cheff's six-year ministry, Hope Church was served by the Reverend Thomas W. Davidson for twelve years, from the end of the roaring twenties through most of the Great Depression. Then the Reverend Paul E. Hinkamp served as moderator for two years. The Reverend Marion de Velder served from 1939 to 1959—with a period away to serve as associate pastor of the First Church in Albany, New York, from November 1951 to April 1952 and occasional absences related to his duties as president of General Synod 1958–59. De Velder, whose tenure was the longest of any of Hope Church's pastors, served through World War II and during the years when many in the baby-boom generation were born.

The Ministry of Thomas W. Davidson

Though its two previous pastors, Bruske and Cheff, had come to Hope Church from Alma and Zeeland, Michigan, respectively, the consistory looked farther eastward for its next pastor. It approved $75 toward traveling expenses for elder John B. Nykerk to take a trip through the East "to make investigations concerning some men who might be candidates for the pastorate of Hope Church."[1]

In July 1925 the congregation voted to call the Reverend Thomas W. Davidson, who was born in Ireland in 1865. He graduated from Methodist College and Methodist Theological School in Belfast. After a six-year ministry in a Congregational church in Montreal, Quebec, he served from 1920 through 1925 as minister to the Reformed Church on the Heights, Brooklyn, New York.[2]

In his letter responding to the call by Hope Church, Davidson stated that he would "accept the call with enthusiasm were it not

---

[1] *Consistorial Minutes*, 6 February 1925, 3:183.
[2] Gasero, *Historical Directory*, 86.

for the fact that acceptance at the salary of $5,000 offered in the call would entail such sacrifice on his part that, in justice to his family, he could not come to Hope Church at that figure. He said that they would gladly come at a salary of $6,000."[3]

The consistory "deliberated long and earnestly over the letter" before arriving at its "unanimous decision that, while a minister's salary of $6,000 would strain the financial ability of Hope Church, with the help of God and the expected growth of the Church under the vigorous leadership of Dr. Davidson, we were justified in meeting his request." Davidson accepted that offer, and he was installed in October 1925.[4]

Thomas W. Davidson

---

[3] *Consistorial Minutes*, 25 July 1925, 3:191.
[4] *Consistorial Minutes*, 25 July 1925, 3:191; 26 October 1925, 3:197.

During the next three months he called on more than 300 families.[5] He made plans to revive the young people's Christian Endeavor group and to start an intermediate Christian Endeavor. Early fruits of his labors were evident on 10 January 1926 when the church received into membership 30 by confession of faith and 27 by letter of transfer.[6] Later in that worship service, nearly 600 people received Communion, the largest number until that time to gather at Hope Church to partake of the sacrament.[7]

In September 1926 he asked Nykerk to furnish him with a list of names and addresses of Hope College students so that he could send them letters of invitation to attend Hope Church. Elder Cornelius Dregman similarly wrote letters to each of the new teachers in Holland to invite them also to Hope Church.[8]

Annual statistics reported at the congregational meeting in April 1927 included the addition of 116 new members, 76 of whom were received by confession of faith and 40 by letter of transfer. Also reported were 18 adult baptisms and 20 infant baptisms.[9]

---

[5] "Holland Church Shows Growth," *Holland City News*, 14 January 1926, 5.
[6] *Consistorial Minutes*, 13 November 1925, 3:199; 4 December 1925, 3:200; 10 January 1926, 3:203.
[7] "Holland Church Shows Growth," *Holland City News*, 14 January 1926.
[8] *Consistorial Minutes*, 2 September 1926, 3:212; 31 October 1926, 3:214–15. Edgar E. Fell, Superintendent of Holland Public Schools 1910–1945, served as elder in Hope Church for many years. John J. Riemersma, Holland High School Principal 1922–1957, was also a Hope Church elder.
[9] *Consistorial Minutes*, 17 April 1927, 3:230–31. Also at that congregational meeting, by unanimous vote, Hope Church contributed $1,000 to the Hope College Chapel Building fund. An additional $700 was contributed by individual church members, making a total of $1,700 donated for the chapel. Known for years as the Hope Memorial Chapel, it was renamed the Dimnent Memorial Chapel in 1959. "A Chronology of Campus Development," *Hope College 2002 Alumni Directory*, 10th ed. (Holland, MI: Hope College), 299. As early as September 1931, however, the *Consistorial Minutes* referred to this as the "Dimnent Memorial Chapel," 3:376.

Ministering to Children

Davidson introduced children's "sermonettes" as part of the morning worship service on the first Sunday of each month to make church more helpful for children and young families.[10] Church member Peggy Prins De Haan remembers some details about Sunday School in the Davidson era:

> My earliest memories of church were as a child in the Sunday School, sitting on tiny wooden chairs, just our size.... [We met] in the large parlor/meeting area ... to sing hymns and songs, heard a short message, and contributed our pennies to the Sunday School collection.... On our birthdays we were made to feel very special. There was a lighthouse-shaped bank with a light in the top that lit when a coin was put in the slot. The birthday child had the honor of holding that bank and inserting coins.[11]

Church member Jo Anne Vander Velde Brooks remembers the singing:

> It was like a fun celebration each Sunday morning when the whole Sunday School gathered for worship, from toddlers to high schoolers. Mrs. [Martha, wife of George E.] Kollen presided with her loving smile and made everyone feel welcome. How we loved to sing 'Onward Christian Soldiers,' 'Stand Up, Stand Up For Jesus,' and 'I Would Be True'. I remember the joy of her calling me forward to sing 'I'll Be a Sunbeam for Jesus,' accompanied by my beaming mother.[12]

---

[10] *Consistorial Minutes*, 21 November 1927, 3:254.
[11] Trudy Vander Haar, ed., *Branches of the Vine: Hope Church 150th Anniversary Special Edition*, January 2012.
[12] Vander Haar, ed., *Branches of the Vine*, January 2012.
Martha Kollen in 1933 was elected the first president of the first conference of the Women's Missionary Union of Holland Classis, a meeting attended by one thousand women. Van Heest, "Women's Societies in Holland Classis," *In Christ's Service*, 7. Kollen was the first woman member of the Holland Board of Education. In memory of her husband, George E. Kollen, she donated land for a public park on the Macatawa lakefront, Kollen Park. http://www.cityofholland.com/parksandcemeteries/kollen-park-heinz-

Church member Lois Hinkamp Boersma remembers Children's Day services and the giving of Bibles to children:

> Children took part in worship only on Children's Day ... in May or early June. Participation in the program required a great deal of memorization and practice. On the small shelf above the wainscoting in the sanctuary there was a row of pots of pansies from the front of the church to the first stained window, each pot covered with some pastel crepe paper. Much time during the service was consumed by me wondering which plant I would receive. These pansies were planted in our garden and were much loved. Later Mrs. [Helen] Wood gave tree seedlings for the Sunday School.... [T]he two [my younger brother] received in successive years grew to ungainly height.
>
> Bibles were given out to those graduating from the Primary Department (3rd or 4th grade) on Children's Day. They were given out by Mrs. Kollen who, it was announced later much to her embarrassment, also paid for them. The Bibles were black with gold edges and had our names imprinted on the front. Although the Bibles came in very good, sturdy boxes, Mrs. Kollen did not give out the boxes, because she wanted the Bibles read and not put away. The Bibles came with the direction from Mrs. Kollen not to put anything on top of them as they were God's Word. How some things stick! I still do not put anything on top of a Bible![13]

Sunday School was popular among the children, but attendance at evening worship services and midweek prayer meetings was slowly declining. When in 1928 a consistory member of the First Reformed Church offered the consistory of Hope Church a possible remedy for attendance problems affecting several churches in Holland—a "revival mission" by the Reverend Martin R. De Haan from Calvary Reformed Church in Grand Rapids—the consistory declined, replying, "our churches in Holland are excellently well

---

waterfront-walkway. Vern Boersma remembers Mrs. Kollen's stipulation that the park never post signs to "Keep off the Grass" because she wanted it to be a playground open to all.
[13] Vander Haar, *Branches of the Vine*, January 2012.

served by their present ministers and ... no need for such a mission seems called for."[14]

Looking Outward to the General Synod and the World

The General Synod of the Reformed Church in America met in Holland in 1929, and Hope Church hosted many of its meetings. The Hope Church choir provided much of the choral music. Other meetings were held in the new chapel on the Hope College campus. Elected president that year was the Reverend Daniel A. Poling, pastor of the Marble Collegiate Church, New York City, and president of World International Christian Endeavor.[15] A major topic of this synod was whether or not to consider uniting with the Presbyterian Church in the United States, but a decision was postponed until the next year.[16]

Davidson presented to the synod a report on the Kellogg Peace Pact. Named for U. S. Secretary of State Frank B. Kellogg, the pact prohibited the use of war as an instrument of national policy except in matters of self-defense. In his speech, Davidson stressed that

---

[14] *Consistorial Minutes*, 24 September 1928, 3:281–82.

Martin R. De Haan in 1929 led the Calvary Reformed Church in Grand Rapids out of the denomination. Calvary Undenominational Church in Grand Rapids, which he started after being deposed as a Reformed Church minister in 1929, became one of the large churches in Southwest Michigan. He left that congregation in 1938 to begin the Radio Bible Class, where he continued to promote his views on premillennial dispensationalism and believers' baptism by immersion. The Radio Bible Class changed its name to RBC Ministries in 1994, and after Martin R. De Haan's son Richard retired, his grandson Mart became president of the organization. http://www.hope.edu/jointarchives/collections/registers/wts/dehaan-m.html and http://www.rbc.org/about/history.aspx.

[15] "Gives Sermon at Synod Meeting," *Holland Evening Sentinel*, 7 June 1929:4, 10. Poling's son Clark V. was one of four Army chaplains honored for giving up their life jackets so others could be saved during the sinking of their troop ship, the *Dorchester*, during World War II.

[16] "Church Union Is Postponed Until the Next Synod, *Holland Evening Sentinel*, 8 June 1929:1–2.

"the church should adopt a constructive program for peace in line with the principles of Christ."[17]

Among missionaries appointed by the General Synod that year was the Reverend Walter de Velder to China.[18] Walter, five years older than his brother Marion, would marry Margaret Otte, the youngest of the children born to Dr. John and Frances Phelps Otte.[19]

Facing the Great Depression

On 24 October 1929, "Black Thursday," Wall Street experienced a crash heard around the world. The Great Depression that occurred after the crash adversely affected most of the world. Holland and Hope Church were not spared.

The early effects were noticed in January 1930 when elder Cornelius Dregman announced at consistory that a large number of members were in arrears in fulfilling pledges of the previous year and were slow to return their pledge cards for the current year. On Sunday, 19 January, the consistory held a special meeting to confer authority upon the treasurer and clerk to borrow $1,000 to pay the current expenses of the church.[20]

The consistory proceeded with its plans to repair, rebuild, and electrify the organ at a cost of $6,000, but scaled back its request for the Kimball Organ Company to add pipes and stops "to make the organ one of the best in the city." Despite elder John B. Nykerk's plea that these additions "would greatly improve the organ, making it on a par with the organ of the Third Reformed Church" and

---

[17] "Synod Considers the Question of Church Training," *Holland Evening Sentinel*, 10 June 1928:1–2.
[18] "Education Today Is Considered at Synod Gathering," *Holland Evening Sentinel*, 11 June 1929:1–2. Walter de Velder and Marion de Velder were both born in Boyden, Iowa. Walter was born in 1907 and graduated from Hope College, and Marion was born in 1912 and graduated from Central College. Gasero, *Historical Directory*, 101.
[19] George B. Scholten, "Crosses on Kulangsu," *Intelligencer-Leader*, 8 March 1940, 7–8.
[20] *Consistorial Minutes*, 10 January 1931, 3:321; 19 January 1931, 3:323.

be "a good business move," the consistory refused by a margin of one vote to allow an extra $330 to the cost.[21]

Davidson volunteered to take a $500 salary reduction for 1931. Four months later, the Finance Committee recommended that the consistory ask him to make an additional $1,000 reduction, bringing his $6,000 salary to $4,500.[22] To this recommendation Davidson responded that, because he "did not want to be a burden to the church financially," he "felt constrained to seek elsewhere for a call." Pastor and consistory reached a compromise at a salary of $5,000.[23] Not only did Hope Church face losses of income in the early 1930s but it also lost three leaders in the deaths of Gerrit J. Diekema, Charles M. McLean, and W. Curtis Snow. Diekema and McLean had served for many years as Sunday School superintendents, and McLean had served consistory for many years as its president pro tem. Brought to Hope College by its president, Edward D. Dimnent, W. Curtis Snow laid the foundation of music education at the college.[24] Choir director and professor of organ and piano at Hope College, he was also a beloved organist, choir director, and director of music at Hope Church.[25]

In addition to responding to diminishing resources, the consistory also responded to several social issues. It endorsed a request that Davidson communicate with Holland Classis and with Michigan education officials "to secure the return and daily use of the Bible in all Michigan Public Schools by appropriate legislation." It also passed a resolution stating its permanent opposition to the "opening of Movie Picture Theatres for business on the Lord's Day."[26]

---

[21] *Consistorial Minutes*, 19 January 1931, 3:324–25.
[22] *Consistorial Minutes*, 13 December 1931, 3:348; 12 April 1931, 3:367.
[23] *Consistorial Minutes*, 21 April 1931, 3:367; 5 May 1931, 3:369.
[24] Wichers, *Century of Hope*, 190. Edward D. Dimnent joined Hope Church in 1900. "Record of Hope Church Holland Michigan 1862–1916." He began serving as elder in 1932. *Consistorial Minutes*, 27 January 1932, 3:396.
[25] *Consistorial Minutes*, 9 January 1931, 3:352; 5 May 1931, 3:370.
[26] *Consistorial Minutes*, 11 September 1931, 3:377; 16 September, 3:378–79.

To devise plans for raising funds to meet an anticipated financial shortfall, the consistory voted to hold a "Smoker" in the church parlors. All men of the church were invited by letter to meet in a smoke-filled room to discuss the financial affairs of the church. As a result of this meeting, five men were added to the Financial Committee of the consistory and thirty men of the church were appointed to help solicit pledges from church members.[27]

In January 1932, the consistory approved a reduction of Davidson's salary from $5,000 to $4,000, reduced salaries for the director of music and janitor, and reduced funds available to committees. At the congregational meeting that year, voting members approved a rotation system for elders and deacons to shorten their terms of service, which until then were virtually unlimited. Deacons and elders could be elected to no more than three consecutive terms of two years each. At least a year had to pass before one who had served six years as deacon or elder

---

[27] *Consistorial Minutes*, 13 November 1931, 3:384; 2 December 1931, 3:386–88; 7 December 1931, 3:390. 18 December 1931, 3:390.

Smoking by men at church meetings was unquestioned until after the mid-twentieth century. In fact, for a Holland Classis meeting held at Hope Church in 1927, Hope Church paid Model Drug Store $4.56 for cigars. *Consistorial Minutes*, 15 March 1927, 3:228.

At an April 1948 consistory meeting, a motion that "Consistory go on record as opposed to smoking in the church parlors" was tabled. *Consistorial Minutes*, 12 April 1948, 8:325–26. Until the early 1960s and then for a time during the ministry of the Reverend Marchiene Rienstra in the mid-1980s, consistory meetings were held in the homes of consistory members. Often they were accompanied by an elaborate lunch. "A number of the men smoked cigars," recalls Lois Boersma, "and I remember our house 'reeking' of smoke for several days afterward" (personal communication to author).

Not until 1 December 1985 was smoking banned from Hope Church. The decision was prompted by the Stewardship Ministry on advice from the church's insurance agency. *Consistorial Minutes*, 19 August 1985, 9 September 1985. An exemption to the ban was granted for some time, however, to those attending Alcoholics Anonymous meetings in the church, providing they pay an increased rent and use smoke filters in their meeting room. *Consistorial Minutes*, 6 January 1986, 13 January 1986.

could be elected again as deacon or elder.[28] (The idea of rotation had been briefly considered in 1901, but for the following three decades it was considered taboo.)[29]

After a run on People's State Bank forced it to close, freezing its accounts for a time in 1932,[30] Hope Church could no longer send its pledged contributions to the denominational Progress Council campaign. Nor could it maintain its giving to the Boards of Domestic and Foreign Missions and to its missionary, the Reverend Willis G. Hoekje.[31] The consistory did, however, try to meet local needs when it approved the purchase of fuel for the homes of two church families, paid someone's hospital bill, and voted "that Hope Church extend temporary relief to welfare cases not coming under the direct jurisdiction of the city Welfare Department."[32]

Despite the financial belt-tightening during 1932, worship services continued and so did the meetings of various church groups. The description of the May meeting of the Women's Missionary society gives a glimpse of vital interest in missions abroad and a hint of the social action in which Hope Church would later engage:

> The monthly meeting of the Women's Missionary society of Hope church was held yesterday afternoon in the church parlors. The devotional period was in charge of Mrs. Jay [Ruth] Den Herder.
> The president, Mrs. P. [Martha] Hinkamp, called on Mrs. F. [Frances] Otte, who gave an account of the recent disturbances in the Amoy mission in China. She told of the property and buildings being occupied by the communist soldiers at mission stations of Thokhe and Chiang-Chow. All the missionaries lost their personal property and were forced to leave these places. They are now at Kulang-Su and Amoy protected by the gun boats of different nations, she said.

---

[28] *Consistorial Minutes*, 8 January 1932, 3:391; 24 January 1932, 3:394; 27 January 1932, 3:396; 22 December 1933, 3:464.
[29] *Consistorial Minutes*, 20 March 1901, 2:83–84.
[30] *Holland Evening Sentinel*, 11 January 1932.
[31] *Consistorial Minutes*, 12 February 1932, 3:400–01.
[32] *Consistorial Minutes*, 9 February 1933, 3:437; 11 September 1936, 4:62.

A brief review was given of the life of Miss Mollie Talmage who recently died. She was a missionary for nearly 69 years....

The principal topic of the afternoon was 'Roving with the Migrants,' a book reviewed by Mrs. Randall C. [Marthena] Bosch.

The migrant camps are composed of different nationalities. The migrant roams from place to place seeking jobs. The job is generally that of picking and selecting fruit and vegetables, getting ready for the canneries.

Many little children accompany their parents, brought up with no ideas of settled homes, Mrs. Bosch stated. They are poor and ignorant without education or any thought of sanitation.

At the close of this review, Mrs. C. L. [Jean] McLean and committee served refreshments and a social hour was enjoyed.[33]

In 1932, the Ladies' Aid Society wrote a letter to the consistory, offering to lend the church $500 interest free. Consistory responded with a letter of thanks and a reassurance that it did not deem the need to be so great as to require this assistance at this time.[34]

In February 1933 Davidson's annual salary was reduced to $3,500 with use of the parsonage. With church funds frozen in closed banks, the consistory voted in March 1933 to pay proportionally the salaries of minister and staff with the available cash on hand.[35]

In November 1934 the consistory set Davidson's salary at $2,500, with the proviso that if the cash collections during 1935 warranted it, an additional $500 would be paid him at the end of 1935. The treasurer's annual report for the year 1934 indicated $3,177.30 impounded in People's State Bank and $414.54 impounded in the Holland City State Bank. The 1935 budget set the pastor's salary at $3,000, and the consistory proposed that the budget for 1936 be the same as for 1935.[36]

---

[33] "'Roving Migrants' Is Topic at Meeting," *Holland Sentinel*, 5 May 1932:5.
[34] *Consistorial Minutes*, 8 April 1932, 3:406. In 1938 the Ladies' Aid Society became the Women's Aid Society. *Consistorial Minutes*, 26 January 1938, 4:139.
[35] *Consistorial Minutes*, 26 February 1933, 3:441; 10 March 1933, 3:442.
[36] *Consistorial Minutes*, 30 November 1934, 3:493; January 1935, 4:5; 13 September 1935, 4:31.

In April 1937 a delegation of the Ladies' Aid Society, including Jean (Mrs. C. J.) McLean, Nell (Mrs. N.) Dykhuizen, and Eva (Mrs. George A.) Pelgrim, addressed the consistory, seeking its support and action in an expansion program. Mary (Mrs. W. M.) Tappan of the delegation reported that the Aid Society had on hand approximately $900 and had in its Building Fund about $1,000. She reported that the cost of redecorating the church would be about $1,500 and that some members of the society approved assuming the expense. Especially needed were improvements to the sanctuary and primary department Sunday School room, better accommodations for the Boy Scouts, and improved kitchen equipment and facilities. Consistory authorized the Ladies' Aid Society to proceed with decorating the sanctuary.[37]

In 1937 Davidson celebrated his 72nd birthday. His hearing was becoming seriously impaired, and he was losing his rapport with the young people in the congregation. The consistory noted a "very evident decline in the attendance at all services of the church, also, the very serious decline of financial support to the church, and a general lack of interest in church affairs." It believed the time was right to seek new leadership. In that era the denomination did not provide ministers retirement benefits, nor were Social Security benefits available for the elderly. So the consistory offered Davidson a severance package. If he would retire on October 1, Hope Church would pay him $3,600 at the rate of $100 per month for three years. In a letter to Davidson on behalf of consistory, deacon Vernon Ten Cate stated that there would be "absolutely no alternative to the proposition made."[38] In other words, Davidson should not expect to receive any more than what was offered.

"It is not without a pang I think of severing my relations with so many good friends and co-workers," Davidson wrote to elder Abraham Leenhouts in submitting his resignation, effective 30 September 1937. The consistory accepted the resignation and later

---

[37] *Consistorial Minutes*, 8 April 1937, 4:101; 30 August 1937, 4:112.
[38] *Consistorial Minutes*, 31 July 1937, 4:114; 26 August 1937, 4:115.

responded to Davidson's request for an advance of $300 in mid-September. It also made plans to rent the parsonage to Esther Snow, whose husband, W. Curtis Snow, had died suddenly in December 1935.[39]

Within a year of his departure from Hope Church, Davidson became pastor of the Twelfth Street Reformed Church, Brooklyn, New York. After the Davidsons' departure, the consistory appointed Paul E. Hinkamp, Hope College pastor, secretary of the faculty, and professor of Bible and religion, as moderator of Hope Church.

Paul E. Hinkamp

---

[39] *Consistorial Minutes*, 17 September 1937, 4:120-22. W. Curtis Snow was survived not only by his wife, Esther, but also by children: Janet, Jean, Murray, and Bob.

Aware of the monthly payment of $100 to Davidson, elder Cornelius Dregman deplored the fact that Hope Church's contributions for missions in 1938 were less than $1,000. In February 1939. elder Albert Van Zoeren noted "a growing resentment on the part of the congregation to Davidson's retirement payments," especially given the knowledge that he had become pastor to another congregation.[40]

The consistory decided to approach Davidson to negotiate a compromise. In a letter to Davidson on behalf of the consistory, deacon Henry Winter indicated that the church closed the year 1938 "with a balance on hand of approximately four hundred dollars and with an outstanding account against it of about three hundred seventy five dollars." To continue making retirement payments to Davidson, it would have to borrow money. Would Davidson accept a compromise settlement?[41]

In reply Davidson wrote that he was "not in the position financially to consider any change." Though he was serving as a minister, his contract with the church and classis was based on the expected three-year "allowance of Hope Church.... The only cash settlement I am in position to accept," he concluded, "is for Hope Church to pay me the balance of its promise."[42]

In August 1939 elder Albert Van Zoeren received a letter written on stationery from the Glen Haven Hotel of Kennebunkport, Maine. The letter, signed by Davidson, thanked Van Zoeren for the one-hundred dollar check which reached him there, where he and his family were spending a few weeks. Davidson acknowledged that his record of payments matched Van Zoeren's and so discharged Hope Church "from any further liability." Closing the note, he

---

[40] *Consistorial Minutes*, 23 June 1938, 4:157; 7 February 1939, 4:182.
[41] *Consistorial Minutes*, 7 February 1939, 8 February 1939, 4:182–83.
[42] *Consistorial Minutes*, February 1939, 4:184.

stated, "We are all enjoying the vacation at this delightful resort in Maine. Best wishes, Cordially yours, Thomas W. Davidson."[43]

Davidson continued to serve as pastor at the Twelfth Street Reformed Church in Brooklyn until 1941 and then as stated supply pastor at the New Lots Reformed Church in Brooklyn until 1945. He died in 1948 at the age of 83.[44]

Marion de Velder Begins His Ministry at Hope Church

Marion de Velder, pastor of the North and Southampton Reformed Church in Churchville, Pennsylvania,[45] was invited to preach at Hope Church on 12 March 1939. At a congregational meeting a week later, he was called to serve Hope Church. Offered an annual salary of $3,000, house-rent, and four weeks paid vacation, he readily accepted.

The day before his installation on 31 August 1939, the consistory instructed the Building Committee to remove the steeple, which had become "a menace to life and property."[46] The long deferral of preventive maintenance during hard times was symbolized by the condition of the steeple upon de Velder's arrival.

The twenty-seven-year-old pastor and his wife, Edith, were eagerly welcomed and readily went to work. One of the first things he did was to add an Education Committee to the standing committees of the consistory (Auxiliary, Boy Scouts, Building and Grounds, Bulletin, Charities, Finance, Membership, Music, Pulpit and Worship, Ushering, and Visitors and Strangers). He made sure that this committee comprised both men (Leon N. Moody, Vernon

---

[43] *Consistorial Minutes*, 14 August 1939, 4:200. Davidson's discharging Hope Church from any additional liability after having received 22 of the 36 promised monthly $100 payments shows a change of heart from his February 1938 note. Perhaps his enjoyable summer vacation at the delightful resort mellowed his spirits.
[44] Gasero, *Historical Directory*, 86.
[45] Gasero, *Historical Directory*, 101.
[46] *Consistorial Minutes*, 30 August 1939, 4:201.

D. Ten Cate, and himself) and women (Frances Yeomans, Eva Pelgrim, and Martha Kollen).[47]

Marion (Mert) de Velder early in his ministry

Church member Robert Snow remembers de Velder as a persuasive man of action:

> Just before Easter in 1939, I received a terse phone call. 'Hello Bob—this is Mert de Velder—we need a cross—get over here!' Once I arrived at the church, we found a scrap lumber pile and some tools,

---

[47] *Consistorial Minutes*, 13 October 1939, 4:207; 3 February 1941, 5:244; 10 March 1941. 5:248.

and fashioned a cross for the Easter service. This was not only my chance to meet the new pastor, but was also an introduction to a new way of doing things. Mert was just a couple of years out of seminary, thus only a few years older than the church youth, and not many years younger than the church membership that was beginning to move into the active leadership of the church. He related well to both groups and he got things moving at a faster pace.

Sermons were more concise, more related to problems of the then-existing society, and included the younger elements of the church membership.[48]

De Velder also replaced Sunday evening worship services with a School for Christian Living, held in the all-purpose room of the church. Each Sunday evening began with a common devotional period, followed by age-grouped learning experiences, and ended with a social time.

Peggy Prins De Haan remembers that the social time included "sandwiches, beverages, and cookies, all prepared by parents or other adults. This activity was frowned on by other churches in Holland but also attracted many high school students from other congregations. I attended a funeral in another church. When asked what church I attended, their response was, 'Oh that church. They serve food there on Sunday night'."[49] The dining halls at Hope College were closed on Sunday evenings, so students were attracted to Hope Church for both physical and spiritual nourishment.

Ever alert to the power of public relations, de Velder likely had a hand in focusing national attention on Hope Church. The weekly magazine of the denomination, the *Intelligencer-Leader*, featured the choir of Hope Church on its 3 May 1940 cover.

---

[48] Vander Haar, *Branches of the Vine*, January 2012.
[49] Vander Haar, *Branches of the Vine*, January 2012.

Hope Church Choir in 1940

Left side:
Back row – left to right: Lawrence Moody, Edward Yeomans, Bruce Van Leuwen, unidentified, unidentified, C. Murray Snow, Clinton Harrison
Middle row – June Baker (later Heasley), Betty Morrell (later Fauls), Mrs. Marion (Edith) de Velder, unidentified, Mrs. Frank (Helen) De Weese, Mrs. Phil (Ruth) Brooks, Mrs. Otto (Margaret) Vander Velde
Front row – Gertrude Slaghuis, Mrs. Gerald (Jane) Breen, Mrs. George (Eva) Pelgrim, Mrs. James (Mildred) Ward, Mrs. Gertrude Wick, Director: Mrs. W. Curtis (Esther) Snow

Right side:
Back row – left to right: Bob Heasley, James B. Hinkamp, LeRoy Alder, Jack Yeomans, George Bosworth, Kenneth De Pree, and Peter Boter
Middle row – Mrs. Arthur (Helene) Visscher, Peggy Hadden (later Hakken), Mrs. (Irene) Sulkers (later Brummer), Fruena Dowstra (later Korstanje), Mrs. Clyde (Ardean) Geerlings, Gertrude Flaitz (later Douwstra), Jean Wishmeier (later Vanden Berg), and Lois Hinkamp (later Boersma)
Front row – Evelyn Kramer (later Van Otterloo), Shirley Shaw (later Goodrich), Betty Daugherty (later Timmer), Helen Ripley (later De Ridder), Phyllis Pelgrim (later White), Harriet Drew (later Elstner)

Enlarged from the cover photograph are the faces of two current members of Hope Church. Between them is choir director Esther Snow. She served as organist and choir director 1935–45 and organist 1945–57.

James Hinkamp   Esther Snow,   Lois Hinkamp
                    choir director   Boersma

Inside the magazine, the "Church Notes" section reported improvements in membership, benevolence, and the church building:

> Hope Reformed Church of Holland, the Rev. Marion de Velder pastor, received thirty-seven new members at the Easter season. The church has also recently assumed the full support of Dr. Willis G. Hoekje, missionary in Japan, and has pledged the sum of $1,000 towards the new Science building at Hope College. The Church School rooms are being improved, with a Junior worship Chapel being outfitted.[50]

Rumblings of World War II

Meanwhile in the background of a prospering and peaceful Hope Church were the rumblings of war-time in Asia and Europe. Consistory minutes for September 1940 report that "600 missionaries

---

[50] "Church Notes," *Intelligencer-Leader*, 3 May 1940, 18. The *Intelligencer-Leader* was the denomination's weekly publication from 1934 through 1943. It succeeded the *Christian Intelligencer* (1834–1935) and preceded the *Church Herald* (1944–2009). http://www.nbts.edu/rcaresources/BibliographyFrameset.htm.

are to be expelled from Japan." Information was received that "Conscientious Objectors must register their objection with the clerk of consistory."[51]

Three months later, de Velder presented to the consistory an application from Hope College freshman Paul Fried, a recent emigrant from Prague by way of England, for a bond as an affidavit of support for Paul's mother in Austria so that she could immigrate to the United States. Under the immigration quota, she was not eligible for entry into the United States. After consulting various officials, the clerk of consistory was instructed to tell Paul Fried that there was no action that the consistory could take to advance his application for a guaranty for his mother's entry into this country.[52]

Paul Fried in 1942 as Hope College sophomore

Paul Fried in 2006

---

[51] *Consistorial Minutes*, 13 September 1940, 5:233. Conscientious objectors are those whose consciences do not allow them to participate in military service. Whether some registered from Hope Church is not known.
[52] *Consistorial Minutes*, 9 December 1940, 5:238 insert; 2 January 1941, 5:238 insert; 3 February 1941; 5:244.

Because of the Jewish ancestry of Fried's family, the lives of his two brothers, his father, and his mother were extinguished in the concentration camps of Germany's Third Reich. After completing his sophomore year, Fried enlisted in the U.S. Army, where his knowledge of German and of Europe made him a valuable member of the Army Intelligence Corps. In 1945 he returned to Hope College and, after graduating, proceeded to Harvard University. After completing his MA degree there, he was invited to serve as a translator for the Nuremberg War Trials. He combined the translating with graduate study at the University of Erlangen from which he earned a doctorate in 1949. In 1953 he returned to Hope College and joined Hope Church. He taught at Hope College, chairing the history department, initiating the Vienna Summer School program, and promoting international education until he retired in 1984.[53]

Though missionaries were being expelled from Japan in 1940 and 1941, Willis G. Hoekje remained in Japan long enough to visit one of Hope College's oldest graduates. In a brief article published in the *Intelligencer-Leader* in May 1941, Hoekje wrote of his visit to Motoitero Oghimi. Frances Phelps Otte had prompted Hoekje to pay Oghimi a visit, and so he made his way to Oghimi's "quiet Japanese home in the suburbs of Tokyo."

Oghimi, a member of Hope College's class of 1879, had lived among other students in Van Vleck Hall when Otte was a child. In 1941, he was ninety-six years old, bowed, frail, and nearly deaf. Hoekje and Oghimi managed to communicate "in scraps of English and Japanese written with a Japanese brush on great sheets of paper." Even into his nineties, Oghimi was writing a Greek-Japanese

---

[53] John W. Hollenbach, "Paul G. Fried, Apostle for International Understanding," in *Into All the World: Hope College and International Affairs*, ed. Robert J. Donia and John M. Mulder (Holland: Hope College, 1985), 7–11.

dictionary for use by Japanese students of the New Testament. Hoekje praised Oghimi as illustrating the "undiscouraged temper of Japanese Christians."[54]

In the 5 December 1941 issue of the *Intelligencer-Leader*, Francis Phelps Otte described the pioneering efforts to bring the gospel and Western medicine to the Amoy (Xiamen) area in Southeast China.[55] Her husband, Dr. John A. Otte, who had died from a disease contracted from one of his patients in 1910, was the first Reformed Church in America medical missionary to China. The Japanese in World War II severely damaged the Hope Hospital for men and the Wilhelmina Hospital for women that Otte built. The Chinese people, however, ensured that these hospitals would be restored, Western medicine would continue to be practiced, the gospel would continue to be preached, and Dr. Otte's life would continue to serve as a model of Christian self-sacrifice. Though the hospitals Otte built are now museums, the legacy of Dr. John A. Otte lives on into the twenty-first century. To celebrate the anniversary of his death, his friends erected a statue, dedicated in 2008, at a new hospital at Jimei, not far from Xiamen.[56]

---

[54] Willis G. Hoekje, "The Oldest Hope Graduate," *Intelligencer-Leader*, 11 June 1941, 14.
[55] Frances Phelps Otte, "Pioneering in Medical Missions," *Intelligencer-Leader*, 5 December 1941, 12–15.
[56] Judy Tanis Parr, John de Velder, and Linda Walvoord de Velder, "A Medical Pioneer," *News from Hope College*, 43, no. 1 (August 2011):12–13.

Statue honoring Dr. John A. Otte at Jimei Hospital near Xiamen

The bombing of Pearl Harbor by the Japanese on 7 December 1941 brought the United States into World War II, and by January 1943 more than fifty from Hope Church were in military service.[57] Between December 1942 and June 1945 the congregation published the twelve issues of *Hope Hi-Lites*, a newsletter of information about the activities and locations of all Hope Church members in the Armed Services. A committee of the Women's Aid Society gathered information from each of the men and women and kept track of where they were.[58] The Women's Aid Society also donated to the

---

[57] *Consistorial Minutes*, 28 January 1943, 6:50.
[58] *Consistorial Minutes*, 28 January 1943, 6:50; 30 January 1946, 7:162.

church a plaque listing all members in the Armed Services, and the Men's Club gave each a New Testament with his or her name in gold.[59]

The consistory interrupted its February 1943 meeting to listen to a radio broadcast by Lt. Mayo Hadden Jr., son of Mayo and Marguerite Hadden, and a grandson of Abraham Leenhouts. Lt. Hadden's description of his experiences in the Air Corps during the African campaign "were listened to very intently."[60]

By January 1946 the Honor Roll plaque listed 109 names of members in the Armed Services during World War II. Hope Church war casualties included Herbert E. Chapman (killed in an airplane crash at Ft. Pickett, Virginia),[61] Carl Gordon Barry (killed in action on the Italian front),[62] Edward Ogden De Pree, William Edward Buteyn (killed in action in Europe), Nelson E. Carter, Clarence John Lokker, and Willard George Pelgrim.[63]

Exploiting World War II Spirit

During the 1940s de Velder inspired the congregation to give and to grow. Hope Church, which in 1939 ranked 129th in the denomination for its benevolences, rose to 7th place in 1943. Also that year, it stood in first place in total gifts for educational purposes in the entire denomination. By January 1943 Hope Church had given more than $11,000 toward a new science building for Hope College.[64]

---

[59] *Consistorial Minutes*, 1 February 1943, 6:54 insert; May 1943, 6:61.
[60] *Consistorial Minutes*, 1 February 1943, 6:51.
[61] *Consistorial Minutes*, May 1943, 6:61.
[62] *Consistorial Minutes*, 26 January 1944, 6:78.
[63] *Consistorial Minutes*, 30 January 1946 7:162 insert; 22 August 1947, 8:290 insert.
[64] *Consistorial Minutes*, 1 January 1943, 6:78. By the end of 1944 the contributions by Hope Church toward the Hope College Science Building exceeded $12,500. *Victory in 1944*, in *Consistorial Minutes*, 2 September 1944, 6:108 insert.

Motivated by de Velder's powers of persuasion, Hope Church in January 1944 began its "Church for Victory" campaign. Among its goals was "Every Pew Filled in 1944." A two-day excursion trip to Chicago was promised and awarded to five children who combined perfect attendance at Sunday School and worship services with Bible memory work, satisfactory Sunday School class work, and good conduct.[65]

He recruited Western Theological Seminary students to lead a "Servicenter" for children in grades one through seven, which met Wednesdays from four to five p.m. Tapping into the patriotic spirit of World War II, "Captains" Bert Van Soest and Marion de Velder and "Lieutenant" John Hains formed their own service corps. Children in grades one and two comprised the "Christian Army," those in grades three and four became the "Christian Navy," and those in grades five, six, and seven joined the "Christian Marines." Each group met for fifteen minutes of recreation with their group, then twenty minutes of united exercises, which included "marching in and out, saluting of the ... American [flag], chorus singing under 'Lieutenant' Hains, offering, story by 'Captain' Van Soest; then Bible study work for the last twenty-five minutes in the respective groups." Every six weeks a child could earn a promotion (from private to corporal to sergeant) for perfect attendance, good responses, and Bible work.[66]

Not to be outdone by their children, the Women's Aid Society of Hope Church in its 1944 annual report to the congregation indicated that the women had organized themselves into five divisions. They were called "the Marines, the Spars, Wacs, Wasps and Waves."[67]

---

[65] *Victory in 1944 for Hope Church* in *Consistorial Minutes*, 1944, 6:78 insert.

[66] "Servicenter Popular with Children," *Victory in 1944 for Hope Church*, in *Consistorial Minutes*, 6:78 insert. During the second year of the Servicenter, children, starting out as cadets, could advance to gunner, bombardier, navigator, and copilot. Seminarian Harlan Steele replaced John Hains, joining Bert Van Soest and Marion de Velder in leading this children's ministry. "Servicenter Marches On!" *Victory in 1944*, in *Consistorial Minutes*, 6:118 insert.

[67] The Women's Aid Society also reported having put up twenty-eight quarts of donated peaches. 24 January 1945, *Consistorial Minutes*, 6:118 insert.

The final page of the first *Victory in 1944 for Hope Church* booklet proclaimed what de Velder saw as the legacy, identity, and mission of Hope Church:

> Throughout its 82 years, the place occupied by Hope Church in Holland's religious life has been of a definite, distinctive pattern. To appreciate the consistency with which it has adhered to its role, one need only compare the characteristics of present day Hope Church with those that were inherent in the church at its founding in 1862.
>
> In that year of great national crisis, with the battles of Antietam and Fredericksburg determining our destiny, Holland was but a self-centered Dutch settlement,[68] dominated in all its activities by the Dutch language. Those who had filtered in from the outside were known as "the Americans", foreigners who found the Dutch tongue a barrier to their affiliating with the Dutch church. To serve the spiritual needs of these "Americans"—outsiders without a church home—Hope Church was established. Thus, it was Holland's first Americanized Dutch church, the first place of worship within the denomination throughout the entire Dutch area to adopt the English language for all of its services.
>
> Ever since, Hope Church has remained true to the spirit of its founders. It has been the "outsiders" haven, the sanctuary of those who seek spiritual uplift in a religious atmosphere congenial to their own varying denominational backgrounds. Sensitive to the

---

[68] De Velder's claim about Holland's being a "self-centered Dutch settlement" in 1862 ought to be modified by the fact that on the first day of recruiting soldiers for the 25th Michigan Volunteer Regiment on August 14 of that year, fifty-five Dutch immigrant young men from Holland enrolled. E. J. Masselink, "Holland, Michigan Residents in the Civil War: Dutch Settlers Quickly Signed up in Civil War," *Holland City News*, 30 November 1961; http://www.migenweb.net/ottawa/military/civilwar/dutchcw.htm. Alida J. Pieters credits Holland's preachers for inspiring active support for the Union: "This young community freely sent its sons to the Civil War under the influence of powerful preachers who aroused the patriotic enthusiasm of the people by their fiery sermons and in sending their own sons practiced their preaching. The rolls of the army shows that more than four hundred of these young men volunteered for service with the Union forces." *A Dutch Settlement in Michigan* (Grand Rapids: Reformed Press, 1923), 96.

progressive development of Holland, Hope Church has provided the open door which has brought Holland's liberal-minded into the religious stream of the community.

Interesting confirmation of the place Hope Church occupies in our community is to be found in the denominational character of its present membership. Since 1925, 352 persons have been received into membership by letters of transfer, coming from 16 different denominations--32% Reformed, 24% Presbyterian, 16% Methodist, 9% Congregational, 5% Baptist, 3% Christian Reformed, 11% from ten others. Approximately 70% have been from 15 denominations other than Reformed.

From this fact it can be appreciated that Hope Church is in reality Holland's interdenominational, community church. As such, it is distinguished by tolerance, breadth of outlook, and goodwill, all solidly grounded in the fundamental teachings of the Gospel and the Protestant tradition. Its constituency is of progressive attitude, practical in mind and action. Within it are the forces and elements which make for vigorous growth and profound impact upon community affairs.

We of Hope Church are not indifferent to our inherent strengths; we know they impose upon all of us a responsibility to make the position of Hope Church ever more commanding in the community. We shall not allow these strengths to become latent; we will employ them, through individual deed and devotion, to build an ever greater, more Victorious Church. Let us then, in complete unity and accord, plan comprehensively, act courageously, and give wholeheartedly for the larger place Hope Church should have in our hearts, our lives, and our community.[69]

A summer issue of the *Victory in 1944 for Hope Church* booklet described "Summer Maneuvers" for the children of Hope Church, led by "Officer in Charge," Bert Van Soest. From 3:30

---

[69] *Victory in 1944 for Hope Church*, in *Consistorial Minutes*, 26 January 1944, 6:78 insert.

to 5:30 p.m. on Mondays, there would be tennis and archery for girls older than twelve. The same time on Tuesdays would be "Christian Commands" for boys younger than twelve. Wednesdays would be devoted to junior softball and Thursdays to senior softball. On Fridays there would be recreation for girls younger than twelve.[70]

Also offered to the children were a Daily Vacation Bible School during the second and third weeks of June and a Junior Church, led by the children's "pastor," seminarian "Uncle Bert Van Soest." "In every respect the Junior Church," according to the booklet, "will be a miniature duplication of the organized Church. The boys and girls will elect their own elders, deacons or deaconesses; they will probably have their own choir and church envelopes."[71]

In 1944, after Willis G. Hoekje was removed from Japan and reassigned to work with "Resettlement of Japanese Americans," Hope Church transferred its missionary support from him to the Reverend John P. and Mrs. Virginia Muilenburg, who were preparing to begin missionary service in China.[72]

---

[70] *Victory in 1944 for Hope Church*, in *Consistorial Minutes*, 1 May 1944, 6:98 insert.
[71] *Victory in 1944 for Hope Church*, in *Consistorial Minutes*, 1 May 1944, 6:98 insert. Note "deaconesses." The opportunities denied women would be offered to the girls attending Junior Church.
[72] *Consistorial Minutes*, 14 July 1944, 6:99; May 1945; 7:138 insert. Hoekje died 10 January 1949 in Wyckoff, New Jersey. De Velder conducted his funeral at Hope Church.

John P. and Virginia Muilenburg and children, missionaries to China and the Philippines, supported by Hope Church 1944–1959. From oldest to youngest, their children are Peter, Jonathan, and Steven.

Supporting Community and Denominational Enterprises

In September 1944 the Hope Church consistory received from the Reverend William Van't Hof and Clarence De Graaf, both from Third Reformed Church, a request to consider establishing "an old people's home in this city under the sponsorship of the Reformed and Christian Reformed Church." Consistory appointed Paul E.

Hinkamp to attend a meeting about the project and report back.[73] This was the beginning of what would become Resthaven Care Community. The current chief executive officer of this ecumenical, community-serving enterprise is Hope Church elder Charles D. Vander Broek, great-great-great-grandson of Albertus C. and Christina J. de Moen Van Raalte.[74]

At the end of 1945, Hope Church had a "substantial financial balance." Elder John J. Riemersma suggested and consistory approved that the denominational weekly magazine be sent to every family of the church. The cost for three hundred subscriptions was $300. Within four years, however, consistory voted to discontinue this plan, replacing it with subscriptions for the *Church Herald* at a group rate for those members wishing to receive the publication.[75]

A photograph, likely taken at Easter 1945, of the church sanctuary shows the Christian and American flags. At that time the center aisle of the church did not extend to the chancel area. On the raised platform are two partially visible pulpit chairs.

In 1946 Hope Church began supporting workers at the Southern Normal School, a teacher's college for African-Americans, in Brewton, Alabama. Persons supported with a missionary share of at least $900 per year were teacher Mary Ada Cater (1946–48), farm director Alonzo Harvey (1949–56), manual arts director Conn V. Miller (1956–1957), Jethro J. Woodson (1957–63), Viola Sutton (1962–77), and Mitchell Culliver (1963–66).[76]

In 1946 the consistory was invited to send representatives to the First Reformed Church of Holland to attend an organizational

---

[73] *Consistorial Minutes*, 8 September 1944, 6:105.
[74] Bruins et al., *Albertus and Christina*, 93.
[75] *Consistorial Minutes*, 17 December 1945, 7:155; 14 November 1949, 9:382.
[76] *Consistorial Minutes*, 31 May 1946, 7:177; 12 January 1948, 8:307; 12 December 1949, 9:394 insert; 10 September 1956, 15:1033; 12 November 1956, 15:1042; 14 October 1957, 16:1082; 11 February 1963, 22:1327, 12 December 1966, 25:no page number.

meeting for Camp Geneva.[77] Hope Church has been sending young people to Camp Geneva ever since its beginning.

Hope Church sanctuary in 1945

---

[77] *Consistorial Minutes*, 11 July 1946, 7:181.

Remodeling the Sanctuary and Modernizing the Parish Hall

Known throughout the denomination for his abilities of persuasion and fund-raising, de Velder accepted a call to serve the denomination for six months spanning 1946–47, promoting its United Advance Fund campaign. In his absence, consistory members took on additional responsibilities, including supervision of the remodeling and redecorating of the church and church parlors. The organ was rebuilt and relocated. The chancel was redone with a new pulpit, lectern, and Communion table dedicated to de Velder; and the organ pipes were no longer visible. The church's front entrance of the church was remodeled, the parish hall was modernized, and a new two-floor addition at the northwest corner of the church was built for the Sunday School and other church organizations.[78]

In 1947 a wood sculpture of the Last Supper was installed in the chancel. Created of Appalachian white oak[79] and modeled on Leonardo Da Vinci's fifteenth-century Last Supper mural located in Milan, Italy, the ecclesiastical sculpture was given in memory of Albert C. Keppel by his wife, Kate De Vries Keppel;[80] the couple had been members of Hope Church for more than three decades.[81] According to their daughter Ruth, Albert C. Keppel was so deeply impressed by seeing one of Alois Lang's Last Supper woodcarvings on a vacation trip to California that Kate later decided to honor his memory by donating to Hope Church a similar work of art.[82]

---

[78] "Holland Classis News," *Church Herald*, 9 January 1948:20. *Rejoicing in Hope ... Romans 12:12* [centennial booklet], 1962, 7.
[79] Sheryl De Jonge, "Creating and Preserving Ecclesiastical Art and the Lord's Supper by Alois Lang," n.d., 13. W91-1034. Hope Church, Holland, Michigan, box 12, Joint Archives of Holland.
[80] "Wood-Carver to Discuss His Work in Hope Church," *Holland City News*, 23 October 1947, 3.
[81] *Record of Hope Church Holland Michigan 1862–1916*.
[82] Carol Bechtel, "Interview with Miss Ruth Keppel in Her Home on August 6, 1981," 1981:19. http://www.hope.edu/jointarchives/Oral%20Interviews/1980/Keppel,Ruth.pdf
  Albert Keppel's father was Teunis Keppel, consistory president of Holland's First Reformed Church in 1882—in Ruth Keppel's words, "one of the originators of the Ninth Street Christian Reformed Church." After

The carver of the sculpture, Alois Lang, was born in 1871 in Oberammergau, Bavaria, where he learned his craft. He moved to the United States in 1890 and carved elaborate mantelpieces for homes in Boston. In 1903 he moved to join the American Seating Company in Manitowoc, Wisconsin, and in 1927 he moved with that company when it came to Grand Rapids.[83]

Last Supper woodcarving by Alois Lang

Alois Lang was featured on the *Time* magazine cover of 12 May 1930, mainly because he was chosen to play the part of Jesus in the Oberammergau Passion Play that year. The magazine account mentioned that Alois Lang was a bee-keeper and a wood-carver, especially known for his "innumerable wooden Christs."[84]

---

his marriage and the birth of their first daughter in 1908, Albert Keppel transferred from Ninth Street Christian Reformed Church to Hope Church, where his wife, Kate DeVries, had been a member since 1894. "Record of Hope Church Holland Michigan 1862–1916."

The Lang carving that the Keppels saw on their California trip most likely was one in the All Saints Church of Pasadena, a church noted for its long history of inclusion (http://en.wikipedia.org/wiki/All_Saints_Episcopal_Church_ (Pasadena,_ California). For a list of places containing wood sculptures by Alois Lang, see http://en.wikipedia.org/wiki/Alois_Lang.

[83] http://en.wikipedia.org/wiki/Alois_Lang.

[84] "In Oberammergau," *Time*, 12 May 1930:36. http://www.time.com/time/magazine/article/0,9171,752526,00.html

Alois Lang on Time *magazine cover, 12 May 1930*

Among other churches containing his woodcarvings are the Rockefeller Chapel in Chicago, Christ Church in Boston, and Park Congregational Church in Grand Rapids.[85] Churches containing Last Supper woodcarvings by Alois Lang include Trinity Lutheran Church in Grand Rapids, Peachtree Christian Church in Atlanta, Georgia, and churches in Indiana, Illinois, and Wisconsin.[86]

---

[85] http://en.wikipedia.org/wiki/Alois_Lang. Given the fame of the sculptor's creator and the beauty of the memorial gift to Hope Church, it is a curious understatement that in the *Consistorial Minutes* the only reference to this memorial gift is a remark by elder Peter Van Domelen Jr. that a "small piece of carving broken out of the Chancel panel would be replaced as soon as the American Seating Company resumed operations following a strike." *Consistorial Minutes* 12 June 1950, 9:422.
[86] De Jonge, "Creating and Preserving Ecclesiastical Art ...," 13.

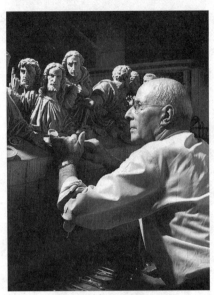

Alois Lang at work

While the installation of the woodcarving and the remodeling of the sanctuary were under way, Hope Church worship services were held in the Hope [Dimnent] Memorial Chapel. The 1947 annual congregational meeting was held in the Masonic Temple Building.[87]

Learning from Missionaries

Perhaps the consistory and those busily remodeling the church envied John Muilenburg's sojourn in a Chinese culture that seemed to run on a slower clock and calendar. A letter to Hope Church from Muilenburg from Kulangsu, Amoy, Fukien, China, c/o H. Poppen 10 June 1946 was tucked into the *Consistorial Minutes*:

> Dear Friends:
> After many months of wandering and waiting I have finally arrived in beautiful Fukien province. This section is surpassingly

---

[87] *Consistorial Minutes*, 3 October 1946, 7:189–90; 17 December 1946:200; January 1947:259–60; 12 April 1948, 8:328 insert.

beautiful. I was quite unprepared for such loveliness of scenery as I find here. In the first place the harbor of Amoy is superb. It is large and deep. It is perfectly protected by headlands which extend far out into the ocean. Within the harbor are many islands, of which Kulangsu is one and Amoy another. The whole thing is ringed with rather high mountains sometimes blue, sometimes purple, sometimes lost in the clouds. This morning I came down the river from Changchow, a city thirty miles from Amoy. I left Changchow just as dawn was breaking. The red and orange colors were flooding the skies. The high mysterious mountain tops were wreathed about with the early morning mists. Along the river edge walked farmers going off to their fields. They looked very picturesque in their high coolie hats. I was on a small launch which went very slowly, but that I didn't mind because I was so enjoying the loveliness of the summer morning. I was actually thankful that I could make the trip on this launch rather than in an automobile or train. I would have reached my destination sooner but also would have missed the intimate contact with Mother Nature. You know, I am beginning to feel sorry for you in America. I have the impression that modern efficiency is robbing you. Well, at any rate, I like it here....

I get a real lift every time I attend church. The congregations are large. How they sing!... [A] Christian group ... of [about thirty] freshmen in Amoy University (a non-Christian institution) ... met in an unlighted room with no furniture but saw-horses for seats. The afternoon was dark and rainy. But the light of God's spirit was there. They read their Bibles, shared insights, prayed, sang hymns etc. for a period of three hours. My back was breaking but my spirit soared. There was the real thing. These youths pledged themselves to speak to somebody about Christ every day. I believe that many actually do it.[88]

A letter from John and Virginia Muilenburg in 1947 described dangers of man-eating tigers that had devoured four people in Tungan, China, where they were living. Two of those people were within one hundred yards of the Muilenburgs' house.[89]

---

[88] *Consistorial Minutes*, 3 October 1946, 7:192 insert.
[89] *Consistorial Minutes*, 19 August 1947, 8:290 insert.

Their letter in November 1948 described economic, political, and military conditions that prompted them and other missionaries to leave China:

> The price of rice is the all-consuming question. The party that can give the people cheap rice will in the end win China. It is the appalling poverty that gets us down. We live in a constant state of moral tension. We are representatives of Christ and out to live by his absolute ethic. Should we not become poor to help the poor? We remain 'rich' in a nation of poor people. How far must we go to show Christ's love for His little ones? That is the question. Of course, you all have the same basic question only it doesn't smack you in the face every time you step outside your door.
>
> As we write this letter the situation is precarious in the extreme. By the time you receive this letter we may also be behind the iron curtain. What will happen to our work then is still an open question. We do know that God has sent us here to preach the gospel of the incarnation of God in Christ. We intend to keep at that job until we can no longer do so.[90]

In September 1950 the Muilenburgs arrived in San Francisco, having been forced to leave China by Communist advances against the Nationalists in the Amoy area and by the hostility of the Chinese people against American intervention in Korea. From 1952 to 1967 the Muilenburgs served as missionaries to Chinese people living in the Philippines.[91] In 1959 Hope Church transferred its support from the Muilenburgs to the Reverend and Mrs. Gordon De Pree, who were also serving in the Philippines.[92]

---

[90] *Consistorial Minutes*, 6 December 1949, 8:353 insert.
[91] *Consistorial Minutes*, 10 December 1951, 10:510 insert. Gasero, *Historical Directory*, 278. In the *Consistorial Minutes* of Hope Church little is mentioned about the Korean conflict other than that as of 20 May 1954, "twenty-one of our men are serving their country."
[92] Moderator Paul E. Hinkamp's annual report in *Consistorial Minutes*, 28 January 1960, 18:1188 insert.

Focusing on Religious Education

In 1948 the consistory, seeking to build a "keener interest on the part of students, teachers, and parents," took steps to hire Hope Church's first paid, full-time, professionally educated director of religious education. In June 1949 the consistory hired Elsie B. Stryker for the position. "She was a gem," remembered Lois Boersma. "She worked tirelessly at the children's Sunday School and promoted a number of dramas for which she made costumes on her own time."[93]

Elsie B. Stryker

---

[93] Personal communication to the author. Elsie Stryker later served in the denomination's Department of Children's Work and as a librarian in the New Brunswick Seminary Library.

Since the early 1940s, Hope Church had provided a two-week Vacation Bible School for elementary school children. Beginning in the early 1950s, it worked with Third Reformed Church and the Methodist Church to present a combined Vacation Bible School experience in the three church facilities, a tradition which continued for thirteen consecutive years.[94]

In February 1950 the consistory thanked Milton L. Hinga for his effective leadership as a teacher of the College Bible Class for twenty-five years. Attendance in his class averaged more than one hundred in the late 1940s.[95] The Consistory also thanked John J. and Madeline Riemersma for their "loving ministry in preparing the elements for Holy Communion services during the past twenty-nine years."[96]

In June 1950 de Velder's alma mater, Central College in Pella, Iowa, granted Hope Church's pastor an honorary Doctor of Divinity degree. Perhaps inspired by the women who made a robe for Phelps to wear on becoming the first president of Hope College, or more likely sensing that de Velder was considering opportunities beyond Hope Church, elder Peter Van Domelen Jr. on behalf of the consistory and church presented him with a robe. With it came the jovial stipulation from consistory that de Velder should "continue

---

[94] *Consistorial Minutes*, 1 May 1944, 6:98 insert; 8 May 1950, 9:415; 22 January 1963, 22:1323 insert. In 1970 young people participating in a Caravan Program worked with members of the Third Reformed Church and First United Methodist Church to provide a one-week Vacation Bible School for children unaffiliated with any church. *Consistorial Minutes*, 29:13 April 1970. In the 1980s Hope Church sent several teachers to assist with Vacation Bible School at other local churches. *Consistorial Minutes* 44:5 March 1984. (After September 1966 pages of *Consistorial Minutes* are unnumbered and hence are referred to by volume and date.)
[95] "Holland Classis News," *Church Herald*, 9 January 1948, 20.
[96] *Consistorial Minutes*, 26 January 1950, 9:396 insert. Hinga continued teaching the college Bible class for six more years, retiring for health reasons in 1956 (*Consistorial Minutes*, 24 January 1957, 15:1046 insert). Though Communion services then were held once a quarter, the nearly three-decade commitment by the Riemersmas is praiseworthy. John J. Riemersma also served Holland High School for a long time. Beginning as a teacher in 1920, he served as principal from 1922 through 1957.

his Pastorate at Hope Church until the new Clerical Robe was entirely worn out."[97]

The religious education of children and young people continued to be taken very seriously. Like elementary and high schools, Hope Church's Sunday School held parent-teacher meetings. In January 1951, for instance, thirty parents of the junior high group of the Church School met at the home of Mr. and Mrs. C. C. Wood, where they were informed about the content of the next quarter's instruction and met in small groups in consultation with the teacher.[98]

The Visual Aid Committee of Hope Church's Board of Christian Education became the nucleus of an interchurch organization known as the Audio-Visual Aid Association of Holland. In 1950 it held six meetings with fourteen churches, Holland Public Schools, Holland Christian School, and the Boy Scouts to demonstrate the use of audio-visual equipment, preview current films and film strips, and share a growing library of materials.[99]

Chiefly responsible for this ecumenical cooperation was Hope Church's director of religious education, Elsie B. Stryker. On at least one occasion she also conducted the opening worship services of the School for Christian Living.[100]

In addition to using audiovisual aids to enhance religious instruction, Hope Church employed drama. Under the leadership of Ethelyn Metz, in March 1951 Hope Church produced the play "Joseph of Arimathea," complete with construction of stage sets, borrowing of props, and applications of make-up. The room formerly used to store coal became the new storage room for stage props. During the Christmas season the play "Why the Chimes Rang"[101] was produced.

---

[97] *Consistorial Minutes*, 25 June 1950, 9:423.
[98] *Consistorial Minutes*, 8 January 1951, 10:455–57.
[99] *Consistorial Minutes*, 25 January 1951, 10:454 insert. (Page numbering in this volume is not sequential.)
[100] *Consistorial Minutes*, 12 February 1951, 10:462.
[101] *Consistorial Minutes*, 12 March 1951, 10:471; 11 February 1952, 11:522 insert.

Meetings, Meetings, Meetings

A highlight of the Men's Club in 1950 was the appearance of the Honorable Gerald R. Ford as guest speaker at its October meeting. By December, memberships in the Hope Church Men's Club reached 130.[102]

To help newcomers feel welcome at Hope Church and to create "a spirit of good fellowship," various married couples were appointed to stand at the three doors of the main Eleventh Street entrance and greet all those coming into the church. In late 1951 a Mr. and Mrs. Club was organized and as their first project sang Christmas carols to the shut-ins of the congregation.[103] The Mr. and Mrs. Club in its early years met twice a month; in later years it met every other month. As members grew older, they came to prefer decaffeinated coffee. At one of the spring meetings Brim coffee cans were used as vases for daffodils. No longer wanting to limit its membership to couples, the group whimsically decided to call itself the Brim Bunch. The coffee brand vanished in the 1980s, but the Brim Bunch is thriving into the twenty-first century.[104]

A regularly published church news letter, first called *Hope Church Parish News* and then *Hope Church News*, also began in 1951.[105] That year the Women's Aid Society reported receipts in excess of $4,000 for its serving of dinners to Hope Church and other organizations, various baked good sales, and a rummage sale. A portion of those funds went toward the purchase of a grand piano for the sanctuary. In 1952 women published a Hope Church cookbook.[106]

---

[102] *Consistorial Minutes*, 9 October 1950, 9:433; 11 December 1950, 9:446.
[103] *Consistorial Minutes*, 10 June 1951, 10:488; 10 December 1951, 10:510.
[104] Lois Boersma, "History of Brim Bunch," n.d. W91-1034, box 12, Hope Church, Holland, Michigan, Joint Archives of Holland.
[105] *Consistorial Minutes*, 9 April 1951, 10:480; 10 June 1951, 10:488; 10 December 1951, 10:510.
[106] *Consistorial Minutes*, 11 February 1952, 11:522 insert.

Not to be outdone by the Women's Aid Society, the Women's Club of Hope Church reported their service as waitresses for each of the dinners prepared by the Women's Aid Society. The Women's Club, boasting an average attendance of eighty-seven, began each of its meetings with a dinner in the parish hall. During 1951, the women gathered and packed twenty-five boxes of clothing for shipment to U.S. Foreign Service officer James Dyke Van Putten and chaplain Harold J. Hoffman to distribute to needy families in Korea. Each month several club members made, packed, and mailed a box of cookies and candy to each of the nineteen Hope Church members in military service.[107] Imagine how—in a time before automatic washing machines, dryers, permanent press, and one-stop shopping—women could find the time to attend all of the women's meetings and perform so many services.

De Velder Accepts Call to First Church, Albany

After ministering to Hope Church for eleven years, Mert de Velder announced his resignation, effective at the end of October 1951, so that he could accept a call extended to him by the First Church in Albany, New York. A letter signed by the entire consistory pleaded with him to stay:

> We feel it our duty to state the unanimous conviction that your work in Hope Church, in the community of Holland and in this center of the Reformed Church is not finished. Your unfailingly inspiring sermons, your administrative ability, your teaching skill, your hold on young people, your pastoral care, are exactly suited to the needs of Hope Church, as is evidenced by its growth and present flourishing condition. The City of Holland with its peculiar problems, needs

---

[107] *Consistorial Minutes*, 11 February 1952, 11:522 insert. The Women's Aid Society, which included lunch and an afternoon meeting, was attended mainly by women who had school-aged children. The Women's Club, which included dinner and an evening meeting, was attended mainly by business women, teachers, and mothers of preschool children.

a man of your stature to give continuing leadership and guidance on moral and spiritual issues. College students, who come in large numbers from various backgrounds, need in this critical period of their lives a church home and a pastor who understands and inspires them. Their attendance in larger numbers at Hope Church leads us to feel that we must speak for them. Your influence on the ministers who have studied at Western Seminary is far-reaching and the opportunity grows greater with each succeeding class and as Hope Church under your leadership increases in prestige and service....

We believe your talents, your temperament and your pioneering spirit, are best suited to building here in Holland a Hope Church that will in every way (in plant, in staff, and in service) match and even surpass the church to which you are now called.[108]

Despite a spontaneous outpouring of pleas and letters from the congregation and the consistory's promise of an increase in salary and other financial remuneration, the de Velders replied that they "felt most convincingly and united that God's will could only be served by accepting this call."[109]

After de Velder's departure at the end of October 1951, Paul E. Hinkamp served as moderator, responsible for various administrative tasks. The consistory appointed the Reverend James E. Wayer as part-time assistant pastor.[110] Wayer had returned to Holland to retire after serving the First Reformed Church in Holland 1919–39 and the Racine Reformed Church in Wisconsin 1939–49.[111] Though he was first hired only to serve until a full-time pastor would be called and though not included among the official list of pastors serving Hope Church (he is not listed among Hope Church's ministers in Gasero's *Historical Directory*), he made thousands of calls on potential new members, and to shut-ins, the ill, and the dying during the ten years he continued to serve as assistant pastor.[112]

---

[108] *Consistorial Minutes*, 2 October 1951, 10:497 insert.
[109] *Consistorial Minutes*, 4 October 1951, 10:497; 8 October 1951, 10:499.
[110] *Consistorial Minutes*, 12 November 1951, 10: 503.
[111] Gasero, *Historical Directory*, 454–55.
[112] *Consistorial Minutes*, 13 November 1961, 20:1288.

James Wayer

Responding to Denominational and Classis Issues

As had happened in 1929 and 1930 with the attempts to merge the Reformed Church in America with the Presbyterian Church of the United States, an attempt at merger with the United Presbyterian Church of North America in 1949 also failed. Though the General Synod approved the merger, it failed to garner the necessary votes among the classes; three-fourths of the classes would have had to agree to the merger by a three-fourths margin in each classis.[113]

---

[113] Lynn Japinga, "On Second Thought: A Hesitant History of Ecumenism in the Reformed Church in America," in *Concord Makes Strength: Essays in Reformed Ecumenism*, ed. John. W. Coakley. Historical Series of the Reformed Church in America, no. 41 (Grand Rapids: Eerdmans, 2002), 18.

In December 1948 Mert de Velder and Hope Church's delegate to classis, Paul E. Hinkamp, had expressed disappointment that the vote by Holland Classis on the merger was nine churches making no response, six noncommittal, seven opposed, and only four in favor.[114] Though the Hope Church consistory could not sway Holland Classis and the denomination to unite with the United Presbyterian Church of North America, it continued to encourage cooperation and ecumenical relationships locally.

In 1952 and 1953 the consistory also tried unsuccessfully to influence Holland Classis on another issue. Hope Church went "on record as being against any division of the Classis of Holland."[115] A member of the Holland Classis since the Michigan Classis was disbanded and its classis boundaries were rearranged in 1923, Hope Church suspected that a multiplication of classes in the Midwest was a move to enlarge voting power over classes in the East. When Holland Classis voted to divide itself into what became Holland Classis and Zeeland Classis, the vote was eighteen in favor, and ten against.[116]

On another vote related to matters coming from Holland Classis, the Hope Church consistory, contrary to the congregation's reputation for being progressive, voted in September 1952 to retain the status quo. To a "recommendation that the word 'male'

---

[114] *Consistorial Minutes*, 13 December 1948, 8:347.
[115] *Consistorial Minutes*, 10 March 1952, 11:523; 13 April 1953, 12:586.
[116] A straw vote by churches resulted in what the clerk of Hope Church consistory called "a laughable grab-bag method of division.... First Reformed Church of Central Park, Holland, at the extreme west end of the Holland Classis, would elect to join the Classis of Zeeland. The same was true of the Beechwood Reformed Church, to the northwest of Holland. On the other hand, the Second Reformed Church of Zeeland, as well as the Vriesland Reformed Church and the Bentheim Reformed Church, both located in the eastern part of the present classis, would elect to continue as members of the Holland Classis." *Consistorial Minutes*, 13 April 1953, 12:586 insert.

be deleted from Article IV, Section 2, of the Constitution" (to allow for the election of women to the offices of deacon and elder) the vote was "Nay 9 and Yea 7."[117]

The de Velders Return to Hope Church

Six months after the de Velders' farewell from Hope Church, elder John J. Riemersma, vice-president of the consistory, conveyed to the consistory the news he had received via telephone call from de Velder. Apparently, "God's will" had been duly served in this brief time. De Velder stated that he had resigned as associate pastor of the First Church in Albany, that his resignation was accepted, and "he would be pleased to be considered as a candidate for minister of Hope Church."[118]

Within a week de Velder returned to Holland to "further explore and discuss the renewing of his Pastorate at Hope Church." At a congregational meeting called within days of his visit, the vote with 488 ballots cast was 431 for calling him. Irwin J. Lubbers moved to "express a unanimous vote."[119] In the May 1952 *Hope Church News*, de Velder acknowledged the reason for his change of heart: "he did not care to continue indefinitely without preaching duties, but wanted to go to a church of his own."[120] And, so like the beloved John Tallmadge Bergen and his family near the end of the nineteenth century, the de Velders returned to Hope Church, where they resumed their thriving ministry.

---

[117] *Consistorial Minutes*, 8 September 1952, 11:550. The vote was likely to provide guidance to Hope Church's delegates to classis, which was to meet the next evening.
[118] *Consistorial Minutes*, 20 April 1952, 11:531.
[119] *Consistorial Minutes*, 20 and 29 April 1952, 11:533–35.
[120] *Hope Church News*, 22 May 1952, 1

Planning for the Expansion of Hope Church

So that de Velder could focus on his gifts for preaching and administration, Wayer was retained part-time to call on people and to conduct the weekly evening prayer services.[121] By 1952 Hope Church needed to make more room for a growing congregation with an increasing number of children in the Church School. It was time to plan for expansion.

As a temporary measure to accommodate overflow crowds in the morning worship services, folding chairs were set up near the back of the sanctuary and loud-speaker equipment was installed in the church parlors. The public address system was discontinued, however, in 1954. Nearly a decade later an experiment to introduce closed circuit television broadcasting to the church parlors met with mixed results.[122]

During 1953 de Velder represented the denomination as a delegate to the Conference on Evangelism sponsored by the National Council of Churches in Christ. He also was appointed chair of the General Synod's Committee on Christian Education.[123] In his report to the General Synod on behalf of the Standing Committee on the Board of Education, he proclaimed the importance of reaching out to the children of the church:

> Our country is a land of children. Over 10,000 babies are born every day. We have over 4,000,000 children under the age of 5, an increase of 53.3 per cent in the last decade. The children's department should be considered our first line of defense and our greatest opportunity. The proper training of our children, and of those to be won in evangelistic outreach, must be a major concern of the Board of Education and of every church. When we win and hold the children, the youth will not stray, and the adult will remain loyal to our Lord and His Church. Youth work and adult work can become

---

[121] *Consistorial Minutes*, 29 April 1952, 11:537.
[122] *Consistorial Minutes*, 8 September 1952, 11:549; 8 February 1954, 13:925; 13 May 1963, 22:1335.
[123] *Consistorial Minutes*, 11 May 1953, 12:587–89.

so much more successful if we have a deep Christian influence on the children.[124]

On 1 November 1953 Holland radio station WHTC produced the first of its broadcasts of Hope Church worship services. Started as an experiment, these broadcasts have continued for more than half a century as a ministry of outreach to the community and to those unable to attend worship services. Also that year the denomination began promoting and broadcasting a radio program called *Temple Time* to "preach the Gospel of Salvation to those who have never heard," especially in countries such as Japan, India, and Arabia.[125]

"In recent years," stated de Velder, "we have progressed from worry over empty pews to the work of setting many chairs to seat our growing congregation." The consistory formed a Church Expansion Committee to seek and acquire properties owned by Jennie Sprietsma and Martha Sherwood near the church for use as classrooms and choir rehearsal facilities. That committee also recommended hiring an architect to assist in the study of long-range building needs.[126]

After Elsie B. Stryker resigned as director of Christian education in early 1954 to assume a similar position at the Salem Evangelical and Reformed Church in Rochester, New York,[127] the consistory added to the responsibilities of director of Christian education those of

---

[124] *The Acts and Proceedings of the One Hundred and Forty-Seventh Regular Session of the General Synod of The Reformed Church in America Convened in Central College, Pella, Iowa, June 1953* (New York: Department of Publication and Sales, 1953), 75–76.

[125] *Consistorial Minutes*, 12 October 1953, 12:603–4, 9 November 1953, 12:909 insert.

[126] *Consistorial Minutes*, 12 October 1953, 12:605 insert; 14 December 1953, 12:911; 27 January 1955, 13:975 insert. The Sprietsma property was purchased and became the East Church House. In 1956 property owned by Velda Van Hartesveldt on Tenth Street was acquired, a house on the lot was dismantled, and the land was converted into a parking lot. *Consistorial Minutes* 11 June 1956, 15:1030; 38:14 December 1978 insert.

[127] *Consistorial Minutes*, 11 January 1954, 12:922 insert. She later served as Director of Children's Work for the RCA and as a librarian in the New Brunswick Seminary Library.

director of youth and called the Reverend Harold A. Colenbrander, a former Navy chaplain (1944-46) and minister of the Hudsonville Reformed Church (1946-51),[128] to become minister of Christian education and youth work. He served from May 1954 until April 1955, when he accepted a call to the Hope Reformed Church of Sheboygan, Wisconsin.[129]

Harold A. Colenbrander

In the spring of 1955, Hope Church honored four members who together had devoted 108 years of service to Christian education. Edward J. Yeomans served as secretary and treasurer of the Church School for twenty-five years. Eva Pelgrim was a teacher and department superintendent for thirty years. Milton Hinga taught the College Bible Class for thirty years, and Carol Van Putten was a teacher and superintendent of the kindergarten department for twenty-three years.[130]

---

[128] Gasero, *Historical Directory*, 73.
[129] *Consistorial Minutes*, 10 May 1854, 12:943; 11 April 1955, 14:986.
[130] *Hope Church News*, May 1955:1.

FACING CHALLENGES FROM 1925 TO 1960   227

Church School leaders honored in 1955: Edward J. Yeomans, Eva Pelgrim, Milton Hinga, and Carol Van Putten

In June 1955 Joan Van Riper became the director of education and youth work.[131] In his annual report for 1955 de Velder stated that forty-five new members were received, a net gain of twenty-three more than in 1954. Total contributions by all church organizations amounted to $71,632.76, averaging $102 per member, "the highest in our history," and triple the giving of 1945. After three years of study, the time was right, he said, for Hope Church to "launch" and "engage in an expansion program of major and even breath-taking proportions."[132]

In February 1956 de Velder read to consistory a message he had written that he confessed had long been on his conscience. In it he cited Hope Church's five weakest points: our Sunday evening program, parent meetings for the Church School, choir participation and rehearsals, mid-week prayer services, and week-day Bible

---

[131] *Consistorial Minutes*, 12 June 1955, 14:991; 14 November 1955, 14:1002. She served until June 1958.
[132] *Consistorial Minutes*, 26 January 1956, 14:1012 insert. These figures for 1956–1959 and into the Reverend William C. Hillegonds's term of ministry continued to grow, each year representing new highs in membership, Church School enrollment, and total giving.

School. Without naming names, he leveled blame at church members who preferred to make Sunday evenings a social time with family and friends or to "watch 'thrilling' television programs" at home instead of spending "an hour or so in God's House." Parental indifference, he added, contributed to low attendance at young people's meetings and great difficulty in retaining volunteer youth group sponsors. For all too many members Sunday morning worship was their only participation in the life of the church. Unless changes were made, he concluded, "our own and our children's spiritual welfare is at stake."[133]

The consistory took de Velder's admonitions seriously and created a composite summary of responses to problems that, though not unique to Hope Church, were not to be ignored. Among the suggestions made were to condense the many activities and focus more on doing a few things well, to stress family participation, to encourage marginal members to take church commitments more seriously, and to focus more on spiritual upbuilding than on building expansion.[134] In addition, a study group assigned to make recommendations regarding church programs urged that a Sunday School teachers' training program be started, a questionnaire "to uncover hidden talent and willing workers" be mailed, and de Velder be relieved of recruitment responsibilities for the School of Christian Living so that he could instead focus on conducting a Bible study for the Adult Fellowship.[135]

In June 1956 a special congregational meeting was called to vote on plans to expand Hope Church at its current location. The close vote of 212 affirmative and 204 negative revealed no consensus.[136] Meanwhile, the consistory purchased the Phillips Brooks home

---

[133] *Consistorial Minutes*, 13 February 1956, 15:1013 insert.
[134] *Consistorial Minutes*, 16 March 1956, 15:1018 insert.
[135] *Consistorial Minutes*, 10 September 1956, 15:1036.
[136] *Consistorial Minutes*, 14 May 1956, 15:1025. Carol Myers recalls de Velder's comment to her about the consequences of this close vote: The day after the vote "Gerrit Van Zoeren called Mert to see him and told him he had been prepared to donate money for building the education wing had the congregation approved it. In the end Hope College got Van Zoeren Library."

and property at 99 West Eleventh Street, near the Pine Avenue intersection, to become a parsonage and investigated purchase of a vacant lot at the corner of Tenth and Pine. The existing parsonage at 79 West Eleventh Street would be used for eight junior and senior high Church School classrooms, an assembly room, space for choir rehearsals, and studies for the pastor and minister of music. Its basement would be used for meetings of Boy Scouts and for storage.[137]

In May 1957 a joint meeting of the Executive Committee and Church Expansion Committee voted to drop plans for the building project voted on in 1956, disband the Church Expansion Committee, and appoint a new Church Building Committee.[138] The consistory met that month at the new Central Reformed Church in Grand Rapids, perhaps with an openness to influences from a new church in the bigger city. De Velder introduced Central's new minister of music to the consistory. At that meeting, the consistory agreed that the new Church Building Committee would include at least three women, and it voted nine to five to employ a full-time minister of music at Hope Church.[139] Two months later, the consistory hired Kenneth C. Schellenberger for the position.[140]

The sizable Carollers and Cherubs choirs in 1957 illustrate the need to construct an education wing.

---

[137] *Consistorial Minutes*, 8 October 1956, 15:1039; 12 November 1956, 15:1046; 24 January 1957, 15:1046 insert; 14 October 1957, 16:1087 insert. The former parsonage became known as the West Church House.
[138] *Consistorial Minutes*, 7 May 1957, 16:1062 insert.
[139] *Consistorial Minutes*, 13 May 1957, 16:1065–67. The new Church Building Committee comprised George Heeringa, Frank D. Kleinheksel. Lawrence W. (Bill) Lamb Jr., church treasurer John D. Plewes, Paul Winchester, Phyllis White, Hester Gronberg, Lois Boersma, June Marsilje, Joan Van Riper, and Marion de Velder. *Consistorial Minutes*, 17 June 1957, 16:1072.
[140] *Consistorial Minutes*, 7 July 1957, 16:1073.

Carollers choir in 1957

The Carollers are depicted on the east side of the parsonage, which was removed in 1961 to make room for an education wing.

Left portion:
Back row – left to right: Barbara Duey, David Meek, Cathy Witty, Scott Wyman, Mary Rich, Anne de Velder
Middle row: Diane Rottschaefer, Dean DeRidder, Kurt Hopkins, Diane Vanderham, Julie Haworth, Margo Hakken
Front row: Thomas Working, Mary Pat Boersma, Jean Thomas, Gail Van Raalte, Melodie Wise, Pamela White

Right portion:
Back row – left to right: Gregory Green, Darrell Dykstra, William Beebe, Deborah Klomparens
Middle row: Craig Hills, Dennis Ferris, Lesley Den Herder, Claudia Vander Heuvel
Front row: Libbie Ann Hanson, Judith Barber, Susan Brooks, Joan Geuder, Roberta Hallan

Cherubs choir in 1957

Back row – left to right: Margaret Lubbers, Gerald Klomparens, Marilyn Barber, Loren Howard, Suzanne Swartz
Second row from top: Sally Jo Hallan, Merry Hakken, Craig Hall, Patricia Hinkle, Peter Mass
Third row from top: Janet Steininger, Stephen Hinkle, Melissa Klomparens
Fourth row from top: Lauralee Hayward, Martha Wilkinson, Claire Morse
Front row: Virginia Evans, Nancy Karsten

Back row – left to right: Debra Ridenour, Susan Beebe, Christine Dinger, Gary Ferris, James Brooks
Second row from top: Stephen Hills, Thomas Thornhill, Alicia Swartz, Linda Freestone, Andrea Klomparens
Third row from top: Heidi Vander Heuvel, James White
Fourth row from top: Kathleen DeWitt, Susan Rottschaefer, Barbara Geuder, Ann DeRidder
Front row: Mark Van Dokkumburg, Dennis Barber, Charles Ridenour

In the late fifties, the chancel had an aisle opened to display the Communion table, the Last Supper wood carving behind the table, and the Bosch memorial Communion window above the wood carving.[141] The organ pipes were invisible, and the choir was split, seated in pews at the sides of the chancel. The organ was at the far east side of the chancel.

Chancel in the late 1950s

De Velder reported in May 1957 that he had received a call "to serve the Board of Domestic Missions" of the RCA. The consistory urged him to stay, pledging its "continued support and full cooperation in the program so auspiciously begun." The following month de Velder was elected vice president of the General Synod.[142]

---

[141] According to the anonymous "Portraits of the Past: Written for the 125th Anniversary of Hope Church," 1987, 6, Hope College President Edward D. Dimnent, who was also an elder of Hope Church, designed the Bosch memorial rose window.

[142] *Consistorial Minutes*, 29 May 1957, 16:1069 (the specific capacity in which he was called to serve was not indicated in the minutes); 17 June 1957, 16:1072.

In September 1957, the consistory approved that there be two church services each Sunday morning, at least from September through Christmas. It agreed to employ Suren Pilafian from Detroit to make a comprehensive structural, architectural, and mechanical survey of the church and suggest three plans: one for complete demolition, another for partial demolition, and a third for a step-by-step rebuilding that would lead eventually to all new construction.[143]

From June 1958 to May 1959, de Velder served as president of the General Synod and spent much of his time visiting churches and denominational centers and performing tasks of denominational leadership. A combination of strong lay leadership and reliance on specialized ministers within the congregation helped sustain Hope Church while its senior pastor was often away. At the 1959 General Synod, held at Buck Hill Falls, Pennsylvania, de Velder concluded his presidential address by drawing from John Calvin's words to inspire renewed devotion to Christ:

> We know that our real need is rededication of our lives to Christ, that God may truly have *first place* in our living. Now, as in answer to this need and on the 450th Anniversary of the birth of our great spiritual leader, John Calvin, we have chosen for the General Synod theme for 1959-60, his personal motto: "My Heart I Offer Thee, Lord, Promptly and Sincerely." And so, may you and I have indelibly impressed upon our lives during these sessions and in the months ahead, this seal and motto (hanging before us). That ALL OF US, and all those we represent—may with hand outstretched, with open palm lifted upward and holding the symbol of a flaming heart—daily offer ourselves with burning love and in complete devotion to God in Christ through the Holy Spirit.[144]

---

[143] *Consistorial Minutes*, 9 September 1957, 16:1073–76.
[144] *The Acts and Proceedings of the One Hundred and Fifty-Third Regular Session of the GENERAL SYNOD of The Reformed Church in America Convened in The Inn Buck Hill Falls Pennsylvania June 1959*. vol. 43, no. 1. (New York: Department of Publication and Sales), 254.

In May 1959, de Velder reported to the consistory that the Church Building Committee had chosen John H. Vander Meulen to draw up "a master plan for the rebuilding of the entire Hope Church plant and submit detailed specifications for the education wing as the first step in the program." He also called for a group meeting of the leaders of all of the church's organizations to consider the purposes of each in relation to the total purpose of the church.

In response to this and to direction from the denomination, the Hope Church Women's Missionary Society, Women's Aid Society, and Women's Club disbanded and formed a single Guild for Christian Service.[145] Gladys Hinga was its first president.[146] The purpose of the denomination-wide Guild for Christian Service was "to unite all the women of the Church in order to make Christ known throughout the world, to deepen the spiritual life of each of its members, and to develop a personal responsibility for the whole mission of the Church, through a program of Prayer, Education, Giving and Service."[147]

In August Marion de Velder and his wife, Edith, wrote a letter to the consistory and congregation of Hope Church, telling of their acceptance of a call to the Central Reformed Church in Grand Rapids. "You have withheld no good thing from us," they wrote, "and have made our stay of twenty years in your midst so pleasant and fruitful that it will always be a precious chapter in the book of memory."[148]

Though he served Hope Church longer than had any other pastor, and though he motivated the congregation to grow and give

---

[145] As Lois Boersma recalled, "all churches were asked to establish guilds and circles. Prior to this time, Hope women had a very active Aid, a Missionary Society and a Women's Club. It took diplomacy and willingness to concede to pull this together and form a Guild" (personal communication to the author).
[146] *Consistorial Minutes*, 11 May 1959, 18:1156–57.
[147] *Consistorial Minutes*, 28 January 1960, 18:1188 insert. *By-laws of the Guild for Christian Service of Hope Church, Classis of Holland, Reformed Church in America*. W91–1034. Hope Church, Holland, Michigan, box 5, Joint Archives of Holland.
[148] *Consistorial Minutes*, 18 June 1959, 18:1161 insert.

more than perhaps any pastor before or since, two decades were not long enough to see the congregation through a productive building campaign and a centennial celebration. But who could fault him for accepting a call to a larger church that had recently built a new facility in a bigger city? After serving two years as pastor at Central Reformed Church, de Velder responded to a call by the denomination to serve first as the stated clerk for the General Synod 1961–1968 and then as the first general secretary of the Reformed Church in America 1968–1977. After serving the denomination, the de Velders returned to Hope Church. From 1983 to 1992, he served as a part-time assistant minister of pastoral care.[149]

Marion de Velder in about 2000

---

[149] Gasero, *Historical Directory*, 557. *Consistorial Minutes*, 52:15 February 1993.

Windows and Woodcarving

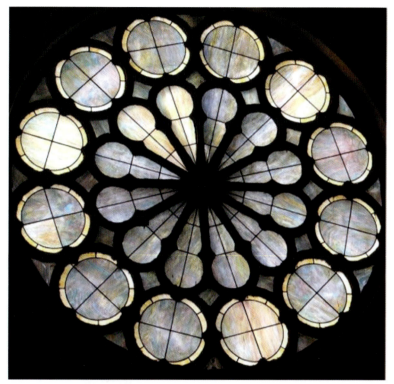

One of three rose windows in the sanctuary

In the early 1920s plans were made to install circular rose windows and ten memorial windows in the church sanctuary.[1] The subjects of the memorial windows were chosen by a committee of the consistory, and the windows were created and installed by J. & R. Lamb of Fifth Avenue, New York. Except for the Jesus windows in the center of each group, the assignment of subject to memorial was made by lot.[2] The windows were dedicated on the first Sunday of August 1924.

---

[1] *Consistorial Minutes*, 9 March 1922, 3:105.
[2] "Windows Are Dedicated at Hope Church," *Holland City News*, 7 August 1924:3.

The east windows depict persons from the Old Testament (pictured in order of mention directly left, and left to right below). The Moses window was given in memory of John Coatsworth Post, 1854–1903, the first child baptized in Hope Church. The Elijah window was given in memory of Mrs. Jane C. Vander Veen Boyd, 1872–1922. The Good Shepherd window was given in memory of the Reverend Philip Phelps Jr., DD, founder of Hope Church and first president of Hope College, and his wife, formerly Margaret Anna Jordan. The David window was given in memory of Henry Boers, MA, Mrs. Louise Birkhoff Boers, and Henry Boers Jr. The Isaiah window was given in memory of John H. Kleinheksel and Anna Vera Kleinheksel.

East windows in the church sanctuary

The west windows depict persons from the New Testament (pictured in order of mention right, and then left to right below). The St. Paul window was given in memory of Mary Alcott Diekema, 1858–1910. The St. John the Baptist window was given in memory of Gerrit John Kollen, LLD, former president of Hope College, and his wife, Mary W. Van Raalte Kollen. The St. John the Evangelist window was given in memory of Ellen Grace Dean, wife of John Tallmadge Bergen, DD. The Christ Blessing the Little Child window was given in memory of George Kollen, 1871–1919. The St. Stephen window was given in memory of Ida Sears McLean, 1865–1910.

West windows in the church sanctuary

In 1947 Kate Keppel donated to Hope Church a wood sculpture of the Last Supper in memory of her husband, Albert C. Keppel. The sculpture was carved by one of America's foremost woodcarvers, Alois Lang. It is framed in a case of scroll-worked wood with a long column on each end topped with angels.[3]

Last Supper woodcarving by Alois Lang in the chancel

In the late 1940s, Emma Bosch and the Randall C. Bosch and Gerald J. Bosch families donated a rose window in memory of Nicodemus Bosch. Originally placed above the Last Supper woodcarving on the north wall of the chancel, it was removed to accommodate pipes for a new organ installation in 1965 and now is in the wall separating the Blanche Cathcart Library from

---

[3] "Wood-Carver, to Discuss His Work in Hope Church," *Holland City News*, 23 October 1947. For other views of this woodcarving, see pages 210 and 234.

the Gathering Area. The window, with a Communion chalice at the center, symbolizes the "communion in Jesus Christ which is essential to ... our worship, fellowship and social ministry."[4]

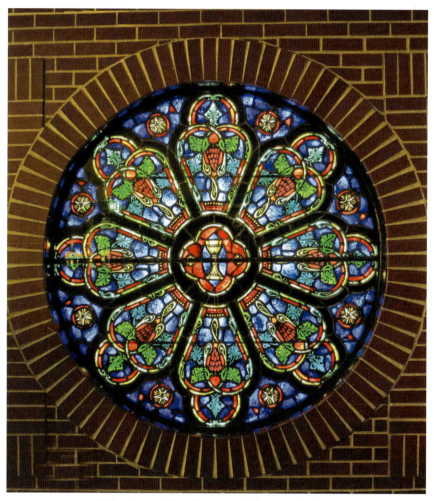

Nicodemus Bosch memorial rose window

---

[4] *Our Time for Rededication*, 1982.

In 1982 the John Vander Broek family donated six facet-slab glass windows to the Parish Life Center (Commons I) in memory

ADVENT
The purple color suggests the penitential time, a time of preparation. The small slip of green with pure white flower is still in the womb of the earth. Above is the water and the Tree of Life reaching up to the heaven. Through the golden leaves the pale tip of the new moon is seen through the tree. Purple is also the royal color and here heralds the coming of the King. The white flower of purity and faith is also associated with the Virgin Mary, as is the moon which is a symbol of the eternal feminine.

CHRISTMAS
The Sun is rising bringing new life, the pure gold of unity and wholeness to light the world. Like a halo it appears above the purple where the manger cradles the new born King. A brighter ray of light above suggests the Spirit now incarnate upon earth below. The alpha and omega signs appear in the band of brown or flesh tones suggesting the sense of earth and humanity.

EPIPHANY
The guiding star shines in the heaven as a message to mankind that Christ is born. Below, the candle lights the darkness expressing the theme of Epiphany as Christ's light shows forth to the world.

of Gertrude Vander Broek. Designed and described by J. Hector, the windows depict the natural seasons and the Christian calendar.

LENT
The deep tones of red and purple suggest the sacrificial blood and the wine, symbols of the Passion of Our Lord crucified. Below the Cross is the Chalice and the green leaf, sign that the earth is soon to spring into new life.

EASTER
The white lilies appear in a field of flowers and bright greenery with many tulips. At the top of the window upon wings outspread appears the word HOPE, for this is the time of the Resurrection of the Lord.

PENTECOST
The Dove, image of the Holy Spirit, descends to earth with tongues of flame. The image of Holy Baptism is expressed in the meeting of the Fire and the Water—the Spirit touches the Water of life. The Sun appears amidst the leaves of the Tree in rich summer greens, completing the seasons. So as in the beginning is in the end—fruit, seed, flower and fruit again.

Eleanor DePree Van Haitsma created a cut-glass window for the meditation room of Hope Church.

The stained glass design is intended to capture the eye in order that it may guide the mind and soul toward God. The lower section, by its humble place and horizontal shape, reminds the worshiper that he lifts up his soul from the midst of life on earth. The middle and upper sections together contain a cross, the sign of the sacrifice of Christ who in his life and death linked heaven and earth. Discerned in the upper section is a triangle, the ancient symbol of the Trinity.

In the upper left corner, God the Father is represented by the sun whose moving flames show him to be the living God, the source of light, warmth, and power. God the Son stands between the father and those who look toward him. Christ is positioned slightly in front of God to emphasize that he is a gift put forth by the father to be the agent of reconciliation, the guide to life eternal, and the perfect demonstration of his love for man. The hand of Christ, centered at the left, with its visible wound recalls the suffering of the Savior for his people, but because he is risen, the cross stands empty as a triumphant emblem of forgiveness, joy and hope. The dove portrays the descent of God the Holy Spirit upon all flesh, and the overlapping of the symbols of Father, Son, and Holy Spirit declares that God is one.

The tree in the center of the design represents the life of man, growing upon earth, but able to reach heavenward through Christ. The moon and stars recall the beauty of the night with its gifts of quiet, rest, and coolness. The wheat and grapes symbolize both the Holy Communion and the daily nourishment of the body, while the long blue streaks suggest the blessings of falling rain. Since God loves all people, the human figures across the lower portion picture every race with their equality before the Creator reflected in their similarity of design. With outstretched arms all receive the gifts of God which descend from him, through Christ, through tree and earth, into the waters flowing all about them.

The remarkable printing of the doxology signifies that it is to be read with a shout of joy in the heart   —Eleanor DePree Van Haitsma

6 ... Engaging in Social Justice Actions

As he had done after Thomas W. Davidson's departure in 1937 and after Marion de Velder's first departure in 1951, Paul E. Hinkamp served as moderator after de Velder's departure in 1959. James Wayer continued to lead the weekly prayer meetings and call on people.[1]

In preparation for calling a pastor, Hope Church conducted a self-study and considered the kind of pastoral leadership it was seeking. The study characterized Hope Church as both a college church and a community church. Hope Church considered its "most significant evangelical activity" as " providing a church home away from home to a large segment of the students at Hope College." As a community church, the congregation saw itself welcoming new families from a variety of Protestant denominations. It also saw itself as "a strong member of the RCA" with a "major responsibility for supporting and providing leadership" to the denomination.[2]

Ministries of William C. Hillegonds and John R. Walchenbach, 1960–66

In March 1960 the congregation voted to advise the consistory to call the Reverend William C. Hillegonds, a native of Chicago and graduate of Hope College and Western Theological Seminary. He was in his fifth year as pastor of the Brighton Reformed Church in Rochester, New York.[3]

---

[1] *Consistorial Minutes*, 14 September 1959, 18:1170–71.
[2] *Consistorial Minutes*, 12 October 1959, 18:1171 insert. There was no Presbyterian church in Holland until 1958. With the exception of the Old Wing Mission conducted by the Reverend George N. and Arvilla Smith in the 1840s, there has never been a Congregational or United Church of Christ in Holland.
[3] *Consistorial Minutes*, 17 March 1960, 19:1204. The vote was 293 yes and 16 no.

William C. Hillegonds

Hillegonds wrote, "With fear in my heart because I am aware of my own limitations and the bigness of the task you have asked me to undertake and with a deepening sense of the strength and love of God, I have accepted your 'call.'" In contrast to de Velder's confidence in knowing God's will in response to a call, Hillegonds added with a note of humor, "I wonder if God ever makes his will as plain as the Dakotas are flat."

In contrast to Davidson, Hillegonds requested a salary less than the $7,000 annual salary offered. Explaining his request, he stated a principle that he and his wife followed: "Since part of the discipline by which we live is never to leave one church for another at a salary larger than we have been receiving, we are asking that the figure in the written 'call' be reduced by $1,000. This means the salary should be $6,000 plus a $500 car allowance. This is what we are presently receiving here."[4]

By his excellent preaching Hillegonds endeared himself not only to the congregation but also to Hope College students, who attended worship services more frequently and in greater numbers than they had in earlier years. Hope Church held two identical worship services on Sunday mornings, and both drew crowds.

After the retirement in 1961 of calling pastor Wayer after ten years of service, Hillegonds enlisted elders to help call on people. The consistory divided the congregation into thirteen zones, each with an elder responsible to visit members in his zone,[5] a practice that continues with some modifications into the twenty-first century.

As de Velder had done, Hillegonds sought and used the services of two seminarians. William de Forest and Ervin Roorda—assisted by Roorda's wife, Andrea—performed many of the tasks that had been done by Shirley Kiefer, who had resigned after serving as director of religious education 1958–1961.[6]

One of the persistent problems still unresolved, however, was the need for additional space for an expanding congregation, especially space for a growing religious education program. In June 1960 the consistory approved employing a professional financial organization to assist the congregation in raising the funds for carrying out a building program. The consistory approved the firm aptly named "Ketchum, Inc.," to raise $300,000 for stage one of the proposed building program, construction of educational facilities and church offices. Building on that momentum, the consistory voted to proceed with the plan if the congregational vote was favorable by a simple majority. Within days, by a vote of 152 to 35, the congregation approved the plans to build, and by a

---

[4] *Consistorial Minutes*, 29 April 1960, 19:1227 insert.
[5] "Hope Church Evangelism Self Study," *Consistorial Minutes*, February 1963, 22:1328 insert.
[6] *Consistorial Minutes*, 13 February 1961, 20:1260; 10 April 1961, 20:1265; 11 September 1961, 20:1280; 13 November 1961, 20:1288.

vote of 139 to 39 it approved the use of Ketchum, Inc., to raise the funds.[7] Meanwhile consistory authorized purchase of the house of Gertrude Flikkema at 55 West Eleventh St. to be used temporarily for senior high Church School classrooms.[8]

The goal was to build an education wing in time for Hope Church's centennial celebration in 1962.[9] To the standing committees of consistory (Educational, Finance, Membership & Evangelism, Music, Property, Worship, Ushering, Stewardship, and Staff) were added Building and Centennial.[10]

In his report to the 1962 congregational meeting, Hillegonds presented his vision for Hope Church:

> In this the 100th year of Hope Church in Holland, Michigan, we should become increasingly aware that our reason for existence is not that we are so terribly different from other Christian congregations in our community; that we are liberal and other congregations stuffily conservative; that we are uninhibited in some of our social practices while other communities of believers in our midst are so mired in legalism as to be where we were in attitude and behavior fifty years ago. Let us not be known only for our difference but for our likeness to the New Testament church which saw herself as an instrument of God in his move to reshape the world according to the way and wishes of his Son....
>
> As God hovers over a world not without its crises, let Hope Church be one of his instruments in showing all who pass our way the whence of our coming, the why of our being here and the eternal destiny of man's eternal soul. This is to honor the past. This is to make meaningful the present. This is to help the world realize another and another dawn.[11]

---

[7] *Consistorial Minutes*, 13 June 1960, 19:1234; 20 June 1960, 19:1237; 12 September 1960, 19:1239; 10 October 1960, 19:1241; 12 October 1960, 19:1243.
[8] *Consistorial Minutes*, 10 April 1961, 20:1266 insert; 25 January 1962, 21:1296 insert.
[9] *Consistorial Minutes*, 13 November 1961, 20:1288 insert.
[10] *Consistorial Minutes*, 25 January 1962, 21:1288 insert.
[11] "Report of the Minister," *Consistorial Minutes*, 15 January 1962, 21:1296 insert.

Women's Groups Form Guild and Circles

Though the women of Hope Church had reduced the number of their organizations to one Guild for Christian Service in 1959, a summary of the activities of the Guild for 1960 shows the women's dedication to reshaping the community and world in ways pleasing to Christ. Ten "circles" were organized to meet once a month. The entire Guild, which had 249 members, also met once a month for lunch and a program.

Guild programs presented in 1960 included a book review of *Africa Disturbed*, a presentation by Dr. Bernadine De Valois on "The Population Explosion throughout the World," and a presentation by Emma Reeverts and Lillian Van Dyke on the needs of the people in Chiapas, Mexico. The Guild supplied workers and donations for the Hope College Village Square, an annual fund-raising event by RCA women to support Hope College. Guild members also placed flowers in the sanctuary each Sunday and provided decorations for Easter and Christmas. They served appreciation dinners for the choir and Sunday School in addition to the seven Guild luncheons and three dinners, four Men's Club dinners, and two receptions for organizations outside Hope Church.[12]

Florence Jenks prepared meals that were taken to feed migrant children. Many women from the Guild provided both volunteer service and financial support in the migrant camps.[13]

Ministering to Migrant Workers

Attention by members of Hope Church to the needs of migrant workers can be traced at least as far back as 1932, when Marthena Bosch presented a book review of *Roving with the Migrants* to the Women's Missionary Society.[14] Of the dues collected from the two

---

[12] *Consistorial Minutes*, 26 January 1961, 19:1254 insert.
[13] Communication from Carol Myers. *Consistorial Minutes*, 26 January 1961, 19:1254 insert.
[14] "'Roving Migrants' Is Topic at Meeting," *Holland Sentinel*, 5 May 1932:5.

hundred students attending the Daily Vacation Bible School held by Hope, Third Reformed, and the Methodist churches in 1951, $75 was given in support of a migrant missionary project at South Haven.[15]

Dr. Vern Boersma, a Hope Church elder, remembers that migrant workers first came in large numbers to Holland after World War II. Farmers and the H. J. Heinz Company were looking for an inexpensive source of labor to replace the German prisoners of war who had helped them grow, harvest, and process pickles during the war.[16] The first migrant workers were a few Caucasian families from Arkansas and Hispanic families from Texas who included Holland in their annual migrations. These migrations started in late spring in Berrien and Van Buren Counties with strawberry picking, proceeded in the summer to Allegan and Ottawa Counties with cucumber harvesting and blueberry picking, and ended in the autumn in northern Kent County with apple picking.[17]

In the early 1950s the Health Department and compassionate farmers who grew blueberries would call Dr. Boersma to care for migrant laborers or their family members who became ill. Other migrant workers with medical needs were referred to Dr. Boersma by Everett Vanden Brink, a Christian Reformed Church elder who began missionary work with Hispanic men hired to work at Heinz. Said Boersma,

> I soon discovered that unless the employer brought these people in they had no transportation. I made numerous calls to the fields and migrant bunk houses and realized how desperate the health

---

[15] *Consistorial Minutes*, 17 September 1951, 10:495.
[16] Vern Boersma, "My Work with Migrants," W91-1034. Hope Church, Holland, Michigan, box 12, Joint Archives of Holland.. During World War II, one of the tasks assigned to German Prisoners of War housed at Camp Lakeview in Allegan was to help farmers raise and harvest pickles. More than forty German POWs worked at the Heinz pickle factory in Holland. Jim Hayden, "Allegan Co. POW Camp a Reminder of Local History," *Holland Sentinel*, 21 May 2011. http://www.hollandsentinel.com/feature/x157795564/Allegan-Co-POW-camp-a-reminder-of-local-history.
[17] Boersma, "My Work with Migrants."

care was for these people with no money, no insurance, and often not wanting to be asked too many questions.... I secured a house-trailer to pull behind my car and took it out into the various fields on Wednesdays and some Saturday evenings to do a little preventative care and education.... Katherine Groenevelt became director of the Health Department nurses and she was extremely helpful. She saw my house-trailer clinic and immediately supplied me with a nurse assistant.[18]

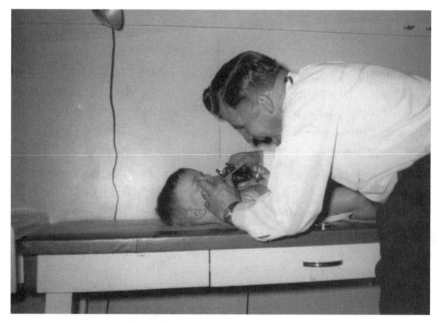

Dr. Vern Boersma, Hope Church elder and volunteer physician in migrant ministry

Dr. Boersma remembers responding one night to a call to one of the bunk houses in a blueberry field. In a ten-by-twenty-foot bunk house lived a family with seven children.

> There was one central light in the middle of the room and several of the kids had fevers so I prepared to sit down on a bunk along the wall and have the kids come one at a time and stand in front of

---

[18] Boersma, "My Work with Migrants."

me. As I prepared to sit down on a blanket there, the father, Jose, grabbed my arm and said, "No, no, not there." I stood erect and lifted the lumpy blanket only to find a 2-year-old underneath with a completely cleft lip and palate.... They were hiding him. The kids had measles and a couple needed antibiotics but I later referred that little guy with the cleft palate to a Grand Rapids plastic surgeon who gladly repaired the congenital defect. Jose and his family settled in Holland and Jose became the bass drummer for the Salvation Army Band, which performed on the corner of 8th and Central on Saturday nights.[19]

Dr. Boersma also remembers Tino Reyes and Lupita Cantu, who later became Tino's wife, as children of some of the first migrant families. Boersma gave Lupita and other children immunization shots in the blueberry fields. Later Tino Reyes assumed increasing levels of responsibility, working thirty years for the H. J. Heinz Company and becoming executive director of Latin Americans United for Progress (LAUP). Lupita Reyes became director of Social Services at Holland Hospital and helped develop the Holland Community Health Center on River Avenue. Said Boersma, "I have many Hispanic friends who though less well known have also gone from migrant survivors to community leaders."[20]

Nurse Katherine Groenevelt learned about what the Berrien County Health Department was doing to bring health care to migrants, and later she and Boersma worked with Berrien County officials to establish the West Michigan Migrant Authority to seek state and federal aid for improving health care for migrant workers and their families.[21] In 2004 Hope College honored Boersma for his donation of "medical services to numerous community organizations. His service included organizing the Ottawa County Migrant Health Clinic, of which he was medical director for 25 years."[22]

---

[19] Boersma, "My Work with Migrants."
[20] Boersma, "My Work with Migrants."
[21] Boersma, "My Work with Migrants."
[22] "Campus Notes, *News from Hope*, December 2004, 3.

Holland's Church Women United group—consisting of women from Hope, Third Reformed, and the Methodist church, with several Christian Reformed Church women—assisted migrant families by providing babysitting. Their migrant ministry began in western Ottawa County in July 1958. Hope Church member R. E. Barber donated a station wagon, and Eva Pelgrim was the migrant ministry's first chair. Services provided later included Vacation Bible Schools for children, thrift sales, health services, and counseling.[23]

Exploring Hope Church's Identity and Purpose

In a self-study report done in 1963, Hope Church acknowledged that its members were more heavily involved with "a wide variety of community activities" than with "specific church activities," such as evangelism. "The prevailing attitude of the congregation, traditionally, toward evangelism has been cool or even negative. The term is not a popular one—perhaps because it is misunderstood or thought of in a very limited connotation."[24]

The report affirmed that some members "have taken a leadership role in organizing help for the agricultural migrants." It acknowledged that there are "few boards or projects such as fund drives in which members are not taking a leading part, e. g., United Fund, March of Dimes, Community Concerts, Tulip Time, fund drives for hospital, college, old folks home, Y.M.C.A., etc. A disproportional amount of the community leadership comes from Hope Church membership."[25]

---

[23] "Migrant Ministry Program Starts Monday in County," *Holland City News*, 17 July 1958:6.
[24] "Hope Church Evangelism Self Study," *Consistorial Minutes*, February 1963, 22:1328 insert. The congregation's attitude toward evangelism had changed considerably over the years since the 1901 prayer meeting revival services led by the evangelist C. C. Smith, who was affiliated with the Moody Bible Institute. That revival added 121 members to Hope Church, 35 of whom were adults baptized by pastor Bergen. *Consistorial Minutes*, May 1901, 2:89–90.
[25] "Hope Church Evangelism Self Study," *Consistorial Minutes*, February 1963, 22:1328 insert.

Hillegonds concluded the self-study with his own assessment:

> The greatest single opportunity that this church has had to fulfill its mission to members of the community not a part of this church is its service to the college student.... There is need for more of the members of the church to be involved in this mission and to recognize this as a mission.[26]

Constructing the Education Wing and Celebrating the Centennial in 1962

With George Heeringa as chair of the Building Committee and John Vander Meulen hired as architect and Arthur Reed as building consultant, construction of the education wing was completed in the fall of 1962. As a former pastor invited to speak at the dedication of the education wing and centennial anniversary services on 21 October 1962,[27] de Velder chose as his text Hebrews 11:30–40 and as his sermon title "The Best Is Yet To Be."[28]

In the introduction to the centennial historical booklet, Hillegonds offered his wisdom about the legacy of Hope Church:

> All of us ... can be grateful to all of the people who through one hundred years helped to keep alive what in our hands remains a vital, searching, active congregation. Joseph Parker was thinking of us too when he wrote, "Our yesterdays follow us; they constitute our life and they give character and force and meaning to our present deeds."
>
> Each day we live this life we receive from yesterday to give to tomorrow.[29]

---

[26] "Hope Church Evangelism Self Study," *Consistorial Minutes*, February 1963, 22:1328 insert.
[27] *Consistorial Minutes*, 31 October 1961, 20:1286; 13 November 1961, 20:1288 insert; 9 July 1962. 21:1308.
[28] *Rejoicing in Hope...Romans 12:12: Hope Church 1862 1962*, 1962:12–13.
[29] *Rejoicing in Hope*, 1. Joseph Parker (1830–1902) was a Congregational preacher in England who was noted for his stimulating sermons. http://en.wikisource.org/wiki/1911_Encyclop%C3%A6dia_Britannica/Parker,_Joseph

1962 education wing from the courtyard

The annual report for 1962 announced that Church School attendance "has increased at least 15% over last year—the enrollment now standing at 345—and several rooms are already filled to capacity." In addition to all Church School classes meeting at 9:30 a.m. in the new education wing, classes for toddlers through those in the fourth grade were offered at 11:00 a.m. A staff of forty teachers and superintendents aided the educational program.[30] The 1963 self-study reported that students and their parents "make up half of the Sunday morning congregation."[31]

---

[30] *Consistorial Minutes*, 24 January 1963, 22:1323 insert.
[31] "Hope Church Evangelism Self Study," *Consistorial Minutes*, February 1963, 22:1328 insert.

1962 education wing, north side

John R. Walchenbach Becomes Associate Pastor

In January 1964 Hope Church extended a call to the Reverend John R. Walchenbach, pastor of the Reformed Church of Hopewell Junction, New York, to become an associate pastor. He accepted and was installed in April.[32]

---

[32] *Consistorial Minutes*, 30 January 1964, 23:1353, 13 April 1964, 23:1360.

John R. Walchenbach

Suddenly, on 22 November 1963, President John F. Kennedy was assassinated. Two days later, the Reverend Arthur H. Jentz Jr., Hope Church member and Hope College religion professor, preached in Hope Church a sermon setting forth what meanings might be drawn from that dark event. Using Isaiah 6:1–8 as his text and commentary on the recent event, Jentz testified:

> When times are relatively peaceful, when we are prosperous, when our trust can be placed in a human leader, or in our own capabilities, it is rather difficult to see God.... We do not see Him because we are not looking for Him. We see ourselves in terms of what we have, we see our powerful nation, we see our leaders, and we worship the works of our own hands....
> Let us benefit from the present crisis to examine the nature of our own being: our trusts, our allegiances, our loyalties....
> In a time of radical crisis, Isaiah saw "the Lord, high and lifted up." Lifted up above the world's sham securities, the finite loyalties and goods of mundane existence. And the seeing implied a way of life:

Whom shall I send, and who will go for us?
Here I am! Send me.[33]

Arthur H. Jentz Jr.

Perhaps in response at least in part to Jentz's sermon, the consistory in 1964 created a "Christian or Social Action Committee." The Reverend John Piet was appointed chair, and its first members were Paul Fried, Ronald Dalman, Bernadine De Valois, Eva Pelgrim, and Lois Ten Cate.[34]

---

[33] Arthur H. Jentz Jr., "Sermon on the Death of President John F. Kennedy," 24 November 1963. H91-1034, box 7, Jentz, Arthur H. Jr. (1934–1993), Joint Archives of Holland. Jentz was ordained as elder in 1972.

Asked at a forty-year Hope College class reunion which Hope professor most impressed and influenced him, Wesley Granberg-Michaelson, RCA General Secretary 1994–2011, replied, "Dr. Jentz." Granberg-Michaelson was also favorably influenced by Hope College chaplain William Hillegonds, who encouraged him and others to lead in the development of a student church at Hope College in the mid-1960s. Wesley Granberg-Michaelson, *Unexpected Destinations: An Evangelical Pilgrimage to World Christianity* (Grand Rapids: Eerdmans, 2011), 47–48.

[34] *Consistorial Minutes*, 8 June 1964, 23:1365.

Despite this promising beginning toward expressing Christian faith in social justice actions, the writer of the report from the Board of Christian Education in 1965 lamented the declining attendance at Sunday evening activities:

> The *Covenant Life Curriculum* has been well received and proved to be stimulating to young people and adults. Still, there are areas of improvement. One still wonders why, in view of the exciting adult education program offered, there is only a relatively small percentage of Hope Church members enrolled in a study course. While we delight in broadening ourselves in almost every area of life, still the deepening of our faith gives way to other Sunday evening activities. What is the answer to this? Is the program not varied enough? Viewing the course offerings, this can hardly be the case. Do we still think of Christianity as a passive affair, with attendance at services meeting the requirements of our faith? Are we afraid to learn, or expose ourselves in confrontation and dialogue with others? Or is Sunday evening more wisely given over to family get-togethers rather than church? This may well be the case, and if so, we must either do some re-scheduling, asking ourselves which of the demands of our time are most important, or drop the program which lies on the exciting frontier of the church's growth.[35]

On Sunday evenings in the 1960s Hope Church was not alone in trying, often unsuccessfully, to direct people's attention to Christian education and worship when they would rather stay home to be entertained by watching the *Ed Sullivan Show*, *Walt Disney's Wonderful World of Color*, and *Bonanza* on television. It was difficult

---

[35] *Consistorial Minutes*, 28 January 1965, 24:1385 insert. Introduced in the 1960s, the *Covenant Life Curriculum* was used by the Presbyterian Church in the United States, Reformed Church in America, and several other closely related denominations. Among the books studied by Hope Church classes were a Bible study titled *The Mighty Acts of God*, taught by Frank Sherburne, Herbert Marsilje, and Jean Protheroe; *Go from Your Father's House*, taught to college students by D. Ivan Dykstra; and *Christian Dimensions in Marriage* and the *Nature and Mission of the Christian Family*, taught by James Harvey and John Hollenbach.

for many families with children to escape the allure of "when you wish upon a star."

Sunday morning worship was well attended, however. In April 1965 deacon Lawrence Green reported to the consistory that about fifty people "were turned away from last Sunday's second service," and he anticipated "a very large turn away from the Easter Sunday second service."[36]

Establishing a Day Care Center

Despite declining attendance at some Sunday evening classes in Hope Church's School for Christian Living, a group of adults in a class titled "The Church in Mission" became energized. As the class began examining "the changing mission of the church and our own community's areas of need," it envisioned some ways to go beyond study to action. In 1965 the class proposed to the consistory that Hope Church establish a day care center for children. The church's education wing could provide classroom space five days a week to provide day care and education to young children in the community.[37]

Carol Van Putten informed the "Church in Mission" class about the needs reported by the Department of Social Welfare. Without the subsidized services of a day care center, some families in Holland were leaving children unattended while parents worked, and other families were leaving small children in the care of an older child who should be attending school. A study group of members Jo Anne Brooks, Carol Van Lente, Bess Schouten, Mary Tellman, Libby Hillegonds, Lura Vanden Bos, Ruth De Wolfe, Jane Den

---

[36] *Consistorial Minutes,* 12 April 1965, 24:1393.
[37] *Consistorial Minutes,* 24:9 August 1965 and insert. (Because after page 1399 of the minutes the page numbering is incorrect and because soon after that minutes lack page numbers, from here to 1995, when online minutes are cited, the minutes and insertions will be identified by volume:date instead of by volume:page number.)

Herder, John J. De Valois, and Bernadine De Valois took further steps to develop a day care center.[38]

Encouraged by Church Women United—an ecumenical group of women from several denominations in Holland—and the Hope Church consistory, Jo Anne Brooks investigated how best to proceed. When she learned that Holland's Michigan Migratory Opportunity, Inc. (MMOI) was trying to establish a day care center, she urged that Hope Church provide the facilities and MMOI secure the funding. The Federal Government's Economic Opportunity act of 1964 and other migrant legislation helped extend services to needy people.

When the Hope Church Day Care Center, later called the Early Learning Center, was opened in April 1966, it enrolled twenty-two children ages 2-and-1/2 through 5.[39] "These children," said Jo Anne Brooks, "will receive instruction similar to that of 'Head Start,' which will help them develop socially, physically and mentally."[40]

In 1972 Hope Church member Dorothy Cecil served as director of the Holland Day Care Center, which expanded to two locations. Children between the ages of 2-and-1/2 and 4 were cared for at Hope Church, and 4- and 5-year-olds were cared for at the Third Reformed Church. Children were served a hot breakfast, hot lunch, and two snacks each day.[41] Hope Church continues to provide space for Child Development Services of Ottawa County in its education wing.

---

[38] *Consistorial Minutes*, 24:9 August 1965 insert.
[39] "Day Care Center Enrollment Has 22 Area Pre-Schoolers," *Holland City News*, 28 April 1966:3.
[40] *Consistorial Minutes*, 24:8 November 1965 insert.
[41] *Consistorial Minutes*, 31:28 November 1972.

Children in Hope Church's Day Care Center

Sacred Dance in Churches

Not only was Jo Anne Brooks instrumental in opening Hope Church's education wing to become the home the Holland Day Care Center, she was also active in promoting dancing—more specifically, sacred dance—in Hope Church and other Reformed churches in Holland. In the early 1960s, Jo Anne Brooks, Libby Hillegonds, and Elsie Lamb invited recently hired Hope College dance instructor Maxine H. De Bruyn to teach them and others to dance as an expression of worship. Brooks, who had seen the Lord's Prayer and various Scripture passages presented in dance at a conference in Colorado, recommended including liturgical dance as part of a worship service at a Reformed Church Women's conference at Camp Geneva in the fall of 1960. De Bruyn agreed to teach liturgical dancing.[42]

---

[42] Una H. Ratmeyer, *Hands, Hearts, and Voices: Women Who Followed God's Call* (New York: Reformed Church Press, 1995), 187.

Sacred Dancers, from left to right: Jane Den Herder (Park), Jo Anne Brooks, Shirley Bosch, and Maxine De Bruyn

The Lord's Prayer in dance was so well received at the conference that others wanted to learn about liturgical dance from De Bruyn. To appeal to those whose moral scruples forbade dancing in church, the group first called itself the Holland Rhythmic Choir, but by 1974 the group became known as the Sacred Dance Group of Holland. Dancers from Hope Church included Maxine De Bruyn, Jo Anne Brooks, Elsie Lamb, Shirley Bosch, Dorothy Cecil, Libby Hillegonds, Jane Den Herder, and Jean Protheroe.

Introducing the first Rhythmic Choir dance at Hope Church in 1961, director of Christian education Shirley Kiefer described its purpose:

> Worship is the art of offering the total self to God. Part of this is the act of lifting our voices in songs of praise through hymn and anthem. But ours is an offering of body, mind, and will unto God as

well, and perhaps there is no more fitting way to express this total offering than through the symbolic movement of the whole body in rhythmic worship. Many churches today are rediscovering this form of worship used in the early church (and also by the early Hebrews) and through it are finding a new awareness of the act of worship as being more than words—a dramatic presentation of the whole self to God.[43]

Over the next twenty years, the group grew to include women from other denominations—Methodist, Lutheran, Presbyterian, and Christian Reformed.[44] Maxine De Bruyn taught dance at Hope College for more than four decades, and for many years she taught sacred dance and led exercise classes at Hope Church.

Not all saw sacred dance as "the art of offering the total self to God." Responding to an article in the *Church Herald* about sacred dance in worship services in some Holland churches, someone from McBain, Michigan, expressed being "shocked to read about dancing in the aisles of the Reformed Churches in Holland, Michigan as well as some other churches." He concluded:

> The old Dutch Reformed people must have been sleeping when Satan came slithering in on the ground floor of the church and is trying to destroy the very foundation on which the church was built.
>
> I have never read an article in the *Herald* so cunningly or craftily written as the one about the sacred dance....
>
> When will there come an end to this nonsense?...
>
> Lord help us get back to the old time religion. It's good for all of us.[45]

---

[43] Hope Church Bulletin, 7 May 1961.
[44] Ratmeyer, *Hands, Hearts, and Voices: Women Who Followed God's Call*, 187.
[45] *Church Herald*, 12 February 1977. By 1977 Hope Church sacred dance had been part of worship services in local churches for well over a decade and continues to be a part of some worship services to the present time.

The First Years of
Glen O. Peterman's Ministry,
1966–71

In August 1965 Hillegonds asked the consistory to release him from his duties as pastor of Hope Church in September so that he might become college pastor at Hope College.[46] Though he and his family remained in Holland, they soon left the parsonage, and Hope Church was faced with having to find another minister.[47]

Associate pastor Walchenbach agreed to serve as needed but indicated that he had no interest in becoming senior pastor. His plans after serving Hope Church were to continue his education.[48]

In April 1966 the consistory called the Reverend Glen O. Peterman as senior pastor,[49] who was serving in his sixth year as pastor of the First Reformed Church in Pella, Iowa. He accepted the call and was installed 3 June 1966.[50]

---

[46] *Consistorial Minutes*, 24:26 August 1965.
[47] In memory of Hillegonds, who died in 2007, Hope Church donated $500 to the Hillegonds Endowed Scholarship at Hope College in honor of his ministry as pastor of Hope Church. Minutes 2008\Consistory 01.doc, 3 January 2008.
[48] *Consistorial Minutes*, 25:20 January 1966.
[49] The consistory had consulted with Marion de Velder for his recommendations about whom to consider calling. Among the list of five men he suggested was Glen O. Peterman. Others recommending Peterman were former Hope College president Irwin Lubbers; Western Seminary president Herman J. Ridder, and Hillegonds. The congregational vote advising consistory to extend the call was 113 to 76. *Consistorial Minutes*, 25:10 January 1966, 21 March 1966, 4 April 1966.
[50] *Consistorial Minutes*, 25:4 April 1966, 9 May 1966 13 June 1966.

Glen O. Peterman

Also in June, Walchenbach reported his plan to leave Hope Church to begin studies for a master's degree at Pittsburgh Theological Seminary. Assuming many of the tasks performed by Walchenbach was Charlotte Heinen, who had worked with Peterman in Pella. She agreed to work at Hope Church on a one-year renewing contract basis as director of Christian education. Peterman welcomed her at the September consistory meeting and invited her to attend consistory meetings.[51]

Peterman reported at the annual congregational meeting in December that Hope Church "changed from two ministers and two Sunday morning services to one minister and one service."[52] Unstated was the fact that, like the fabled pied piper of Hamelin, pastor Hillegonds had attracted many Hope College students to follow him—not as in the fable to their deaths but certainly to

---

[51] *Consistorial Minutes*, 25:13 June 1966, 12 September 1966. She served Hope Church for two years before transferring to the Garden Grove (CA) Community Church, which later became known as the Crystal Cathedral. *Consistorial Minutes*, 28: 17 March 1969.

[52] *Consistorial Minutes*, 25:15 December 1966.

a dearth of youthful congregants at Hope Church. He not only served as chaplain for Hope College from 1965 through 1978, but he helped the college establish its own student church congregation, which began in the spring of 1966.[53] Many Hope students were worshiping at Hope College's Dimnent Memorial Chapel instead of at Hope Church.

Facing Declining Church Attendance

In April 1967 Holland Classis scheduled meetings to consider "Why the Reformed Churches, Holland Classis, are not growing."[54] Declining rates of growth were experienced not just in Hope Church and Holland Classis but also in the entire denomination and in mainline Protestant churches generally. "After reaching its apex of 224,000 active communicants in 1967," according to a study of the Reformed Church by Roger J. Nemeth and Donald A. Luidens, "growth rates began a slow rate of decline in the late 1960s and by the early 1970s the denomination's membership was rapidly shrinking." Between 1967 and 2001 total RCA membership declined by more than 17 percent.[55]

American society, after experiencing the effects of the baby boom from 1946 to 1964, was seeing the reduction of a demographic

---

[53] "The Student Church presented the student body with much more than a Sunday service; it provided opportunities for discussion and dialogue with outside speakers, faculty, and other students; opportunities to see the challenge of the church's task in places like Harlem and Appalachia on spring vacation trips; opportunities to work and give help in a wide range of areas." Among those on the board of trustees of the student church was Wesley Michaelson. *1967 Milestone, Hope College, Holland, Michigan*, 32.
[54] *Consistorial Minutes*, 26:10 April 1967.
[55] In 2001 RCA membership was about 185,000 communicant members. Roger J. Nemeth and Donald A. Luidens, "Fragmentation and Dispersion: Postmodernity Hits the RCA," in *Reformed Encounters with Modernity: Perspectives from Three Continents*, ed. J. Jurgens Hendriks, Donald A. Luidens, Roger J. Nemeth, Corwin E. Schmidt, and Hijme Stoffels. Conference Proceedings of the International Society for the Study of Reformed Communities (ISSRC). Stellenbosch, South Africa, 2001:126.

bulge—first in fewer infant baptisms, then in lower Sunday School attendance, followed by a tapering off of youth fellowship attendance. Membership in some of the organizations at Hope Church also declined. As of September 1967, the report to consistory from its Organizational Life Committee indicated a loss of some vitality: a Fireside Fellowship had ceased to be, as had the Mr. and Mrs. Club, and the Men's Club found itself with nobody willing to be president for the coming year.[56]

At its October meeting, the consistory broke into several discussion groups to assess the health of the congregation and report their findings. "Many felt that women should be allowed on Consistory, even though the Constitution of the R.C.A. prohibited such action." Upon learning that the Guild would like one of its members to sit in at consistory meetings, Peterman said that consistory meetings are "open until we vote to go to executive meeting."[57]

Engaging in Ecumenical Activities

In 1968 as in 1930 and 1949, the General Synod voted on whether to merge with Presbyterians—this time with the Presbyterian Church of the United States, also known as the Southern Presbyterian Church—to form a Presbyterian Reformed Church in America. The vote by the General Synod was 193 for and 103 against merger. However, in the second step toward union, approval by two-thirds of 46 classes of the Reformed Church and three-fourths of the 79 presbyteries of the Presbyterian Church of

---

[56] *Consistorial Minutes*, 26:11 September 1967.
[57] *Consistorial Minutes*, 26:9 October 1967.

the United States, the attempt at merger failed.[58] Holland Classis, by a vote of 20 to 33, aligned itself with classes defeating the merger.[59]

Despite decisions at the denominational level, Hope Church continued to cooperate with other local denominations in a variety of activities. During the early 1970s Hope Church provided the leadership to form Churches United for Social Action (CUSA) "to explore, plan, implement and coordinate various Christian action programs and concerns in the greater community of Holland."[60] Founding member churches of CUSA also included Holland's Grace Episcopal, St. Francis de Sales Catholic, First Presbyterian, First United Methodist, Third Reformed, and Christ Memorial, and Zeeland's Second Reformed Church. CUSA supported the Community Action House and a coffee house ministry.[61] In 1971 Hope Church redirected its support from the City Mission to the Community Action House, an organization for "Helping People Find Help."[62] The Community Action House for more than forty years has been helping people find food, clothing, and housing. It also operates the Community Kitchen at Western Theological Seminary. For decades Earl and Char Laman have advocated for and assisted in providing food for the hungry in our community.

---

[58] Had the second step succeeded, a third step would have been to go back to the RCA's General Synod and Presbyterian Reformed Church in America's General Assembly for a concluding vote. *Consistorial Minutes*, 27:10 June 1968; 28: 14 April 1969.
[59] *Consistorial Minutes*, 14 April 1969 insert.
[60] *Consistorial Minutes*, 29:16 November 1970 insert.
[61] *Consistorial Minutes*, 29:16 November 1970 insert. For more about the development of the 261 Coffee House on East Eighth Street, see "Community, Churches Back Youths' 261 Coffee House," *Holland Sentinel*, 15 August 1969, 7.
[62] *Consistorial Minutes*, 30:8 December 1971.

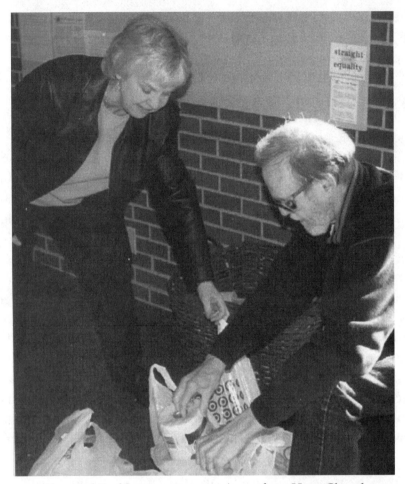

Char and Earl Laman transport items from Hope Church to the Community Kitchen

In 1973 Hope Church and the First United Methodist Church began a shared tradition. On the first Sunday of their summer schedule, the congregations worshiped together. Afterward, they enjoyed a meal of barbecued chicken. This tradition lasted at least through 1980.[63] When the First United Methodist Church was de-

---

[63] *Consistorial Minutes*, 34:9 June 1975, 35:12 January 1976, 40: 19 May 1980.

stroyed by fire on 24 January 1979, Hope Church opened its doors to the Methodists the following evening for a service of unity and dedication. After meeting for worship in Hope College's Dimnent Memorial Chapel for two years, the Methodists returned to a new sanctuary and fellowship hall across from Hope Church on Tenth Street.[64] When the sanctuary of Hope Church was renovated in 1984, the First United Methodist Church let Hope Church worship there.[65]

When the St. Francis de Sales Catholic Church was destroyed by fire in 1995, Hope Church deacons designated the Christmas offering that year as a gift to that church for rebuilding. Elders waived the Hope Church building use fee for weddings for all St. Francis members while their church was being rebuilt.[66] St. Francis de Sales held funerals, worship services, and a Good Friday service at Hope Church while its new sanctuary was being built.

Hope Church's ecumenical ties reach well beyond Holland. For decades it has included in its annual budget the Michigan Council of Churches, National Council of Churches, and World Council of Churches.

Forming a Christian Action Commission

In his report for 1967, Peterman expressed concern about the spiritual health of the congregation as measured by attendance at worship services. Observing that less than half of the total membership of Hope Church attended worship services regularly, he called the congregation to a new purpose that would reach past Hope College to respond to the needs of a wider community:

---

[64] http://.www.fumcholland.org/about/history
[65] *Consistorial Minutes,* 44:11 June 1984.
[66] *Consistorial Minutes,* 54:18 September 1995 insert, 18 December 1995.

Hope Church was organized and founded with the purpose of carrying out a particular ministry to the college community.[67] The founder of Hope Church was also the president of the Holland Academy, which later became Hope College.... With the inception of a Hope College student church, this particular relationship ... has been severed by Hope College.[68] This makes it imperative that Hope Church discover for itself a new sense of mission and purpose....

I believe that Hope Church can play a significant role in being the leaven ... in the life of our community. This has been done to a great degree as evidenced by the Day Care Center, which is held in our church, the use of our facilities by the Alcoholics Anonymous, and our participation in the City Mission and the Migrant Ministry north of town. There are many more social problems which exist in our community.... On some of these critical social problems I believe a church like Hope Church could and should speak. This speaking should be done not solely by the minister in the pulpit on Sunday morning, which might serve to alienate and antagonize members of the church, but rather should be done by the consistory in response to a careful study of responsible members of the church. I would like to recommend that the consistory approve the appointment of a "Christian Action Commission" ... to study the social, economic and political problems of our community, state and nation; [and] to recommend policy, positions and steps of action to be taken by Hope Church.... Hope Church has among its membership many people who are the leaders of the community and are involved in its power structures. Hope Church can play a significant role in the community, and this may very well be its mission in the next decades.[69]

---

[67] Peterman, like several others, failed to realize that half of Hope Church's charter members and most of Hope Church's first members were English-speaking people who settled in Holland as part of America's expansion westward and were not affiliated with the Holland Academy or Hope College. For more details about the composition of the congregation of Hope Church during its earliest years, see Appendix B. For a list of Hope College faculty and staff who became members of Hope Church, see Appendix F.
[68] Peterman apparently viewed Hillegonds's creation of a student church at Hope College as a breach of good faith between Hope College and Hope Church, a form of sheep-stealing.
[69] Apparently the Christian or Social Action Committee that was formed in 1964 in Hillegonds's time had lost some of its steam. The Christian Action Commission would have more members. *Consistorial Minutes*, 26:2 November 1967 insert.

In December 1967 the former Organizational Life Committee was replaced by a new Christian Action Committee, which would focus on social issues. Members of this committee included Jo Anne Brooks, Dorothy Cecil, the Reverend James I. Cook, Ronald Dalman, the Reverend D. Ivan Dykstra, Ruth Green, Robert Hall, Charlene Herrinton, Janice Mahaney, and Suzanne Neckers.[70]

As one of its first actions, the Christian Action Committee urged support for a 10-mill taxation levy to meet the financial needs of local public schools. The committee drafted a resolution, which consistory endorsed, and sent it on to Holland Classis for its support. Holland Classis, however, voted "no action" in response to the resolution.[71] A year later the Christian Action Committee "moved for the endorsement by Hope Church of a community college and the supporting millage in the forthcoming election." This time the process of endorsement was not to seek the approval of Holland Classis but to publicize this recommendation in the *Hope Church News* and *Holland Sentinel*.[72]

In 1970 the Christian Action Committee took a stand on another issue, one affecting the entire denomination, when it recommended that the consistory officially favor an amendment to the Constitution of the Reformed Church in America to "drop the word 'male' from the list of requirements for holding office in the Reformed

---

In promoting formation of a Christian Action Commission, Peterman was mirroring the history of the RCA, which in 1955 formed a Christian Action Commission to investigate and report to the denomination on social issues such as poverty, unemployment, women's rights, homosexuality, prison reform, and abortion. This commission grew out of the Committee on Social Welfare, which was created during the 1930s, the successor of an earlier Committee of Public Morals, which had focused in previous decades on temperance and Sunday observance. Dennis N. Voskuil, "Piety and Patriotism: Reformed Theology and Civil Religion," in *Word and World: Reformed Theology in America*, ed. James W. Van Hoeven. Historical Series of the Reformed Church in America, no. 16 (Grand Rapids: Eerdmans, 1986), 128–29.

[70] *Consistorial Minutes*, 26:11 December 1967; 27:8 January 1968.
[71] *Consistorial Minutes*, 27:11 March 1968; 8 April 1968.
[72] *Consistorial Minutes*, 28:23 June 1969.

Church." The consistory passed the recommendation, adding an amendment to ensure that a letter be sent to Holland Classis to recommend its support.[73]

By 1970 the General Synod had voted to allow women as well as men to be eligible for election as deacon or elder, and the next step in the process was to seek approval by two-thirds of the classes. Within each classis a simple majority would determine its vote. In Holland Classis the proposed amendment that elders and deacons "shall be chosen from the members of the church in full communion who are at least twenty-one years of age" carried by a vote of 25 to 20. But an accompanying amendment that ministers of the Word "are those men and women who have been inducted into that office by ordination in accordance with the Word of God and the order established by the church" was defeated by a vote of 22 to 23.[74] Neither amendment was approved by two-thirds of the classes.

Serving through Task Forces

In March 1969, the consistory, with the approval of the Reverend Herman J. Ridder, president of Western Theological Seminary, hired professor James I. Cook as director of Christian action for the 1969–70 program year. Cook's mission during this time (a sabbatical year from his teaching) was to "seek out the areas and problems of need for Christian action in the community of Holland and ... elicit the resources of Hope Church to meet those needs, hopefully establishing interest groups or 'task forces' from among the membership of Hope Church." He would work not only with Hope Church members but also with a core group of several juniors at the seminary.[75]

---

[73] *Consistorial Minutes*, 29: 9 February 1970.
[74] "Resume of Holland Classis Minutes of 9 and 10 March 1970," after *Consistorial Minutes*, 29:24 February 1970 insert.
[75] *Consistorial Minutes*, 28:17 March 1969 insert.

James I. Cook

At a worship service in September 1969, Peterman and Cook presented a dialog sermon introducing the Christian action projects and inviting participation. At the annual congregational meeting in November, Peterman stated that the "major work of the church is service" and "a pastor's main duty is to equip the congregation for service."[76]

Cook presented progress reports to consistory on the work of eight task forces:

- Suicide Prevention. People responded to phone calls from those considering suicide.
- Tutoring. Ten volunteers met on a one-to-one basis with junior high students referred by teachers and counselors.
- Kandu Industries. Seven people helped handicapped persons.
- Family-to-Family. Several couples helped first-time home-owners to find, purchase, and maintain their homes.

---

[76] *Consistorial Minutes*, 28:12 November 1969.

- Faith-to-Faith. Six members and seminary student teams met regularly at Third Reformed Church with fifteen handicapped young people.
- Big Brother. Eight men volunteered to be friends with or mentors for fatherless boys.
- Open House. Seven families volunteered to invite college students for dinner to provide an occasional alternative to dormitory life.
- Telecare. Ten people made daily phone calls, each to a particular elderly person living alone to ensure his or her health and well-being.[77]

Hope Church members Walter and Betsy Martiny in the Family-to-Family task force assist first-time home-buyers

In May 1970 the *Church Herald* featured Hope Church's Christian action projects in an article written by Cook about the origin and success of this ministry:

> Holland, Michigan, a small town by many standards, has many more needs than we can meet. Opportunities for meaningful involvement in response to Christ literally surround the church. Our program is only a small beginning in one place. We hope it will

---

[77] *Consistorial Minutes*, 28:8 December 1969; 29:24 February 1970.

encourage other beginnings in the many communities served by congregations of the Reformed Church in America.[78]

Hope Church member John De Haan as Big Brother

Many of the Christian action ministries continued for years. The Suicide Prevention task force, for example, was the first such crisis intervention program in West Michigan. It later was sustained by the Association of Holland Churches and became one of the missions of the Crisis Intervention Service of Holland and more recently the Holland/Ottawa County Helpline.[79]

---

[78] James I. Cook, "A Task Force Ministry," *Church Herald*, 15 May 1970:23.
[79] *Consistorial Minutes*, 29:13 April 1970. http://suicidehotlines.com/michigan.html

Tutoring of children was continued by Hope College's Higher Horizons program. In 2003 under the direction of Judy Vander Wilt, Hope Church began participating in Kids Hope USA, a program of church-school partnerships that pair church members with children in mentoring relationships. Started in Western Michigan in 1995, Kids Hope USA is now based in Zeeland, Michigan, and has spread to seven hundred churches in thirty denominations in thirty-three states. Since the start of Hope Church's participation, more than seventy-five volunteers have served as mentors, substitute mentors, or prayer partners for mentors working with children from Vanderbilt Charter Academy.[80]

Responding to community needs has expanded to include caring for creation. The first observation of Earth Day occurred in San Francisco on 21 March 1970. At the April meeting of the Christian Action Committee, Karen Mulder proposed that "Hope Church join the Holland Area Environmental Action Council," and Hope Church soon supported Mulder's membership on that council.[81] This was the beginning of what has developed into a Caring for Creation group. Under the leadership of Peter Boogaart in the twenty-first century, Caring for Creation conducted an energy audit of Hope Church, developed a rain garden, sponsored many hikes to regional parks, and invited various speakers to educate the congregation about environmental issues.

---

[80] Minutes 2003\Consistory 06.doc, 9 June 2003. Hope Church bulletin insert, 28 August 2011.
[81] In subsequent years, April 22 became the annual date for Earth Day, now celebrated in many countries. *Consistorial Minutes*, 29:11 April 1970, 11 May 1970. In 1990 a Recycling task force was formed with Mark Baron as its first chair. *Consistorial Minutes* 49: 4 June 1990.

Ministries of Glen O. Peterman and Marlin A. Vander Wilt, 1971–77

In 1970 the congregation voted to continue the task forces ministry and strengthen youth ministry by calling an additional full-time minister.[82] In the following year, the consistory called the Reverend Marlin A. Vander Wilt to become associate pastor.[83] He was given primary responsibility for Christian education. He had responsibility for Fish Club, the junior high youth group; Peterman had similar responsibility for High Hopes, the senior high group.

Marlin Vander Wilt

---

[82] The vote was 125 yes and 67 no.
[83] *Consistorial Minutes*, 29:8 June 1970, 30:6 June 1971.

Serving through Mission Trips

As early as 1962, senior high youth had raised funds, planned, and participated in a week-end mission trip to Chicago, where they worked at the Inner Church Parish.[84] This was the first of what became a tradition of mission trips, some for young people and others for people of all ages.

After a trip to the Mott Haven Reformed Church in the Bronx, New York, in 1971, the Senior High Youth Fellowship worked on various projects to raise money to buy a bus for that church.[85] Several Hope Church members responded to the Reverend Richard Detrich's invitation to the dedication of a new facility at Mott Haven in 1972 and enthusiastically persuaded consistory to recommend to the congregation a goal of raising $5,500 above budget to support the Mott Haven Project.[86]

Someone at the congregational meeting in 1972 questioned support for a project as far away as the Bronx instead of closer to home. Paul Elzinga responded by describing the "enthusiasm of our young people to [meet] Mott Haven's young people," the gift of the Microbus from our youth group last year, and the youth group's financial support of the anti-drug program there. "The trip which Hope Church people made to Mott Haven's dedication of a new sanctuary was a highpoint in the spiritual lives of all who went.... Their reception for Hope Church people at 2:00 a.m. was the prelude to a spirit-filled weekend of worship and dedication."[87]

Mission trips have continued to be vibrant, faith-nurturing experiences of youth groups at Hope Church. In 1991, for example, ten members of Fish Club participated in a service

---

[84] *Consistorial Minutes*, 22:1328 insert.
[85] *Consistorial Minutes*, 30:15 March 1971.
[86] *Consistorial Minutes*, 31:11 September 1972, 13 November 1972.
[87] *Consistorial Minutes*, 31:5 December 1972. This support for an Eastern church mirrors the kind of support Hope Church and other churches in Holland received from the East a century before.

project in which they helped clean a house for Holland's Housing Opportunities Made Equal (HOME) organization.[88] In 1992 members of High Hopes worked for a week with Habitat for Humanity to help build a home in West Virginia.

Many adults and young people also have put their faith into action by participating in trips to places such as Educational Concerns for Hunger Organization (ECHO) Ministries in North Fort Myers, Florida, and Water Missions International in Charleston, South Carolina. At ECHO Farm, people learned about hunger issues and performed farm chores. ECHO Farm provides seeds that are compatible with soils and climates where food crops are otherwise difficult to produce. At Water Missions International people assembled water purification equipment that was later transported to and installed in places such as Chiapas, Mexico; and Haiti. In 2007 a Think Hope silent auction, organized by the Community/World ministry, raised more than $10,000 for Water Missions.[89] Mission projects such as these enable Hope Church members to help people relieve hunger and drink safe water. They see direct results of their financial contributions and their service. Those helping to install water purification systems in Mexico, for example, better understand the difficulties of living without the conveniences many in our community take for granted.

---

[88] *Consistorial Minutes*, 50: 5 December 1991.
[89] Minutes 2007\Consistory 06.doc, 18 June 2007.

*Karen and Larry Mulder take a work break
at Barrio Sable Girls School, Chiapas, Mexico, 2002*

*Ian and Jim McKnight (on the left) begin to assemble
components for a Living Water Treatment system
at Water Missions International in 2007*

Starting Early Worship

Vander Wilt promptly established a Youth Council. Chaired by Hermina (Mickie) Lamb, it was made up of all high school Church School teachers and two young people from each grade. The Youth Council was asked to suggest new forms of ministry they would like to provide. The council defined youth ministry as youth and adults together seeking to "serve the social and spiritual needs of youth and ... encourage meaningful ways of serving others."[90]

While Peterman's main ministries were administration and worship, Vander Wilt guided the Christian education and Christian action ministries. Peterman also did most of the pastoral calling and visited the sick and homebound, and Vander Wilt also worked with various ecumenical community projects.[91]

Leola Ralph, who taught the seventh-grade Sunday School class in 1974, recalls the beginning of the Early Worship services then. Almost none of the seventh graders attended worship services, and she asked them why.

The services were too "stuffy," one said.

"Would they attend a more modern service?" she asked.

Their answer was a resounding "yes." So Leola Ralph asked the ministers if an informal more contemporary worship service were possible.

"Yes, but it would have to start as early as 8:30 in the morning." Knowing how fond seventh-graders are of sleeping in, she wasn't sure what response she would receive from her class, but they responded, saying that they would try it.

She had ideas of what the young people were looking for. Leola Ralph with her husband, George, and the ministers, planned and led the first few services. The Worship Committee recommended Early Worship services to the consistory, which approved them, first

---

[90] *Consistorial Minutes*, 30:6 June 1971, 13 September 1971, 31:28 November 1972.
[91] *Consistorial Minutes*, 31:28 November 1972. *Journey Inward – Journey Outward: Hope Church*, n.d., 7.

as an experiment and then as an established practice. Attendance grew, and others in the congregation took part in planning and leading the informal worship services. The services gave members of the congregation the opportunity to experiment with new and varied forms of worship, including drama, dialog, and drawing, among other forms. Early Worship has continued to meet during the program year ever since 1974.[92]

Starting Intergenerational Worship Activities

In 1975 Vander Wilt proposed that a Seder supper be celebrated as part of the Maundy Thursday observance. Civic leader Barbara Padnos, a stalwart advocate for social services such as the Community Action House, which she helped establish, was invited to provide instruction about Jewish traditions informing the Seder service.[93]

Vander Wilt also introduced worship and activities for children and adults during the Christian seasons of Advent and Lent. Advent family nights on Sundays included wreath-making, children's craft activities, a pot luck supper, and singing. On Wednesday nights during Lent children were included in adult groups that did not include their parents. This fostered new relationships between children and adults. Advent and Lent meetings deepened people's understandings of seasons in the church year.

Another intergenerational activity in which Hope Church has participated since the early 1980s was an annual CROP Hunger Walk. Sponsored by Church World Service, CROP Hunger Walks raise money to feed hungry people locally and throughout the world.[94]

---

[92] Communication from Leola Ralph to the author. *Consistorial Minutes*, 33:11 March 1974.
[93] "Annual Consistorial Report for 1975," *Consistorial Minutes*, 35:9 February 1976. Also communications from Carol Myers and Marlin Vander Wilt.
[94] *Consistorial Minutes*, 41:9 March 1981.

Serving Needs of Refugees and Homeless Young Women

During nearly two decades of American involvement in the Vietnam War, little if any mention is made of it in the minutes of the consistory and the various ministries of the church. Apparently, Hope Church neither rallied support for the war, as it had with World Wars I and II, nor did it protest the war, though various members may have done so. Sgt. Gordon Douglas Yntema, son of members Dwight and Cynthia Yntema, "gave his life while serving with the Special Forces in Vietnam."[95] The soldier was one of sixteen men from Holland who died in military service during the Vietnam War.[96]

As the war ended, Hope Church considered supporting a refugee family. In September 1975, the consistory authorized the Christian Action Committee to recruit a task force to bring a Vietnamese family to Holland. The task force collected money and explored employment and housing possibilities. By December, however, no family was "known to wish to come to this climate," though there was a possibility of receiving two single men.[97] In 1976 Hope Church worked with Harderwyk Christian Reformed Church to support the Nguyen Van-Chanh family.[98]

In 1977 Hope Church transferred funds left from its earlier refugee family project to a group foster home project. Members Wayne and Lucie Kramer expressed interest in using their house at 24 East 18th Street as a group foster home for teen-aged girls. A task force organized and supervised the project. Barbara Veurink, Judy Vander Wilt, Nancy Rock, and others assisted in preparing the

---

[95] *Hope Church News*, February 1968:1. Awarded an Army Medal of Honor posthumously, he was buried in Pilgrim Home Cemetery. He was survived by his wife, Peggy, and their three daughters: Elizabeth, Jane, and Julie. http://en.wikipedia.org/wiki/Gordon_Douglas_Yntema. He was baptized in Hope Church in 1947 but did not become a communicant member.
[96] http://www.vetfriends.com/memorial/mem_alphab.cfm?war_id=4&states_ID=24&page_id=1&city=city
[97] *Consistorial Minutes*, 34:8 September 1975, 10 November 1975, 8 December 1975.
[98] *Consistorial Minutes*, 35:14 June 1976, 36:14 February 1977, 10 October 1977, 14 December 1977.

house for its new purpose. By October 1977, two girls were living in the group foster home. In 1978, after considerable discussion, the Board of Deacons turned management of the home over to Bethany Christian Services.[99]

In 1980 Cuban president Fidel Castro allowed several thousand Cubans to leave for the United States. Among those who left via the Mariel boatlift were members of the Pardo family—Jose (Pepe), his wife, Olga, and their daughters, Marlen and Surlen. Jose Pardo was a brother of Mary Santamaria, who with her husband, Richard (Ricardo), and their sons, Rick and Kiki, had joined Hope Church in 1976. Vern and Lois Boersma headed a committee of Hope Church volunteers to find a home, furnishings, clothing, financial assistance, and English instruction for the Pardo family. Hope College offered a temporary home in a house that would later become Sutphen Cottage on Thirteenth Street. Hope Church members worked with the Santamaria and Pardo families to clean, paint, and furnish the home. Debbie Fike began tutoring Surlen Pardo in English, and others in the family attended English as a second language classes offered locally.

The Pardo family moved into this refurbished home in August 1980, and a month later *Hope Church News* conveyed their thanks for the prayers, generosity, and assistance in making their resettlement in Holland "a beautiful and rewarding experience." They found a church home in the Spanish-speaking Capilla la Encruzijada.[100]

In 1988, an Asian refugee family arrived: Thi Luom Pham and her son, Anh Vu. The congregation helped pay them $500 monthly for their living expenses. In 1990 Thi Luom, Pham's

Luom and Ahn Vu Pham

---

[99] *Consistorial Minutes*, 36:9 May 1977 insert, 38:10 April 1978.
[100] "Cuban Refugee Project, *Hope Church News*, 15 June 1980:2, 23 June 1980:3, 30 June 1980:5, 14 July 1980:3, 15 September 1980:3.

nephew, arrived, and the church supported him in his settling in Holland.[101] In 1992, Hope Church undertook support for another refugee family, the Nguyens.[102]

Accepting Peterman's Resignation

In 1975 the consistory slowly but steadily determined that a change in pastoral leadership would be necessary.[103] On 5 May 1976, at a specially called meeting of consistory moderated by the Reverend Robert Hoeksema of Holland Classis, Peterman read his letter of resignation as minister of Hope Church. A motion to accept his resignation was unanimously passed. Consistory agreed to provide Peterman two months' salary and the balance of his vacation time with pay. Elder Vern Boersma announced Peterman's resignation at the following Sunday's worship services.[104] In 1977 Peterman accepted a call to the Neshanic Reformed Church, where he served as pastor for sixteen years.[105]

After the departure of Peterman, the Staff (Personnel) Committee received names of more than three dozen ministers to consider but quickly focused on one. It recommended to consistory that a call be extended to Vander Wilt to become the senior pastor. Consistory unanimously passed a motion to do so. The congregation by

---

[101] *Consistorial Minutes*, 47:31 May 1988, 8 August 1988, 49:4 June 1990.
[102] *Consistorial Minutes*, 51:15 April 1992, 25 June 1992, 21 December 1992.
[103] *Consistorial Minutes*, 34:10 March 1975 insert. Charles Steketee was clerk of consistory then; he served in that role from 1973 to 1993. *Consistorial Minutes*, 32:10 September 1973, 52:14 November 1993.
[104] *Consistorial Minutes*, 35:5 May 1976. Peterman's letter of resignation was not included in minutes of consistory or of the elders. *Hope Church News* provided no information about the resignation. According to Vern Boersma, vice-president of consistory at that time, the reasons for resigning cited in Peterman's letter were not the real reasons for his departure. The real reasons were related to unprofessional conduct.
[105] Gasero, *Historical Directory*, 304. The Neshanic Reformed Church is in New Jersey.

an overwhelming margin supported the motion of the consistory, and Vander Wilt was installed as senior pastor.[106]

Meanwhile, Marion de Velder, after serving as the first general secretary of the RCA 1968-77, chose to return to Hope Church in his retirement.[107] The consistory named him "Pastor Emeritus" of Hope Church, and he assisted Vander Wilt with visitation and preaching.[108]

Writing the Mission Statement

Looking toward a more focused vision for Hope Church under new leadership, the consistory in 1977 decided to develop a Mission Statement and a five-year plan for putting it into practice. These would begin at its September retreat at Castle Park Lodge. "Come prepared to dream, to struggle, to think, to share and to decide," Vander Wilt announced.[109]

At the retreat, the consistory resolved to proceed toward the restoration/renovation of the church facility, improve communications within the church, and complete a mission statement as outlined at the retreat. Elder David Myers and deacon George Ralph soon turned an outline and notes from the retreat into a Mission Statement:[110]

HOPE CHURCH
STATEMENT OF MISSION

> Now there are varieties of gifts, but the same Spirit,
> and there are varieties of service, but the same Lord,
> and there are varieties of works, but it is the same God

---

[106] The congregational vote to call Vander Wilt as senior pastor was 124 yes and 8 no. *Consistorial Minutes*, 36:10 January 1977, 14 February 1977, 6 March 1977, 10 October 1977.
[107] Gasero, *Historical Directory*, 101. Before serving as general secretary of the RCA, he served as pastor of the Central Reformed Church, Grand Rapids, MI, 1959-61 and as stated clerk of General Synod 1961-68.
[108] *Consistorial Minutes*, 37:10 October 1977.
[109] *Consistorial Minutes*, 37:15 August 1977 insert.
[110] *Consistorial Minutes*, 36:16-17 September 1977.

> who inspires them all in every one. To each is given
> the manifestation of the Spirit for the common good.
> I Corinthians 12:4–7

Hope Church affirms the unity which binds together diverse people as the church universal. Unity is possible and diversity is celebrated because the church is the very body of Christ.

No single congregation can fulfill equally all of the functions for which the Spirit equips the whole people of God. Hope Church recognizes that she is the representative, in one special time and place, of the body of Christ. In this spirit, Hope Church has established the following goals:

<u>To Pioneer</u>: Aware of our own heritage as a pioneering people, Hope Church aspires to creativity and excellence in worship, Christian nurture, governance, and outreach. We aim to experiment courageously and, when an experiment proves unsuccessful, to press ahead in new directions and with new methods.

<u>To Be Open</u>: Hope Church seeks to maintain the diversity in which she finds strength. We welcome people with varied interests, talents and backgrounds. We strive to be a community in which each member listens to and has genuine concern for all other members.

<u>To Grow in Faith</u>: Hope Church aims to grow, not merely in numbers, but more importantly, in depth of Christian commitment. We seek to be faithful to our calling as the people of God by identifying and eliciting each member's particular gifts and directing these in obedience to God's Word.

<u>To Lead in Christian Action</u>: Hope Church seeks to be servant to the human community, both locally and worldwide. We aim to serve both institutionally and through the total lives of our people.

> For just as the body is one and has many members,
> and all the members of the body, though many, are one body,
> so it is with Christ. For by one Spirit we were all
> baptized into one body—Jews or Greeks, slaves or free—
> and all were made to drink of one Spirit.
> Corinthians 12:12–13[111]

Embraced by verses from Paul's first letter to the Corinthian church, the mission statement has withstood the test of more than

---

[111] *Consistorial Minutes*, 38:13 February 1978.

three decades. With only a few minor revisions made to it since 1977,[112] the mission statement stands as a faithful guide to the congregation.

Ministries of Marlin A. Vander Wilt and Paul R. Fries, 1978–82

To serve as co-pastor with Vander Wilt, Hope Church called the Reverend Paul R. Fries in 1978. He accepted the call and with his family moved to Holland from New Jersey, where he served as a professor of theology at New Brunswick Theological Seminary for ten years. As Vander Wilt had done, Fries purchased a house.[113]

Fries was given primary responsibility for planning worship and for preaching in both the Early Worship and later worship services. Vander Wilt was given primary responsibility for administration of staff and consistory, direction of Christian education and youth

---

[112] Changes through 2011 include the following: Removal of all underlining, changing "works" to "working" in the first scripture passage, removing the final sentence from the first scripture passage, enclosing both scripture passages within double quotation marks, adding parentheses around the scripture citations, changing "church universal" to "Church Universal," changing "church is the very body" to "Church is the very Body," changing "the representative" to "one representative," changing "body of Christ" to "Body of Christ," changing the four infinitive phrase headings to all capital letters, and changing "and, when an experiment" to "and when an experiment," and changing "grow, not merely in numbers, but more" to "grow—not merely in numbers—but, more."

[113] *Consistorial Minutes*, 38:15 May 1978, 24 May 1978, 12 June 1978. In June 1973, at the recommendation of the Property Committee and consistory, the congregation voted to approve selling the parsonage and providing Peterman a housing allowance equal to that being paid to Vander Wilt. The parsonage, located at 99 West 11th Street, had been purchased in 1957 after the previous parsonage, immediately west of the church, was converted into church school classrooms, assembly room and offices before being removed to make way for the education wing. *Consistorial Minutes*, 32:9 April 1973, 14 May 1973, 24 June 1973.

ministry, and coordination of student interns. They shared pastoral care and began lectionary-based preaching at Hope Church.[114]

Paul R. Fries

Fries saw his ministry at Hope Church as a way to learn how a seminary can better prepare students for parish ministry. He established long-range planning for the Early Worship services. Several times a year, he, worship leaders, and musicians met together to read lectionary texts for upcoming months, discuss their meanings and themes, and plan the liturgy for those services.

To put into practice the "grow in faith" portion of the mission statement, Hope Church in 1980 began a comprehensive study of the Bible by means of the Bethel Bible Series. James I. Cook and Marlin Vander Wilt attended the requisite classes to teach the series. Cook

---

[114] Lectionary-based preaching is a practice followed by many mainline denominations. The Revised Common Lectionary contains for each Sunday a passage from the Old Testament, a Psalm, one of the Gospels, and another passage from the New Testament. The prescribed readings repeat every three years.

recruited a class of nine or ten people who committed to a two-year class covering the Old Testament in the first year and the New Testament in the second year. When he began the second year, Vander Wilt recruited a class of fourteen people who committed to a two-year class. After the conclusion of Cook's class, Karen Mulder taught three congregational-phase classes of one year each in an abbreviated version of the Old and New Testaments. The Bethel Bible Series, said Vander Wilt, "gave a Biblical foundation to a large segment of the Hope congregation."[115]

Remodeling in the Early 1980s

In 1964 the congregation had purchased a new organ from the Reuter Company of Lawrence, Kansas,[116] but after construction of the education wing in 1962, it had put off renovation of the church sanctuary. With the arrival of Fries as co-pastor, attention centered on deciding whether to build a new church and parish hall on the current site, to extensively remodel the existing facility, or to continue to make minor repairs.

In February 1978, elder Geraldine Dykhuizen reported to consistory that the rose window on the east side of the church sanctuary was "in acute danger of being blown out at any time." While decisions about whether to remodel or rebuild were being considered, some needs could not wait. In the late 1970s and early '80s, the consistory approved this and other similar necessary repairs.[117] In his first annual report to the consistory, Vander Wilt stated, "The single five-year goal adopted last year was that we 'be in a totally renovated and functional facility within five years.' We are on the way!"[118]

---

[115] Communications from Marlin Vander Wilt December 2011 and January 2012.
[116] *Consistorial Minutes*, 23:21 September 1964.
[117] *Consistorial Minutes*, 37:14 November 1977.
[118] *Consistorial Minutes*, 38:30 September 1978 insert. Vander Wilt also proposed in this report the start of monthly executive leadership meetings

Parish hall in mid-twentieth century

To learn the wishes of the congregation, a questionnaire was prepared. Among questions asked were which parts of the church should be kept in a new or renovated church facility. By far, the Last Supper carving and the stained-glass memorial windows in the sanctuary were favored.[119] Many added comments:

"I think the slanted sanctuary floor, together with the semi-circular seating, contributes to the feeling of community in worship," Carol Myers wrote.

"Hope Church people played a significant role in the history of Holland," wrote Martha Kaiser. "How wonderful it would be to have the historically significant building to show our children ... an old building preserved, but used in creative, adaptive fashion to minister to today."[120]

---

to develop the agenda for consistory meetings. A month later the consistory approved establishing a "a monthly executive review session."
[119] *Consistorial Minutes*, 39:2 January 1979 insert. Of the 221 responses returned, 86% wanted to keep the carving and 80% the windows. Less important were pulpit and lectern (44%), exterior brick appearance (37%), bell tower (32%), present pews (29%), and Eleventh Street entrance (28%).
[120] *Consistorial Minutes*, 39:2 January 1979 insert.

Stanley Rock wrote: "I think that it is important that Hope Church reflect a sense of continuity and history using elements of the past, yet thrusting itself into God's future."[121]

In December Lawrence W. (Bill) Lamb Jr., reporting for the Building Committee, announced Diekema and Hamman of Kalamazoo as the architectural firm for planning construction and renovation. Consistory approved engaging this firm.[122]

In August 1980 the congregation authorized the consistory to construct a Parish Life Center (the area consisting of Commons I and II, the choir room, main offices, and the central hallway), renovate the education wing, and repair the sanctuary. It also approved $700,000 to be raised over three years to include costs of construction and a 10 percent outreach goal for two projects: the RCA Church Growth Fund and the Cook Center for Theological Research at Western Theological Seminary.[123] In February 1981 the consistory approved a bid of $600,000 from Lakewood Construction Company to serve as contractor for the building project.[124] The 1874 Hope Church sanctuary, which in 1902 became a parish hall, was razed in 1981.[125]

The bell tower of the 1874 church, however, was kept. After a fire destroyed Van Raalte Hall on the Hope College campus on 28 April 1980, Veneklasen bricks salvaged from the fire were used to make repairs to the church. There was a close match between the bricks of Van Raalte Hall built in 1903 and the Hope Church sanctuary completed in 1902. More than two hundred bricks were replaced,[126] another connection between Hope College and Hope Church.

---

[121] *Consistorial Minutes*, 39:2 January 1979 insert.
[122] *Consistorial Minutes*, 39:10 December 1979.
[123] *Consistorial Minutes*, 40:7 August 1980. Unlike the close vote to expand the church facility in 1957, the 182 yes to 11 no vote in 1980 was a clear mandate to proceed.
[124] *Consistorial Minutes*, 41:9 February 1981.
[125] *Our Time for Rededication*, 1982, 2. Note the interior of the parish hall in the following picture and compare it with the interiors of the 1874 church shown in chapter 2.
[126] Wichers, *Century of Hope*, 134. *Holland Sentinel*, 30 May 1980.

East view of church and parish hall before Parish Life Center was built

East view of church after Parish Life Center was built

The new Parish Life Center was dedicated on 10 January 1982, the beginning of a year-long celebration of rededication. Architect Gerry Diekema presented the keys, and Lawrence W. (Bill) Lamb, chair of the Design and Construction committee, and Clarence J.

Becker, general chair of the building project, were recognized for their efforts.[127]

In the booklet for the dedicatory service, Vander Wilt and Fries expressed gratitude to the people who through the previous 120 years had "worked to place in our hands a living, searching and vital congregation" and described anticipated improvements to the education wing and sanctuary:

> We build upon the foundations of the past, a fact which is symbolized by the preservation of the bell tower which was built in 1874. The courage and strength of these pioneers continue to give impetus and character to our present ministry....
>
> Plans to refurbish the Education Center reflect a new interest in adult education, the need for a youth center and more adequate space for elementary and pre-school and the Holland Day Care Center. Finally, we anticipate the re-decoration of the sanctuary to enhance our worship.[128]

Not only was the bell tower from the 1874 church preserved but also the Nicodemus Bosch memorial window, which had graced the chancel from the mid-1940s until 1965, found a new home in the north exterior wall of the new east entrance. That would be its location from 1981 until 1995.[129]

The new Commons I area in the Parish Life Center contained six facet-slab glass windows depicting seasons of the Christian and natural calendars. The six windows were a gift of the John Vander Broek family in memory of Gertrude Vander Broek.[130] The new facility also contained a music room, parlor, kitchen, and several administrative offices. "The intent has never been to provide for our own comfort," stated the dedicatory booklet, "but always to

---

[127] *Our Time for Rededication*, 1982.
[128] *Our Time for Rededication*. The education wing was later called the education center.
[129] This window was removed from the chancel to accommodate pipes for a new organ installed in 1965. *Consistorial Minutes*, 33:14 January 1974. Between 1965 and 1981 the window was crated and safely stored in the church basement.
[130] See pages 239–46 for these and other memorial artworks in Hope Church.

keep the ministry of Jesus Christ alive and growing at Hope Church, reaching out in the center of our community."[131]

Amid the new construction and plans for rededication, Fries received a call from the Board of Theological Education to rejoin the faculty of New Brunswick Seminary as a professor of theology and ministry. He accepted that call, and his pastoral relationship with Hope Church ended two months later.[132] In May, the consistory changed Vander Wilt's title from co-pastor to senior pastor.[133]

On 27 June 1982, Hope Church held a service of dedication for its restored bell tower and steeple. At that service, the Reverend James Van Hoeven, pastor of the First Church in Albany, New York, one of the oldest Reformed churches in America, presented a gift from that congregation to Hope Church.

The gift, a rooster weathervane made of beaten brass, came fresh from the Netherlands. The weathervane was a replica of the oldest church weathervane in the United States. The original, now in the First Church's museum, had topped the steeple of that church since 1656. Symbolizing the cock that crowed when Peter denied Christ, it was a call to be true to the faith.

Rooster weathervane, a gift from First Church, Albany

---

[131] *Our Time for Rededication.*
[132] *Consistorial Minutes,* 41:23 November 1981, 42:13 January 1982 insert.
[133] *Consistorial Minutes,* 42:24 May 1982.

In presenting the gift, Van Hoeven stated that it commemorated the visit by the Reverend Isaac N. Wyckoff from Albany to the Holland colony in 1849 to invite Albertus C. Van Raalte and his followers to join the Dutch Reformed Church in the United States. Wyckoff was also the pastor to whom Phelps had confessed his faith and by whom he was ordained.[134] In accepting the weathervane, elder Ekdal Buys, vice-president of the Hope Church consistory, commented:

> I trust, Reverend Jim, that your journey here did not parallel that of Dr. Wyckoff. History tells us that he used stagecoach from Pittsburgh to Cleveland, then steamboat to Detroit, and finally [came] to the shores of Black Lake by a team and wagon. With Dr. Van Raalte and others he followed the Indian Trails, from one clearing and settlement to another. His purpose was to influence the colony to merge with the Reformed Church in America. Dr. Wyckoff and his companions even swam the Black River to reach Groningen and spent the evening with the Rev. [Cornelius] Vander Meulen in Zeeland. It is interesting to note that in Zeeland they were 'lavished with bread, butter, and coffee' before departing for Vriesland.[135]

During 1982, plans for renovating the sanctuary proceeded. The chancel lighting was improved. Pairs of pews on the east and west sides of the chancel were removed, and a removable railing was extended across the chancel from east to west. The organ console was turned 90 degrees so that the organist would face the center of the chancel, and a mirror was removed. The Last Supper woodcarving was cleaned, repaired, and oiled.[136] On 24 October 1982 Hope Church celebrated the renovation with a community open house with the First United Methodist Church, which had recently completed the rebuilding of its church after the fire that had destroyed it in January 1979.[137] Additional renovations to

---

[134] "In Memoriam, *Anchor*, October 1896, 10.
[135] "Rooster Weathervane," http://www.hopechurchrca.org/rooster.html.
[136] *Consistorial Minutes*, 42:25 August 1982 insert.
[137] *Consistorial Minutes*, 42:11 October 1982.

restore the sanctuary to more nearly resemble its 1902 design were made in 1984.[138]

Sanctuary after 1984 renovations

Reflecting on the changes to the structure of Hope Church during several decades, James B. Hinkamp, who grew up in this church and returned to it in 1999 after living away from Holland for more than sixty years, concluded:

---

[138] Note the presence of flags near the front. Citing several authorities, the Worship Ministry in 1989 recommended not displaying the American flag and the "so-called Christian flag" anywhere on the church premises. *Consistorial Minutes*, 48:22 May 1989. The consistory later approved a policy not to have flags in the sanctuary. *Consistorial Minutes*, 50:17 June 1991. For the Fourth of July Sunday in 2011 the American flag was displayed in the narthex "as a sign of honor, gratitude and respect." Hope Church bulletin, 3 July 2011.

> One of my greatest joys is to sit in our sanctuary and enjoy its appearance. It is much the same today as it was when the market crashed in 1929. A few doors have disappeared, the pulpit platform has disappeared and some pew positions have been changed, but the general appearance is unchanged: The chandelier, rose window, the side windows; the overall impression is the same. Our ancestors did it right and it still has the peaceful and worshipful atmosphere that it has always had.
> But changes do take place. Our church parlors have been completely modernized. We now have an excellent kitchen, church offices, and meeting rooms. All of these were essentially non-existent back then.[139]

In May 1983 Vander Wilt—who had shepherded the congregation through the planning, financing, and construction of the Parish Life Center and the beginnings of renovation of the sanctuary—received a call from the American Reformed Church in Orange City, Iowa. He accepted that call, and the consistory began to form a search committee to find first a senior pastor and then an associate pastor.[140]

In the months before he left, Vander Wilt introduced the consistory and congregation to serving Communion by intinction, helped the consistory establish an Endowment Fund Board, and urged the church to investigate possible uses of a computer to assist in administrative and educational tasks. Ekdal Buys became the first chair of the Endowment Fund Board, and Frank Sherburne wrote a

---

[139] Jim Hinkamp also remembers a tale about the belfry tower: "More than sixty years ago—maybe seventy years—a rope was stretched through the trees between the Hope Church belfry and that of the Methodist Church a short block away. This enabled a man in the Hope Church belfry to surreptitiously ring the Methodist Church bell [one night]. This caused great consternation, especially since the door to the Methodist belfry had been fastened shut. Finally it was opened and the secret was out. Men with flashlights began tracing the rope through the trees to Hope's belfry. All this was visible to the man in Hope's belfry who took the hint and left the scene of the crime. He has not been apprehended to this day." Vander Haar, *Branches of the Vine*, January 2012.
[140] *Consistorial Minutes*, 43:9 May 1982, 31 May 1983, 13 June 1983.

report recommending uses for a computer and creation of a Computerization Feasibility task force.[141]

In the dozen years Vander Wilt served as associate pastor, co-pastor, and then pastor, he guided Hope Church through a difficult time of transition, helped its members to continue to work with other Holland churches in Christian actions of service and social justice, and prompted and helped celebrate major renovations of the church facility. Like the Bergens and the de Velders, Marlin Vander Wilt and his wife, Judy, would return to Hope Church.

Peacemaking

In the early 1980s, Hope Church elders Elsie Lamb and Jo Anne Brooks were translating their Christian faith into actions that challenged the status quo in the nation and world. With a passion for world peace, they attended a World Peacemakers gathering in Washington, D.C., and returned to Holland with plans to start a Holland Peacemakers group. In 1982, the Holland World Peacemaker group began arranging workshops, planning vigils, and protesting America's role in the proliferation of nuclear weapons.[142]

On 18 November 1983 the *Holland Sentinel* published on its opinion page two letters from Hope Church members. The first was a letter from Elsie Lamb and thirty other Holland Peacemakers protesting the production of missile engines by Williams International of Walled Lake, Michigan:

> We, the Holland Peacemakers, endorse the action proposed by the Covenant for Peace scheduled for Nov. 27–Dec. 2, 1983.
> This action will be a daily non-violent blockade of Williams International....
> We as a group of individuals feel called to peacemaking. The pleas for dialogue have been ignored. The deployment of Cruise and Pershing II missiles is now imminent.

---

[141] *Consistorial Minutes*, 43:13 June 1983, 11 July 1983.
[142] Ratmeyer, *Hands, Hearts, and Voices*, 56.

> We feel that, at this time, Christian Peacemakers ... are being placed in the position of choosing between obedience to civil law or obedience to the higher dictates of Christ.
>
> In pursuit of peace and justice for our world we give our endorsement of Covenant for Peace as they follow the higher dictates of Christ.[143]

Elsie Lamb not only wrote the letter but also put her words into actions, and she faced the consequences:

> I joined fifty other protesters at Williams International, the largest manufacturer of cruise missile engines at Walled Lake, Michigan. Six of us linked arms and blockaded and prayed at the plant entrance at 6 a.m. on the first day of Advent. I was arrested and jailed for eight days and nights.
>
> I found myself in a large cell with eight other women who had been arrested on various charges.... In general, I was where I was supposed to be, unafraid and enjoying these new friends.[144]

Elsie Lamb

Elsie Lamb and other protesters were found guilty of trespassing and placed on probation. She paid a fine, and once a month for one year she reported to authorities in Pontiac.[145] The editor of the *Holland Sentinel* rebuked her: "Civil disobedience must be

---

[143] "Readertorials," *Holland Sentinel*, 18 November 1983.
[144] Ratmeyer, *Hands, Hearts, and Voices*, 56.
[145] Ratmeyer, *Hands, Hearts, and Voices*, 56–57.

answered. Although people have the freedom to express themselves, the tactics used by Lamb ... should not be condoned."[146] Two letter-writers berated her action: "Lamb and her other law-breaking associates are dupes of the KGB and hamper our effort to avoid war through military power," wrote one. "Lamb's naive, un-American activities send the wrong signal to Moscow and give aid and comfort to the Godless Soviet nation,"[147] wrote another.

But six letter-writers came to Lamb's defense, the most exemplary among them from her friend and Hope Church deacon, Jo Anne Brooks. Chiding the editor, she wrote:

> I am amazed at your lack of understanding of civil disobedience when our whole country was founded on the proposition that man should never surrender his ultimate loyalty to the state. Civil disobedience has been justified by responsible authorities—from Socrates, St. Peter and Thomas Jefferson to those who helped give birth to our nation, to the abolition of slavery, the right of women to vote, the achievement of religious liberty, the recognition of the rights of organized labor, and the securing of the civil rights of minority groups.
>
> The cost to the taxpayer for their court proceedings and jailing are minuscule compared to the costs of continued nuclear buildup—$1.5 trillion—in the next decade. Even President Reagan's top economic advisor, Martin Feldstein, has said recently that defense spending is a major cause for the country's record deficits and a serious threat to economic recovery.[148]

Undaunted, Elsie Lamb continued to make peacemaking trips, not just in Michigan but around the world. Under the auspices of the World Council of Churches, she traveled to the Soviet Union for a US/USSR Church Relations seminar in 1983, "a time when then

---

[146] "Elsie Lamb's Crusade," *Holland Sentinel*, 8 December 1983.
[147] "Readertorials," *Holland Sentinel*, 20 December 1983.
[148] "Readertorials," *Holland Sentinel*, 14 and 15 December 1983.

President Ronald Reagan called the Soviet Union 'the evil empire'.... The people there were just like me and you—they want peace."[149]

"Upon my return from the trip to the Soviet Union," said Lamb, "I shared my slide presentation, Faces of Russia, with more than one hundred congregations in Michigan and Wisconsin. I saved all the offerings I received and used them to send another young woman to the Soviet Union."[150]

Among others from Holland area churches, Elsie Lamb traveled with RCA missionary Wendell Karsen to China in 1987. With a group of students from Western Theological Seminary led by Sonja Stewart, professor of religious education, she traveled to El Salvador and Nicaragua in 1990.

In 1995 with Jo Anne Brooks, Elsie Lamb traveled to Okinawa and Hiroshima, Japan, with the Japan North America Commission of the National Council of Churches to study issues of war and peace from 1945 to 1995.[151] The two represented the Reformed Church in America, but paid their own way. They took with them 1,000 Hope Church bulletins folded into paper cranes. According to a legend in Japan, "if one folds 1,000 paper cranes it will be a protection from illness."

> The legend became famous by a little girl who died from leukemia 10 years after the atomic bombing ... by Allied forces in response to the Japanese attack on Pearl Harbor. The girl made more than 900 paper cranes in her hospital bed before she died. Since then making paper cranes has been a sign of peace.[152]

---

[149] John Burdick, "Hope Church on Mission of Peace," *Holland Sentinel*, 17 February 1995. She covered her own costs. *Consistorial Minutes* 44:4 January 1984.
[150] Ratmeyer, *Hands, Hearts, and Voices*, 57.
[151] Ratmeyer, *Hands, Hearts, and Voices*, 57.
[152] Burdick, "Hope Church on Mission of Peace."

Speaking for the congregation, the Reverend Dennis L. TeBeest stated, "The making of the cranes has been a way for us to share prayers for healing and for peace. For Elsie this is incredibly holistic. All of her life has been wrapped up in the peace of Christ."[153]

"As Christians," said Elsie Lamb, "we admit that both sides did violent things.... We have to forgive and move on to peaceful reconciliation."[154]

Advocating Civil Rights for Homosexual Persons

The second letter published on the opinion page of the 18 November 1983 *Holland Sentinel* was from the consistory of Hope Reformed Church, signed by Larry Mulder, its vice-president:

> Representative [Jim] Dressel has sponsored a bill (Bill 5000) which would prohibit discrimination on the basis of sexual orientation. While sincere Christians debate homosexuality, there is only one response a Christian can make to another human being: To love my neighbor as myself.
>
> Is the homosexual my neighbor? Perhaps the Reformed Church in America Theological Commission's statement on Homosexual Rights will help each of us to consider this issue. The statement says:
>
> "Approval of the homosexual orientation or acts is not a prerequisite to firm support of basic civil rights for homosexual persons....
>
> While we cannot affirm homosexual behavior, at the same time we are convinced that the denial of human and civil rights to homosexuals is inconsistent with the biblical witness and Reformed theology." (Minutes of the General Synod, Reformed Church in America, June 1978, page 239.)[155]

---

[153] Burdick, "Hope Church on Mission of Peace."
[154] Burdick, "Hope Church on Mission of Peace."
[155] "Readertorials," *The Holland Sentinel*, 18 November 1983. Four days earlier, consistory had approved this letter. *Consistorial Minutes* 43:14 November 1983. Republican Jim Dressel, a former Air Force pilot, was in this third term as state representative from Ottawa County when he

Unlike Lamb's letter, Mulder's letter prompted few responses. More readers were critical of the decision made by the superintendent of West Ottawa Schools to allow Representative Dressel to speak to high school students "on rights for homosexuals." "Neither God nor man can condone homosexuality. It is not normal. It is not an alternative. It is a perversion. It is sin," wrote the Reverend Mark Zimmer.[156]

In contrast, Hope Church elder David Myers expressed his hope that local legislators would have the "wisdom, compassion, and courage" to distinguish between being justly intolerant of "reprehensible sexual acts by either homosexuals or heterosexuals" and supporting "basic human rights for persons, regardless of their unchosen sexual orientation."[157] The consistory's letter to the *Sentinel* was another step in Hope Church's journey toward full inclusion of all—regardless of race, gender, physical handicaps, or sexual orientation—into membership and into ministries.

---

introduced HB 5000, a bill to add "sexual orientation" to the state's Eliott-Larsen Civil Rights Act. Dressel was defeated for re-election the following year and later served as president of the Michigan Organization for Human Rights. Todd VerBeek, "Jim Dressel (Oct. 14, 1943–Mar. 27, 1992)," *Network News*, May 1992. Republished at http://toddverbeek.com/diffangle/JimDressel.html

[156] "Readertorials," *Holland Sentinel*, 28 November 1983. Zimmer was from a denomination other than the Reformed Church in America.

[157] "Readertorials," *The Holland Sentinel*, 10 December 1983.

7 ... Expanding Inclusion

Hope Church has a long history of embracing inclusion. It was a pioneer in welcoming people of non-Dutch ethnic groups. It was the first church in Holland to allow both women and men to vote to call ministers (1878) and elect deacons and elders (1879). It was the first Reformed Church in Holland to build a ramp for those in wheelchairs and among the first churches in America to install a loop system to aid people with hearing loss. It was among the first Western churches in the denomination to elect women as deacons and elders. It was a leader in preparing for the participation of children in the Lord's Supper. It was first in the denomination to call a woman to become its senior pastor (though not the first to call a woman as sole pastor). It was the first Reformed Church congregation in Holland to welcome into membership and into consistory those who are homosexual.

Welcoming People of Various Ethnic Groups into Membership

As early as 1872, Hope Church welcomed into communicant membership Motoitero Oghimi, Kumaje Kimura, and Rio Zon Tsugawa—three young men from Japan who were students in the Hope Preparatory School and Hope College.[1] In 1930, it received into membership Abraham Naoum, a Hope College student from the United Protestant Mission of Iraq, and requested financial aid from the Classical Board of Benevolences for his studies.[2] In 1930

---

[1] *Elders' Minutes of Second Reformed Protestant Dutch Church of Holland, Michigan*, 1 June 1872:27–28.
[2] *Consistorial Minutes*, 3:21 September 1930. The student, having been befriended by missionary John Van Ess and sent to Hope College, graduated in 1933. After graduate study at Massachusetts State College in pharmacy, he returned to Iraq, where he became a businessman, taught English, and served as a translator. His daughter Margaret (Maggie) Naoum and

it also welcomed into membership its first African-American member, James Dooley, a student at Hope College, by letter of transfer from the Zion African Methodist Episcopal Church of Brewton, Alabama.[3] His parents were the first of many at the Southern Normal School in Brewton who were supported by the Reformed Church in America over a span well over a half-century.[4] In 1991 Asian-American Alan Yamaoka was elected as deacon,[5] and in 1993 African-American Fronse Smith was elected as an elder.

Allowing Women to Vote to Call Pastors and Elect Consistory Members

As early as 1878, the Hope Church consistory invited both men and women to vote to call a minister. Beginning in 1879, it allowed men and women to elect consistory members.[6] These advances were perhaps the earliest recognition in a Reformed Church west of New York that women and men are equally capable in decision-making and leadership. Further progress would be slow until nearly a century later the Reformed Church in America began to allow women to serve as ordained deacons, elders, and ministers of Word and Sacrament.

---

granddaughter Sarah Naoum attended Hope College. Abraham Naoum and his wife moved in 1992 from Iraq to Kalamazoo, MI, where they lived with their daughter for more than a decade before the couple died.
[3] *Consistorial Minutes*, 3:25 September 1930, 13 December 1930. James Dooley was also the first African-American graduate of Hope College. "United in Vision," *News from Hope* 43, no. 3 (December 2011):11.
[4] Gasero, *Historical Directory*, 702–04.
[5] His parents, Ted and Yukiko Yamaoka, with Ted and Toshi Sasamoto were received by adult baptism in 1952.
[6] *Consistorial Minutes*, 1: 10 October 1878, 5 December 1879. In the Reformed Church in America, the decision of when women are allowed to vote in congregational meetings is left to each congregation's consistory to decide.

Improving Accessibility

Meanwhile, Hope Church made worship more accessible to all, including those afflicted by polio and those experiencing hearing loss. Church member Helen De Weerd remembers what attracted her and her husband to Hope Church:

> My husband, Millard, had not walked since he had polio at age five. We wanted to be married in church, but at that time there was no church in town that was handicapped-accessible. Riding around one day we noticed a very rough wooden ramp leading to the Hope Church entrance. We went in, introduced ourselves to the minister, and asked if he would marry us. He agreed and said that if we kept coming to Hope Church, a more permanent ramp would be built. It was.
>
> The wedding was set for five o'clock on a certain afternoon. 5:20 came along; then 5:30 and still no pastor. We were getting quite concerned. Finally the pastor and his wife, wearing shorts, arrived along with an exchange student similarly attired. No excuses were made and the wedding proceeded.
>
> It was two weeks later when we invited the pastor and his wife over for dinner that the story came out. They had been on their way for a game of miniature golf. Riding past the church, the pastor's wife remarked on some cars parked in the lot. 'What's going on?' she said. Said he, 'Nothing that I know of ... oh was that wedding today? I thought it was tomorrow.'
>
> I am sure that this was an act of providence. I believe that if the wedding had been postponed it would have been hard to get Millard back again for that ordeal. We have always been happy that we 'happened' upon Hope church.[7]

The minister was the Reverend Hillegonds, and the wedding was on 12 July 1962.

---

[7] Vander Haar, ed. *Branches of the Vine*, January 2012.

Helen and Millard De Weerd

To make Hope Church more accessible to those living in retirement homes, the consistory began to explore bus transportation to and from Hope Church for residents of Freedom Village and Resthaven's Warm Friend. On 17 December 2000, the first busload arrived. The bus was full, and many people have found this a welcome means of transportation, a way to enable them to participate in worship and community.[8]

Addressing the Needs of Those with Hearing Loss

To aid those with hearing difficulties and those unable to come to church, Hope Church as early as 1 November 1953 began to broadcast its traditional worship services on Holland radio station

---

[8] Exploration of transportation for residents of Freedom Village began in 1995. *Consistorial Minutes*, 54:21 August 1995. Minutes 2000\Consistory 12.doc, 18 December 2000. In 2011, as an experiment, bus transportation was also provided to residents of Waverly Meadows and Appledorn. Minutes 2011\Consistory 06.doc, 13 June 2011.

WHTC.[9] Responses to the broadcasts, which began as an experiment, were encouraging. "Our radio ministry ... each Sunday is proving to be the best job of public relations that Hope Church has undertaken," the *Consistorial Minutes* reported. "Our own shut-ins and hard of hearing are very appreciative."[10] Helpful as the radio broadcasts were, allowing listeners to turn up the volume to suit their needs, they did nothing to include them within the congregation during worship services.

Elder David Myers encouraged the installation of advanced hearing-enhancement systems. But, even after an infrared system with receivers was installed in Hope Church in 1995, people rarely used the assistive-hearing headsets. Some found the system inconvenient, and others perhaps were too embarrassed by their hearing condition to be seen using them.

A major advance came after Myers experienced the dramatic difference made by induction hearing loop technology.[11] When he was attending a worship service in the eight-hundred-year-old Iona Abbey in Scotland, which had installed an induction loop system, he at first found it difficult to hear the amplified music and the words of the speaker. But when he switched on the telecoil (T-coil) function of his hearing aid, "the result was dramatic. The babble of people was replaced by the sweet harmonies of musicians playing in front of microphones across the Abbey. My mouth fell open. It was like listening to a CD over a headset. I was in ecstasy, feeling a little like the blind man who, having adapted to blindness, now reveled in the vision restored by Jesus. The scales had fallen from my ears. With the T-coil ... on I was in auditory heaven."[12]

---

[9] *Consistorial Minutes*, 12 October 1953, 12:604.
[10] *Consistorial Minutes*, 20 May 1954, 12:943 insert.
[11] The hearing loop, or induction loop, is a thin strand of copper wire that radiates electromagnetic signals. When a hearing aid or cochlear implant with a telecoil (T-coil) sensor that can pick up these signals is turned on, the telecoil filters out background sounds, picking up, amplifying, and transmitting only sounds coming from a microphone.
[12] David Myers, "Do You Hear What I Hear?" *Church Herald*, February 2002, 30.

The combination of a hearing loop in a room with a T-coil in a hearing aid effectively includes people in worship services who were previously excluded. This form of assistive listening, said David Myers, is "the equivalent of a wheelchair ramp for people who used to be socially isolated because of their hearing loss."[13]

David Myers

Myers soon had a hearing loop installed in his home, and he provided incentives for its installation in 2002 in Hope Church's sanctuary and Commons I as he had for the installation of the infra-red system. Soon after the hearing loops were installed, ten people began using them, and the number has been steadily increasing.[14] Myers, working with the Holland Community Foundation, subsidized the addition of hearing loops in places on the Hope College campus and around Holland. He persuaded the Grand Rapids

---

[13] David Myers, quoted by John Tierney, "A Hearing Aid That Cuts Out All the Clatter," *New York Times*, 23 October 2011. http://www.nytimes.com/2011/10/24/science/24loops.html
[14] Myers, "A Hearing Aid," *New York Times*.

airport to add hearing loops and has made it one of his avocations to advocate for hearing loop technology.[15]

Others are joining the campaign, giving new hope to people disappointed with the inadequacies of their hearing aids. "If we build it, they will come," Myers said. "I see no reason why what's happened here in West Michigan can't happen across America."[16] "This," he added, "is truly a case of the churches (indeed, the churches of Holland, of which Hope Church was one of the very first), leading the culture."[17]

Including Women in Church Leadership

Adding a ramp to improve access to Hope Church and adding a hearing loop system were faster and easier than the lengthy deliberations within the Reformed Church in America to acknowledge the spiritual gifts of women, hear their voices, and open doors for them to the offices of deacon, elder, and minister of Word and Sacrament. By the end of 1972, after more than a half-century of debate and votes in the General Synod and among classes, the denomination voted to allow women to be elected deacons and elders. Hope Church wasted no time in electing women to the consistory. Elder Elizabeth (Betty) Becker began serving in 1972. Deacon Audrey

---

[15] Among the many books he has written is *A Quiet World: Living with Hearing Loss* (New Haven: Yale Univ. Press, 2000), "a journal of his experiences with hearing loss, interspersed with information about the psychology of hearing and new hearing technologies." http://www.davidmyers.org/Brix?pageID=6
[16] Myers, quoted by Tierney, "A Hearing Aid That Cuts Out All the Clatter."
[17] David Myers, personal communication 24 October 2011.

Navis and elders Hermina (Mickie) Lamb and Bernadine Siebers De Valois, began serving in 1973.[18] Women have been elected to these offices regularly ever since.

Elder Hermina Lamb later became director of children's education at the Central Reformed Church in Grand Rapids.[19] She had a degree in religious education and also served as director of children's education in Holland's First Reformed Church and Grace Episcopal Church. After being re-elected elder, she became in 1982 the first woman to be elected senior elder in Hope Church.

Hermina (Mickie) Lamb (Van Eyl)

Bernadine Siebers De Valois had wanted to be a missionary since childhood. After graduating from Hope College's pre-med program, she graduated from Rush Medical College in Chicago in 1934. For more than five years she served as assistant surgeon at the Christian Medical College and Hospital in Vellore, India. After additional medical studies in Canada, she returned to Vellore in 1945 and established the Department of Otorhinolaryngology (ear, nose, and throat), where she taught

---

[18] *Consistorial Minutes*, 31:5 December 1972. The first overture to the General Synod to allow women to serve as deacons and elders came in 1918. The long denominational debate about women serving as deacons, elders, and ministers is summarized by Edwin G. Mulder, "Full Participation—A Long Time in Coming!" *Reformed Review*, vol. 42, no. 3 (Spring 1989), 224–46.

[19] *Consistorial Minutes*, 34:12 May 1957.

medical and nursing students. In 1946 she married John J. (Jack) De Valois, an agricultural missionary in India, whose wife Harriet, Bernadine's close friend, had died in 1944.

The De Valoises served in India until 1959 and then for World Neighbors, a self-help organization that placed them in Central and South America and in Africa. They joined Hope Church in 1963, and from 1964 to 1973 Bernadine worked part-time at Pine Rest Christian Hospital in Grand Rapids, Michigan.[20]

Doris Mazurek in 1980 was the first woman elected as senior deacon. Jean Cook in 1985 was the first woman to serve as vice-president of consistory at Hope Church.

John J. and Dr. Bernadine S. De Valois

Women also have been appointed regularly as delegates to the Classis of Holland, the Particular Synod of Michigan, and the General Synod. Carol Myers, an elder delegate to Holland Classis beginning in 1988, became the first woman to serve as its vice-president in 1994 and its president in 1995.[21] At the denominational level she served on the Commission on Worship 1981-88, becoming

---

[20] Una H. Ratmeyer, *Hands, Hearts, and Voices: Women Who Followed God's Call* (New York: Reformed Church Press, 1995), 75-77. In her book Ratmeyer includes information not only about De Valois but also about five other Hope Church women who followed God's call: Maxine De Bruyn, Elsie Lamb, Lynn Japinga, Carol Myers, and Eloise Van Heest. "Certainly there are many other faithful women from the congregation," comments Carol Myers, "but it is significant that so many from Hope Church [six of ninety-six women from the denomination] were selected for this book lifting up the stories of RCA women." Communication from Carol Myers, 28 October 2011.

[21] Communication from Carol Myers 28 October 2011. The Reverend Cindi Veldheer DeYoung served as president of Holland Classis in 2000. Minutes 2000\Consistory 03.doc, 14 February 2000.

the first non-ordained person to serve as moderator of this commission in 1986, serving in that role through 1988. She served on the New Brunswick Theological Seminary Board of Trustees 1993–97. Among the General Synod task forces on which she served were Tithing (1990–92), Baptism and Membership Terminology (1994–95), Consistories (1998–2000), and Revision of Disciplinary and Judicial Procedures (1994–97). She served on the Commission on Church Order 1997–2003 and was its moderator 2000–2003. She was a delegate to the General Synod in 1991, 1997, and 2001 and also attended synod as a delegate for the Worship Commission, the Church Order Commission, and the New Brunswick Theological Seminary trustees for several years.[22]

Carol Myers

The first woman from Hope Church to serve as a delegate to the General Synod was Elsie Lamb in 1977.[23] Also at the national denominational level, Hope Church members Jean Cook, Eloise Van Heest, and Trudy Vander Haar chaired RCA Women's Triennials for the years 1980, 1986, and 1989, respectively.[24] Hope Church member Fritzi Sennett represented Holland

---

[22] Communication from Carol Myers 28 October 2011.
[23] *Consistorial Minutes*, 36:22 March 1977.
[24] Kansfield, *Letters to Hazel*, 234–35. Before Mina Buys joined Hope Church in 1977, she served as national president of the First Triennial held in 1962.

Classis on the Board of Managers for the denomination's National Department of Women's Work.[25]

Jean Cook   *Trudy Vander Haar*

Eloise Van Heest served the denomination in several roles. In the late 1970s, she cochaired the Committee on Sexist Bias in the RCA Liturgy with her husband, the Reverend Gerard Van Heest, and she was the facilitator of the Task Force on Women. In 1982-84 she coordinated the Council for Christian Education and served as liaison for Christian education to groups in the Reformed Church and other denominations. Over the years, she has designed, written, and edited many educational resources for various Reformed Church agencies, including materials for more than twenty-five seminars. In 1992 she was chosen "Educator of the Year" by Christian Educators of the Reformed Church in America (CERCA), and in 1994 she was elected president of that organization. She also served as secretary of the Board of Trustees of Western Theological Seminary for seven years, and for four years on the Board

---

[25] Van Heest, "Women's Societies in Holland Classis," in *In Christ's Service: The Classis of Holland and Its Congregations 1847-1997*, 7.

of Theological Education, first as its vice-moderator and then as its moderator.[26]

Eloise Van Heest

While serving the denomination, she also served Hope Church. She was elected elder in 1982 and became administrative associate, a half-time position in which she supervised all other non-ordained staff and recruited and co-ordinated volunteers at Hope Church. From 1990 through 1994 she was given additional responsibilities and employed full-time as Hope Church's associate for administration and Christian education.[27]

The first two women to teach full time in the Religion Department of Hope College were members of Hope Church. Associate professor Janet Everts has taught there since 1985, specializing in New Testament. The Reverend professor Lynn Japinga has taught at Hope College since 1992, specializing in the history of American religion and in feminist theology.[28]

---

[26] Ratmeyer, *Hands, Hearts, and Voices*, 12–3. *Consistory Minutes*, 51:16 January 1992.
[27] *Consistorial Minutes*, 48:6 February 1989, 52:12 April 1993.
[28] http://www.hope.edu/academic/religion/fac_staff/everts.html
http://www.hope.edu/academic/religion/fac_staff/japinga.html

Janet (Jenny) Everts   *Lynn Japinga*

In 1998 the Reverend Carol Bechtel, Hope Church member and professor of Old Testament at Western Theological Seminary, was elected as General Synod Professor of Theology, the first woman to hold that office. In 2007–08 she served as vice-president of the General Synod, in 2008–09 as its president, and in 2009–10 as moderator of the General Synod Council.[29]

Hope Church elder the Reverend Leanne Van Dyk became professor of Reformed theology at Western Theological Seminary in 1998. Since then, she has been promoted to dean of the faculty, academic dean, and dean and vice president of Academic Affairs.[30]

Carol Bechtel   *Leanne Van Dyk*

[29] http://www.westernsem.edu/files/2912/7492/3045/CV-Bechtel.pdf
[30] http://www.westernsem.edu/files/2612/7505/2828/CV-VanDyk.pdf

Inviting Children and Youth into Greater Participation

Soon after becoming an elder in 1973, Hermina (Mickie) Lamb urged the consistory to prepare families for allowing children to partake of the Lord's Supper. Although the 1973 General Synod defeated a proposal to admit children to the sacrament of the Lord's Supper, Lamb saw the likelihood of its future passage and wanted Hope Church to be ready. She proposed to the consistory that the Worship Committee study questions raised by including children in receiving the Lord's Supper and recommend ways that children could learn about the sacrament and about church membership.[31] In 1986 children received grapes and crackers during Communion time.[32] In 1988 the denomination approved admitting baptized children to the Lord's Supper. Hope Church was ready, having provided parents information to aid their children's understanding of the sacrament. Children were prepared to receive the sacrament, and elders were aided in their oversight of Communion.[33]

In 1978, the consistory approved the addition of a junior high representative (Jeffrey Mulder) and a senior high representative (Deborah Fike) to attend consistory meetings. The young people would have speaking but not voting privileges.[34]

In 2005 Hope Church introduced an annual Children's Sabbath, a way for church members to affirm the baptismal vows they make to support baptized children. Children on this day assist in the worship service and distribute a "reverse offering." In this offering, members of the congregation, instead of contributing to an offering

---

[31] *Consistorial Minutes*, 33:11 March 1974.
[32] Worship Ministry minutes stated, "Children receive grapes and crackers during communion time." Whether this occurred in Early Worship only or in Children in Worship was not indicated. *Consistorial Minutes*, 45:17 March 1986.
[33] *Consistorial Minutes*, 47:27 June 1988, 17 July 1988.
[34] *Consistorial Minutes*, 38:30 September 1978. Several months later the Board of Elders decided to replace attendance by youth representatives at all consistory meetings with invitations made only to meetings in which something of interest to young people would be discussed. *Consistorial Minutes*, 39:12 March 1979.

plate, each take from it a piece of paper with the name of a family with children and make a commitment to pray for them over the next year. "Updates are placed in the bulletin throughout the year telling which children are graduating, going to camp, participating in a mission trip, and so on, so that their prayer pals can stay informed. Since people draw new names each year," said Jocelyn Van Heest, children's ministries coordinator, "the children get to know a number of adults in the church, and vice versa."[35]

Ministries of Marchiene Rienstra and Dennis L. TeBeest, 1984-88

After the Reformed Church voted to allow women as deacons and elders, momentum was building toward taking the next step. In 1975 the consistory drafted a letter in support of the ordination of women to the ministry of Word and Sacrament and sent the letter to delegates to and consistories of Holland Classis and to women students of Western Theological and New Brunswick Theological Seminaries.[36]

Four years later, a judicial action of the General Synod to allow women to serve as ministers of Word and Sacrament was supported by the required number of classes. Hope Church's search committee, formed after the Reverend Vander Wilt received a call to serve the American Reformed Church in Orange City, Iowa, worked promptly. Within six months of that call, the committee recommended calling the Reverend Marchiene Vroon Rienstra to be senior pastor. The congregation voted overwhelmingly that consistory call Rienstra, pastor of the Port Sheldon Presbyterian Church in West Olive, Michigan.[37]

---

[35] "Congregation Prays for Children," *Reformed Church in America Today*, October 2010.
[36] The likely purposes of the letter were to influence a classis vote and show support for women students at the seminaries who were preparing for pastoral ministry. *Consistorial Minutes*, 34:10 February 1975, 10 March 1975.
[37] *Consistorial Minutes*, 43:9 May 1983, 7 November 1983, 4 December 1983. The vote was 263 yes and 26 no.

Marchiene Rienstra

Rienstra accepted the call "with great joy, and a profound sense of the marvelous leading of God."[38] On 5 February 1984 Holland Classis installed Rienstra as senior pastor of Hope Church, the first church in the Reformed Church in America to place a woman in that position (though in some other congregations women were serving as sole pastors). Denominational and faith traditions represented in that service included not only ministers from her Christian Reformed Church heritage but also Reformed Church ministers; the Reverend John Francis of Holland's First United Methodist Church; Rabbi Phillip Sigal of Ahavas Israel, Grand Rapids; and Sister Joan Mary Williams of St. Francis de Sales Church.[39]

Born during her parents' journey by boat from America to India and living in India and Pakistan until age fourteen, Rienstra brought to her ministry perspectives and insights from other cultures and

---

[38] *Consistorial Minutes*, 43:12 December 1983 insert.
[39] "New Hope Church Minister a 'First' in RCA," *Holland Sentinel*, 3 February 1984, A8.

other religions. Her parents, medical missionaries Dr. John and Theresa Vroon, grew up as members of the Christian Reformed Church but later transferred to the United Presbyterian Church of North America, which in the 1940s more readily supported their ministry as medical missionaries.[40] A graduate of Calvin College in 1963 and Calvin Seminary in 1978, Rienstra was the first woman to receive a master of divinity degree from that seminary[41] and the first woman to petition the Christian Reformed Church to allow her ordination. The denomination denied her request, but she was invited by the United Presbyterian Church to be ordained in 1979 and to serve as pastor of a church start in Port Sheldon, Michigan.[42] She answered her call to ministry by going outside the Christian Reformed Church, which did not approve women as candidates for ministry of the Word until 1996.[43]

Her installation as senior minister at Hope Church met with some criticism. A Baptist church pastor rebuked Hope Church for calling a woman pastor, but his letter to the editor of the *Holland Sentinel* was effectively countered by a response from the Reverend John H. Piet, professor of Bible and missions at Western Theological Seminary and an elder at Hope Reformed Church:

> Did Hope Reformed Church do wrong and depart from the authority of the scriptures when it installed a woman as its pastor, as Rev. Mark Mayou suggests in his letter of Feb. 8? Hope Church believes it did right; and, taking the scriptures seriously, acted in accord with its teaching....
>
> When Hope accepts a woman on confession of faith, it believes, as Paul suggests [in 2 Corinthians 5:17 and Galatians 3:27–28], that

---

[40] Arkie Van Raalte, "Church and New Pastor: Pioneering Together," *Holland Sentinel*, 9 February 1984, A3. In the late 1950s the Christian Reformed Church asked Dr. John Rienstra to be its first medical missionary in Africa.
[41] Van Raalte, "Church and New Pastor: Pioneering Together," *Holland Sentinel*, 9 February 1984, A9.
[42] Jonesetta Lassiter, "New Heights: The Rev. Marchiene Rienstra Breaks New Ground for Women in RCA," *Muskegon Chronicle*, 28 January 1984.
[43] "Women in Ecclesiastical Office," http://www.crcna.org/pages/positions_women_office.cfm

the created order has been reversed and that every member of the body of Christ has an equal standing before God....

St. Paul challenges all of us when he says, "If we live by the Spirit let us also walk by the Spirit (Gal 5:25)." One fruit is love, so let us dialogue rather than choose sides. Hope Church is ready for that."[44]

Dennis L. TeBeest Becomes Associate Pastor

In October 1984, the congregation voted that consistory call the Reverend Dennis L. TeBeest to assist Rienstra as associate pastor. Currently serving as associate pastor of First Reformed Church of Kalamazoo, he accepted that call, beginning what would become a twelve-year ministry at Hope Church.[45]

Dennis L. TeBeest

---

[44] "Readertorials: Rather Than Choose Sides Hope Church Ready for Dialogue," *Holland Sentinel*, 10 February 1984, A5. The Reverend Mark Mayou was pastor of a Baptist church in Holland.
[45] *Consistorial Minutes* 44:28 October 1984. The vote was 120 yes, 10 no, and 1 abstention.

Congregational Care and Children in Worship

Not long after her arrival, Rienstra proposed replacing "task forces" with "ministries" comprising the following: Worship, Christian Education, Community and World, Stewardship, Prayer, Pastoral Care, Fellowship, and Hospitality.[46] The "Consistorial Report" for 1984 noted a "variety of liturgical forms, ... ecumenical emphasis, ... a strong spiritual Christian atmosphere ... 'Living with God' prayer courses, ... emphasis on prayer and spiritual disciplines," and "giant steps forward in congregational care."[47] Among positives listed in the "Consistorial Report" for the following year were more involvement of laypeople and children in worship, meditative singing, and more frequent Communion and sacramental emphasis.[48]

Rienstra introduced music from around the world and especially from the Taize Community for congregational singing. In the mid-1980s music from the Iona Community off the coast of Scotland was introduced to Hope Church. Later John Bell, a composer of much of the music of Iona, visited Western Theological Seminary and introduced the music to local Reformed Churches. Using biblically based texts coupled with simple melodies, the music of Taize and Iona spared Hope Church from the "worship wars" that pitted contemporary praise music against traditional hymns.

Hope Church also enriched worship experiences for children. In 1986 the Church School superintendent, Jocelyn Van Heest, attended a Children's Worship Conference at Western Theological Seminary, which included sessions about "Children in Worship." The following year, Nancy Page, Julie Campbell, Lauren Heyboer, and Jan Veurink learned more about how this program could be introduced to the children of Hope Church. By 1988, Children in Worship completed its first full year with an average of fifty

---

[46] *Consistorial Minutes* 44:12 November 1984, 45:14 January 1985.
[47] *Consistorial Minutes* 44:31 December 1984.
[48] *Consistorial Minutes* 45:31 December 1985.

children from kindergarten through fifth grade participating.[49] This program continues into the twenty-first century to provide children with worship experiences and Bible stories presented in ways that engage the children's sense of wonder.

Ann Piet Anderson leading Children in Worship

Encouraging Denominational Ecumenism

Illustrative of an ecumenical emphasis in the mid-1980s was elder William Schutter's interest and action toward bringing the Lutheran, Presbyterian, and Reformed churches "into full communion fellowship."[50] Consistory voted to recommend to Holland Classis approval of the following as an overture to General Synod:

---

[49] *Consistorial Minutes* 45:20 October 1986, 46:16 February 1987, 47:11 September 1988.
[50] *Consistorial Minutes* 45:4 March 1985, 47:14 March 1988. The Reverend William Schutter and his family joined Hope Church in 1979 when he began teaching at Western Theological Seminary; he was installed as elder in 1984. They left in 1988 after he accepted a call to Arcadia Reformed Church in Newark, NY. Gasaro, *Historical Directory*, 350.

The Classis of Holland overtures General Synod to respond to The Lutheran-Reformed dialogues and <u>An Invitation To Action</u>, p. 126, by requesting the Theological Commission to determine whether The Augsburg Confession of 1530 or The Westminster Confession of 1647 with American alterations contain any doctrinal impediment which would prohibit their adoption by the RCA, and to make its report to Synod in 1986.[51]

Holland Classis supported the overture,[52] and three months later the General Synod adopted a recommendation based on the substance of the overture.[53] This was the only overture originating in Hope Church that successfully moved through Holland Classis to adoption by the General Synod.

The overture initiated by Schutter was one step in a process that had begun in the Reformed Church in 1962, when representatives from the Reformed and Lutheran churches in the United States began official conversations about working more closely together. By 1998 the Reformed Church in America, the Evangelical Lutheran Church in America, the Presbyterian Church U.S.A., and the United Church of Christ agreed to an ecumenical partnership. The resulting *Formula of Agreement* affirmed that the four participating denominations

---

[51] *Consistorial Minutes* 45:13 March 1985.
[52] "Minutes," *Classis of Holland, RCA,* 26 March 1985. W96-1217. Classis of Holland, Joint Archives of Holland.
[53] The recommendation approved by General Synod was "To respond to the Lutheran-Reformed dialogues and *An Invitation to Action* by requesting the Theological Commission to determine whether The Augsburg Confession of 1530 and other Lutheran symbols of faith contain any doctrinal position which would prohibit our wholehearted affirmation of the action requested in this document and to report this to Synod of 1986." *Acts and Proceedings of the 179th Session of the General Synod, June 17–21, 1985* (State College, PA: Jostens Printing and Publishing, 1985), 65:150–51.

recognized the validity of each other's baptism, encouraged the sharing of Holy Communion, and permitted ministers from one denomination to serve in the other denominations.[54]

Cooperating with Other Churches in the Neighborhood

What Churches United for Social Action (CUSA) was in the 1970s, a group of churches working together to serve needs within the Holland community, the Four-Parish Council, later named the Inter-Parish Council, was in the 1980s. Begun in 1982 by Hope and Third Reformed Church, First United Methodist Church, and St. Francis de Sales Catholic Church, it expanded to include the Spanish (*Iglesia Hispana*) Christian Reformed Church and focused on the needs of the central city of Holland.

In 1984 the Four-Parish Council requested Holland City Council to establish a program to register, inspect, and certify rental housing in order to protect the health and safety of occupants, the legitimate interests of landlords, and the decency of the central city neighborhood.[55]

The Four-Parish Council established Kids' Clubs in various churches. A poster for the 25 September 1985 initial gathering invited kids to various churches from 3 to 5 p.m. First- and second-graders went to St. Francis de Sales Catholic Church. Third- and fourth-graders went to Hope Church. Fifth- and sixth-graders went to Third Reformed, and seventh-graders and

---

[54] In 1987 the four denominations approved participation in the *Formula of Agreement* during each of their denominational meetings. Leaders and various members from these denominations gathered at the University of Chicago's Rockefeller Chapel on 4 October 1998 to formally celebrate the "full communion." "A Formula of Agreement," https://www.rca.org/sslpage.aspx?pid=432. See also "A History of Lutheran/Reformed Dialogues," https://www.rca.org/sslpage.aspx?pid=431.

[55] Document in "Parish Council" folder in main office file cabinet at Hope Church.

up went to the First United Methodist Church. This ecumenical ministry intended to "provide well supervised activities ... meet the spiritual, social and emotional needs of the youth in our immediate neighborhood" and provide a positive influence as an "alternative to delinquency."[56]

The Kids' Clubs were the forerunners of Holland's Boys and Girls Club. Kalamazoo had a successful Boys and Girls Club with which the Reverend Dennis L. TeBeest was familiar. He and Elly Muiderman from the Third Reformed Church were the Inter-Parish Council leaders who created the Holland Boys and Girls Club as an affiliate of Boys and Girls Clubs of America.[57] The club first met in the Center for Community Education building in 1991 and in the following years met also in five elementary schools and West Middle School. In May 1997 the former Bethel Reformed Church on Van Raalte Avenue at Eighteenth Street became the home for the Boys and Girls Club.[58] In 2009 a $4 million, 25,000 square-foot North Side Center was built at Riley Street and Butternut Drive.[59]

The Inter-Parish Council in 1988 organized a Carol Sing for Peace, cosponsored by World Peacemakers, and a St. Nicholas Day celebration. In 1992 the Inter-Parish Council invited people from many Holland churches to a "celebration of Christian Unity in Prayer" held 19 January. The following year the council and Habitat for Humanity built a home at 10 East 15th Street for a family. By 1993 Fourteenth Street Christian Reformed Church and Maple Avenue Ministries joined the Inter-Parish Council.[60]

---

[56] Document in "Parish Council" folder in main office file cabinet at Hope Church.
[57] Communication from Carol Myers, 21 December 2011.
[58] "Our History," Boys and Girls Club of Greater Holland, http://www.bgch.org/page1286469.aspx.
[59] http://www.mlive.com/news/grand-rapids/index.ssf/2009/05/adam_bird_grand_rapids_press.html. Key supporters of Holland's Boys and Girls Club over the years include Hope Church members Gerrard and Edna Haworth, Dr. Tom and Sharon Arendshorst, Larry and Karen Mulder, and Jeff and Jeri Mulder. http://www.hollandsentinel.com/news/news_community/x1179097345/Community-Shapshot-Boys-Girls-Club.
[60] Documents in "Parish Council" folder in main office file cabinet at Hope Church. *Consistorial Minutes*, 52:25 January 1993, 15 February 1993.

In 1995 the consistory of Hope Church listened to a representative of the Inter-Parish Council introduce parish nursing as a program that individual churches could support. The consistory affirmed the efforts of the Inter-Parish Council "to explore and further define the parish nursing program in order to meet the health care needs of the congregation and community." The consistory also directed elder Ann Piet Anderson to assess the interest of Hope Church medical professionals in this program.[61]

Churches in the Inter-Parish Council worked together at the turn of the twenty-first century to provide noon Lenten services, sponsor Vacation Bible School, and build houses for Habitat for Humanity. But consistory minutes of 14 April 2003 indicated the demise of this community ecumenical organization: "this structure may be ending having served its purpose. Many of the things originating with this [council] are functioning well on their own."[62]

Celebrating the 125th Anniversary in 1987

In the midst of all of this outward-focused activity, Hope Church also celebrated its 125th anniversary in 1987. Appointed by the Worship Ministry to establish a Fine Arts Committee to "assess the church's art collection and develop a visual arts format for the halls and walls of the church," Edith de Velder with Helena Winter, Winifred Hollenbach, and Marian Vanderham gathered photographs of former and current pastors for display during the celebration.[63] She also advocated creation of a needlepoint crest of the RCA for unveiling at the church's anniversary. Dr. James Ward produced the crest.

---

[61] *Consistorial Minutes*, 54:17 April 1995.
[62] Minutes 2001\Consistory 05.doc, 14 May 2001. Minutes 2003\Consistory 04.doc, 14 April 2003.
[63] *Consistorial Minutes*, 45:20 October 1986, 46:19 January 1987.

RCA crest in needlepoint created by James Ward

Kristine Bradfield created a needlepoint image of Hope Church.

Hope Church in needlepoint created by Kristine Bradfield

And, lo and behold, needlepoint crosses also came to pass in the collection plates. Kay MacKenzie, who also created ornaments of Christian symbols for the Advent Chrismon tree, designed the crosses for the collection plates, and Pat Daily, Marilyn Cook, and others completed them in needlepoint.[64]

Needlepoint symbols in collection plates

---

[64] Communications from Kay MacKenzie in December 2011.

As part of the anniversary celebration in mid-July, members and friends gathered at Hope College's Maas Center for a heritage dinner followed by a skit, "Portraits of the Past," and the Reverend Marion de Velder's overview of the church's history. The following Sunday, a continental breakfast was served in the church's courtyard, after which pastor Rienstra preached a sermon focusing on the future. The choir that day comprised former and present choir members, led by Brian Carder, director of music. Commenting on Hope Church's 125th anniversary, de Velder stated, "Hope Church did everything first, and got roundly criticized, but eventually other churches followed."[65]

A Passage to India and Mission to China

Beginning in the summer of 1987, Hope Church conducted "Passage to India," a major congregational year-long adult class on India. Coordinated by elder Phillip Van Eyl, the class informed the congregation on the history, culture, economy, and religions of India and how best to respond to that country's needs. As a result of the study, Hope Church sponsored a student, Merci Renabai, from Ranipet, India, in her studies at Western Theological Seminary.[66]

Also in the summer of 1987, Randall and Carol Braaksma made plans to teach in China under the auspices of the Foundation for East-West Trade Development. Hope Church began to contribute toward support for Randall Braaksma in 1988.[67] Living in Beijing not far from Tiananmen Square during the student protests in the spring of 1989, he described events and analyzed their implications:

> The events in Beijing disrupted our lives in a relatively small way by forcing us to return to the United States; they shattered the

---

[65] "Hope: A Pioneering Church Turns 125," *Holland Sentinel*, 17 July 1987, A8.
[66] *Consistorial Minutes*, 46:9 February 1987, 47:11 September 1988. She was but one of many students supported over many years by scholarship assistance through Hope Church's Community/World Ministry.
[67] *Consistorial Minutes*, 46:11 May 1987, 47:11 January 1988 insert.

lives of many Chinese, literally and spiritually. Hope has always been a precious commodity in China. During the middle of May it seemed to be reproducing itself every day. It was there aplenty when people—young and old, students, workers, educators, professionals, and even Communist party members—joined in the early, exuberant demonstrations. It was there in the wee hours of the morning as Beijing residents milled around ... discussing freedom. It was there in Tiananmen Square, in the faces of the students, dazed by hunger and sickness. Now, after the massacre and the arrests, hope is once again rare.[68]

In 1992 Randall and Carol Braaksma were appointed to serve in China as World Mission Program Associates of the RCA. Hope Church supported them through a Partnership in Mission share, and the Braaksmas served in China through 1994.[69]

Rienstra's Illness

In September 1987 Marchiene Rienstra was diagnosed with breast cancer. She underwent surgery and began a series of chemotherapy and radiation treatments. During that time she was granted a nine-month leave of absence. Dennis TeBeest and Eloise Van Heest were assigned additional responsibilities, and the Reverend Ruth Zwald Staal, a church member who had received her MDiv degree from

---

[68] "A Black Day," *Church Herald*, September 1989, 28. See also in the same issue Randall Braaksma, "China: Crisis of Faith," 24–28.
[69] *Consistorial Minutes*, 51:20 January 1992, 14 June 1992. Gasero, *Historical Directory*, 711. The desire to support and build a close relationship with a missionary family is evident in minutes from the Community/World Ministry: "Community / World wants to build close ties with a family working in world mission. In the past our relationships with our mission families have been distant—Hope Church sends money to the RCA for their support; they send us occasional letters. We want a closer relationship. We want to increase the focus of Hope Church on mission activities, inform the congregation about another culture, and involve the congregation in the work of a mission family. The return of Randy, Carol and John Braaksma, a member family of our church, to China as Mission Associates of the RCA provides us with a unique opportunity to achieve this goal." *Consistorial Minutes* 51:27 July 1992.

Western Theological Seminary in 1984 and worked with the young people of the church part-time, was assigned more hours and given the title, "youth minister."[70]

In May 1988 Rienstra asked the consistory to allow her to become a "part-time senior pastor" with a revised job description.[71] Members of a Leadership Committee and the Executive-Personnel Committee struggled with how best to employ the leadership gifts of Rienstra, TeBeest, de Velder, and Van Heest.[72]

Redefining the Pastoral Roles of Rienstra and TeBeest

In June 1988 the congregation voted on whether to require Rienstra as senior pastor to work full time. The vote was close, with 51 percent voting for requiring Rienstra to work full time as senior pastor and 48 percent voting against this requirement. After considering the congregation's vote, the consistory called TeBeest to serve as senior pastor and Rienstra to become pastor of worship.[73]

Among other pastoral reflections at the annual congregational meeting in September, TeBeest declared, "Christ is writing a letter to the world and we are that letter." Added Rienstra: "We are unique because we at Hope are still the church that will take anybody. We honor the gifts and contributions of women. We are a church where people from other parts of the greater church can feel at home. We foster a balance between head, heart and hands."[74]

The years 1987 and 1988 brought many achievements. With a starting fund of $60,000 from memorial donations, an Endowment

---

[70] *Consistorial Minutes,* 44:10 September 1984, 46:14 September 1987, 24 September 1987, 44: 12 October 1987, 3 November 1987, 46:31 December 1987, 47:4 January 1988, 11 January 1988, 18 April 1988. Staal was, however, allowed a three-week maternity leave in the midst of taking on this additional work.
[71] *Consistorial Minutes,* 47:9 May 1988.
[72] *Consistorial Minutes,* 47:26 May 1988, 31 May 1988, 12 June 1988.
[73] *Consistorial Minutes,* 47:27 June 1988, 12 July 1988, 10 October 1988.
[74] *Consistorial Minutes,* 47:11 September 1988.

Fund board was incorporated.[75] Plans were begun to increase parking space and enable a driveway between Tenth and Eleventh Streets near the church's east entrance.[76] Twenty-two members completed an intensive two-month "Equipping Laypeople for Ministry" pastoral care training program. Hope Church developed a sister-church relationship with the Church of the Good News in Chicago. It began a long tradition of an all-church summer weekend at Cran-Hill Ranch.[77]

By December 1988, however, Rienstra resigned to pursue a different calling,

> to enter a life of greater silence, solitude, and simplicity.... a different kind of ministry.... the opportunity to share the gifts God gives me through spiritual direction, writing, retreats and teaching.... Being at Hope Church no longer feels as if it 'fits' the person I have become and am becoming, or the ministry to which I am being called....[78]

With "very deep regret" consistory accepted the resignation of Marchiene Rienstra.[79]

Rienstra did pursue her other callings. Elder Francis Fike summed up the legacy she left Hope Church:

> Marchiene is a highly grace-gifted woman whose tenure as pastor has had long-lasting influence in Hope Church. She stirred the depths of our spiritual life by her example and by her instruction in prayer; she preached with power and authority that illuminated

---

[75] The first members of this board were Ekdal Buys (chair), Clarence Becker, Lawrence W. (Bill) Lamb Jr., George Heeringa, Peter Van Pelt, Joyce Seaman, and Phyllis Hooyman. *Consistorial Minutes,* 46:12 October 1987, 3 November 1987.
[76] Eventually the house on the Grigsby property at 66 West 10th Street east of the church was razed to created this space for parking and driveway. *Consistorial Minutes,* 46:14 December 1987.
[77] More than one hundred attended the first weekend at Cran-Hill Ranch. *Consistorial Minutes,* 47:11 September 1988. Cran-Hill Ranch is located in Rodney, MI, about five miles east of Big Rapids.
[78] *Consistorial Minutes,* 47:5 December 1988.
[79] *Consistorial Minutes,* 47:7 December 1988.

biblical texts; her ecumenical spirit brought our attention to the value not only in other Christian viewpoints beyond the Reformed, but in other religions as well. She introduced us to the worship service of healing, and offered comforting presence in time of loss and grief. She continues those contributions to us and to the wider public through her roles as spiritual director, writer and explorer of spiritual disciplines.[80]

Ministries of Dennis L. TeBeest and Toni L. Macon, 1989–90

At its January 1989 retreat, the consistory decided to call a second ordained person to lead a relational youth ministry and preach occasionally. It also affirmed the continuing work of Marion de Velder and Eloise Van Heest. In February the Executive Committee recommended that Van Heest be hired full time as administrative associate and director of Christian education for children and adults.[81]

Under TeBeest's leadership as senior pastor, more detailed planning occurred for all worship services. The ministers, music staff, and two representatives from the Worship Ministry met twice each year for an overnight retreat. (When away on vacation, the James Brooks family opened its lakeside home for these retreats.) Together those attending the retreat would read scripture passages specified by the lectionary for the upcoming six months, identify worship themes, establish the environment for the worship services (banners, Communion table settings, liturgical art), and select some of the music. The goals were thematic integrity and meaningful worship.

---

[80] Communication from Francis Fike, 1 December 2011.
[81] *Consistorial Minutes*, 48:21 January 1989, 6 February 1989.

Toni L. Macon

In 1989, the consistory called the Reverend Toni Louise Macon, a recent MDiv graduate of Colgate Rochester Divinity School, as associate pastor.[82] At the annual congregational meeting in September TeBeest reported, likely with a sense of relief, "After two years of staff vacancies we are now a full team."[83]

In 1990 the Stone Ridge Reformed Church of Marbletown, New York, called Macon to become its sole pastor. She served there for six years before returning to Michigan to become a co-pastor at the Church of the Savior in Coopersville, Michigan.[84] Also in 1990, member Todd Engle designed and carved a processional cross and later a baptismal font for the church.[85]

---

[82] *Consistorial Minutes*, 48:25 June 1989. The vote was 125 in favor, 12 opposed. *Consistorial Minutes*, 48:10 July 1989. Gasero, *Historical Directory*, 248.
[83] *Consistorial Minutes*, 48:10 September 1989.
[84] Gasero, *Historical Directory*, 248.
[85] *Consistorial Minutes*, 49:18 June 1990.

*Baptismal font and processional cross
created by Todd Engle*

Planting a Peace Pole

In June 1990, Hope Church, encouraged by Elsie Lamb, accepted a peace pole donated to Hope Church by the Holland Peacemakers.

The peace pole was planted on the grounds of Hope Church and is currently located north of the Parish Life Center (Commons I).[86]

Hope Church's peace pole

Despite the presence of the peace pole, members of Hope Church, like most Americans, did little to protest the 1991 War on Iraq and

---

[86] *Consistorial Minutes,* 49:4 June 1990.

the post-9/11 U.S. invasions of Afghanistan and Iraq. Though the January 1991 Executive Committee minutes mentioned "prayers of concern in regard to the pending possibility of war,"[87] nothing in minutes of 1991 expressed protest of the War on Iraq. In October 2002, the consistory discussed a request from Holland Peacemakers to allow that organization "to have a table in the gathering area on Sunday for the purpose of making available 'A Statement of Conscience, Not in Our Name.'" By a vote of ten yes, twelve no, with two abstentions, the request was denied.[88]

In 1991, the consistory approved the Reverend Mary T. Van Andel as interim associate pastor.[89] In the early 1990s she and her husband, Ben Sikkink, established a house of prayer, or spiritual retreat center. They named it Bethabara, which in the gospel of John means "place of passage or crossing." The relationship of Hope Church with Bethabara continues into the twenty-first century.[90]

In 1991, Hope Church became a registered Michigan Historic Site with an official marker installed near the southwest corner of the sanctuary.[91]

Mary T. Van Andel

---

[87] *Consistorial Minutes*, 50:14 January 1991.
[88] Minutes 2002\Consistory 10.doc, 14 October 2002.
[89] *Consistorial Minutes*, 50:21 January 1991, 5 February 1991.
[90] *Consistorial Minutes*, 50:11 September 1991, 51:21 June 1992.
[91] Funds from the estates of members Janet Mulder, archivist at Hope College; and Eva Van Schaak, professor of botany at Hope College, paid for the historical marker and landscaping around it. *Consistorial Minutes*, 27 July 1992 insert.

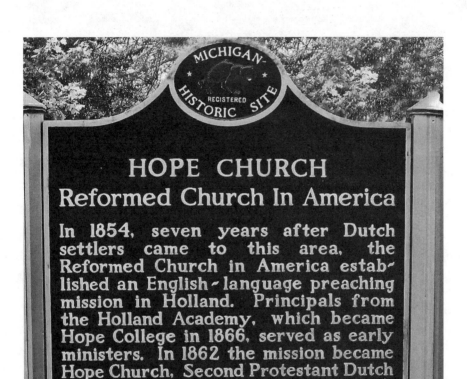

Historical marker facing east[92]

---

[92] Pioneer School and Holland Academy principals who served as early ministers of Hope Church were the Reverends Fred P. Beidler, John VanVleck, and Philip Phelps Jr. "Academic and Administrative Personnel 1847 through 1960," *Hope College 2002 Alumni Directory*, 10th ed. (Holland, MI: Hope College, 2002), 305.

Historical marker facing west

Ministries of Dennis L. TeBeest and Ruth Zwald Staal, 1991–97

Ruth Zwald Staal

In 1991 the consistory called Ruth Zwald Staal to become associate pastor.[93] As an ordained pastor and member of Hope Church, she had become increasingly active in youth work at the church and had been given the title of youth pastor in 1987. In 1990–91 she was program director at Camp Geneva.[94]

In 1992 TeBeest was granted a sabbatical leave to work on a master's degree at the University of Notre Dame's Center for Liturgy. In his absence, the Reverend James I. Cook served as interim pastor.[95] TeBeest enhanced Hope Church's understanding of liturgy and the sacraments. The number of Communion services in the church year, including Maundy Thursday and Christmas Eve, increased to seventeen. Holy Communion was a part of each Early Worship service as well. He introduced the Tenebrae service to the observance of Holy Week. During the Tenebrae service candles are gradually extinguished while various scripture passages are read aloud. Characteristics of worship at Hope Church that have proceeded well into the twenty-first century include lectionary preaching introduced in the Vander Wilt years, Taize and Iona music intro-

---

[93] The vote was 135 yes and 11 no. *Consistorial Minutes*, 50:22 July 1991, 18 August 1991, 16 September 1991.
[94] Gasero, *Historical Directory*, 371.
[95] *Consistorial Minutes*, 51:15 April 1992, 27 April 1992.

duced in the Rienstra years, and liturgical awareness developed in the TeBeest years.

In spring of 1992 de Velder retired from his part-time position as assistant minister of pastoral care. In June the Reverend Delbert Vander Haar took on that part-time position, serving as assistant minister of pastoral care until the end of 1998.[96] He had been pastor at the Trinity Reformed Church in Fulton, Illinois, and the Bethel Reformed Church in Sheldon, Iowa, before providing denominational leadership in youth work, family life ministry (with his wife, Trudy), and stewardship development. Immediately before coming to Hope Church, the couple served the Union Church in Yokohama, Japan. Working with the Pastoral Care Committee at Hope Church, Vander Haar proposed the creation of a prayer chain; anyone could notify one of the pastors of a need for prayer, and the pastor would begin the notification process that would pass the prayer request along the chain of those who would pray in response to the need.[97]

Delbert Vander Haar

---

[96] *Consistorial Minutes*, 52:15 February 1993, 2 June 1993. Minutes 1998\Consistory 10.doc, 19 October 1998.
[97] Gasero, *Historical Directory*, 409. Minutes 1998\Consistory 02.doc, 16 February 1998.

Expanding the Kitchen, Gathering Area, and East Entry

In memory of his wife Dorcas, Gerrard Haworth donated $175,000 to Hope Church to expand and upgrade the kitchen and improve the east entrance area. The consistory expanded this project to include repairing the heating system of the education wing and replacing its windows. It created the Renewing Hope Building Fund and set a project goal of $800,000.[98]

Improvements to the east entrance area included the removal of restrooms which were near the Blanche Cathcart Library, and the addition of new restrooms, a large storage closet, and a large space eventually called the "Gathering Area." The Nicodemus Bosch memorial window was moved from the east entrance's north wall to the wall between the Gathering Area and the Blanche Cathcart Library.[99]

The renovated building was dedicated on 22 October 1995. The bulletin for the service stated:

> Today we dedicate a building which reflects the changing life and ministry of Hope Church. Hospitality, fellowship and education are vital to the life of the church.... We worship God in the sanctuary, but we continue to share our triumphs and sorrows over a cup of coffee in the hallway, or as we gather for church school.[100]

---

[98] *Consistorial Minutes*, 52:14 July 1993 insert, 30 August 1993; 53:18 April 1994. The new kitchen included exhaust fans, expanded countertop space, and expanded storage. The building fund goal was later reduced to $625,000. *Consistorial Minutes*, 53:6 September 1994; 54:11 September 1995.
[99] Blanche Cathcart, a member of Hope Church since 1895, was an elementary school teacher for forty-seven years, twenty-six of them in Holland. She died at the age of ninety-seven in 1979 and willed a sum of money to Hope Church "to be used for its educational library." *Holland Sentinel*, 5 February 1979. *Consistorial Minutes*, 39:13 August 1979, 10 December 1979 insert.
[100] "Dedicated to Hope: The Renewing Hope Building Project," 1995. W91-1034, box 12, Hope Church, Holland, Michigan, Joint Archives of Holland.

*East view of church showing enhanced entrance
and new kitchen addition to north, 2011*

Remarking on Hope Church's building, with its changes over more than a century, elder Cecil Williams commented that the "architecture of Hope Church certainly suggests wide diversity! And uniqueness!... And one finds the same quirky differences and commonalities among the worshippers!"[101]

Countering Apartheid by Giving Scholarships to South Africans

For many years the Community/World Ministry had designated scholarships for international students at Hope College and Western Theological Seminary as part of Hope Church's benevolent stewardship. In 1993 as an attempt toward removing apartheid in South Africa, especially in its Reformed churches, elder Jane Dickie invited Hope Church to promote peaceful change in South Africa by providing scholarships to South Africans in Reformed churches. Unlike other measures, such as removing all investments from South African businesses, this form of social action would seek justice by "empowering South African Christians, through education,

---

[101] Cecil Williams, "Speaking Our Faith," *Hope Church News*, August 2010 (Vol. 53, No. 7), 6.

to contribute to productive change." The consistory endorsed this effort by proposing a South African Education Fund.[102]

Welcoming People of Homosexual Orientation as Members

In 1991 Douglas (Doug) Abell joined Hope Church by reaffirmation of faith and David (Dave) Van Heest by letter from the Christ Memorial Reformed Church of Holland. They joined Hope Church after Christ Memorial, knowing that Van Heest and Abell were Christian men living in a committed homosexual relationship, denied membership to Abell. As Van Heest tells it, after two weeks of their attending Hope Church, elder Frank Sherburne asked them, smiling, "Well, Dave and Doug, when are you two going to join Hope Church?"[103]

Feeling welcome, the partners asked to join Hope. The elders and TeBeest agreed that there was no reason in the Church Order why Van Heest and Abell should not be received as members with full privileges. The two joined and became active in various ministries. Sitting side by side in worship, they became faithful members in attendance, stewardship, and service. De Velder, in his pastoral visits with some of the older people in the congregation who doubted the rightness of the church's acceptance of this couple, responded to their concern with ready counsel: "These young men have suffered SO much already. We must welcome them."

At the annual congregational meeting in 1993, Nancy Rock, chair of the Nominations Committee, presented the slate of elders: Vern Boersma, Ann Piet, Fronse Smith, and David Van Heest. Someone made a motion to accept the printed slate. But then questions were raised about one of the elder nominees. All elder nominees were asked to leave the room while extensive discussion took place.

---

[102] *Consistorial Minutes*, 52:8 August 1993 letter, 30 August 1993.
[103] *Consistorial Minutes*, 50:20 October, 1991 and communication from David Van Heest summer 2011.

A substitute motion that the slate of nominations be accepted and the individual candidates for elder be voted on by ballot failed. Another motion that the vote for the slate of elders be taken by secret ballot carried. While these votes were being counted, the congregation elected the slate of deacons and conducted its other business. Then Rock, having received the results of the counted secret ballots, announced that the slate was approved. Those who were at this meeting remember hearing an audible sigh in response to the announcement.

At that point, David Van Heest asked permission to address the congregation. He said that he did not want to be a cause for division in the congregation and asked that his name be removed from the slate of elected elders. He added also that he did not want people to assume that the need to understand and minister to people who are homosexual would go away by his stepping aside. A motion carried that Van Heest's spot would be filled by someone whose name would be supplied by the Nominating Committee and who would be elected by a mail-in vote.

Ruth Zwald Staal then made the following motion: "That we, as a congregation, commit ourselves to prayer, study and discussion of the issues of homosexuality, implemented through a task force representing diverse opinions, to form ways for that dialogue, and to form a statement of our beliefs after the action of General Synod 1994." The motion carried, and thus began two years of planning for and carrying out the "process for moral discernment" at Hope Church.[104]

A Homosexuality task force was formed, comprising Steve Hoogerwerf as chair, Doug Abell, Kristen Gray, Karmen Kooyers, Laura Myers, Isla Van Eenenaam, Ekdal Buys, Gary Rizner, Dave Nieboer, John Beyer, Mary T. Van Andel, and John Hollenbach.[105]

---

[104] *Consistorial Minutes*, 52:14 November 1993. Also communications from Doug Abell, Dave Van Heest, Vern Boersma, Carol Myers, Ann Piet Anderson, and Marlin Vander Wilt. The elder later elected by mail vote was Carolyn Hoffman.
[105] *Consistorial Minutes*, 53:2 January 1994.

They proposed a detailed process of moral discernment, put the process into practice, and then formulated a statement of beliefs, which was endorsed by consistory and reported to the congregation.[106]

After an "eighteen-month season of dialogue and discernment regarding issues of homosexuality and leadership in the church," the consistory, guided by the Hope Church Mission Statement, offered to the congregation four resolutions:

> Resolution 1: We as a consistory accept persons with committed same-gender relationships as complete Christians without limitation of church privilege, including ordination.
> Resolution 2: We believe that, at this time, we will best recognize our place in the Body of Christ by honoring the denominational practice of not placing persons engaged in committed same-gender sexual relationships in ordained roles of service in the church.
> Resolution 3: We will continue to welcome all people into Hope Church on the basis of faith itself, trusting that the Holy Spirit will work in our midst to call us to ever more faithful lives.
> Resolution 4: We will engage in speech and behavior which enriches persons of faith among us, and we will actively offer the acceptance and freedom to struggle with hard issues such as sexual orientation. We will listen to one another's struggles and honestly share our own.[107]

The document concluded with an affirmation of faithfulness and love:

> God will continue to lead us in faithful ways. The ways of God are the ways of love. The ways of God are the paths toward wholeness.

---

[106] The planning report is "A Process for Moral Discernment at Hope Church (Revised 4-25-94)." The concluding report is "Hope Church Holland, Michigan A Report to the Congregation from the Consistory," 16 October 1995 (Revised 15 April 1996), "Subject: MORAL DISCERNMENT Regarding the issues of homosexuality and ordained leadership in the church." Both reports are in W91-1034, box 12, Hope Church, Holland, Michigan, Joint Archives of Holland.
[107] "Hope Church Holland, Michigan A Report to the Congregation from the Consistory," ... "Subject: MORAL DISCERNMENT," 6–7. Note how Resolution 3 resembles the response of Hope Church to Freemasons in 1867 (see page 57).

The ways of God are the steps of encouragement. The ways of God are the roads that bring us always into closer fellowship with our neighbors and with our God.

May our love overflow more and more.[108]

In the church photo directory of 1994, the first photograph of families within the congregation was one that portrayed Doug Abell and David Van Heest. In 1995 David Van Heest was appointed chair of the Outreach/Hospitality Ministry. He also served as vice-chair of a ministerial Search Committee in 1998.[109]

Doug Abell and David Van Heest

Facing a Difficult Time of Transitions

Although the report of the Personnel Committee to the consistory in 1995 indicated high evaluations of TeBeest and Staal, and chair Ron Gensemer praised Hope Church's "strong leadership,"[110] minutes of the Executive Committee and consistory meetings of 1996 revealed

---

[108] "Hope Church Holland, Michigan A Report to the Congregation from the Consistory,"... "Subject: MORAL DISCERNMENT," 8.
[109] *Consistorial Minutes*, 54:20 February 1995. Minutes 1998\Consistory 05.doc, 18 May 1998.
[110] *Consistorial Minutes*, 54:13 November 1995.

issues that were interfering seriously with their ministries. Elder Cecil Williams, a psychologist with a career in Human Relations, was a member of the Personnel Committee at that time.

Recalling conversations and events of that time, Williams provided details and insights that help explain what happened and the changes that were made to prevent similar difficulties from recurring. "The problems were a combination of strong personalities and structural or systemic processes," said Williams. "The two pastors were maturing in a structure that was not helpful. As a result of the difficulties, several people with management experience on the Personnel Committee took steps to prevent such difficulties from recurring."

"Until the 1990s," said Williams, "Hope Church had hired ordained ministers and let them develop their various gifts for ministry. There was little definition of roles for pastors."

> We hired a senior pastor or an associate pastor with the understanding that the associate pastor would report to the senior pastor as part of a "chain of command." There were no formal job descriptions....
>
> A structural problem that contributed to friction between Ruth Staal and Dennis TeBeest was that Ruth received direction though Dennis on what the church expected her to do. Consistory and Personnel would tell Dennis what they wanted, and then Dennis conveyed this to Ruth, and he was expected to monitor her carrying out of the tasks assigned her.
>
> Meanwhile Ruth wanted to broaden her own leadership in more areas of Hope Church beyond exclusively with the youth of the church. This desire led to misunderstandings and failures to communicate in many areas of congregational life, ultimately ending in Ruth's resignation.[111] In the following year Dennis accepted a call to a church in New Jersey.[112]

---

[111] After she resigned in August 1996, the consistory voted to extend her salary and benefits to the end of the year and give her $5,000 as an educational and professional development fund to use through September 1997. Minutes 1996\Consistory 08.doc, 19 August 1996. Minutes 1996\Consistory Special 09B.doc, 7 September 1996.

[112] In June 1997 TeBeest reported having received a call to another church.

As a result of difficulties between associate pastor and senior pastor that were inherent in the "chain of command" model, the Personnel Committee [working with an Advisory task force chaired by Richard Cook] did three things to improve the system:

1. No longer would there be a chain of command with associate pastor reporting to senior pastor. Instead both would report to the Personnel Committee.

2. Instead of each person following the dictates of his or her gifts, the Personnel Committee wrote detailed job descriptions for pastors and eventually all of Hope Church staff. Job descriptions were written not for hierarchical senior pastor or associate pastor but for a more parallel partnership, each responsible for specific duties but supporting each other with their separate gifts.

3. To assist the congregation after this transitional period, two interim pastors were soon hired.[113]

In 1997, Hope Church was coping with more than the departure of its two pastors, each of whom did much good work and was loved by many in the congregation. Also that year, organist Barbara Borr Veurink took a leave of absence of several months for cancer surgery and subsequent treatments, and custodian Happy Rodriguez was unable to work for several months after surgery.[114] Janet Bast (Elzinga), the church administrator, reported difficulties in the startup of new computer software, problems with building security, and some significant repair needs of the church building.[115]

Minutes 1997\Consistory Special 6B.doc, 23 June 1997. Later that summer he accepted a call to become senior pastor at the Preakness Reformed Church in Wayne, New Jersey.
[113] Conversation with Cecil Williams by the author 1 January 2012.
[114] Minutes 1997\Consistory 05.doc, 19 May 1997. Executive Committee Special 07.doc, 18 July 1997. Minutes 1997\Consistory 11.doc, 20 October 1997.
[115] Minutes 1997\Executive Committee Special 07.doc, 18 July 1997. Minutes 1997\Executive Committee 08.doc, 1 August 1997.

Ministries of Interim Pastors Arthur Van Eck and Evelyn Diephouse 1997–98

In September 1997, the Classis of Holland appointed the Reverend Ken Eriks as classis supervisor for Hope Church. Also that month, the consistory appointed the Reverend Arthur Van Eck as interim minister and the Reverend Evelyn De Jong Diephouse as interim associate minister. "Having a period of interim pastors was helpful," said Cecil Williams, "Van Eck and Diephouse did an outstanding job calming things down."[116]

Arthur (Bud) Van Eck   *Evelyn De Jong Diephouse*

By November, Hope Church had appointed a Search Committee chaired by the Reverend James I. Cook. In December the consistory directed the Personnel Committee to develop job descriptions for two ordained ministers that encompassed three areas of ministry: worship/witness, congregational life, and Christian formation.[117] At the 1997 congregational meeting, Van Eck set forth three goals

---

[116] Conversation with Cecil Williams by the author 1 January 2012.
[117] Minutes 1997\Consistory Special 09.doc, 1 September 1997. Minutes 1997\Executive Committee 09.doc, 4 September 1997. Minutes 1997\Consistory 09.doc, 15 September 1997. Minutes 1997\Consistory 11.doc, 17 November 1997. Minutes 1997\Consistory 12.doc, 15 December 1997.

for his interim ministry: to maintain the viability of Hope Church, to reinforce the laity of the church, and to provide a time of fellowship and reconciliation.[118]

Extending Sympathy to a Friend of Hope Church

During this time of transition, a response to the death of a friend of Hope Church and a "thank you" for that response highlight a facet of Hope Church's participation in ecumenical relationships. In response to the death of Barbara Padnos, who had provided instruction for Hope Church's Seder services, the consistory asked its vice-president Carol Myers to write a letter of sympathy to Stuart Padnos and passed a motion that Hope Church contribute $50 to Temple Emanuel in Grand Rapids in memory of his wife. Minutes of May 1997 report that a thank-you note was "received from Stuart Padnos for the gift given to Temple Emanuel in memory of Barbara Padnos."[119]

Like so many notes and letters alluded to in the consistory minutes, this one is not included with the bound volumes or computer directories. But the letter and the thank-you note came forth for this history.

The letter expressed gratitude for Barbara Padnos's "willingness to share faith and practice in helping us experience Seder in all its fullness." It also conveyed the intent of the monetary gift from Hope Church to Temple Emanuel, to "honor Barb and respect the faith tradition we hold in common."[120]

A handwritten thank-you note, written on deckled-edged note paper, its front bearing a copy of a painting titled "Fare Well" completed by Barbara Padnos a few days before her death, conveyed the thanks of Stuart Padnos to the consistory and members of Hope Church:

---

[118] Minutes 1997\Congregational Meeting Annual 11.doc, 23 November 1997.
[119] Minutes 1997\Consistory 04.doc, 21 April 1997. Minutes 1997\Consistory 05.doc, 19 May 1997.
[120] Copy of letter provided by Carol Myers.

There could be no testimony more meaningful to Barbara's life than your fine donation in her memory to Temple Emanuel.

As you enter our home the first piece of art you see is a Ben Shahn lithograph quoting the 133 psalm. "Behold how good and how pleasant it is for brethren to dwell together in Unity." It is the only piece of art we own which will never be moved from that location by my choice. I have trouble reading your letter because tears invariably cloud my vision. Thank You seems totally inadequate.

Stuart[121]

Ministries of Kathryn Davelaar and Gordon Wiersma, 1998–2007

The changes proposed by the Personnel Committee and put into effect by the consistory ensured smoother working relationships in the shared ministries that began in the last decade of

Kathryn Davelaar

---

[121] Note provided by Carol Myers.

the twentieth century and continued into the present century. A nonhierarchical model for ministry with complementary roles for pastors, each using personal gifts in ministry, each reporting to the Personnel Committee and directed by the consistory, has been working well.

In 1998 the Search Committee worked first with a list of candidates for a minister of Word and witness position and then with a list of candidates for a minister of congregational life position. In August Hope Church called the Reverend Kathryn Davelaar as minister of Word and witness. Leaving her position as associate minister of the Third Reformed Church in Holland, where she had served for five years, Davelaar began her ministry at Hope Church in September 1998.[122]

In April Hope Church called the Reverend Gordon S. Wiersma as minister of congregational life. Leaving his ministry of the previous four years as co-pastor of the North and Southampton Reformed Church in Churchville, Pennsylvania, Wiersma began serving in Hope Church in August 1999.[123] Both Davelaar and Wiersma grew up in Christian Reformed churches and, like Rienstra, graduated from Calvin College.

In 1999 Hope Church began a $550,000 capital fund campaign titled, "Hope 2000: Assuring Our Future." The campaign entailed plans for "Looking Inward, Looking Outward and Looking to the Future." At the congregational meeting, campaign chair Fred Leaske thanked the committee and congregation for pledges totaling $604,325. Money received from the campaign and from a later restoration project campaign was used to reinforce trusses above the sanctuary and supports below the sanctuary, repair plaster cracks,

---

[122] Minutes 1998\Consistory 04.doc, 20 April 1998. Minutes 1998\ Congregational Special 08.doc, 2 August 1998. The vote was 188 yes, 27 no, and 1 abstention. Minutes 1998\Consistory 08.doc, 17 August 1998.
[123] Minutes 1999\Congregational Mtg Special 04.doc, 18 April 1999. The vote was 179 yes and 2 no. The North and Southampton Reformed Church was the congregation where Marion de Velder had served for two years before accepting the call from Hope Church in 1939.

Gordon S. Wiersma

repair the organ, install hearing loop systems in the sanctuary and Commons I, refurbish and reposition pews to allow more leg room, shorten some pews to accommodate wheel chairs, improve temperature controls, add air conditioning, protect windows, replace west entrance doors, and add and improve landscaping.[124]

---

[124] Minutes 1999\Consistory 01.doc, 18 January 1999. Minutes 1999\Consistory 03.doc, 15 March 1999. Minutes 1999\Congregational Mtg. Special Capital Fund 04.doc, 25 April 1999. Minutes 1999\Annual Congregational Mtg 11.doc, 21 November 1999. Minutes 2000\Annual Congregational Meeting 11.doc, 19 November 2000. Minutes 2001\

In April 2000, Wiersma reported that the application submitted by Hope Church to Holland Community Hospital for a parish nurse program was approved and there was money in the 2000 budget to support a parish nurse for twenty hours a week, though a future commitment to this ministry would require consistory decisions about funding. In July Barbara Sychowski was hired. She served from August 2000 to August 2002, when she resigned. Parish Nurse Marjorie Taylor served part-time from April 2003 through 2009.[125]

Wiersma developed a two-year Growing In Faith Together (GIFT) class for eighth- and ninth-graders and wrote a curriculum for the class to help the students explore issues of faith and church life. The class has helped prepare young people to join the church by confession of faith.[126] Wiersma and Davelaar also promoted the Belhar Confession by frequently incorporating parts of it in worship liturgies.

In 2001 member Connie Thornhill presented to the Executive Committee the idea for a memorial garden where ashes of deceased persons could be buried. The consistory approved the creation of a memorial garden. David Van Heest soon reported that a suitable site, procedures for using it, and a brochure had been prepared.[127] The memorial garden has received the ashes of several individuals with room for many more.

Consistory 05.doc, 14 May 2001. Minutes 2002\Executive Committee 01.doc, 7 January 2002. The goal of the restoration project campaign was $250,000.00. Minutes 2002\Consistory 06.doc, 10 June 2002.
[125] Minutes 2000\Consistory 04.doc, 10 April 2000. Minutes 2000\Consistory 07.doc, 30 July 2000. Sychowski resigned because she found it necessary to find a full-time position. Minutes 2002\Consistory 09.doc, 9 September 2002. Minutes 2003\Executive Committee 04.doc, 31 March 2003. By May 2009 Marjorie Taylor had secured employment at Holland Hospital. Minutes 2009\Consistory Meeting 05.doc, 11 May 2009.
[126] Minutes 2000\Consistory 04.doc, 10 April 2000.
[127] Minutes 2001\Executive Committee 10.doc, 1 October 2001. Minutes 2001\Consistory10.doc, 8 October 2001. Minutes 2003\Consistory 01, 13 January 2003. Minutes 2003\Consistory 06.doc, 9 June 2003.

In 2002 Hope Church purchased the house at 92 West Tenth Street. Hope Church then worked with Good Samaritan Ministries on a Community Housing Partnership through HUD to refurbish and manage the house for use as a transitional home for families.[128]

In 2003 in reaction to what many perceived as the denomination's and regional synod's preoccupation with efforts to produce many new churches with increasing membership, Hope Church considered alternative ways toward church growth. It found a useful model in Natural Church Development (NCD). NCD presented a way for churches to study who they are and then learn how to develop and improve their spiritual health. Based on methods developed by Christian A. Schwarz and used by churches across many denominations, NCD was introduced to the consistory of Hope Church by the Reverend Vicky Menning. The consistory approved use of the NCD survey, and a representative sample of the congregation completed it. The pastors used its results to develop a "plan using the eight characteristics of a healthy church and involving the entire congregation."[129] The eight characteristics comprised empowering leadership, gift-oriented ministry, passionate spirituality, functional structures, inspiring worship services, holistic small groups, need-oriented evangelism, and loving relationships.[130]

Encouraged by the NCD process, an Ideas ministry was started to collect ideas and distribute them to appropriate ministries. A Gifts team was formed to find ways for the membership to experience gift-oriented ministry. Gifts was the theme for the 2006 consistory retreat and Wednesday Lenten programs. Spiritual Gifts was the topic of a six-week adult education series led by Karen Mulder in

---

[128] Minutes 2002\Executive Committee 11.doc, 4 November 2002.
[129] Minutes 2003\Consistory 10.doc, 13 October 2003. Minutes 2004\Executive Committee 02.doc, 2 February 2004.
[130] Christian A. Schwarz, *Natural Church Development: A Guide to Eight Essential Qualities of Healthy Churches* (St. Charles, IL: Churchsmart Resources, 1996).

the autumn of 2006. In January 2007 several members whose gift was writing presented a pair of adult education classes on relationships between writing and Christian faith. The theme for the 2007 stewardship campaign was "Celebration of Our Gifts."[131]

On 12 September 2004 the congregation bestowed on its highly talented organist, Barbara Borr Veurink, the title, "Organist Emerita." After nearly four decades of splendid service as organist and director of children's choirs, she was honored at her retirement by a party of celebration.[132]

Barbara Borr Veurink, organist

---

[131] Minutes 2006\Consistory 01.doc, 9 January 2006. Minutes 2006\Consistory 02.doc, 13 February 2006. Minutes 2007\Executive Committee 08.doc, 8 August 2007.
[132] Minutes 2004\Consistory 08.doc, 9 August 2004.

Advocating Inclusion for All

In 2001 Doug Abell and David Van Heest were appointed to the Memorial Garden Committee and Van Heest was elected deacon. Pastors Davelaar and Wiersma reported to the Executive Committee that there has been "some community response but no formal Classis response" to Van Heest's election to the office of deacon.[133] In 2004 Doug Abell was elected deacon. Also in 2004 the consistory added "sexual orientation" to the list of classes protected by the section on harassment in its "Non-Ordained Staff Employment Policy Guidelines."[134]

In 2004 the consistory of the Grace Community Church submitted to Holland Classis an overture "to declare by resolution that no person who continues in unrepentant homosexual behavior be ordained to the offices of Deacon, Elder and Minister of Word and Sacrament."[135] Holland Classis held a special session in November 2004 to discuss the issues presented by the Grace Community Church consistory. In the spring of 2005, Holland Classis denied three overtures regarding prohibition of homosexuals from leadership in the RCA. The Executive Committee of the classis proposed and classis approved an alternative to a polarizing vote. Guided

---

[133] Minutes 2001\Executive Committee 11, 5 November 2001. As in recent previous elections of deacons and elders, a Nominations Committee consisting of several members of the "retiring" class of consistory, a pastor, and several long-time members, selected candidates for deacon and elder from a list of names provided by members of the congregation. Candidates from the list were ranked by perceived gifts for ministry as elders or deacons, and they were contacted to ascertain their willingness to serve if elected. From those willing to serve, a single slate of deacons and of elders was voted on at a congregational meeting. The election of elders and deacons at the 2001 congregational meeting was by voice vote. There were no "no" votes for either slate of elders or deacons. Minutes 2001\Annual Congregational Meeting 11.doc, 18 November 2001. Minutes 2001\Executive Committee 12, 3 December 2001.
[134] Minutes 2004\Consistory 04.doc, 12 April 2004.
[135] Holland Classis minutes, 28 September 2004:3. "Overture from Grace Community Church," Holland Classis, January 2005 session.

by processes used in Hope Church's year of discernment,[136] the committee proposed "an alternate route," a third way:

> Instead of voting again ... or simply settling into separate camps held together by an uneasy truce of silence—might we covenant together to ... pursue a different model?... Might there be a plot of common ground where all of us can agree to stand together on this issue so we also can move forward together in Christ's mission for Holland Classis? We are proposing an accountable, definite timetable of biblical study, dialogue, and prayer.... We ask that we make a commitment, to God and to each other, to engage in a period of intentional reflection and shared discernment to the pastoral challenges raised by the presence of homosexual persons in our congregations and communities.[137]

While the discussion about homosexual people in church leadership was occurring in Holland Classis, the Reverend Norman Kansfield, president of New Brunswick Theological Seminary, had become a lightning rod in the East. He was attracting complaints for having officiated at the marriage ceremony of his daughter Ann, a recent graduate of that seminary, to Jennifer Aull on 19 June 2004. The marriage took place in Massachusetts, where same-sex marriages had recently been ruled legal. About his action and Ann's plans to become a pastor in the RCA, Norman Kansfield stated, both of us "are struggling to find a way ... that people can be blessed by the full, regular and joyful participation in the life of the church."[138]

In January 2005 the consistory of Hope Church wrote a letter of encouragement to Norman Kansfield:

---

[136] Minutes 2004\Consistory 08.doc, 9 August 2004. Minutes 2005\Executive Committee 02.doc, 7 February 2005. Minutes 2005\Consistory 02.doc, 15 February 2005. Minutes 2005\Consistory 04, 11 April 2005.

[137] "Recommendations to the Classis from the Executive Committee," Classis of Holland, 2005. In minutes of the Holland Classis Executive Committee on 1 March 2005, this document was referred to as "A Third Approach for Addressing a Divisive Issue."

[138] Anthony Ramirez, "Seminary Votes Out Leader Over Daughter's Gay Wedding," *New York Times*, 21 February 2005. http://www.nytimes.com/2005/02/12/nyregion/12seminary.html

Dear Brother in Jesus Christ,

....Your choice to preside at the marriage of your daughter, Ann, and daughter-in-law, Jennifer, is such an example of the love, mystery, and complexity with which our humanity challenges each of us. Your actions invite us to think prayerfully about the choices we make in the human contexts we encounter.

We also believe as a consistory that you and your family are brothers and sisters in Christ, and we celebrate all that you have contributed to growing and enriching the body of Christ within the Reformed Church and beyond. We look forward with hope to your continued ministry to us and to the RCA....

We pray that the impending conversation you have with the RCA's leadership will be a joyful and hopeful one for you and your family and one from which we will all grow as a church family....

>   Sincerely,
>   The Consistory of Hope Church
>   Holland, Michigan[139]

In February 2005 the board of New Brunswick Theological Seminary voted not to extend the contract of Kansfield as president.[140]

The General Synod, in June of that year, put Kansfield on trial. Because he was a theological professor, he was not tried by a classis but by the General Synod, the first such trial in more than a century. By a roughly three-to-one majority, the delegates found Kansfield guilty of acting "contrary to our faith and beliefs as affirmed by the holy Scriptures and the decisions of the General Synod concerning the relationships of active homosexuality."[141] They voted to suspend him from the ministry "until he changes his views to fall

---

[139] Consistory Documents 2005\N Kansfield letter of support 1-12-05.doc
[140] Anthony Ramirez, "Minister Faces Church Trial for Performing Gay Wedding," *New York Times*, 17 June 2005. http://www.nytimes.com/2005/06/17/nyregion/17priest.html
[141] Anthony Ramirez, "Minister Cited for Performing Gay Wedding," *New York Times*, 18 June 2005. http://www.nytimes.com/2005/06/18/nyregion/18priest.html There were 245 delegates who voted.

in line with church doctrine, and to strip him of his standing as a professor of theology in the church."[142]

In the months leading up to Kansfield's trial, a number of his friends who were in sympathy with his views and actions spoke out. Via e-mail they communicated support and solidarity with Kansfield. In response to the trial, his friends agreed to keep the voice for full inclusion of lesbians, gays, bisexuals, and transgenders (LGBTs) alive, to "serve the church in communicating God's love for all people." David Van Heest, Doug Abell, and some others from Hope Church attended a Holy Relationships conference at New Brunswick Theological Seminary in October 2005.[143] From this conference came forth an organization called Room for All, which was incorporated "to support, educate and advocate for the full inclusion of LGBT people in the RCA."[144]

Kathryn Davelaar was installed as president of the Holland Classis for 2006, the year in which the classis presented a four-session series of dialogues about homosexuality. Hope Church was well represented at the dialogue meetings held at Western Theological Seminary. The dialogues in Holland Classis were a pilot project for a process under the leadership of the Reverend John Stapert that spread across the denomination over two years—though not all classes chose to participate—and served as a model for responding to divisive issues. Reporting the results of the dialogues about homosexuality, the planning team concluded,

> Because none of us has all the answers, we have much to learn from others in the body of Christ. We value Christian fellowship and our collective desire to use good judgment without being judgmental. We acknowledge that we need to minister to and with homosexual

---

[142] Ramirez, "Minister Cited for Performing Gay Wedding."
[143] Minutes 2005\Consistory 08.doc, 8 August 2005. Also in 2005 a book coauthored by David Myers and Letha Dawson Scanzoni, *What God Has Joined Together?: A Christian Case for Gay Marriage*, was published by HarperCollins. In a subsequent edition of the book the question mark was removed from the title.
[144] "History," http://roomforall.com/about-us/history/

persons, but we also acknowledge that the texture and shape of such ministries will vary among churches in Holland Classis. We affirm the importance of openness and honesty in dealing constructively with this issue. Since we are not of one mind, we need to resist the temptation to compel one church to imitate another in its perspective or approach. Love and grace are needed in our ministries, particularly as we proclaim God's call to fidelity and chastity. While God's love is unconditional, our response to that love brings responsibility to follow God's call upon each of us. We trust the Holy Spirit to guide us—as congregations and as a classis—to be faithful to the One who has called us out of darkness into God's marvelous light.[145]

Ministries of Gordon S. Wiersma and Jill R. Russell, 2008–

In February 2007 Davelaar expressed to a combined meeting of the Executive and Personnel Committees "her sense that it was time for a completion of her ministry at Hope Church."[146] Davelaar became interim pastor at the Lynnwood Reformed Church in Schenectady, New York, and later accepted a call to the Reformed Dutch Church of Claverack, New York.

A search committee, chaired by the Reverend Paul Smith (who was also an elder), worked for more than a year to update the church profile, place advertisements for a co-pastor, and interview candidates. The Reverend Jill R. Russell, unanimously approved by consistory and congregation, was called. She began her ministry at Hope Church in September 2008.[147]

---

[145] "Report of the Holland Classis Dialogue Planning Team," *Holland Classis Stated Session*, May 2006.
[146] Minutes 2007\Executive-Personnel Committee 02-21 Special.doc, 21 February 2007.
[147] Minutes 2008\Consistory Minutes 06.doc, 9 June 2008. Minutes 2008\Congregational Meeting 6-22-08.doc, 22 June 2008. Minutes 2008\Consistory Meeting 08.doc, 11 August 2008.

Jill R. Russell

Like Davelaar and Wiersma, Russell graduated from Calvin College. Like Wiersma, she grew up in Southwest Michigan, received her MDiv degree from Princeton Theological Seminary, and served churches outside Michigan before coming to Hope Church. She introduced to the congregation Appreciative Inquiry and Restorative Circles. One of the first occasions to practice Appreciative Inquiry was in responding to the removal of funding for the parish nurse program in 2009.[148]

---

[148] Minutes 2008\Consistory Meeting 09.doc, 9 September 2008.

In 2005 Holland Hospital had informed churches that it would no longer provide funding for parish nursing programs. To keep Hope Church's part-time parish nurse, the church would need to increase her salary by $7,500, which the consistory did. In 2008 and 2009 the Personnel Committee and consistory worked on staff restructuring. They proposed dropping all funding for the parish nurse program, replacing the facilities manager position held by David Hawley with a custodial position by Ric Beltran, and reassigning tasks performed by the church administrator, Janet Bast Elzinga, who retired in 2008, and by the finance manager, Joan DeJonge (Wall), to Laurie Beyer Braaksma and Karla Kammeraad-Bos.[149]

Some members of the congregation wanted to revisit the decision to drop the parish nurse position, and efforts were made to extend the parish nurse position held by Marjorie Taylor for fifteen hours a week through June 2009. A Congregational Care Study Group was formed under the leadership of Jill Russell to explore ways the congregation could attempt to fill the gap made by the loss of the parish nurse. Russell employed Appreciative Inquiry processes in the study group's consideration of what pastoral care and congregational care practices functioned well in the past. In the study, congregation members "identified the relationships they share with one another as the primary place they receive care at Hope Church." Additionally, the study found that there was a "great deal of convergence between what people value about the care they have received from Hope Church in the past and the vision they have for how Hope Church could become the ideal caring church in the future."[150] Among the group's recommendations approved by consistory were changing the name of Pastoral Care ministry to Congregational Care ministry, changing Anchor

---

[149] Minutes 2005\Consistory 11.doc, 14 November 2005. Minutes 2008\Consistory Minutes 06, 9 June 2008.
[150] Minutes 2008\Consistory Meeting 10.doc, 13 October 2008. "Congregational Care Study Group Report to the Consistory," approved by the consistory on 8 June 2009.

Groups to Care Groups, and changing the Anchor Line to the Care Line; encouraging Congregational Care ministry members to pray with and maintain personal and direct contact with each member of their Care Group; and developing a plan to identify and support small groups.[151]

In 2011, with approval by the congregation,[152] the consistory added a part-time parish nurse and a part-time youth director to the staff. In April, Hope Church contracted with Resthaven for one of its At Home nurses, Danita Robards, to begin serving as the Hope Church nurse for eight hours per week. Hope Church member Anne Duinkerken was hired as a part-time youth ministry director.[153]

As part of her continuing education, Russell attended Restorative Circles training in October 2010. For the season of Epiphany in 2011 she introduced a "Season of Reconciliation," a time-span that would coincide with national observances such as Martin Luther King Jr. Day and Black History Month. Russell stated that the purpose for this season came from our call as Christians to the "ministry of reconciliation" (II Corinthians 5:17–20) and invited the congregation to explore "what this might mean in our relationship to God, with the people in our lives, and ... on the way we live together in community."[154] She introduced Restorative Circles at a weekly small group discussion in January and February 2011. In May Restorative Circles were introduced to members of other churches in Holland, and a group called Holland Restorative Circles was formed.[155]

---

[151] Minutes 2009\Consistory Meeting 06.doc, 8 June 2009. Minutes 2009\Consistory Meeting 09.doc, 14 September 2009.
[152] A special congregational meeting was held in October 2010 for consistory to respond to questions from the congregation and hear their responses to possibility of hiring two part-time staff members.
[153] Minutes 2011\Consistory 04.doc, 11 April 2011. Minutes 2011\Executive Committee 08.doc, 01 August 2011. The "employer of record" for the nurse position is Resthaven. Minutes 2011\Consistory 02.doc, 14 February 2011.
[154] Russell, "And Finally...," *Hope Church News*, November 2010:10.
[155] Minutes 2010\Consistory 10.doc, 10 October 2010. Minutes 2010\

Focusing on Multicultural Diversity

Prompted by the RCA's call for a "multiracial future freed from racism," Hope Church's Community/World ministry began to focus in 2009 on expanding multicultural diversity at Hope Church. In August the consistory hosted a Celebrating Multicultural Diversity dinner, to which it invited the congregation. Those attending were encouraged to share responses to the question: "How can we shape our life as a congregation to reflect our call and commitment to be an inclusive community?" Lois Maassen described the changing demographics of Holland, and Kay Hubbard described the history of diversity in the church and opened discussion for all to consider their hopes and fears regarding multicultural diversity. In small groups people discussed what pursuing diversity might look like in worship, hospitality, spiritual formation, and outreach.[156]

One of the ideas springing from August's multicultural diversity celebration was a resource fair or open house, an occasion when various agencies experienced with racial diversity issues would be invited to Hope Church to present information about their groups and missions. Local churches of various denominations would be invited to this event.[157] At an open house held at Hope Church on 14 November 2009, representatives from the Alliance for Cultural and Ethnic Harmony, Lakeshore Ethnic Diversity Alliance, Latin Americans United for Progress, and others provided information to those attending from several congregations.[158]

Other initiatives for diversity included inviting the Reverends Andrés Fierro, Roberto Jara, Andy Nakajima, Angela Taylor-Perry, and others from various ethnicities to be guest preachers on various

---

Consistory 12.doc, 13 December 2010. Russell, "And Finally...," *Hope Church News*, January 2011:11. Minutes 2011\Consistory 03.doc, 14 March 2011. http://hrcircles.wordpress.com/
[156] Minutes 2009\Consistory Meeting 08.doc, 10 August 1009.
[157] Minutes 2009\Consistory Meeting 09.doc, 14 September 2009. Minutes 2009\Consistory Meeting 10.doc, 12 October 2009.
[158] Minutes 2009\Consistory Meeting 12.doc, 7 December 2009.

Sundays at Hope Church; singing songs and hymns from non-U.S./European countries on the fifth Sundays of various months; and attending Summits on Racism held at Hope College.[159]

In the autumn of 2010 an adult education class was presented, titled "Multicultural Diversity: Holland, the RCA, and Hope Church." Holland Public Schools' Superintendent Brian Davis, Lakeshore Ethnic Diversity Alliance Executive Director Gail Harrison, and others discussed the changing demographics of Holland and how to bring about a future enriched by our growing diversity.

At the final session of this series, a banner designed by Christopher Wiers was unveiled. Embraced by a pair of Old and New Testament passages—Psalm 133:2 and II Corinthians 5:17:18—it states Hope Church's commitment to multicultural diversity.[160]

In spring 2011 an adult education class viewed and discussed the DVD titled *Race: the Power of an Illusion*. Hope Church also sent several members to participate in Western Theological Seminary's Multi-Racial Journey 2010–11 Initiative.[161]

The Multi-Racial Journey Initiative prompted Hope Church representatives to participate in the Neighborhood Connections ministry. Supervised by the Good Samaritan Center and funded in part by AmeriCorps, the ministry is an ecumenical effort that also includes St. Francis de Sales Catholic, First United Methodist, and Third Reformed churches.[162] Among its goals is to work side-by-side with people in the neighborhood of these churches to strengthen community.

---

[159] Minutes 2009\Consistory Meeting 12.doc, 7 December 2009. Minutes 2011\Executive Committee 04.doc, 4 April 2011.
[160] Note that the opening verse, "How very good and blessed it is when kindred dwell together in unity," is the same verse quoted in the thank-you note from Stuart Padnos on page 358.
[161] *Hope Church News*, September and October 2010 and February and March 2011. Participants in the Multi-Racial Journey were Gordon Wiersma, Jill Russell, Ric Beltran, John Koch, Lois Maassen, Kyle Vohlken, and Beverly Zell. Minutes 2010\Consistory 03.doc, 8 March 2010.
[162] Minutes 2011\Executive Committee 08.doc, 1 August 2011. Minutes 2011\Executive Committee 11.doc, 7 November 2011.

> How very good and
> blessed it is when kindred
> dwell together in unity.
> Psalm 133:1

**Hope Church is committed
to multicultural diversity
as an expression
of our faith in Jesus Christ.
This commitment is integral to our life
as a community of faith
and to our work
as peacemakers and reconcilers
in God's world.**

> If anyone is in Christ,
> there is a new creation:
> everything old has passed away;
> see, everything has become new!
> All this is from God,
> who reconciled us to God
> through Christ,
> and has given us the
> ministry of reconciliation.
> II Corinthians 5:17-18

Multicultural diversity banner

Advocating for Gracious Acceptance and Justice for All

During 2010 several Hope Church members supported the causes of Hope Is Ready, a Hope College student group which among other things was questioning Hope College's 1995 policy on homosexuality. The consistory sent a letter to the Hope College Board of Trustees, urging its members to "consider removing the 1995 'Institutional Statement on Homosexuality' from Hope College policy."

April 15, 2010

Dear Hope College Board of Trustees,

>We, the consistory of Hope Church RCA, are aware of recent events that have challenged Hope College's 1995 "Institutional Statement on Homosexuality." We value the long-standing relationship between Hope Church and Hope College. We take seriously the 1971 "Covenant of Mutual Responsibilities" of the Reformed Church in America that calls RCA congregations and RCA colleges to engage in relationships of mutual support, encouragement, and trust. We affirm the deep commitments of the college administration and the Board of Trustees for the flourishing of the college community.
>
>Because of the values and commitments identified above, we respectfully request that the Board of Trustees consider removing the 1995 "Institutional Statement on Homosexuality" from Hope College policy. We are concerned, particularly, that the document claims that "the witness of Scripture is firm in rejecting the moral acceptability of homosexual behavior. . ." We observe that this is simply not the case. Serious, committed, thoughtful Christian people have profound disagreements on the witness of Scripture with respect to homosexuality in particular and Christian sexual ethics in general. This statement does not express the kind of careful, complete theological and biblical reflection that Hope College seeks to embody.
>
>In addition, the statement tends to use social/psychological categories that are no longer seen as valid in the growing literature on sexual orientation. For example, the use of "homosexual behavior" is a term that perhaps seemed clear fifteen years ago, but now signals an inadequate and untenable distinction between

actions and orientation. Hope College's own academic standards invite a careful reconsideration of this kind of language.

We are also very concerned about the witness of Hope College to its students. Students who are gay or lesbian and struggle to find acceptance and worth will be damaged by an affirmation of this 1995 Statement by the Board of Trustees. All students will be formed in their own patterns of hospitality and mature reflection by observing the actions of the Board in response to the petitions the Board has recently received. We can well understand the difficulties these public petitions pose to the Board. But we believe this may well be an opportunity for the Board to model the virtues and values of the gospel, including care, gracious acceptance, faithful living, and openness to the Spirit of God.

Sincerely,
Hope Church RCA Consistory[163]

Hope Church members and the consistory also supported Holland Is Ready, a group that formed to support Hope Is Ready and to support efforts by Holland citizens to include sexual identity among the classes currently protected by Holland ordinances governing housing and employment. In 2010 the consistory submitted "an overture to request that Holland Classis make a public stand to support a civil rights ordinance that includes sexual orientation."[164]

---

[163] Minutes 2010\Consistory Meeting 04.doc, 12 April 2010 addendum.
[164] The consistory supported the overture because it reflected the RCA position of affirming "human and civil rights to homosexuals" and "such a statement would be a witness from the Holland Classis to the Holland community expressing a united voice of justice and faithfulness from the Holland Classis congregations." Minutes 2010\Consistory Meeting 08.doc, 9 August 2010. The overture submitted by Hope Church was modified slightly by the Classis Executive Committee, mainly by inclusion of the entire sentence quoted from the *Minutes of General Synod 1978*, before the overture was presented at the classis meeting.

The overture stated:

> The Holland Classis of the Reformed Church in America is committed to serving our community in the name of Jesus Christ. As many congregations, numerous ministries, and thousands of members, we are blessed by God to be part of the vibrant Holland community. We seek to be a presence of unity, reconciliation and justice with our neighbors.
>
> We are aware of the current discussion in our community surrounding the consideration of amending a civil rights ordinance in the City of Holland. In the midst of this atmosphere, the Holland Classis RCA offers this statement: The position of the Reformed Church in America is that the denial of human and civil rights based on sexual identity is inconsistent with the biblical witness and Reformed theology.[1] In faithfulness to this position, the Holland Classis expresses its support for every civil rights ordinance that affirms the value and dignity of each person. In the midst of many theological, political, and social differences, valuing civil rights for all serves the Holland community well.
>
> We offer this statement with conviction and humility, as we seek to be faithful to God and to serve our community with gratitude and joy.
>
> ---
>
> [1] "While we cannot affirm homosexual behavior, at the same time we are convinced that the denial of human and civil rights to homosexuals is inconsistent with the biblical witness and Reformed theology." (*Minutes of General Synod 1978:* 233–239)[165]

The Holland Classis of the RCA approved Hope Church's overture by voice vote. An additional motion was made to send the approved overture to the Holland City Council and its Human Relations Commission.[166] Despite the overture and the unanimous

---

[165] "Minutes: Classis of Holland, Reformed Church in America Stated Session at Maplewood Reformed Church Tuesday, ... [September] 28, 2010," 2–3. http://www.hollandclassisrca.org/documents/classis/2010-9-28%20 CommitteeReports.pdf.

[166] "Minutes: Classis of Holland, Reformed Church in America Stated Session at Maplewood Reformed Church Tuesday, ... [September] 28, 2010," 2–3. http://www.hollandclassisrca.org/documents/classis/2010-9-28%20 CommitteeReports.pdf

endorsement by the Human Relations Commission to amend the city's human rights ordinances to add sexual orientation and gender identity as protected classes, on 16 June 2011 the Holland City Council voted five to four against amending the ordinances.[167]

Becoming a "Room for All" Church

In January 2009, the Adult Education ministry presented a three-week series titled, "Homosexuality, the RCA, and Hope Church." Lynn Japinga summarized thirty years of denominational responses to homosexuality. Kristen Gray described the Holland Classis four-session dialogue of 2005. Doug Abell, David Van Heest, and Steven Hoogerwerf described the events leading to the year of moral discernment and the outcomes of that process in the mid-1990s. The DVD titled *Seven Passages*, which explores the ways that various gay Christians have responded to key scripture passages, was shown and discussed. A panel that included David Van Heest, Doug Abell, Kristen Gray, and the Reverend Marlin Vander Wilt discussed the creation of Room for All, the "Welcoming and Affirming" progress within Classis of New Brunswick congregations, and how the United Church of Christ and Presbyterian Church USA are responding to issues of homosexuality.[168] In March the consistory unanimously approved posting Hope Church contact information on websites for www.gaysinfaithtogether.org and www.gaychurch.org as a means of indicating that Hope Church "is a welcoming place for gay, lesbian, transgendered, and bisexual people."[169]

Under the leadership of David Van Heest, Room for All held meetings with members of various Reformed churches in the Holland area. Led by the Room for All board of directors, including Van

---

[167] Annette Manwell, "Holland Could Face Long Battle over Human Rights Changes," *Holland Sentinel*, 18 June 2011. http://www.hollandsentinel.com/homepage/x1425876953/Holland-could-face-long-battle-over-human-rights-changes

[168] *Hope Church News*, January 2009.

[169] Minutes 2009\Consistory Meeting 03.doc, 9 March 2009.

Heest, the first national conference, "Making Room for All," was held at the Central Reformed Church in Grand Rapids in October 2009. In April 2010 Hope Church hosted regional training for RCA churches seeking to become more inclusive, and in 2011 another national conference was held at the Central Reformed Church.

In a January 2011 adult education series, the Reverend James Brownson presented a four-session series titled "Deepening the Church's Debate about Same-Sex Relationships." This was augmented by a two-session class in April. In the first session a panel presented efforts toward inclusion by the RCA denomination, by Hope College, and by Western Theological Seminary. In the second session speakers representing Parents, Families and Friends of Lesbians and Gays (PFLAG), Holland Is Ready, and Room for All described community responses toward inclusion.[170]

In addition to supporting the Room for All organization, Hope Church also developed a supportive relationship with the Greenpoint Reformed Church in Brooklyn, New York, the church served by the Reverends Ann Kansfield and Jennifer Aull. The senior high youth group, High Hopes, took mission trips there to assist with distributing food and maintaining the church facility in 2009 and 2011.

In January 2012 the congregation indicated overwhelming support for becoming a Room for All congregation.[171] The following month consistory by a unanimous vote approved the "Room for All Affirmation" and added Hope Church to the sixteen Reformed churches already on the roster.[172]

---

[170] *Hope Church News*, April 2011. Brownson is the James and Jean Cook Professor of New Testament at Western Theological Seminary.
[171] The vote was 111 in favor, 7 opposed, with 3 abstentions. "Update on the Room for All Affirmation process,: Hope Church bulletin 12 February 2012:8
[172] All sixteen of the previously signing churches are in New Jersey and New York. Hope Church is the first church west of New York to sign the roster. For the current roster of Room for All churches, see http://roomforall.com/welcoming-and-affirming/roster-of-room-for-all-churches-in-the-reformed-church-in-america/

Clark MacLean and Jon Jerow prepare to paint window frames at the Greenpoint Reformed Church

Bethany Wiersma paints at the Greenpoint Reformed Church on a 2011 High Hopes mission trip

Looking Back, Forward, Inward, and Outward

Many would agree that this expanding inclusion is in accord with the spirit prevailing since the founding of Hope Church in 1862. From its earliest years, Hope Church welcomed those who spoke Dutch and those who spoke English. It welcomed members from a variety of denominations. It welcomed Holland residents and Hope College faculty and students, even students from as far away as Japan.

Hope Church cultivated relationships with churches in the East. As a member of the English-speaking Michigan Classis until 1923, Hope Church was not drawn into or damaged by the secessions that disrupted relationships among churches in Holland Classis. As a pioneer in recognizing the gifts of women, Hope Church as early as 1878 allowed women members to vote to call a minister and as early as 1879 allowed them to elect deacons and elders.

In the twentieth century Hope Church cooperated with other Holland Reformed churches and with churches of other denominations and with St. Francis de Sales Catholic Church to reach out to migrant worker families, provide day care to children, and respond to other needs of the community. Two members, Elsie Lamb and Jo Anne Brooks, founded the Holland Peacemakers organization. Hope Church advocated for equal justice in housing and employment opportunity for all and elected a gay man to consistory.

In the twenty-first century Hope Church joined several other Reformed churches in supporting, educating, and advocating for the "full participation of lesbian, gay, bi-sexual and transgender (LGBT) persons in all aspects of the life and ministry of the Reformed Church in America as compelled by the inclusive love of God revealed to us by our Lord and Savior Jesus Christ."[173]

---

[173] Certificate of Incorporation, Room for All, Inc., Article 4.

Hope Church was the home of thirteen of Holland's forty-one mayors[174] and eight of Hope College's twelve presidents.[175] Seven presidents of the General Synod were affiliated with Hope Church: Philip Phelps Jr. (1864), Charles Scott (1875), Ame Vennema (1907), Marion de Velder (1958), Lester Jacob Kuyper (1970), James I. Cook (1982),[176] and Carol Bechtel (2008). In addition, Marion de Velder served as stated clerk of the General Synod (1961–68) and then general secretary of the RCA (1968–77).

In 2012, the sesquicentennial year of Hope Church, the Reformed Church in America is asking congregations to seek answers to three questions: "How is God working within you? Through you? Ahead of you?"[177] If you have read this history of Hope Church, you have learned how God has worked through this congregation and its ministries to pioneer, to be open, to grow in faith, and to lead in Christian action. To paraphrase the motto of our state—If you seek a church where God is at work, look around you.

---

[174] They were Bernardus Ledeboer, 1868–72; Edward J. Harrington, 1872–74 and 1892–93; Henry Kremers, 1889–90; Oscar Yates, 1890–92; Gerrit J. Diekema, 1895–96; William Brusse, 1900–02; Henry Geerlings, 1904–06 and 1936–44; Jacob G. Van Putten, 1906–08; Nicodemus Bosch, 1912–16, 1918–20, and 1932–36; Earnest Brooks, 1928–32; Robert Visscher, 1955–61; Lawrence W. (Bill) Lamb Jr., 1971–73; and Philip A. Tanis, 1987–89 (though Tanis joined Hope Church after serving as mayor). http://www2.cityofholland.com/mayors/

[175] They were Philip Phelps Jr. (1866–78), Charles Scott (1878–93), Gerrit J. Kollen (1893–1911), Ame Vennema (1911–18), Edward D. Dimnent (1918–31), Irwin J. Lubbers (1945–63), Calvin Vander Werf (1963–70), and John H. Jacobson (1987–99). *Hope College 2002 Alumni Directory*, 10th ed. (Holland, MI: Hope College, 2002), 298.

[176] Gasero, *Historical Directory*, 689.

[177] "Discernment Discovery Process," https://www.rca.org/discernment

Appendix A: Consistory Members

Below in chronological order of their first installation to office are lists of Hope Church deacons and elders.[1] Though many individuals served several terms, they are listed only once per office.

Deacons

1862	William B. Gilmore	1898	Frank D. Haddock
1864	James Sipp	1901	William Wing
1864	Peter Sakkers	1902	Gerrit Van Schelven
1867	William A. Shields	1902	George Van Landegend
1867	John Te Winkle	1902	Fred Betts
1868	Richard H. Heald	1902	John G. Kamps
1868	Ernst Herold	1906	Henry R. Brush
1868	Thomas Emerson Annis	1906	Charles C. Wheeler
1872	J. O. Bakker	1909	Bastian D. Keppel
1872	Matthew Scott	1910	Egbert E. Fell
1875	Wilson Harrington	1911	Cornelius J. Dregman
1876	Henry Baum	1913	Abraham Leenhouts
1877	Isaac Bangs	1913	John B. Nykerk
1880	Albert Dutton	1916	August Heuer
1885	Oscar E. Yates	1916	Peter Van Domelen
1886	Peter H. Wilms	1917	James O. Scott
1887	William Brusse	1917	Arthur Visscher
1887	Bernard J. De Vries	1917	George L. Lage
1887	Dirk B. K. Van Raalte	1920	Henry Winter
1889	F. J. Schouten	1920	William J. Olive
1892	Ulke De Vries	1920	Hoyt Post
1893	George W. Browning	1923	John J. Riemersma
1895	Henry Boers	1923	Joseph Rhea
1896	George Souter	1924	Chester L. Beach

---

[1] Sources of information 1862–1916 are *Consistorial Minutes*, 1, and "Record of Hope Church Holland Michigan, 1862–1916." Both are at W91-1034, Hope Church, Holland, Michigan, Joint Archives of Holland, the first in box 1 and the second in box 11. Information after 1916 comes from volumes of *Consistorial Minutes*. Information after 1995 comes from Hope Church's computer files.

Deacons (continued)

1926	George W. Van Verst	1953	Leonard R. Swartz
1928	Edward J. DePree	1953	Lawrence A. Wade
1928	Milton L. Hinga	1954	I. Herbert Marsilje
1929	Irwin J. Lubbers	1955	Vern Boersma
1930	Gerrit J. Van Zoeren	1955	Robert Vanderham
1931	Kenneth DePree	1956	Paul Winchester
1932	W. Tappan	1957	Lester J. DeRidder
1932	Randall C. Bosch	1957	George Steininger
1932	George A. Pelgrim	1957	Roy D. Klomparens
1933	Albert Van Zoeren	1959	James Brown
1933	John Vander Broek	1959	Lawrence Green
1933	W. C. Kools	1959	Clarence Hopkins
1934	Merrick W. Hanchett	1960	John De Haan
1934	H. J. Kleinheksel	1960	Arthur Hills
1936	Vernon Ten Cate	1960	Raymond Wilkinson
1936	Edward J. Yeomans	1961	Loren Howard
1937	Otto Vander Velde	1961	Harold Thornhill
1940	Bruce M. Raymond	1961	Robert Van Zanten
1941	Clyde Geerlings	1962	William Hakken
1941	Peter Van Domelen, Jr.	1962	William Hinga
1941	William G. Winter	1962	Herbert Thomas
1941	Harold J. Karsten	1963	Bryan Athey
1941	Leon N. Moody	1963	Arthur Becker
1943	Malcolm Mackay	1963	Richard De Witt
1943	J. Harvey Kleinheksel	1963	William Sanford
1944	Andrew G. Sall	1964	William De Long
1945	Gerrard W. Haworth	1964	Paul Elzinga
1945	Marvin C. Lindeman	1965	Donald Cochran
1945	C. R. Trueblood	1965	Wilmer A. Forberg
1945	Russell H. Welch	1965	Robert MacLeod
1946	George Heeringa	1965	Blaine Timmer
1946	Theodore H. Carter	1966	Louis Robbert
1946	James K. Ward	1966	Carl Selover
1947	Clarence J. Becker	1966	James Van Lente
1947	Frank E. De Weese	1966	Charles Myers
1948	Charles E. Drew	1966	Robert Bernecker
1949	Adrian G. Buys	1967	Nelis Bade
1950	Millard C. Westrate	1967	Harold Ketchum
1951	Harold J. Haverkamp	1968	Chris Den Herder
1952	Lawrence W. (Bill) Lamb Jr.	1968	Larry Ter Molen
1953	Bruce G. Van Leuwen	1968	Brian Ward

Deacons (continued)

1968	Jack Westrate	1981	Clare Heyboer
1968	Edward Helbing	1981	Richard Cook
1969	Richard Trask	1981	Tom Page
1969	John Tysse	1982	Jane Dickie
1969	Kenneth Zuverink	1982	Judy Mastenbroek
1970	Theodore Bosch	1982	Jeffrey Mulder
1970	Larry Mulder	1983	Barbara Boer
1970	John Workman	1983	Ella Weymon
1971	Dwight Ballast	1983	Marcia Smit
1971	William Beebe	1984	James Heisler
1971	Ronald Dalman	1984	Phyllis Hooyman
1972	Kelwin Bakker	1984	Michael Van Lente
1972	Alfred Smith	1984	Piet Van Pelt
1973	Audrey Navis	1984	William Van Dyke
1973	William E. Price	1985	Steven Bassett
1973	J. Norman Timmer	1985	Dorothy Bradish
1974	Robert Bolte	1985	Neva Jackson
1974	Gary Beckman	1985	Robin Klay
1974	Fred Birdsall	1986	David Medema
1974	Ruth Steininger	1986	Timothy Stall
1975	John Feininger	1987	David DeBlock
1975	Michael Gerrie	1987	Michael Floch
1975	Fred Leaske	1987	Marvin Israels
1976	Gerald Boeve	1987	Terry Pott
1976	George Ralph	1987	James Wiley
1976	Carl Flowerday	1987	Pat Daily
1977	Barrie Richardson	1988	Kristine Bradfield
1977	Richard Santamaria	1988	Steve Exo
1977	Jack Vander Broek	1988	Anne Mulder
1977	Jeffrey Green	1988	Greg Oppenhuizen
1978	Doris Mazurek	1989	William Bryson
1978	Richard Persinger	1989	Robert Grant
1978	Arthur Seibert Jr.	1989	Howard Huyser
1979	Robert Benzenberg	1989	Mark Laman
1979	Nancy Rock	1990	Joan De Jonge
1980	Randall Braaksma	1990	Ben Sikkink
1980	Gary Hodgson	1990	Martin Wick
1980	Fronse Pellebon-Smith	1991	Paul Battjes
1980	Joyce Stempfly	1991	John Foster
1981	William Anderson	1991	Pat Tysse
1981	David Dirkse	1991	Alan Yamaoka

Deacons (continued)

1992	Mark Baron	2001	Kevin Rosenau
1992	Keith Marcus	2002	Lois Maassen
1992	Sam Martin	2002	David McGraw
1992	Charles Vander Broek	2002	Tom Stryker
1993	Dave Gosselar	2002	David Van Heest
1993	Greg Green	2003	Ric Beltran
1993	Mark Rhoades	2003	Miriam Boogaart
1993	Tom Lampen	2003	Duane Kooyers
1994	Art Buys	2003	Theresa Reagan
1994	Tim Cook	2004	Norman Chambers
1994	Rachelle Oppenhuizen	2004	Kyle Vohlken
1994	Loretta Smith	2004	Brian Yost
1994	Jean Nelson	2005	John Armstrong
1995	Ron Gensemer	2005	Doug Abell
1995	Jeff S. Mulder	2005	Michelle Israels
1995	Bob Snow	2006	Betsy Kaylor
1996	Ted Reimer	2006	John Roe
1996	Gary Rizner	2006	Marilyn Sytsma
1996	Kris Witkowski	2007	Judith Boogaart
1997	Jason DeVries	2007	Bert Duinkerken
1997	Michael Israels	2007	Tim Jarzembowski
1997	Kim McGraw	2007	Michelle Johnson
1997	Mark Sneller	2008	John Fleming
1997	Jocelyn Van Heest	2008	Mary Mokma
1998	Brad MacLean	2008	Nancy Stryker
1998	Amanda Price	2009	Judy Bos
1998	Lynn Raymond	2009	Michael Henry
1998	Jeff Snyder	2010	Beth Beltran
1999	John Foster	2010	Stephanie Beyer
1999	Janice Fike	2010	John Koch
1999	Jackie Kroll	2010	Jim McKnight
1999	Cory Steeby	2011	Michael Kolk
1999	Jim Vander Woude	2011	Henry Luttikhuizen
2000	Julie Clough	2011	Barbara Osborn
2000	Jean McFadden	2011	Claire Rumpsa
2000	Barb Osborn	2012	Tom Arendshorst
2001	Jean Den Herder	2012	Judy Bultman
2001	Joy Fleming	2012	Joyce Teusink
2001	Mark Kuyers		
2001	Doug Nibbelink		

Elders

1862	Bernardus Ledeboer	1944	Arthur A. Visscher
1862	Bernardus Grotenhuis	1944	Milton L. Hinga
1864	Theodore Romeyn Beck	1946	Irwin J. Lubbers
1867	William B. Gilmore	1946	Peter Van Domelen Jr.
1869	Charles F. Post	1950	J. Harvey Kleinheksel
1872	Thomas Emerson Annis	1951	John W. Hollenbach
1877	Henry Baum	1952	Russell H. Welch
1878	Ernst Herold	1953	Otto Vander Velde
1882	Charles A. Dutton	1954	James K. Ward
1883	Cornelis Doesburg	1956	Randall C. Bosch
1885	Gerrit J. Kollen	1956	Adrian G. Buys
1892	Dirk B. K. Van Raalte	1956	Charles E. Drew
1898	Charles S. Dutton	1957	Gerrard W. Haworth
1898	Wilson Harrington	1959	Lawrence Wade
1902	Henry Boers	1959	Harold Hakken
1902	Charles Howell	1960	Dwight Ferris
1902	Charles M. McLean	1960	George Heeringa
1906	William Brusse	1960	Lawrence W. (Bill) Lamb Jr.
1911	Bernard J. De Vries	1960	Leonard Swartz
1913	William Wing	1960	William G. Winter
1915	John H. Kleinheksel	1961	Richard Vanden Berg
1917	John B. Nykerk	1962	Vern Boersma
1917	Abraham Leenhouts	1963	Arthur Hills
1920	Egbert E. Fell	1964	Wilbur Cobb
1920	Bastian D. Keppel	1964	Harold Karsten
1923	Cornelius J. Dregman	1964	William Vander Lugt
1927	Jacob Lokker	1964	Titus Van Haitsma
1932	William J. Olive	1965	Lester De Ridder
1932	John J. Riemersma	1965	Frank Sherburne
1932	Edward D. Dimnent	1965	Bruce G. Van Leuwen
1933	William Tappan	1965	Jack Plewes
1935	Kenneth DePree	1966	James I. Cook
1935	Leon N. Moody	1966	John J. De Valois
1938	W. C. Kools	1966	Robert Vanderham
1939	Merrick W. Hanchett	1967	John K. Vander Broek
1940	Paul E. Hinkamp	1967	Harold Thornhill
1942	Henry Winter	1968	Paul Winchester
1942	John Vander Broek	1969	Lawrence (Larry) Green
1942	Edward J. Yeomans	1969	Walter Martiny
1943	Clifford B. Hopkins	1969	Charles Steketee
1944	George A. Pelgrim	1970	Bryan Athey

Elders (continued)

Year	Name	Year	Name
1970	Robert Cavanaugh	1983	Bill Seaman
1970	Millard De Weerd	1983	John Piet
1971	Frank Moser	1984	Ronald Dalman
1972	John De Haan	1984	Charles Myers
1972	Elizabeth Becker	1984	William Schutter
1972	Francis Fike	1984	Nancy Rock
1972	Arthur Jentz Jr.	1985	Gary Hodgson
1972	Louis (Bud) Robbert	1986	Richard Campbell
1973	Bernadine De Valois	1986	Jean Martin
1973	Lawrence Geuder	1986	Doris Mazurek
1973	Hermina (Mickie) Lamb	1986	Michael Hansen
1974	Robert A. King Jr.	1986	Paul Smith
1974	Louis J. Stempfly Jr.	1987	Larry Dickie
1974	James Van Lente	1987	Robert Hoekstra
1975	Jane Breen	1987	Karen Mulder
1975	John Tysse	1988	Jeffrey Green
1975	Chester Smith	1988	Isla Van Eenenaam
1976	Geraldine Dykhuizen	1988	Phillip Van Eyl
1976	Edward Helbing	1988	Robin Klay
1977	Elsie Lamb	1989	Joanne Hoff
1977	David Myers	1989	Carol Myers
1978	Helen De Weerd	1989	Eileen Nordstrom
1978	Clarence Hopkins	1989	Gary Rizner
1978	John Workman	1990	John De Haan Jr.
1979	Jean Cook	1990	Peter Everts
1979	Christopher Kaiser	1990	Cecil Williams
1979	Herbert Marsilje	1991	Edna Haworth
1979	John Nordstrom	1991	Carolyn Zeek
1980	Gary Beckman	1992	Ruth Beckman
1980	Ekdal Buys	1992	Kay Hubbard
1980	Joan Fike	1992	Kay MacKenzie
1980	Donald Luidens	1992	Richard Smith
1980	Judy Mastenbroek	1993	Marcia Bradsell
1981	Jo Anne Brooks	1993	Kathryn Brownson
1981	Richard Cook	1993	Kristen Gray
1981	J. Norman Timmer	1993	John Schmidt
1982	Peggy De Haan	1994	Ann Piet
1982	Eloise Van Heest	1994	Fronse Pellebon-Smith
1982	Fred Leaske	1994	Carolyn Hoffman
1983	Larry Mulder	1995	Roy Berry
1983	Darell Schregardus	1995	Dorothy Bradish

Elders (continued)

1995	Martin Wick	2008	Dave Boelkins
1995	Joyce Seaman	2009	Char Laman
1996	Laurie Baron	2009	Marilee Nieuwsma
1996	Carol Braaksma	2009	David DeBlock
1996	Bette Williams	2010	Peter Hintz
1997	Les Beach	2010	Rachelle Oppenhuizen
1998	Bill Bryson	2010	Leanne Van Dyk
1998	Mary Buys	2011	Keith Derrick
1998	Earl Laman	2011	Lois Maassen
1998	Nancy Vande Water	2011	Ronald Mulder
1999	Ed Anderson	2012	Jane Dickie
1999	Renie Geary	2012	Mark Sneller
1999	Clare Heyboer		
1999	James Piers		
2000	Peter Boogaart		
2000	Cathy Green		
2000	Kathy Mulder-Sheridan		
2001	George Kraft		
2001	Ben Sikkink		
2001	Ann Sneller		
2002	Milt Nieuwsma		
2002	Jan Smith		
2002	Cindi Veldheer DeYoung		
2003	Anne Dirkse		
2003	Paul Elzinga		
2003	Curtis Gruenler		
2003	Loretta Smith		
2004	Carla Beach		
2004	Bob Bos		
2004	Jane Schuyler		
2004	Trudy Vander Haar		
2005	Peg Luidens		
2005	Sam Martin		
2006	Charles Vander Broek		
2006	AnnaMae Vander Woude		
2007	David Klooster		
2007	Judy Parr		
2007	Ed Van Dam		
2007	MaryJo Waters		
2008	Kim McGraw		

Appendix B: Early Members

The table on the following pages contains membership information about people who joined Hope Church during its first five years.[1] Joining by "certificate" is equivalent to joining by transfer from another congregation. Joining by "reconfession" is equivalent to joining by reaffirmation of faith. The column heading "Date of Dismissal" indicates when the member transferred to another congregation. Information under the "Comments" column was provided by one of the pastors, either Philip Phelps Jr. or Abel T. Stewart.

---

[1] Data in this appendix are from four sources, all at W91-1034, Hope Church, Holland, Michigan, Joint Archives of Holland, in the Theil Research Center:
1. *Records Hope Reformed Church Holland, Mich.*, 2–17. At the top of the first page of this book is the statement: "Record of Members of Hope Church made out by me Abel T. Stewart Aug 1874." Because the original records may have perished in the Holland fire of October 8 and 9, 1871, Rev. Stewart, the first pastor of Hope Church, likely reconstructed these records predating the fire from his and Hope Church members' memories. This marbled-cover book is in box 10.
2. *Records Hope Ref. Prot. Dut. Ch., Holland, Michigan.* vol. 1. This leather-bound book (very similar to the identically spined first book of *Consistorial Minutes*) is in box 11.
3. *Consistorial Minutes*, vol. 1. This is the leather-bound volume bearing "Records Hope Ref. Prot. Dut. Ch., Holland, Michigan" on its spine. This volume, found and purchased after being lost for nearly a century, is in box 1.
4. *Record of Hope Church Holland Michigan 1862–1916*. This typed alphabetical list of members and membership data sorted by member last name is in box 10.

	Name	Relation to Other Member	Date of Membership	Joined by
1	Bernardus Ledeboer, M. D.	husband of Allida Goetschuis	20 July 1862	certificate
2	Allida Goetschuis Ledeboer	wife of Bernardus Ledeboer	20 July 1862	certificate
3	Bernardus Grotenhuis		20 July 1862	certificate
4	Margaret Anna Jordan Phelps	wife of Rev. Philip Phelps Jr.	20 July 1862	certificate
5	William Brokaw Gilmore		20 July 1862	certificate
6	Henry Denison Post	husband of Anna Coatsworth, brother of Charles F. Post	20 July 1862	re-confession
7	Anna Coatsworth Post	wife of Henry D. Post	20 July 1862	re-confession
8	Charles Francis Post	brother of Henry D. Post, husband of Charlotte Taylor	20 July 1862	re-confession

From	Date of Dismissal	To	Comments	Died
Cong. Ch., Grand Rapids, MI	8 April 1873	Ref. Ch., Paterson, NJ	Reunited March 1877.	10 October 1879
Cong. Ch., Grand Rapids, MI	8 April 1873	Ref. Ch., Paterson, NJ	Reunited March 1877.	1882
First Ref. Dutch Ch., Grand Rapids, MI				3 March 1893
Ref. Dutch Ch., Hastings-on-Hudson, NY	January 1886	Second Ref. Ch., Albany, NY		1907
Ref. Dutch Ch., Fairview, IL.	1871		Married Christina Catharina Van Raalte in 1869. Entered the ministry in 1871.	1884
			Absent too long from previous church to receive a certificate.	20 July 1897
			Absent too long from previous church to receive a certificate.	1906
			Absent too long from previous church to receive a certificate.	1915

	Name	Relation to Other Member	Date of Membership	Joined by
9	Sarah Broadmore (Mrs. Francis Broadmore)		20 July 1862	
10	Elizabeth Welcher Sipp	wife of James Sipp	20 July 1862	certificate
11	James Sipp	husband of Elizabeth Sipp	23 July 1862	confession
12	Eliza Osborn (Mrs. Robert Simmonds)		30 January 1863	certificate
13	Phyllis W. Jacobs (Mrs. Symonds)		30 January 1863	certificate
14	Fannie Symonds		30 January 1863	confession
15	Margaret N. Handley, widow of John S. Bangs		30 January 1863	certificate
16	Lucy Ann Green, (Mrs. Wilson Harrington)		22 May 1863	certificate
17	Peter Sakkers	husband of Johanna V. Sakkers	4 March 1864	certificate
18	Johanna Voorlagen Sakkers	wife of Peter Sakkers	4 March 1864	certificate
19	Marietta Shuler Van Olinda	wife of Owen Van Olinda	4 March 1864	certificate

From	Date of Dismissal	To	Comments	Died
	4 October 1875	Cong. Ch., Grand Ledge, MI		
				1866
	21 March 1870	Pres. Ch., Oakland, NE	"the only case of adult baptism under the missionary pastorate of Dom. Phelps."	
Meth. Epis. Ch., Allegan, MI	1866	a Methodist church		
Meth. Epis. Ch., Chicago, IL	1866	Meth. Epis. Ch., Holland, MI		
	1866	Meth. Epis. Ch., Holland, MI		
Meth. Epis. Ch., Fillmore, MI	1866	Meth. Epis. Ch.		
First Pres. Ch., Allegan, MI				1892
First Ref. Dutch Ch., Grand Rapids, MI	14 September 1869	First Ref. Dutch Ch., Holland, MI		
First Ref Dutch Ch., Grand Rapids, MI	14 September 1869	First Ref. Dutch Ch., Holland, MI		
First Ref. Dutch Ch., Holland, MI				1907

	Name	Relation to Other Member	Date of Membership	Joined by
20	Eugene Strong		4 March 1864	certificate
21	Henry George Kleyn		4 March 1864	certificate
22	John William Te Winkle		4 March 1864	certificate
23	Enne Jansen Heeren		17 December 1864	certificate
24	John W. Minderhout	husband of Apollonia De Boe	7 January 1865	confession
25	Apollonia De Boe Minderhout	wife of John W. Minderhout	25 May 1865	certificate
26	Isaac Peter Thiebout		25 May 1865	certificate
27	Charlotte Taylor Post	wife of Charles F. Post	17 August 1865	confession

From	Date of Dismissal	To	Comments	Died
Ref. Dutch Ch., Constantine, MI	1865 1876	Jefferson Park Pres. Ch., Chicago, IL (for both dismissals)	Reunited 1873	
Ref. Dutch Ch., Chicago, IL	1873		"Dismissed before my ministry." —A. T. Stewart	
	1869 or 1870		Entered the ministry.	1901
Ref. Dutch Ch., Silver Creek, IL	1870 or 1871		Entered the ministry and within 2 or 3 years entered foreign missions service in India. Became ill there.	fall of 1878
	28 March 1878	First Ref. Dutch Ch., Grand Rapids, MI		
First Ref. Dutch Ch., Holland, MI	28 March 1878	First Ref. Dutch Ch., Grand Rapids, MI		
First Ref Dutch Ch., Holland, MI	1866		Joined with baptized children. "Dismissed before my ministry." —A. T. Stewart	
				25 March 1902

	Name	Relation to Other Member	Date of Membership	Joined by
28	Edwin Jerome Harrington	husband of Matilda Harrington	17 August 1865	confession
29	Matilda Harrington	wife of Edwin Jerome Harrington	17 August 1865	confession
30	Mary Woodyer Sullivan, (Mrs. Daniel McRae)		17 August 1865	confession
31	Ernst Herold	husband of Susanna Bertsch Herold	24 May 1866	confession
32	Susanna Bertsch Herold	wife of Ernest Herold	24 May 1866	confession
33	William Herrick Finch	husband of Charlotte Smith Finch	24 May 1866	confession
34	Charlotte Smith Finch	wife of William Herrick Finch	24 May 1866	confession
35	Thomas Jefferson Boggs		24 May 1866	confession
36	Frances Louisa Albee (Mrs. Robert Finch)		24 May 1866	confession
37	Polly Emily Albee (Mrs. Lee Collins)		24 May 1866	confession

From	Date of Dismissal	To	Comments	Died
	19 October 1871	Meth. Epis. Ch., Holland, MI		1912
	30 October 1867	Pres. Ch., Canada		
				1903
				1906
				1895
				1910
	1866		"Dismissed or left ... before my settlement." —A. T. Stewart	1911
	1874	Cong. Ch., Grand Haven, MI		

	Name	Relation to Other Member	Date of Membership	Joined by
38	Rachel Bogert Ledeboer (Mrs. James Ten Eyck)		24 May 1866	confession
39	Anna Sakkers (Mrs. Daniel Bertsch)		24 May 1866	confession
40	William Altamont Shields		1 June 1866	confession
41	Katie Goetschuis Ledeboer	wife of D. B. K. Van Raalte	1 June 1866	confession
42	Mary Evelyn Granger		1 June 1866	confession
43	Frances Jeanette Guy	wife of Rev. Peter Moerdyke	1 June 1866	confession
44	Jonathan B. Stewart	[likely a brother of Rev. Abel T. Stewart]	14 September 1866	certificate
45	Huibert Barendreght	husband of Dinah Barendreght	14 September 1866	confession

From	Date of Dismissal	To	Comments	Died
	January 1873	Ref. Dutch Ch., Fairview, IL	Returned 1878.	
	March 1879	Meth. Epis. Ch., Holland, MI		
	1886	Pres. Ch., Macomb, IL		
	8 April 1876	Ref. Ch,, Paterson, NJ	Returned March 1877.	14 June 1926
			"Could never find Mrs. Granger. Never saw her unless at her reception by Doctor Phelps." —A. T. Stewart	
	14 June 1870	Ref. Dutch Ch. of Macon, MI		
	14 November 1873	First Ref. Dutch Ch., Grand Rapids	Reunited 1 June 1872.	
First Ref. Dutch Ch. of Tarrytown, NY			"United in order to help the church." —A. T. Stewart"	
	28 February 1872	Pres. Ch., Kalamazoo		

	Name	Relation to Other Member	Date of Membership	Joined by
46	Mrs. Cornelia Gale		14 September 1866	confession
47	Irene L. Beck	wife of Prof. Theodoric Romeyn Beck	30 November 1866	certificate
48	Eliza Jane Stewart	wife of Rev. Abel T. Stewart	30 November 1866	certificate
49	Phebe Ann Osborne	mother of Jane Elizabeth Sipp	30 November 1866	certificate
50	Jane Elizabeth Sipp	daughter of Phebe Ann Osborne	30 November 1866	certificate
51	Peter Moerdyke	husband of Frances Jeanette Guy	30 November 1866	certificate
52	Dinah Barendreght	wife of Huibert Barendreght	30 November 1866	confession
53	Joseph Oxner	husband of Mary Wilhelmina Oxner	6 December 1866	confession
54	Mary Wilhelmina Oxner	wife of Joseph Oxner	6 December 1866	confession

From	Date of Dismissal	To	Comments	Died
	1874	a church in New York		
Baptist Ch., Wendell, MA	1890	Pres. Ch., Brooklyn, NY		
First Ref. Dutch Ch., Tarrytown, NY				
34th Street Ref. Ch., New York City, NY				1871 or 1872
34th Street Ref. Ch., New York City, NY		34th Street Ref. Ch., New York City, NY		1 July 1881
First Ref. Dutch Ch., Holland, MI	1870		Entered the ministry.	
	28 February 1872	Pres. Ch., Kalamazoo, MI		

The data reveal that of the first fifty-four members who joined Hope Church before 1867 approximately one-third had Dutch surnames such as Ledeboer, Grotenhuis, Sakkers, Van Olinda, Kleyn, Te Winkle, Heeren, Minderhout, Barendreght, and Moerdyke; approximately two-thirds had British surnames such as Post, Coatsworth, Broadmore, Osborne, Jacobs, Symonds, Handley, Green, Strong, Taylor, Harrington, Woodyer, Finch, Smith, Boggs, Albee, Granger, Guy, Stewart, Gale, and Oxner.

As early as 1864, Philip Phelps Jr. noted the increasingly American character of the congregation:

> The changes incident to a new community and especially the increase of the American element had been continually modifying the character of the congregation. Among the growing American population, there were very few who had had a previous acquaintance with the American Reformed Dutch Church. On the contrary they were composed of all Denominations—and many of them without special religious training. The enlistment into the army during the civil war drew away many young men who had been in the habit of attending the English service once on the Sabbath until at length in 1864, the congregation had become mainly Americans, that term being used to denote those not belonging to the Holland colonists.[2]

Paul Hinkamp, who had access to early membership lists but not the first volume of *Consistorial Minutes*, stated that Hope Church came about in response to a desire of some for worship services in English:

> Only seven years after the founding of the colony under the leadership of ... Van Raalte, a small group of people in Holland found the use of the Dutch language of little value to them in divine services. This group began to hold services in the English language in 1854 in the "red schoolhouse," under the auspices of the Board of Domestic Missions of the Reformed Church in America. Among

---

[2] *Consistorial Minutes*, 1:6.

the preachers who conducted services ... all [were] connected with the Holland Academy.[3]

In 1967 the Reverend Glen O. Peterman, perhaps influenced by Hinkamp's connection of the preachers (but not necessarily the congregation) with the Holland Academy, stated erroneously that Hope Church "was organized and founded with the purpose of carrying out a particular ministry to the college community."[4] Others later understated the numbers and influence of non-Dutch Americans among Hope Church's earliest members.

Elton Bruins, in his history of the Third Reformed Church, characterized the Second (Hope) Reformed Church in its origins as

> a small and struggling congregation composed mostly of Hope Academy and College faculty who had been recruited in the East. The second church was true to the Dutch Reformed faith but its services were in English. The Dutch-speaking members of First Church were certainly not ready for that innovation, so there was no inclination for members of First Church to affiliate with the second church.[5]

Later in his book, however, Bruins acknowledged non-Dutch residents of Holland in addition to Hope College faculty as the impetus for an English-speaking congregation:

> There was in the city a nucleus of American people of non-Dutch descent. Isaac Fairbanks, who preceded Van Raalte to the area, became a prominent member of the city and served in many city offices. Hope College brought English-speaking people of Reformed Church in America background from the East to serve on the faculty. Hope Reformed Church had been founded in 1862 by members of the college community in order to have an English-speaking Reformed church.[6]

---

[3] "Hope Church, Reformed Church in America, Holland Michigan: 1862-1942," 1942:5.
[4] *Consistorial Minutes*, 26:2 November 1967 insert.
[5] Bruins, *Americanization of a Congregation*, 2nd ed., 10.
[6] Bruins, *Americanization of a Congregation*, 2nd ed., 37. See also 67. Bruins's characterization is echoed by Mary Kansfield's "English-speaking residents

Isaac Fairbanks became one of the first members of Holland's Methodist Episcopal Church in 1861. More to the point, however, were charter members such as the two Ledeboers, the three Posts, Broadmore, and Sipp, who were not affiliated with Holland Academy or Hope College. Of the fifty-four members who joined Hope Church before 1867, the vast majority were neither faculty members nor their spouses. Nor were they students of Holland Academy or Hope College. The exceptions include these:

(1) Margaret Anna Jordan Phelps, wife of Philip Phelps Jr.;
(2) Irene L. Beck, wife of professor Theodoric Romeyn Beck;
(3) Eliza Jane Stewart, wife of Abel T. Stewart (he was acting instructor in mental and moral philosophy and sacred rhetoric at Hope College and minister of Hope Church);
(4) Peter Moerdyke, teacher of Latin and Greek;
(5) Frances Jeanette Guy Moerdyke, wife of Peter Moerdyke;
(6) William Altamont Shields, teacher of rhetoric and English literature;
(7) William Brokaw Gilmore, a student and tutor, from Fairview, IL;
(8) John Te Winkle, a student; and
(9) Enne Jansen Heeren, a student.[7]

Not all of the earliest professors and administrators of Holland Academy and Hope College who were in Holland within the first ten years of Hope Church's start became members of Hope Church. Those whose names are not included in Hope Church lists of members joining before 1872 include the Reverends Peter John Oggel, John Mason Ferris, and Albertus Bernardus

---

of the community (especially the members of the college faculty and their families from the East)" in "Francis Davis Beardslee and the Leading Ladies of Holland, Michigan, 1912-1917," in *Tools for Understanding: Essays in Honor of Donald J. Bruggink*, ed. James Hart Brumm, Historical Series of the Reformed Church in America, no. 60 (Grand Rapids: Eerdmans, 2008), 72.
[7] "Historical Sketch," *First Catalogue and Circular of Hope College*, 9; and *Second Annual Catalog and Circular of Hope College 1866-7*, 3.

Veenhuizen. Oggel, professor of sacred literature, was not affiliated with Hope Church, though he occasionally preached in the early years when Philip Phelps Jr. was out of town before Abel T. Stewart arrived. Ferris was professor of logic, rhetoric, and English literature; Veenhuizen was professor of modern languages and literature.[8]

Twenty-five of the first fifty-four members who joined Hope Church before 1867 came by certificate of transfer, twenty-five joined by confession of faith, three joined by re-confession of faith, and one joined by a method not indicated. Only one, James Sipp, was baptized as an adult, a practice rare also in Holland's First Reformed Church. Most members of First Church came as baptized or confessing members from Reformed churches in the Netherlands, and the addition of non-baptized adult members through evangelism was rare.[9]

Among the first members transferring into Hope Church, five came from Reformed Protestant Dutch churches in New York, four came from Holland's First Church, four came from Reformed Protestant Dutch churches in the Michigan Classis, and three came from Reformed Protestant Dutch churches in the Illinois Classis. Those transferring from other denominations include three from Methodist Episcopal churches, two from Congregational churches, one from a Presbyterian church, and one from a Baptist church. Unlike its Dutch-speaking sister churches—First and Third Reformed—English-speaking Hope Church during its first five years took in no direct transfers from churches in the Netherlands.

Of the first fifty-four members who joined Hope Church during its first five years, twenty-seven eventually transferred to other congregations. Of these, six transferred to Reformed Protestant Dutch churches in New York and New Jersey, four

---

[8] "Historical Sketch," *First Catalogue and Circular of Hope College*, 9; and *Second Annual Catalog and Circular of Hope College 1866-7*, 3.
[9] De Vries and Boonstra, *Pillar Church in the Van Raalte Era*, 79.

transferred to Reformed Protestant Dutch churches in the Michigan and Illinois Classes, and two transferred to Holland's First Reformed Church. Seven joined Presbyterian churches, six joined Methodist Episcopal churches, and two joined Congregational churches. For the relatively new and growing community that Holland was in the mid-nineteenth century, this coming and going of members was not unusual.

Appendix C: Descendants of Albertus C. and Christina J. de Moen Van Raalte Who Became Members of Hope Church

Though Albertus Christiaan and Christina Johanna de Moen Van Raalte never joined Hope Church, most of their children did, as did many of their grandchildren. Of their seven children who lived past infancy, the youngest five became members of Hope Church: Benjamin, Dirk Blikman Kikkert, Christina Catharina, Maria Wilhelmina, and Anna Sophia.[1]

When the names of those included in a Van Raalte family photograph taken during the summer of 1911[2] are matched with the membership lists of Hope Church, eighteen of the twenty-one pictured were members of Hope Church at one time or another. Those in the picture who were not Hope Church members were Albertus (Allie) Van Raalte, Albertus Van Raalte's wife Edna Pillsbury, and Estelle Kollen Pelgrim's husband Jacob (Jay) Carleton Pelgrim.

---

[1] The best source of information about descendants of Albertus C. and Christina J. de Moen Van Raalte, including those who became members of Hope Church, is Elton J. Bruins et al., *Albertus and Christina: The Van Raalte Family, Home and Roots* (Grand Rapids: Eerdmans, 2004). Information about the first generation of Van Raaltes who became members of Hope Church comes mainly from the membership list in *Records 2d. R. P. D. C. Holland Michigan, Book 2,* W91-1034, box 11, Hope Church, Holland, Michigan, Collection, Joint Archives of Holland and *Record of Hope Church Holland Michigan 1862–1916,* W91-1034, box 10, Hope Church, Holland, Michigan, Collection, Joint Archives of Holland.
[2] Bruins et al., *Albertus and Christina,* 184–85.

Some of the Van Raalte family in about 1911

Left side
Front row, seated from left to right: Kate Ledeboer Van Raalte (widow of Dirk D. B. K.), Benjamin Van Raalte, Orlando (Andy) Reimold (sitting on Benjamin's lap), Christina Van Raalte Gilmore
Standing, from left to right: Julia (Lu) Van Raalte Reimold, Lena Kollen (niece of Gerrit J. Kollen), Wilhelmina (Minnie) Van Raalte, Frank De Moen Kleinheksel, Edna Pillsbury (wife of Albertus), Albertus (Allie) Van Raalte, Adeline (Addie) Huntley Van Raalte (wife of Ben Jr.)

Right side
Front row, seated from left to right: John H. Kleinheksel, Anna Sophia Van Raalte Kleinheksel, and Gerrit J. Kollen (widower of Maria)
Standing, from left to right: Christina (Tia) Pfanstiehl Van Raalte (wife of Allie), Christina (Chris) Van Raalte Van Putten, Albertus Van Raalte, Anna Van Raalte Keppel, Estelle Kollen Pelgrim, Jay Carleton Pelgrim (husband of Estelle), and Albertus (Raalte) Van Raalte Gilmore[3]

---

[3] Bruins et al., *Albertus and Christina*, 185.

The First Generation

Benjamin Van Raalte (1840–1917)[4]

Dirk Blikman Kikkert (D. B. K. Van Raalte) (1844–1910)[5]

Christina Catharina Van Raalte Gilmore (1846–1933)[6]

Maria (Mary) Wilhelmina Van Raalte Kollen (1850–1905)[7]

Anna Sophia Van Raalte Kleinheksel (1856–1914)[8]

---

[4] Although there is no record of Benjamin's joining Hope Church, consistory minutes state that in response to a congregational meeting resolution to appoint a committee constituting the pastor, a member of consistory, and a member of the congregation to estimate the expense of painting the church, the pastor, "Deacon Harrington and Benjamin Van Raalte" were appointed. *Consistorial Minutes*, 7 January 1884, 1:187–88.

Elton J. Bruins's file on Benjamin Van Raalte at the Theil Research Center contains a note stating, "Rec. of Benjamin Van Raalte the sum of twenty Dollars being Pay in full for his pew rent for the year 1875" signed by William Harrington, and "five Dollars for pew rent to July 1st, 1881," signed by I. F. Bangs, treasurer, Hope Church. According Bruins et al., *Albertus and Christina*, 147, a pew rental receipt was found in Benjamin's wallet shortly after he died in 1917.

[5] Though he did not join Hope Church by confession of faith until 1886, his wife Katharine (Kate) Goetschius Ledeboer, daughter of charter members Bernardus and Allida Goetschuis Ledeboer, joined by confession of faith in 1866. He served as deacon beginning in 1887 and as elder beginning in 1892. Both remained members of Hope Church until his death in 1910 and her death in 1926.

[6] She joined Hope Church in 1869 upon marrying charter member William Brokaw Gilmore. Transferring her membership from the Congregational Church of Olivet, MI, where she was attending Olivet College (Hope College was not yet admitting women students), she was the first of Albertus C. and Christina Van Raalte's children to join Hope Church and was the first organist of Hope Church. *Consistorial Minutes*, 1:58.

[7] Her membership was transferred from Holland's First Reformed Church to Hope Church in March 1880. The membership of her husband, Gerrit John Kollen, had been transferred from the Reformed Church of Overisel, MI, to Hope Church in September 1879. *Records Hope Ref. Prot. Dut. Ch., Holland, Michigan*. 1:42. W91-1034, Hope Church, Holland, Michigan, Joint Archives of Holland.

[8] Her membership from Holland's First Reformed Church was transferred to Hope Church in March 1882. The membership of her husband, John Henry Kleinheksel, was transferred from Holland's Third Reformed Church in June 1888. *Records*, 1:58.

The Second Generation

Christina (Chris) Van Raalte Van Putten (1861–1921)[9]

Anna Helena Van Raalte Keppel (1862–1947)[10]

Christina Johanna Oggel (1865–1911)[11]

Johanna Maria Wilhelmina (Minnie) Van Raalte (1870–1923)[12]

Albertus C. Van Raalte (Raalte) Gilmore (1870–1955)[13]

Julia Christina Van Raalte Reimold (1873–1952)[14]

Paul Edwin Kleinheksel (1885–1956)[15]

Estelle Marie Kollen (1886–1984)[16]

Anna Vera Kleinheksel (1889–1910)[17]

Albertus Christiaan Van Raalte (1889–1944)[18]

Dirk (Dick) Blikman Kikkert Van Raalte Jr. (1891–1964)[19]

Frank De Moen Kleinheksel (1892–1973)[20]

John Lewis Kleinheksel (1896–1963)[21]

---

[9] Her membership was transferred from Holland's First Reformed Church to Hope Church in 1892. *Records*, 1:70.
[10] Her membership was transferred from the First Reformed Church in Grand Haven in 1897. *Records*, 1:78.
[11] She transferred from Ninth Street Christian Reformed Church in 1897. *Records*, 1:78.
[12] She joined Hope Church by confession of faith in 1892. *Records*, 1:70.
[13] His membership was transferred from the Reformed Church of Havana, IL, in 1885. *Records*, 1:62.
[14] She joined Hope Church by confession of faith in 1891. *Records*, 1:68.
[15] He joined Hope Church by confession of faith in 1901. *Records*, 1:84.
[16] She joined Hope Church by confession of faith in 1901. *Records*, 1:84.
[17] She joined Hope Church by confession of faith in 1901. *Records*, 1:84.
[18] He joined Hope Church by confession of faith in 1901. *Records*, 1:86.
[19] He joined Hope Church by confession of faith in 1905. *Records*, 1:96.
[20] He joined Hope Church by confession of faith in 1904. *Records*, 1:92. His membership was transferred to the First Congregational Church of Muskegon, MI, in 1921.
[21] He joined Hope Church by confession of faith in 1908. *Records*, 1:100.

The Third Generation

	(Born–Died)	Joined Hope Church[22]
Helene Gertrude Keppel Visscher	(1888–1970)	1901
Henry Charles (Carl) Van Raalte	(1893–1974)	1928
Gertrude Christine Keppel Vander Broek	(1895–1977)	1910
Christine Cornelia Van Raalte Van Westenberg	(1895–1987)	1910[23]
Helene Wilhelmina Van Raalte Dalenberg	(1899–1980)	1913
Philip Benjamin Reimold	(1903–1940)	by baptism in 1904[24]
Orlando Jr. (Andy) Reimold	(1910–1977)	by baptism in 1910[25]
Margret Elizabeth (Toodie) Van Raalte Plowe Kleis	(1914–1959)	1928
Derk (Dick Jr.) B. K. Van Raalte	(1916–	1932
Jean Marie Van Raalte Klomparens	(1918–1994)	1934

---

[22] Unless otherwise indicated in this column, each person joined by confession of faith.
[23] This and subsequent membership data come from volumes 2 and 3 of *Hope Church Membership Records*. Volume 2 covers 1910–1970 and volume 3 covers 1971 to the present.
[24] The baptism of Philip Benjamin Reimold took place at the residence of Ben Van Raalte on East Sixteenth Street a short distance west of Country Club Drive.
[25] The baptism of Orlando Reimold Jr. took place at the residence of Ben Van Raalte on East Sixteenth Street.

The Fourth Generation

	(Born–Died)	Joined Hope Church
Helena Anne Visscher Winter	(1914–	1924
Dorothy (Dody) Jane Visscher Frederickson	(1918–2005)	1934
John (Jack) Keppel Vander Broek	(1922–2008)	1937
Gail Joan Van Raalte Fadel	(1946–	1962
Deborah (Debby) Jean Klomparens Bock	(1946–2005)	1960[26]
Melissa Ann Klomparens Ramirez	(1950–	1965[27]

The Fifth Generation

	(Born–Died)	Joined Hope Church
William Garrett Winter III	(1939–	1956[28]
Lynn Anne Winter	(1941–1958)	1956
John (Jack) Keppel Vander Broek	(1943–	1961[29]
Paul Arthur Winter	(1947–	1961[30]
Richard George Vander Broek	(1948–	1963
Charles Donn Vander Broek	(1950–	1965[31]

---

[26] She was removed from membership roll in 1981.
[27] She was removed from membership roll in 1985.
[28] His membership was transferred to the First Presbyterian Church of Hartford, CT, in 1963.
[29] His membership was transferred to the Christ Memorial Church in Holland.
[30] His membership was transferred to the Providence Presbyterian Church of Matthews, NC, in 1985.
[31] He was installed as deacon in 1992 and elder in 2006.

The Sixth Generation

	(Born–Died)	Joined Hope Church
Anna Christine Vander Broek	(1983–	baptized member
Charles William Vander Broek	(1985–	baptized member
Philip John Vander Broek	(1988–	2003

Since the arrival of Albertus C. and Christina J. de Moen Van Raalte in 1847, most of their descendants have moved from Holland. Three of them, however, are full members of Hope Church. They are Helena Anne Visscher Winter, Charles Donn Vander Broek, and Philip John Vander Broek. Baptized members Anna Christine Vander Broek and Charles William Vander Broek bring the total to five descendants of the Van Raaltes who are members of Hope Church in 2012.

Appendix D:
Music and Administrative Staff

Lists of Hope Church choir directors, organists, Sunday School superintendents, directors of Christian education, and church administrators are based generally on information from *Consistory Minutes*. Generally names are listed in chronological order of the person's beginning to serve in a role or position.

Choir Directors

William B. Gilmore, chorister
Huibert Barendreght, chorister
Mr. Downie, chorister
Edmund P. Potter, chorister
Mr. B. J. De Vries, chorister
J. Marion Doesburg, chorister
Darius Gilmore, chorister
Kittie M. Doesburg, chorister
Dr. A. C. Van Raalte Gilmore, precentor
John B. Nykerk, choir director, 1903–21
Miss Van Verst, choir director, 1907
Willis Diekema, 1921–28
Dr. A. C. Van Raalte Gilmore, choir director, 1922
Harris Meyer, 1922
Chester L. Beach, choir director, 1924
Mrs. H. Dunwoody, conductor of choir and junior choir,1926
W. Curtis Snow, choir director,1929, and director of music, 1930–35
Esther Snow, choir director, 1935–45
Robert W. Cavanaugh, senior choir director, 1946-47, 1951–55
Hazel Paalman, 1947–49
Harvey O. Davis, director of music, 1949–51
Peggy Prins De Haan, director of junior choir, 1951–52
Norma Baughman, leader of Cherub choir for ages 5–8
    and Carollers for ages 9–12, 1955
Willard S. Fast, 1955–57

Choir Directors (continued)

Margaret Van Vyven, leader of Cherub and Carollers choirs, 1957
Kenneth C. Schellenberger, minister of music, 1957–59
Anthony Kooiker, director of music,
 including choir and junior and senior high choirs,
 1959–65; 1968–69
Joan Tallis, choir director, 1964
James H. Tallis, supervisor of church's music program, 1965-66;
 choir director, 1966–68
Joan Tallis, junior choir director, 1965
Edna Hollander TerMolen, director of children's choir, 1966
Anthony Kooiker, choir director, 1968
Robert Thompson, director of music, 1968
Anthony Kooiker, director of music, 1968
Prudence Selover, director of junior choir, 1968
Floyd Farmer, director of music, 1969–70
Caron Farmer, youth choirs
Calvin Langejans, choir director, 1970–77
Trish Kliphuis, director of Joy Singers children's choir, 1974
Neta Gensemer, director of Joy Singers children's choir, 1976
Eugene Westra, choir director, 1977–81
Barbara Veurink, youth choir director, 1977
Brian Carder, director of music, 1981–91, 1993–2003
Barbara Veurink, director of children's, youth, and
 handbell choirs, 1981–88
Beth Bichler, director of bell choir, 1983
J. Scott Ferguson, director of music, 1991–93
John Hoyer, director of music, 2003
Amy Kate Hilsman, director of children's choirs, 2003–04
David Schout, music director, 2004–05
Brian Carder, director of music and chancel choir director,
 2005–present
Laurie Braaksma, handbell choir director, 2005–present
Sarah Van Zetten, Joy and Jubilate choirs, 2005
Carol Carder, Joy and Jubilate choirs, 2006–08
Amy Mulder Gould, Techna Theou director, 2007

Organists

Christina Van Raalte
Kate Ledeboer
Gertrude Alcott
Rike Boone
Beca Boone
Minnie Kramer
William. N. Birchby
Anne Floyd
Amy Yates
Miss TeRoller
Christina Van Raalte
   Gilmore, 1902
Miss Huey, 1907
Mrs. E. D. Kremers, 1908
Harris Meyer
Mr. Petit
Martha Robbins
Walter Blodgett
George Dok, 1925
Mrs. Edward De Pree, 1928
Mr. Gosselink, 1928
Mrs. R. Page, 1929
W. Curtis Snow, 1929–35
Esther Snow, 1935–1957
Mrs. Henry Masselink
Anthony Kooiker, 1959–64
Mrs. Robert Barrows, 1964
James H. Tallis, 1966–68
Barbara Borr Veurink, 1968–2004
   Organist Emerita, 2004–2005
David Schout, 2005–2011
Rhonda Edgington, 2012–

Sunday School Superintendents

Philip Phelps Jr., 1863
William B. Gilmore
Charles Scott
William B. Cropley
I. F. Bangs
Albert H. Dutton
Gerrit J. Kollen
Gerrit J. Diekema, 1902,
   1911–16
Charles M. McLean, 1909–11,
   1916–23
John J. Riemersma, 1924–27
George Pelgrim, 1927–31
Leon Moody, 1930
Martha D. Kollen, 1931–41
Leon Moody, 1941–45
Malcolm McKay, 1945–47
Harold J. Karsten, 1947–49
Randall C. Bosch, 1949–59
Elizabeth Becker, 1959–62
William Dow, 1965
Robert Bernecker, 1966
Jane Breen, 1970–86
Jocelyn Van Heest, 1986–93

Directors of Christian Education and Youth

Elsie B. Stryker, director of Christian education, 1949–54
Rev. Harold Colenbrander, minister of Christian education and
　　youth work, 1954–55
Joan Van Riper, director of Christian education and youth work,
　　1955–58
Shirley Kiefer, director of Christian education, 1958–61
Andrea Roorda, assistant in Christian education, 1961–63
Bonnie Bruins, director of Christian education, part-time, 1963
Charlotte Heinen, director of Christian education, 1966–68
William Paarlberg, director of Christian education, 1969–70
Jocelyn Van Heest, Church School coordinator, 1986–93
　　children's ministries coordinator and then director,
　　1993–present
Anne Marcus, co-coordinator of Christian education, 1988;
　　youth director, 2004
Loretta Smith, co-coordinator of Christian education, 1988–97;
　　director of education ministries, 1994–97
Eloise Van Heest, director of Christian education, 1989–94
Ellen Rizner, Church School coordinator, 1993
Loretta Smith, director of education ministries, 1995–96
Margaret Buckley, Church School coordinator, 2001
Wendy Rebhan, Children in Worship coordinator
Jocelyn Van Heest, children's ministries director, 2002–present
Anne Dirkse, youth coordinator, 2004–2005
Dana Boyle, youth coordinator, 2005–2006
Anne Duinkerken, youth ministry director, 2011–present

Church Secretaries

Phyllis Engelsman, 1951–54
Helen Voogd, 1954–58
Florence Thompson, 1958–66
Norma Sprick, 1968–78; office manager, 1979–86
Barbara Veurink, 1968–1978
Joan Fike, 1986
Amy Ingraham, 1986–1994
Marilyn Cook, 1994–96
Kay MacKenzie, 1994–97
Laurie Beyer Braaksma, secretary, 1999;
    ministries coordinator, 2000–present;
    office support, 2006–2008
Carol Yonker, 1999
Barbara Vande Vusse, part-time administrative support,
    2003–present

Church Administrators

Eloise Van Heest, administrative associate, 1982–94
Janet Bast Elzinga, administrator, 1994–2008
Joan DeJonge Walls, finance manager, 2004–11
Laurie Beyer Braaksma, church administrator 2008–present
Karla Kammeraad-Bos, financial administrator, 2008–present

Appendix E:
Members Who Became
RCA Ministers or Missionaries

Hope Church in its first year adopted a system of benevolent collections that included the Boards of Domestic and Foreign Missions.[1] Because many of Hope College's students in the first five decades joined Hope Church and later became ministers or missionaries, Hope Church can rightfully claim credit for nurturing the faith of many who became ministers and missionaries. Following, in chronological order of their joining Hope Church or coming under care of Hope Church and Holland Classis, are their names.[2]

1862–1882

William Brokaw Gilmore
John William Te Winkle
Enne Jensen Heeren
Aleida Vennema Heeren[3]
Peter Moerdyke
Frederick Bakker
Motoitero Oghimi
Albert Angus Pfanstiehl
Charles S. Dutton
Philip Tertius Phelps

---

[1] *Consistorial Minutes*, 1:18.
[2] Information about the earliest members listed comes from "Record of Hope Church Holland Michigan 1862–1916," Hope Church, Holland, Michigan, Joint Archives of Holland.
[3] Enne Jensen Heeren was the first Hope Church member and Hope College graduate to become a foreign missionary. In 1872, the Reverend Albertus C. Van Raalte commissioned him and his wife, Aleida Vennema Heeren, for service in India. He became ill there, returned to the U.S. in 1877, and died in 1878. Wichers, *Century of Hope*, 180; Bruins, *Americanization*, 51; Van Hinte, *Netherlanders*, 411; and Gasero, *Historical Directory*, 168.

1883–1953

William H. Bruins
Frances Phelps Otte (Mrs. John A. Otte), missionary to China[4]
William Stegeman
Jacob J. Van Zanten
Henry Huizenga
Cornelius M. Steffens
John Walter Beardslee Jr.Bernice Takken
    (Mrs. Bernard Rottschaefer), missionary to India
Albertus C. Van Raalte (son of D. B. K. and
    Kate Ledeboer Van Raalte)
Melvin Verne Oggel[5]
James Verburg
Edwin Paul McLean
Anthony Ver Hulst[6]
May De Pree Thoms[7]
Mrs. J. J. Banninga[8]
Bernard Daniel Hakken Jr.[9]

---

[4] Frances Phelps Otte accompanied her husband, John A. Otte, to Amoy, China in 1887. After a family furlough in 1905, she stayed with their four young children in the United States. Her husband served as a medical missionary in the Amoy mission until his death in 1910 from pneumonic plague caught from one of his patients.
[5] At the centennial celebration of Hope Church, Melvin Verne Oggel, Edwin Paul McLean, and Randall Bayes Bosch were honored as "Sons of Hope Church who have entered the ministry." *The Hope Church Historical Booklet 1982: Our Time for Rededication.*
[6] Ver Hulst joined Hope Church in 1909 and entered ministry in the Presbyterian Church in 1913.
[7] According to *Hope Church Reformed Church in America Holland, Michigan ... Eightieth Anniversary*, 1942:20, May De Pree Thoms was an active missionary. According to Gasero, *Historical Directory*, 716, she served in the Middle East 1906–13 and 1918–44.
[8] According to *Hope Church ... Eightieth Anniversary*, 1942:20, Mrs. J. J. Banninga was an active missionary in foreign fields.
[9] According to *Consistorial Minutes*, 9 November 1953, 12:907, Bernard Daniel Hakken Jr. was a member of Hope Church for eight years. According to Gasero, *Historical Directory*, 158, he graduated from Western Theological Seminary in 1953 and was ordained in the Dunningville Reformed Church. He and his wife Donna later served as missionaries to the Philippines, and he served as pastor to several RCA churches.

1954–1973

Paul William Kranendonk[10]
Randall Bayles Bosch[11]
Paul Fries[12]
Lewis and Nancy Scudder[13]
Paul Ransford[14]
Roger W. Rozeboom[15]
David and Nancy Piet[16]

---

[10] According to *Consistorial Minutes*, 10 May 1954 insert, 12:943, Paul William Kranendonk and his wife were members of Hope Church. According to Gasero, *Historical Directory*, 220–21, after graduating from Western Theological Seminary, he served the First Reformed Church of Marion, NY, the first of his pastorates in New York and New Jersey.

[11] According to *Consistorial Minutes*, 28 January 1960 insert, 18:1188 and Gasero, *Historical Directory*, 41, Randall B. Bosch became an associate pastor of the Pompton Reformed Church, Pompton Lakes, NJ, in 1959. He later served as pastor to Reformed churches in Brielle, NJ; Mt. Prospect, IL; Kingston, NY; and Locust Valley, NY.

[12] According to *Consistorial Minutes*, 31 October 1961, 20:1287, Paul Fries was a member of Hope Church and a senior at Western Theological Seminary. According to Gasero, *Historical Directory*, 140, after receiving additional graduate degrees at the University of Utrecht, he became pastor of the Reformed Church in Homewood, IL (1965–67), and taught at New Brunswick Theological Seminary (1968–78) before serving Hope Church as a co-pastor (1978–82).

[13] Lewis R. Scudder III, son of Lewis R. Scudder II and his wife, Dorothy, joined Hope Church in 1961 while a student at Hope College. He and his wife, Nancy, served for at least four decades as a missionary in the Middle East.

[14] Membership records indicate that Paul Ransford was a member of Hope Church 1962–64. According to Gasero, *Historical Directory*, 318, he attended Western Theological Seminary 1965–66 and received his M. Div. degree from Union Theological Seminary in Virginia in 1969. He served Presbyterian churches in KY, AL, and IL before serving as program director for Manitoqua Ministries in Frankfort, IL.

[15] According to *Consistorial Minutes*, 27:8 April 1968 insert, Roger Rozeboom, a Hope College senior and member of Hope Church, came under care of Holland Classis as a ministerial student. According to Gasero, *Historical Directory*, 334, he received his M. Div. degree from Princeton Theological Seminary and served Reformed churches in Blawenburg, NJ, and Littleton, CO.

[16] According to *Consistorial Minutes*, 28:23 June 1969, a missionary-commissioning ceremony was scheduled in June for David and Nancy (Pelon) Piet, both members of Hope Church. David was the son of John and Wilma Piet. According to Gasero, *Historical Directory*, 708, 711–12, David and Nancy Piet served as missionaries in Southeast Asia 1970–73.

1974–1977

Mary T. Van Andel[17]
John E. Schmidt[18]
Steven Robert Brooks[19]
Carol Hector-Braaksma
Randall Braaksma[20]
David Vos[21]

---

[17] Mary Van Andel transferred her membership from the Woodville Christian Reformed Church of White Cloud, MI, to Hope Church in 1974. According to Gasero, *Historical Directory*, 403, Mary T. Van Andel, a graduate of Hope College, Western Theological Seminary, and the Catholic Theological Union of Chicago, was ordained by Holland Classis in 1980. She served as pastor to the Knox Church in Altamont, NY, and the Second Reformed Church in Berne, NY. From 1987 to 1991, she served on the staff of the First Presbyterian Church, Holland, MI, and also in 1991 on the staff of Hope Church. In 1991 she and her husband, Ben Sikkink, founded Bethabara, a ministry of retreat and spiritual direction in Saugatuck. According to information supplied by Van Andel, from 1995 to 2011 she served as staff chaplain for psychiatric care at Holland Hospital. She transferred her ordination credentials to the Presbyterian Church USA and is associate pastor at First Presbyterian Church, Kalamazoo.

[18] While a student at Hope College, John E. Schmidt joined Hope Church by transfer from the First United Methodist Church of Wichita Falls, TX. He transferred to the Christ Memorial Church in Holland in 1977 and received his MDiv degree from Western Theological Seminary in 1979. He served in several administrative ministries in and outside the denomination. Returning to Hope Church in 1991, he served as dean of students at Western Theological Seminary 1985–93 and then as interim pastor at Calvary Reformed Church in Holland 1993–95, when he accepted a call to the Second Reformed Church of Zeeland, MI. Gasero, *Historical Directory*, 343.

[19] According to *Consistorial Minutes*, 32:29 April 1973, Hope Church member Steven Robert Brooks, son of James and Jo Anne Brooks, came under care of Holland Classis. According to Gasero, *Historical Directory*, 50, Brooks received his M. Div. degree from Fuller Theological Seminary and served churches in Nebraska and Colorado.

[20] Randall and Carol Braaksma, who joined Hope Church in 1976, served in the People's Republic of China 1992–94. Gasero, *Historical Directory*, 711.

[21] According to *Consistorial Minutes*, 36:14 February 1977, David Vos joined Hope Church in 1977 while a student at Western Theological Seminary. According to Gasero, *Historical Directory*, 50, Vos was licensed and ordained by Holland Classis and served as minister of the Reformed Church in Prattsville, NY, 1978–80, before additional graduate study followed by ministry in Presbyterian churches.

1978-1983

Carol Cook[22]
Margaret (Peggy) Lubbers[23]
Donald Heringa[24]
James J. O'Connell Jr.[25]
Diane Maodush-Pitzer[26]

---

[22] Carol Cook, daughter of the Reverend James I. and Jean Cook, served as a teacher in Taiwan 1978-79, according to Gasero, *Historical Directory*, 712. She received MDiv and PhD degrees from Princeton Theological Seminary and a MSW degree from Rutgers University. A marriage and family therapist, licensed clinical social worker, and certified pastoral counselor, she taught at New Brunswick Theological Seminary before joining the Louisville Seminary faculty in 2000. http://www.lpts.edu/About_Us/detailview.asp?id=362

[23] Margaret Lubbers served as a teacher in Taiwan 1978-79, according to Gasero, *Historical Directory*, 712.

[24] Donald Heringa became a member of Hope Church while he attended Western Theological Seminary from which he received his MDiv degree in 1979. He was licensed in Holland Classis in 1978 and ordained in Orange Classis in 1979. According to Gasero, *Historical Directory*, 172, his ministry in the denomination included chaplaincy, parish ministry, and direction of pastoral care in a hospital.

[25] According to *Consistorial Minutes*, 38:14 August 1978, James J. O'Connell Jr. joined Hope Church in 1978 before enrolling at Western Theological Seminary. According to Gasero, *Historical Directory*, 290, O'Connell was ordained by Holland Classis in 1981 and served as minister in Reformed churches in Pottersville, NJ, 1981-88 and Carrollton, TX, beginning in 1988.

[26] Diane Maodush-Pitzer joined Hope Church in 1978. According to Gasero, *Historical Directory*, 251, she received her MDiv degree from Western Theological Seminary in 1982 and was ordained by Holland Classis the following year. She served in various denominational ministries in Michigan, including five years as associate pastor of the Servant's Community Reformed Church in Grand Rapids.

1984-1985

John D. De Haan[27]
Dawn Boelkins[28]
Ruth Zwald Staal[29]
Ron Rienstra[30]
Ruth Hawley-Lowry[31]

---

[27] John D. De Haan, son of Peg and John De Haan, was a baptized and confessing member of Hope Church. According to Gasero, *Historical Directory*, 91, he graduated from Western Theological Seminary in 1984 and then served as pastor of the Hope Reformed Church in Vancouver, B.C. for two years.

[28] Dawn Boelkins joined Hope Church by transfer from the Covenant Reformed Church in Muskegon, MI, in 1984. She was licensed and ordained in Holland Classis in 1986. According to Gasero, *Historical Directory*, 35, she served as pastor at the Christ Community Church in Spring Lake, MI, 1987-92. According to information from Western Theological Seminary (http://www.westernsem.edu/faculty/boelkins), in recent years she has taught biblical languages at the seminary for more than fifteen years and more recently with her husband, the Reverend John Schmidt, has been pastor of the Second Reformed Church, Zeeland, MI.

[29] Ruth Zwald Staal and her family joined Hope Church by transfer from the First Reformed Church in Baldwin, WI, after receiving her MDiv degree from Western Theological Seminary and having been licensed and ordained by Classis Wisconsin in 1984. While serving as chaplain at Pine Rest Christian Hospital in Grand Rapids, she worked part time with youth at Hope Church. In 1990 she was program director of Camp Geneva. During 1991-96 she served as associate pastor at Hope Church.

[30] Ron Rienstra, son of Marchiene and John Rienstra, joined Hope Church in 1984 and earned a MDiv degree from Princeton Theological Seminary, and PhD degree from Fuller Theological Seminary. Ordained in the RCA in 1993, he has served as interim pastor and consultant to churches. Since 2006 he has been Visiting Assistant Professor of Preaching and Worship at Western Theological Seminary. http://www.westernsem.edu/faculty/rienstra/

[31] Ruth Hawley-Lowry joined Hope Church in 1985 by transfer from the First Evangelical Covenant Church of Rockford, IL. After graduating from Hope College, she received her MDiv degree from Princeton Theological School and pursued graduate work at the University of Chicago and Western Theological Seminary. Licensed under Holland Classis and ordained in Hope Church, she has served as pastor of churches in New Jersey, Illinois, and Michigan. Gasero, *Historical Directory*, 167.

1986-1996

Cindi Veldheer DeYoung[32]
Barbara Wright[33]
Michael L. Mulder[34]
Jane Vander Haar Van Es[35]
Rowland Van Es[36]

---

[32] In 1986 Cindi Veldheer De Young graduated from Calvin College, joined Hope Church, and came under care of Holland Classis. She received her MDiv degree from Western Theological Seminary in 1990. Licensed and ordained under Holland Classis, she has served as chaplain at several hospitals and hospices in Western Michigan. Gasero, *Historical Directory*, 440. In 2000 she served as president of Holland Classis.

[33] Barbara Wright joined Hope Church and came under its care and that of Holland Classis in 1993. She was ordained under Classis Central Iowa in 1995 and served churches in Iowa and Michigan. Gasero, *Historical Directory*, 473.

[34] Michael L. Mulder, son of Larry and Karen Mulder, was a baptized and communicant member of Hope Church. He attended Fuller Theological Seminary 1994–96 and received his MDiv degree from Western Theological Seminary in 1998. He was ordained in Hope Church 25 July 1999, after which he became pastor of the Servant's Community Church in Grand Rapids. Gasero, *Historical Directory*, 279.

[35] Jane Vander Haar Van Es, daughter of the Reverend Delbert and Trudy Vander Haar, joined Hope Church by transfer from the Trinity Reformed Church in Orange City, Iowa, in 1996. She served with her husband in Nkhoma, Malawi, where their daughters Jenna and Michelle were born; Serekunde, Gambia; and Limuru, Kenya.

[36] Rowland Van Es joined Hope Church with his wife, Jane, in 1996. The couple served as missionaries in Nkhoma, Malawi, 1990–96. After graduating from Western Theological Seminary in 1999, he was ordained in Hope Church in August 1999. With his wife, Jane Vander Haar Van Es, he served in Nkhoma, Malawi; Serekunde, Gambia, 2000–03; and Limur, Kenya, 2004 to the present. Hope Church supported them from 1995 to the present.

1997-2012

Bruce Mulder[37]
Rachel Brownson[38]
Jessica Kast-Keat[39]

Hope Church also has become the congregation of many ordained to specialized ministries, including professors at Western Theological Seminary. In addition to those named above, many ministers and missionaries chose to become active in Hope Church after retirement.

---

[37] Bruce D. Mulder joined Hope Church by transfer from the First Presbyterian Church of Garner, NC. He graduated from Western Theological Seminary in 1999. During the late 1990s he began serving as pastor of congregational care at the Fifth Reformed Church, Grand Rapids, MI. http://www.fifthreformedchurch.org/_blog/Fifth_Reformed_Church_Blog/post/125_Years_of_Ministry/ As of 2011, he was one of the pastors there.
[38] Rachel Brownson, daughter of the Reverend James and Kathryn Brownson, joined Hope Church by confession of faith in 1993. She was ordained at Hope Church by Holland Classis on 6 March 2011.
[39] Jessica Kast-Keat joined Hope Church in 2009 by transfer from the Mars Hill Bible Church of Grandville, MI. She was ordained at Hope Church by Holland Classis on 29 January 2012. Her membership was then transferred to the Classis of New York. In 2012 she is associate pastor at the West End Collegiate Church, New York City.

Appendix F:
Hope College – Hope Church Connections

"The early history of the Second Reformed Protestant Dutch Church of Holland, Ottawa Co. Michigan," wrote the Reverend Philip Phelps Jr., "is closely associated with that of the Holland Academy since grown into Hope College."[1] Though none of the ten charter members of Hope Church was a Hope College faculty member or administrator, the ties binding church and college soon became many and strong.

Phelps came to Holland in 1859 with a dual assignment from the Reformed Protestant Dutch Church. By the Board of Education he was commissioned to be the principal of Holland Academy, and by the Board of Domestic Missions he was commissioned to be a "Missionary Preacher."[2] As principal, Phelps laid the foundations for Hope College. As missionary pastor, he laid the foundations for Hope Church.

His wife, Margaret Anna Jordan Phelps, was a charter member. Another charter member, William B. Gilmore, was a member of the first graduating class of Hope College and later taught in the primary and female department of Hope's Preparatory School.[3]

---

[1] Philip Phelps Jr., "Historical Sketch of the Second Reformed Dutch Church at Holland in Michigan," *Consistorial Minutes [1854–96]*, 1:1.
[2] Phelps, "Historical Sketch," Consistorial Minutes, 1:3.
[3] Wichers, *Century of Hope*, 89.

Of that 1866 class of eight young men four—William B. Gilmore, Peter Moerdyke, John W. Te Winkel, and William A. Shields—were members of Hope Church during their years as Hope College students. Gilmore, Moerdyke, and Te Winkel became ministers in the RCA, and Shields became a Hope College professor.

First graduating class of Hope College, 1866

Upper row: Harm Woltman, Peter Moerdyke, Gerrit Dangremond, and Ale Buursma
Lower row: William Moerdyke, William B. Gilmore, William A. Shields, and John W. Te Winkle[4]

---

[4] Willard Wichers, ed., *The Hope Milestone of 1930* (Holland, MI: Hope College, 1930).

The first women to graduate from Hope College—Sarah Gertrude Alcott (Whitenack) and Frances F. C. Phelps (Otte) in 1882, and Mary E. Alcott (Diekema) and Eliza Phelps in 1885—were members of Hope Church.

First women graduates of Hope College

Upper row: Sarah Gertrude Alcott (Mrs. Erastus Whitenack) and Frances F. C. Phelps (Mrs. John A. Otte)
Lower row: Eliza Phelps and Mary E. Alcott (Mrs. Gerrit J. Diekema)

Following, roughly in order of the year of their being hired by Hope College, are the names of faculty and administrators who were also members or ministers of Hope Church.[5] In cases when the spouse of a Hope College professor was a member and the professor was a member of a classis rather than of Hope Church, the minister/professor is included.

1865	Rev. Philip Phelps Jr. (missionary preacher and first president of Hope College)	1866	Rev. Peter Moerdyke
		1878	William A. Shields
		1878	Gerrit J. Kollen (became third president of Hope College in 1893)
1866	Rev. Theodoric Romeyn Beck (member of New Brunswick Classis; wife was member of Hope Church)	1878	Henry Boers
		1878	John H. Kleinheksel
		1885	James Sutphen
		1885	John B. Nykerk
		1887	Christina C. Van Raalte Gilmore
1866	Rev. Cornelius Eltinge Crispell (member of New Brunswick Classis; wife was member of Hope Church)	1888	Rev. John H. Gillespie (member of Bergen Classis; wife was member of Hope Church)
1866	Rev. William Brokaw Gilmore		
		1893	Erastus A. Whitenack
1866	Mrs. Owen (Marietta Shuler) Van Olinda	1895	Rev. John Tallmadge Bergen (pastor at Hope Church 1889–92, 1900–06)
1866	Cornelis Doesburg		
1866	Rev. Charles Scott[6] (member of New Brunswick Classis; wife was member of Hope Church)	1897	Henry Veghte
		1897	Edward D. Dimnent (became fifth president of Hope College in 1918)

---

[5] Information about Hope College academic and administrative staff comes mainly from *Hope College 2002 Alumni Directory*, 10th ed. (Holland, MI: Hope College, 2002), 305–332. More recent information comes from Hope College catalogs. Membership information comes from Hope Church membership books.

[6] Scott became provisional president of Hope College in 1880 and became the second president of the college in 1886.

1897	James G. Van Zwaluwenburg	1915	Elizabeth Ann Hunt
1900	John W. Beardslee Jr. (member of Michigan Classis; wife was member of Hope Church)	1916	W. B. Pietenpol
		1917	Rev. P. P. Cheff (pastor of Hope Church 1918–24)
		1918	Rev. Paul E. Hinkamp (ordained by Milwaukee Presbytery; wife was member of Hope Church)
1901	John G. Winter		
1902	Rev. John M. Van der Meulen (pastor of Hope Church 1907–09)	1919	Egbert Winter
		1919	Anne G. Visscher
		1920	John (Jack) H. L. Schouten
1903	Rev. Paul F. Schuelke (served German Reformed churches; wife was member of Hope Church)	1921	Clara E. Yntema
		1921	Laura Alice Boyd
		1921	Louise M. Brusse
		1922	Francis M. Vander Veen
		1922	Irene Brusse Ver Hulst
1904	Almon T. Godfrey	1922	Rev. James Wayer (part-time assistant pastor at Hope Church 1951–61)
1907	John Dyce MacLaren		
1908	Frank B. Meyer		
1909	Winifred Durfee		
1911	Rev. Ame Vennema (fourth president of Hope College; member of Kingston Classis; wife was member of Hope Church)	1923	Irwin J. Lubbers (became seventh president of Hope College in 1945)
		1923	Albert H. Timmer
		1924	Ephraim J. Zook
		1925	Bruce M. Raymond
		1925	Earnest C. Brooks
1912	Lambert Eidson	1926	Metta J. Ross
1913	Rev. Milton J. Hoffman (member of Pella Classis; wife was member of Hope Church)	1927	Rev. Edwin Paul McLean
		1927	Adelaide Dykhuizen
		1928	J. Harvey Kleinheksel
		1928	Helen Prisman Karsten
		1929	W. Curtis Snow
1914	John Tillema	1931	Milton Lage Hinga
1914	Magdalene De Pree	1932	Dwight B. Yntema
1914	Rev. George B. McCreary (wife was member of Hope Church)	1934	Evelyn M. Beach
		1934	Carolyn Hawes
		1936	Elizabeth Lichty
		1937	Esther Snow
1915	Arthur H. Heusinkveld	1937	Vernon D. Ten Cate

1938	Rev. William Hilmert (member of Classis Grand Rapids; wife was member of Hope Church)	1949	Mildred Singleton
		1949	Robert C. Vanderham
		1949	John E. Visser
		1950	Mary Louise Bried
		1950	Helen L. Harton
1939	William Schrier	1950	Anthony Kooiker
1940	Robert W. Cavanaugh	1950	Perma Rich
1944	Rev. Lester J. Kuyper (member of Classis South Grand Rapids; president of General Synod in 1970; wife was member of Hope Church)	1952	Lawrence Green
		1952	James Dyke Van Putten
		1952	Ransome Everett
		1952	James H. Hallan
		1952	Arthur C. Hills
		1953	Paul G. Fried
		1954	Lois Bailey
1945	John W. Hollenbach	1954	William Vander Lugt
1945	Alvin W. Vanderbush	1955	Paul E. Reid
1946	Charles R. Wimmer	1956	Ruth De Wolfe
1946	Rev. D. Ivan Dykstra	1956	Eva Van Schaak
1946	Clyde H. Geerlings	1957	Tunis Baker
1946	Charles E. Steketee	1958	E. Jean Protheroe
1946	Louise Van Domelen	1958	John R. May
1947	Norma Baughman	1958	Cornelius Mulder
1947	Marian Anderson Stryker	1959	Frank Sherburne
		1959	John Utzinger
1947	Alice Lammers	1959	F. Phillip Van Eyl
1947	Hazel Paalman	1959	Gerhard F. Megow
1947	Ernest Ellert	1960	Robert S. Brown
1948	Marguerite Hadden	1960	John E. De Pree
1948	Henry S. Maentz	1960	James Loveless
1948	Russell B. De Vette	1960	Barbara Loveless
1948	Ella Hawkinson	1960	William Oosterink
1948	Marian De Weerd Hietbrink	1960	David O. Powell
		1960	Werner Heine
1948	Lotus Snow	1962	Robert Cecil
1948	James Unger	1962	Arthur H. Jentz
1948	Donald F. Buteyn	1963	Isla Van Eenenaam
1949	Dwight Ferris	1963	Calvin Vander Werf (eighth president of Hope College)
1949	Sinnia Billips		
1949	Donald F. Brown		
1949	Harvey O. Davis	1964	Leslie R. Beach

1964	Fred Leaske	1987	Kristen Gray
1964	John Piet	1988	Gregory S. Olgers
1965	Rev. William Hillegonds	1990	Diana Benzenberg
1965	Maxine De Bruyn	1990	Phillip Tanis
1966	George Ralph	1991	Michelle Bombe
1967	Barry L. Werkman	1991	Daina Robins
1967	David G. Myers	1992	Lynn Japinga
1967	George Kraft	1992	Steven D. Hoogerwerf
1967	Mary Tellman	1993	Phillip B. Muñoa III
1968	Francis Fike	1993	Germaine Pellebon-Smith
1970	John Norman Timmer	1994	Steve Bouma-Prediger
1972	Jane R. Dickie	1994	Dierdre D. Johnston
1971	Lee H. Wenke	1994	Kathleen Ten Haken
1973	John Tysse	1996	Teunis [Tony] Donk
1973	Mark Cook	1996	Jeanne M. Jacobson
1974	Jonathan Osborn	1997	Brian Yost
1975	Jim Piers	1997	Curtis Gruenler
1975	Roberta Kraft	1998	William Bloemendaal
1976	Carla Beach	1998	Bob Bos
1977	Donald Luidens	1998	Jon Brockmeier
1978	Barbara Mezeske	1998	Terry Vande Water
1979	Rev. Gerard Van Heest	1998	Carla Vissers
1979	John D. Cox	2000	David Klooster
1979	Robin K. Klay	2001	Thomas L. Bultman
1981	David Van Heest	2003	Mark Pearson
1981	James Heisler	2003	Judith Vander Wilt
1982	Jacqueline Heisler	2005	Teresa Heinz Housel
1983	Mary Linda Graham	2006	Jacquelin Koch
1984	Tom Davelaar	2007	Anne Heath Wiersma
1984	Richard K. Smith	2007	Karen Nordell Pearson
1985	Peg Luidens	2008	Pamela Koch
1985	Janet M. Everts	2010	Rebecca Schmidt
1985	Terrance Pott	2010	Brian Yurk
1986	John Fiedler		
1986	Peter Everts		
1986	Richard Mezeske		
1987	John H. Jacobson Jr. (tenth president of Hope College)		
1987	Julie Fiedler		

Eight of the twelve Hope College presidents—Philip Phelps Jr., Charles Scott, Gerrit J. Kollen, Ame Vennema, Edward D. Dimnent, Irwin J. Lubbers, Calvin Vander Werf, and John H. Jacobson Jr.—were affiliated with Hope Church. The ministers (Phelps, Scott, and Vennema), while being technically members of the classes in which they were ordained, often served both Hope College and Hope Church. Not only were college presidents active in Hope Church, but four of Hope Church's ministers—Philip Phelps Jr., John Tallmadge Bergen, John Van der Meulen, and P. P. Cheff—taught or served as administrators at Hope College.

Appendix G: Ministers

As is evident from the following table about the ministers of Hope Church,[1] most of the ministers serving in the first fifty years of Hope Church received their college and theological school education in the East, came from churches in New York, and went to churches in New York. During the second fifty years, two of the five ministers were born and received their theological instruction outside the USA, and three of the five came to Hope Church from New York congregations. During the third fifty years, most of the pastors were born outside Michigan and attended colleges other than Hope College and seminaries other than Western Theological Seminary. What stands out over the 150 years is the diversity of birthplaces, places of college and theological education, and ministerial locations before and after Hope Church.

Minister	Place and Year of Birth	College/ Seminary	Immediately Before Hope Church	Years at Hope Church
Philip Phelps Jr.	Albany, NY; 1826	Union College, NBTS, New York Univ.	Hastings-on-Hudson, NY	1862–66, stated supply
Abel T. Stewart	Somerville, NJ; 1822	Rutgers College, NBTS	First, Tarrytown, NY	1866–77

---

[1] The main source of information about ministers of Hope Church is Gasero, *Historical Directory*.

Minister	Place and Year of Birth	College/ Seminary	Immediately Before Hope Church	Years at Hope Church
Daniel Van Pelt	Schiedam, Netherlands; 1853	College City New York, NBTS, Rutgers College	Spring Valley, NY	1878–83
Thomas W. Jones	Schuylerville, NY; 1843	Rutgers College, NBTS	Fonda, NY	1883–88
John T. Bergen	Bergen Islands, Flatlands, NY; 1860	Rutgers College, Union TS	Shandaken, NY	1889–92
Henry G. Birchby	Euxton, England; 1853	Lafayette College, Union TS	Presbyterian Church, Smithfield, NY	1892–99
John T. Bergen	Bergen Islands, Flatlands, NY; 1860	Rutgers College, Union TS	South, Brooklyn, NY	1900–06, stated supply
John M. Van der Meulen	Milwaukee, WI; 1870	Hope College, Princeton TC, McCormick TS	Missionary to Oklahoma, Prof at Hope College	1907–09
Edward Niles	York, PA; 1868	Williams College, Union TS	South Bushwick Ref. Ch., Brooklyn, NY	1909–11

Minister	Place and Year of Birth	College/ Seminary	Immediately Before Hope Church	Years at Hope Church
August F. Bruske	Rachen, Prussia; 1847[2]	Adrian College; Drew TS[3]	President of Alma College, MI	1911–16, stated supply
Peter P. Cheff	Rotterdam, Netherlands; 1873	Kampen Theo School, NBTS	First, Zeeland, MI; instructor, Hope College	1918–24
Thomas W. Davidson	Loughgall, Ireland; 1865	Methodist College, Belfast, Ireland; Methodist TS	Church on the Heights, Brooklyn, NY	1925–37
Marion de Velder	Boyden, IA; 1912	Central, NBTS	North and Southampton, Churchville, PA	1939–51
Marion de Velder	Boyden, IA; 1912	Central, NBTS	First, Albany, NY	1952–59
William C. Hillegonds	Chicago, IL; 1922	Hope, WTS	Brighton, Rochester, NY	1960–65
John R. Walchenbach	Paterson, NY, 1935	Hope, NBTS, Pittsburgh TS, Pittsburgh U	Hopewell Junction, NY	1963–66, assistant pastor

---

[2] Michigan Dept. of Public Instruction, "August F. Bruske, D. D.," *Fifty-Ninth Annual Report of the Superintendent of Public Instruction of the State of Michigan* (Detroit, MI: Bagg & Harmon, 1895), 142.
[3] Michigan Dept. of Public Instruction, "August F. Bruske, D. D.," 142.

Minister	Place and Year of Birth	College/ Seminary	Immediately Before Hope Church	Years at Hope Church
Glen O. Peterman	Strasburg, ND, 1927	Central, WTS, San Francisco TS	First, Pella, IA	1966–76
Marlin A. Vander Wilt	Boyden, IA; 1936	Northwestern College, Hope, McCormick TS	First, Albany, NY	1971–77, associate pastor; 1978–82, co-pastor; 1982–83, pastor
Paul Fries	Humboldt, IA, 1935	Muskegon CC, U Michigan, WTS, U Utrecht	Homewood, IL; prof NBTS	1978–82, co-pastor
Marion de Velder	Boyden, IA, 1912	Central, NBTS		1981–92, assistant minister for pastoral care
Marchiene Rienstra	Rangoon, Burma, 1941[4]	Calvin College, Calvin TS	Port Sheldon Presbyterian Church, MI	1984–88, senior pastor

---

[4] "Church and new pastor: pioneering together," *Holland Sentinel*, 9 February 1984:A3.

Minister	Place and Year of Birth	College/ Seminary	Immediately Before Hope Church	Years at Hope Church
Dennis L. TeBeest	Waupun, WI, 1953	Hope, WTS	associate pastor, First, Kalamazoo, MI	1985–89, associate pastor; 1989–97, senior pastor
Toni L. Macon	Middletown, CT, 1957	Marquette U, Colgate-Rochester Divinity School		1989–90, associate pastor
Mary T. Van Andel	White Cloud, MI, 1951	Hope, WTS, Catholic Theol U	associate pastor, First Presbyterian, Holland, MI	1991, interim associate pastor
Ruth Zwald Staal	Hudson, WI, 1956	Northwestern College, WTS	program director, Camp Geneva	1991–96, associate pastor
Delbert Vander Haar	Holland, MI, 1923	Hope, WTS	Yokohama Union Church, Japan	1993–98, assistant minister for pastoral care
Arthur Van Eck	Denver, CO, 1925	Hope, WTS	National Council of Churches	1997–98, interim pastor
Evelyn J. Diephouse	Grand Rapids, MI, 1946	Calvin College; Rutgers U, MEd; WTS	interim, Trinity, Grand Rapids, MI	1997–99, interim pastor

Minister	Place and Year of Birth	College/ Seminary	Immediately Before Hope Church	Years at Hope Church
Kathryn Davelaar	Fremont, MI, 1950	Calvin College, WTS	associate pastor, Third, Holland, MI	1998–2007
Gordon S. Wiersma	Seattle, WA, 1963	Calvin College, Princeton TS	North and Southampton, Churchville, PA	1999–present
Jill R. Russell	Lansing, MI, 1970	Calvin College, Princeton TS	specialized interim minister, Classis New Brunswick	2008–present

Appendix H: A Historical Digest of Hope Church Cookbooks

Because "food has always been a key indicator of who we think we are—and where we aspire to be,"[1] as an anonymous reviewer of *The Essential New York Times Cookbook* sagely commented recently, it's appropriate that a church history devote some space to cookbooks published by the ladies of Hope Church from time to time, going back to 1896.

The preface to Hope Church's first cookbook stated its edifying purpose, which it can be assumed was passed along like original sin to subsequent efforts: "Bad dinners go hand in hand with total depravity, while a properly fed man is already half saved."[2]

Eye-catching recipes from the 1896 cookbook include Dutch soup and calf's foot jelly.

Dutch Soup
Take any soup stock and season to taste, with salt and pepper. Add one cup of rice and boil until the latter is well done. Flavor with celery, cabbage or onion, or all.
—Miss Pfanstiehl[3]

The author of the Dutch Soup recipe could have been any number of women in Hope Church because there were at least two Pfanstiehl families, one of which had seventeen children,[4] of which the first eleven were daughters.[5] Needless to say, Dutch Soup could be modified to feed families small or large.

---

[1] *Newsweek*, 1 November 2010:50.
[2] *Our Cook Book, Receipt Book Published by the Ladies Aid Society of Hope Church, Holland, Mich.* (Holland, MI: Press of John D. Kanters, 1896), i. W91-1034, box 5, Hope Church, Holland, Michigan, Joint Archives of Holland.
[3] *Our Cook Book*, 1896.
[4] "Pieter Frederick Pfanstiehl," *Holland City News*, 16 July 1892:4.
[5] *Holland City News*, 30 December 1882.

The calf's foot jelly recipe is intriguing for many reasons. Is this jelly meant for human consumption? Or is it a farmer's remedy to be applied to the foot of a distressed calf? Given that the author of the recipe was a sister-in-law of the Reverend Henry G. Birchby, was the attempt to prepare food from calves' feet, not letting any part of the calf to go to waste, a veiled plea to increase the minister's salary?

Calf's Foot Jelly
Two dressed calf's feet, or one large veal shank. (Break the shank into six or eight pieces,) or if feet are used, split them in two and remove any fat from them, put them into a stewpan with three quarts of cold water bring slowly to a boil and skim off any scum as it rises. *Boil gently* six hours, or till the liquor is reduced half. Strain through fine sieve and set to cool. Next day carefully remove all fat from top, pour over a little hot water to remove any fat that may remain, and wipe the jelly with a clean hot cloth; turn out of the bowl and cut from the bottom all the sediment. Dissolve the jelly and measure off one quart. Put in preserving pan. Add six ounces of sugar, shells and whites of five eggs, (wash the shells and lightly whip the whites of the eggs.) Grated rind of one lemon and steamed juice of two, one-half ounce of Cox gelatine (this is not needed in winter but always makes you sure of firm jelly.) Dissolve the gelatine with a very little hot water and add to the other ingredients. Stir well together, simmer gently one-fourth of an hour, but *do not stir after* it is warm, throw into the pan a half teacup of cold water and again boil gently five minutes. Cover the pan and stand by stove one-half hour. Wring your jelly bag out of hot water and fasten it between two chairs, put your mould under the bag and strain the whole through. It should run through clear as rock water, but if it should be cloudy, empty the bag but not wash and pass through a second time.

The clearness of all jellies depends so much on the jelly-bag and mine are such a success that I should like to give my plan of making them.

One-half yard double mill flannel, such as we use for ironing blankets. Cut in two and fold each piece like a foolscap. Care must be taken to stitch the sides twice, to secure equal filtration, bind the top with tape and sew on six sets of tape strings. When using tie four sets of strings to a wooden hoop size of bag top and the other two to two chairs placed back to back. You will have two bags, one for light and one for dark jelly.

—Mrs. W. Birchby[6]

---

[6] *Our Cook Book*, 1896.

First question: where does one purchase "dressed calf's feet"? The instructions after "Put in preserving pan" seem rather garbled, making one wonder whether this might be a conflation of two recipes. What do the shells of five eggs contribute to this jelly? And what's the business about wringing a jelly bag out of hot water? When did the jelly bag get into the hot water to begin with? After all the time and effort put into this process, by the time we get out the two chairs and worry about whether or not we'll need to pass this jelly through the jelly bag a second time, some jelly-makers might begin feeling a little shaky.

But read on. If we'll just follow Mrs. Birchby's recipe for making successful jelly bags, all will be well, and we'll have sewn a bag for light jelly and one for dark jelly. All of this boiling, removing of fat, all of this grating and stirring and wringing—not to mention the cutting, folding, stitching, binding and sewing of the jelly bags—seems like way too much work for several jars of calf's foot jelly. Who has this much time on her hands?

By 1904 the Ladies' Aid Society published a third edition of their "RECEIPT BOOK." Many of the recipes from the first edition were republished, but not the recipe for calf's foot jelly. The third edition contained at least seventeen pages of advertisements. The women of Hope Church had secured payments from a wide range of advertisers, including manufacturers of stoves and producers of pills for dyspepsia.

> **WE GUARANTEE**
> **Rexall Dyspepsia Tablets**
> to cure any case of DYSPEPSIA or INDIGESTION that may be caused by the use of this book.
>
> 25c and 45c.   **HAAN BROS.,**   6 E. 8th St.

Rexall dyspepsia tablets advertisement

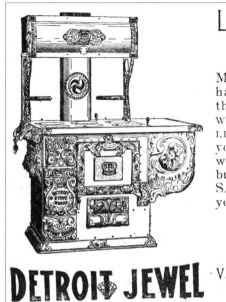

Detroit Jewel range advertisement

Seeking advertisers, designing ads, and managing the money received from advertisers and purchasers of cook books, members of the Ladies' Aid Society of Hope Church demonstrated considerable business acumen.

Recipes from the 1904 cook book include those for noodle soup, little pigs in blankets, and an omelet. If a family at the turn of the century wanted noodle soup, someone had to make the noodles from scratch:

Noodle Soup
Break two eggs in one pint of flour, add a pinch of salt, make a stiff dough, as stiff as possible; divide in three parts and roll out very thin, let it dry until it can be rolled up, then cut very thin with a sharp knife, shaking them so they will fall apart; drop the noodles into stock (made from a beef soup-bone) and boil for one minute. Serve hot.
—Mrs. S. Herold[7]

---

[7] *Receipt Book Published by the Ladies Aid Society of Hope Church, Holland, Michigan.* Third Edition. Press of John D. Kanters, 1904, 14. W91-1034, box 5,

Mrs. M. W. Gillespie, wife of a Hope College professor from the East, offered a variation of a traditional Dutch recipe that would have included sausage and pastry:

Little Pigs in Blankets
Take as many large oysters as are wished, wash and dry them thoroughly with a clean towel. Have some fat bacon cut in very thin slices, cover each oyster with them and pin on with wooden toothpicks. Broil or roast them until the bacon is crisp and brown. Do not remove toothpicks. Serve hot.
—M. W. Gillespie[8]

The intriguing ingredient in Mrs. Van Schelven's omelet recipe is the well buttered spider. It is not an arachnid thrown in for its flavor but a cast-iron skillet.

Omelet
Four eggs, one tablespoonful flour, one cup sweet milk, a little salt. Beat the eggs, whites and yolks separately, mix flour with milk, add the yolks, salt, then the whites. Bake in spider, well buttered.
—Mrs. G. Van Schelven[9]

By 1926, the Hope Church Cookbook was published by the Women's Aid Society of Hope Church. The ladies had become women. It included an index to more than one hundred advertisers of businesses in Holland and Grand Rapids. Recipes selected from that book tell how to make candied tongue, doughnuts, and coffee.

Is there a grocery store in Holland that still sells beef tongue, a delicacy remembered from my childhood? The liquor in the following recipe is more likely synonymous with liquid than alcoholic beverage.

Hope Church, Holland, Michigan, Joint Archives of Holland.
Mrs. S. Herold could have been Sarah Bertsch Herold or Suzanna Herold.
[8] *Receipt Book.*
[9] *Receipt Book.* Mrs. Gerrit Van Schelven's first name was Priscilla.

Candied Tongue
One medium sized tongue, ½ cup vinegar, ½ cup syrup (brown sugar), ¼ teaspoon allspice, ¼ teaspoon cloves, ¼ teaspoon cinnamon, ½ cup seeded raisins, 1 tablespoon salt. Cook tongue in salt water about 2 hours; remove skin and let cool in liquor; mix together vinegar, sugar, spices, and raisins, adding necessary water. Let tongue simmer in above mixture 45 minutes on top of stove. Pour over tongue removed from liquor.
—Mrs. E. P. McLean[10]

Mrs. Hadden's recipe for doughnuts sounds more like how to make fat balls, or *oliebollen*. The dough-shaped tires we now call donuts were in an earlier stage of their evolution shaped more like balls. Scoops of the mixture when dropped into a pan of hot lard, as described in the recipe below, came to resemble little nuts of dough.

Doughnuts
Break 2 eggs in a dish. Mix with 1 large cup of granulated sugar. Add 1 cup of thick buttermilk or sour milk, 2 tablespoons of melted lard, 1 level teaspoon soda. Beat well. Add Lily White flour enough to mix soft and 1 heaping teaspoon of baking powder. When the lard is hot, begin to fry the doughnuts, turning them over as soon as they come to the top.
—Mrs. J. B. Hadden[11]

When my grandmother on the farm made coffee, she cracked open a raw egg and dropped it along with the ground coffee into the coffee pot, a blue granite container that predated percolators and coffee makers. I don't remember whether she tried to separate out the yolk, or whether she put in shell and all. She said the egg collected the grounds and made a tasty, clearer coffee than the eggless coffee would be.

---

[10] *Our Cook Book*, Holland, MI: Women's Aid Society of Hope Church, [1926]:19. W91-1034, box 5, Hope Church, Holland, Michigan, Joint Archives of Holland.
[11] *Our Cook Book*, 1926.

Coffee
To make medium strong coffee use 1 rounding tablespoon good brand coffee to 1 cup cold water. Add 1 tablespoon coffee 'for the pot.' Use shell and white of egg to settle. Let come to a boil very slowly, then set back on stove and let stand for a few minutes, keeping it at boiling point but do not boil. If very strong coffee is desired, increase amount of coffee.
—Committee[12]

Among recipes in the Hope Church cookbook of 1935 are those for roast goose and jugged chicken. The roast goose recipe includes details more related to the butchering than to the cooking:

Roast Goose
Singe, remove pin feathers, and scrub goose in hot soap suds; then remove insides and rinse well in clear, cold water. Wipe dry inside and out, stuff and truss, sprinkling with salt and pepper and roast in a hot oven for 2 hours. For the first hour of roasting, the breast should be covered with buttered paper. Baste every 15 minutes. When done, place on a hot platter and remove skewers and string. Garnish with browned apples and watercress.
—Mrs. N. Dykhuizen[13]

Jugged Chicken
Disjoint a chicken, roll each piece generously in flour and place in layers in a casserole with a tight lid. Salt and pepper and put small pieces of butter over each layer. Nearly cover with boiling water, and bake 2½ hours. Chicken is delicious cooked in this way, and is easily prepared. It does not have to be watched, and the gravy is all made and ready to serve.
—Mrs. J. J. Cappon[14]

---

[12] *Our Cook Book*, 1926.
[13] *The Hope Church Cook Book: Tested Recipes Compiled by Woman's* [sic] *Aid Society of Hope Reformed Church, Holland, Michigan*, 1935:20. W91-1034, box 5, Hope Church, Holland, Michigan, Joint Archives of Holland. Mrs. Dykhuizen's first name was Nell.
[14] *The Hope Church Cook Book: Tested Recipes*, 1935:22.

The *Hope Church 80th Anniversary Cook Book* made the claim that the recipes were tested. In its special section of Dutch recipes are those for making krakaling, hutspot, and balkanbrij.

Krakaling

1 lb. butter   ½ c. water   1 lb. flour

Mix as pie dough. Let stand in refrigerator overnight. Roll like pencil, bring ends together, and twist like figure 8. Dip both sides in sugar and bake until brown on bottom, 375 degrees F.
—Mrs. H. Carley[15]

Hutspot

6 carrots, 6 onions, boil with a small piece of pork. Boil 8 or 10 potatoes; dry them thoroughly and mash. Put the boiled carrots, onions, pork, and potatoes together. Add salt, pepper and a little piece of butter. Stew all together.
—Miss Alice V. Althuis[16]

Balkanbrij (Liver Sausage)

3 lbs. beef liver	1½ tsp. cloves
1 lb. side pork	1 tsp. pepper
1 pt. meat stock	2 c. buckwheat flour
1 pt. water	2 c. or more quick-cooking
1 tbsp. salt	Cream of Wheat

Grind liver and pork. Heat meat with other ingredients. Add Cream of Wheat until you are no longer able to stir the mixture. Put into a mold. When thoroughly cold cut mixture into ½-inch slices and brown in dry frying pan. Serve hot for breakfast.
—Mrs. Albert Van Zoeren[17]

---

[15] *Tested Recipes: Hope Church 80th Anniversary Cook Book* [(Holland: Women's Aid Society of Hope Church, 1942)], 8. W91-1034, box 5, Hope Church, Holland, Michigan, Joint Archives of Holland.
[16] *Tested Recipes,* 1942:10.
[17] *Tested Recipes,* 1942:10. Mrs. Van Zoeren's first name was Irene.

Frances Phelps Otte's scripture cake lists ingredients (with parallel instructions to the right) but gives no directions for the baking. Her citation of the Proverbs verse as a prescription for making a good boy would likely violate the tastes and the moral scruples of many twenty-first-century parents.

Scripture Cake

4½ c. *I Kings* 4:22	4½ c. **Flour**
1½ c. of *Judges* 5:25 (last clause)	1½ c. **Butter**
2 c. of *Jeremiah* 6:20 (second clause)	2 c. **Sugar**
2 c. of *I Samuel* 30:12 (second clause)	2 c. **Raisins**
2 c. of *Nahum* 3:12	2 c. **Figs**
1 c. of *Numbers* 17:8	1 c. **Almonds**
2 tbsp. *I Samuel* 14:25	2 tbsp. **Honey**
Season to taste of *II Chronicles* 9:9	Season with **Spice**
4 of *Jeremiah* 17:11	4 **eggs**
A pinch of *Leviticus* 2:13	A pinch of **Salt**
½ c. of *Judges* 4:19 (last clause)	½ c. **Milk**
2 tsp. of *Amos* 4:5	2 tsp. **leaven** (baking powder)

Follow Solomon's prescription for making a good boy Proverbs 23:14; and you will have a nice cake.
—Frances Phelps Otte, from My Mother's Cook Book[18]

Hope Church also produced a *Hope Church Cook Book Holland Michigan, A Book of Favorite Recipes Compiled by Reformed Church Women of Hope Church 1977* (Kansas City, MO: Circulation Service). In 1991 the Hope Church Women's Guild published a three-ring binder cookbook titled *Hope Church Holland Michigan: Since 1862 Member Reformed Church in America* (Kearney, NB: Cookbooks by Morris Press).

---

[18] *Tested Recipes*, 1942:93.

Appendix I: Missionaries Supported by Hope Church

Listed below in chronological order are the names of foreign and domestic missionaries for whose support Hope Church paid a large share. Additional missionaries were supported by the Women's Missionary Societies. The Women's Bible class for many years sent money to help support missionaries Margaret Rottschaefer in India and Elda Van Putten Hakken in Iraq—to name only two examples.

The Reverend and Mrs. Willis G. Hoekje, Japan, 1907–32, 1940–45

Mrs. B. D. Hakken (nee Elda Van Putten), Arabia

The Reverend John and Mrs. Virginia Muilenburg, China and later the Philippines, 1945–59

Dr. and Mrs. Blaise Levai, India, 1952–58

Mrs. Mary Ada Cater, teacher at Southern Normal School, Brewton, Alabama, 1946–48

Alonzo Harvey, farm director at Southern Normal School, Brewton, Alabama, 1949–56

Conn V. Miller, manual arts director, Southern Normal School, Brewton, Alabama, 1956–57

Jethro J. Woodson, Southern Normal School, Brewton Alabama, 1957–62

Viola L. Sutton, Brewton, Alabama, 1962–77

Mitchell Culliver, Brewton, Alabama, 1963–66

Southern Normal School, Brewton, Alabama, 1978–94, 1996

The Reverend and Mrs. Raymond Denekas, Jackson County Ministries, Kentucky, 1958–63

The Reverend and Mrs. Henry Fikse, Canadian missionaries, 1958–59

The Reverend and Mrs. Carl J. Schroeder, Canadian missionaries, 1959–60

The Reverend and Mrs. Alvin J. Poppen, overseas Chinese in Hong Kong, 1959

The Reverend and Mrs. Gordon De Pree, Philippines, 1959–60

Dr. and Mrs. Everett Kleinjans, India (International Christian University), 1963–77

Dick Doeden, Jackson County Ministries, Kentucky, 1963–68

Katpadi Agricultural Institute, founded in 1920 by Dr. John James De Valois; also Katpadi Campsite, India, 1967–1994, 1996

The Reverend Lewis and Mrs. Nancy Scudder Jr., missionaries to Arabia and later to other parts of the Middle East, 1967–72 and 1974–2007

David and Nancy Piet, Indonesia, 1969–74

The Reverend Julius and Mrs. Wilma Brandt, Middle East (Bahrain, Kuwait), 1977–79

Mr. and Mrs. David Wyma, Taiwan, 1979

The Reverend John and Mrs. Gloria Rottenberg, Middle East, 1979–81

Warren and Janice Greving, Southeast Asia, Taiwan, 1979–84

Louis and Marilyn Sytsma, Chiapas, Mexico, 1982–83

The Reverend Steven and Mrs. Susan Van Bronkhorst, Chiapas, Mexico, 1984–91

David and Char Alexander, Taiwan, 1985–present

Randall Braaksma, China, 1988, 1992–94

Carol Braaksma, China, 1992–94

Peter and Patty Ford, Sudan, 1991

Bruce and Tamar De Jonge, 1991

Rowland and Jane Van Es, Malawi and Kenya, 1995–present

Caleb and Joanna Swart, Ethiopia, 2007–present

Appendix J: A Doggie Story

A little, gray bulldog named Tige has been trying to get my attention for some time. "Let me in, let me in," she has been barking. So before we close the covers of this book, she has a story that Cornelius Vander Meulen[1] has put into words. The events of the story took place a long time ago, sometime between 1900 and 1914.

> Doctor Henry Kremers[2] was, for years, the leading physician in Holland, Michigan—an ideal example of the family doctor of those days, making his daily rounds of visits, ready to respond to need at any time of the day or night.
>
> Alice Kremers, his wife, was a person, in her own way, just as remarkable as the Doctor. She was intellectual. The Kremers had five sons and a little, gray female bulldog named "Tige." The boys grew up and left home but Tige remained. If the boys loved their mother, Tige adored her. It was Mrs. Kremers who provided Tige with food and provided a nice, warm place for her to sleep and who permitted her to curl up at her feet, and sometimes even in her lap. The saddest hours of Tige's life were the occasions, when, for some reason beyond Tige's comprehension, Mrs. Kremers left the house without letting Tige tag along. There were occasions when Tige was compelled to stay alone.
>
> Doctor and Mrs. Kremers ... regularly attended the morning worship service of Hope Church. Just before they left, Mrs. Kremers would escort Tige to her basement quarters and close the door. This

---

[1] Cornelius Vander Meulen (1880–1968), grandson of Zeeland, Michigan, founder the Reverend Cornelius Vander Meulen (1800–76), graduated from Hope College in 1900 and served as Holland's municipal judge for seventeen years. His stories, such as this one, often entertained members of Holland's Century Club.

[2] Not only was Henry Kremers (1850–1914) a leading physician, but he was also mayor of Holland (1889–90) and owned a pharmacy on Eighth Street. He was also president of the Board of Education, a director of a bank, on the board of a sugar company, and one of the organizers of the Holland Furnace Company. http://www2.cityofholland.com/mayors/12.htm

wonderful, woman, being as intelligent as she was, apparently had no conception of the torture of solitary confinement; but Tige had learned to read the signs. When the doctor appeared in his Sunday suit and when Mrs. Kremers wore her Sunday hat and dress, Tige knew that her hour of solitude was at hand.

So, on one particular Sunday morning in October, when the Kremers were ready to start for church, Tige was nowhere to be found. Mrs. Kremers' call and the Doctor's whistle brought no response. Thinking that it would in no way harm Tige to be outdoors for a couple of hours on a beautiful Sunday morning, the Doctor and Mrs. Kremers strolled slowly to the church just a few blocks away,[3] entirely unaware that, a couple hundred feet away and keeping in the shelter as much as possible of hedges, Tige was trailing them. Tige knew she was doing wrong and that if caught she would be reprimanded and chased home, but the dread thought of that awful solitude made her take the risk.

When Doctor and Mrs. Kremers came to the front of the church, Tige was still a couple hundred feet back. When she saw them disappear into the entry, they were just entering the door of the sanctuary on the east side, but some other people were also entering, and Tige was delayed. When she came to the head of the east aisle, Doctor and Mrs. Kremers had disappeared, having seated themselves in the pew. There was Tige—a poor, bewildered, frustrated, little dog. What should she do? Turn around and scamper for home, or continue the search for her beloved mistress? Just then, she spied a friend. From the west side door, the minister of the Church entered, walked on to the platform, and seated himself in the chair directly behind the pulpit.

Now, the minister was not only the Kremers' pastor; he was also a former patient of the Doctor and a close personal friend. He had on numerous occasions been a guest at the Kremers home and had undoubtedly scratched Tige's head. What a joy and relief to find a

---

[3] The Kremers lived at 8 East Twelfth Street at the southeast corner of Central and Twelfth Street in a large house, which from 1919 to 1928 served as Holland's first public hospital. For ten years between 1928 and 1940 it became the home of Hope College's Knickerbocker fraternity. From 1949 to 1992 it served the Netherlands Museum. Lynne B. Weir and Mary Grace York, *City of Holland: Intensive Level Study Areas: Historic Preservation*. (Holland, MI, 1993).

friend among this multitude of strangers! Down the aisle pattered Tige, up the steps; and there she placed herself under the minister's chair. As the minister bowed his head in prayer that the "words of his mouth might be acceptable," Tige, too, assumed an attitude of reverence, placing her head between her two, little, front paws—all this to the great amusement of the congregation, but to the consternation of Doctor Kremers.

The Doctor immediately walked over to the very front pew; and there he sat beckoning to Tige, his lips forming the words, "Tige, Tige", but soundlessly. To no avail! Tige had found sanctuary in the temple of God. She trusted the man of God under whose chair she had found safety. But that Congregation! Oh, no! Tige was a very discerning little dog. She knew that congregations are not always what their Master would have them be; perhaps not what their minister would have them be; possibly not even what a little, gray bulldog would have them be. As for the Doctor! Tige did not like the look in his eye. You see, Tige, perhaps more than any other individual, felt the guilt of the sin she had so recently committed. That look boded no good.

It seemed to her that the safest place for her was just where she was, and there she proposed to say. But, alas! The best laid plans of mice and little, gray bulldogs often go awry. For the Doctor was a man, and men so often, when they failed to gain their ends by persuasion, resorted to force. The Doctor bided his time until the congregation arose to sing a hymn. Then he, too, arose, mounted the platform, grabbed Tige by the collar, carried her down, pitched her out of the side door, then returned to join Mrs. Kremers in their regular pew.

Did Tige get home safely? I am quite positive that she did, for Tige had lived in that neighborhood for the greater part of her dog's life. It was only a short distance from the church to the Kremers' home. Also, since Tige was only a little, gray bulldog, I am sure that when the Doctor arrived home, he was greeted by a wagging tail and that Tige bore no resentment whatever for having been so rudely removed from the Communion of the Saints.[4]

---

[4] Cornelius Vander Meulen, "The Excommunication of Tige," no date. W91-1034, box 12, Hope Church, Holland, Michigan, Joint Archives of Holland.

Appendix K: Chronology

ca. 4 BCE–30 CE	The birth, life, death, and resurrection of Jesus Christ proclaim that God is love.
1509–64	John Calvin breaks from Roman Catholicism and develops Reformed theology.
1566	The Belgic Confession and Heidelberg Catechism become standards of Reformed theology.
1618–19	The Great Synod of Dordt establishes Canons of Dordt.
1628	The Reformed Protestant Dutch Church is established in New Netherland (New York). It is the oldest Protestant Church in the new world with a continuous history.
1847	More than seven-hundred Dutch immigrants, led by Albertus C. Van Raalte, establish a colony in the Black Lake area of what becomes Holland, Michigan.
1848	The Classis of Holland is established and elects Albertus C. Van Raalte president.
1850	The Classis of Holland unites with the Reformed Protestant Dutch Church.
1854	The Reformed Protestant Dutch Church in North America establishes an English-language preaching mission in Holland.
2 March 1860	Albertus C. Van Raalte donates land, and others pledge money and materials for building an English-speaking second Reformed church in Holland.
20 July 1862	Hope Church is organized.
1862–66	Philip Phelps Jr. serves as missionary pastor.
1864	Philip Phelps Jr. is elected president of the General Synod.
25 Dec. 1864	Hope Church dedicates its first sanctuary.
1866–77	Abel T. Stewart serves as pastor.
1866–78	Philip Phelps Jr. serves as president of Hope College.
1867	The Reformed Protestant Dutch Church in North America renames itself the Reformed Church in America.
1868–72	Member Bernardus Ledeboer serves as mayor of Holland.
1869	The first Hope Church parsonage is built.

8–9 Oct. 1871	Fire destroys much of Holland, including Hope Church. The Hope Church parsonage is spared.
1872–74	Member Edward J. Harrington serves as mayor of Holland.
1874	Hope Church dedicates its second sanctuary.
1875	Charles Scott is elected president of the General Synod.
1878	Women and men vote to call Daniel Van Pelt as pastor.
1878–83	Daniel Van Pelt serves as pastor.
1878–93	Charles Scott serves as president of Hope College.
1879	Women and men vote to elect deacons and elders.
1883	Hope Church Ladies' Aid Society is organized.
1883–88	Thomas W. Jones serves as pastor.
1886	Hope Church Women's Missionary Society is organized.
1889–90	Member Henry Kremers serves as mayor of Holland.
1889–92	John T. Bergen serves as pastor.
1890–92	Member Oscar Yates serves as mayor of Holland.
1892–93	Member Edward J. Harrington serves as mayor of Holland.
1892–99	Henry G. Birchby serves as pastor.
1893–1911	Member Gerrit J. Kollen serves as president of Hope College.
1895–96	Member Gerrit J. Diekema serves as mayor of Holland.
1900	Pew rental is replaced by pledging system to support the church.
1900–02	Member William Brusse serves as mayor of Holland.
1900–06	John T. Bergen serves as stated supply pastor.
1901	Revival by C. C. Smith adds more than 100 new members.
1902	Hope Church dedicates its third (present) sanctuary.
1903	Young Ladies' Aid Society donates individual cups for use during Communion, replacing use of a common cup.
1904–06	Member Henry Geerlings serves as mayor of Holland.
1906–08	Member Jacob G. Van Putten serves as mayor of Holland.

1907	Hope Church begins support of missionaries Rev. and Mrs. Willis G. Hoekje in Japan.
1907	Ame Vennema is elected president of the General Synod.
1907–09	John M. Vander Meulen serves as pastor.
1909–11	Edward Niles serves as pastor.
1910	New parsonage is built at 79 West Eleventh Street.
1911–16	August F. Bruske serves as stated supply pastor.
1911–18	Ame Vennema serves as president of Hope College.
1912–16	Member Nicodemus Bosch serves as mayor of Holland.
1918	Member Willard G. Leenhouts is killed in World War I.
1918–20	Member Nicodemus Bosch serves as mayor of Holland.
1918–24	Peter P. Cheff serves as pastor.
1918–31	Member Edward D. Dimnent serves as president of Hope College.
1921	Martha Diekema Kollen donates land to become George E. Kollen Memorial Park.
1924	Hope Church Boy Scout troop is organized.
1924	Ten memorial stained glass windows are dedicated.
1925–37	Thomas W. Davidson serves as pastor.
1927	Member Lida Rogers proposes annual tulip plantings, the origin of Holland's Tulip Time Festival.
1928–32	Member Earnest Brooks serves as mayor of Holland.
1932–36	Member Nicodemus Bosch serves as mayor of Holland.
1934	Hope Church Men's Club is organized.
1936–44	Member Henry Geerlings serves as mayor of Holland.
1939–51	Marion de Velder serves as pastor.
1941	Hope Church replaces the Sunday evening worship service with the School for Christian Living (with refreshments).
1945–63	Member Irwin J. Lubbers serves as president of Hope College.
late 1940s	The Bosch family donates the Communion rose window in memory of Nicodemus Bosch.
1947	Kate Keppel donates "Last Supper" wood carving by Alois Lang in memory of her husband, Albert C. Keppel.

1949	Elsie B. Stryker becomes the first full-time director of Christian education.
1950s	Hope, Third Reformed, and First Methodist churches together begin annual Vacation Bible School.
1951	Mr. and Mrs. Club is organized; later it becomes the Brim Bunch.
1951	*Hope Parish News*, later becoming *Hope Church News*, begins monthly publication.
1952–59	Marion de Velder serves as pastor.
1953	Radio station WHTC begins broadcasting Hope Church worship services.
1955–61	Member Robert Visscher serves as mayor of Holland.
1956	Hope Church purchases house at 99 West Eleventh Street as parsonage. Old parsonage at 79 West Eleventh Street and Sprietsma house become West Church House and East Church House for offices and meeting rooms.
1958	Marion de Velder is elected president of the General Synod.
1960	Men organize Wednesday morning prayer breakfasts.
1960–65	William C. Hillegonds serves as pastor.
1961	Maxine De Bruyn begins Rhythmic Choir, later known as Sacred Dance Group of Holland, at Hope Church.
1961–68	Marion de Velder serves as stated clerk of the General Synod.
1962	The education wing is built.
1963–70	Member Calvin A. Vander Werf serves as president of Hope College.
1963–66	John R. Walchenbach serves as assistant pastor.
1966	Holland Day Care Center opens in the education wing and begins continuous early learning for children.
1966–76	Glen O. Peterman serves as pastor.
1968–77	Marion de Velder serves as general secretary of the Reformed Church in America.
1969	James I. Cook establishes Christian Action task forces.
1969	Hope Church, Grace Episcopal, St. Francis de Sales, and other churches organize Community Action House.

1970	Lester Jacob Kuyper is elected president of the General Synod.
1971–73	Member Lawrence W. (Bill) Lamb Jr. serves as mayor of Holland.
1971–77	Marlin A. Vander Wilt serves as associate pastor.
1972	RCA allows women to serve as deacons and elders. Elizabeth (Betty) Becker is installed as elder.
1973	Dr. Bernadine S. De Valois and Hermina (Mickie) Lamb are installed as elders, and Audrey Navis is installed as deacon.
1974	Hope Church begins Early Worship services.
1978–82	Marlin A. Vander Wilt serves as co-pastor.
1982–83	Marlin A. Vander Wilt serves as pastor.
1978–82	Paul R. Fries serves as co-pastor.
1981–92	Marion de Velder serves as assistant minister for pastoral care.
1982	James I. Cook is elected president of the General Synod.
1982	The former 1874 sanctuary, which became the parish hall, was replaced by the Parish Life Center.
1982	The Vander Broek family donates six facet-slab glass windows in Commons I to honor Gertrude Vander Broek.
1983	Elder Elsie Lamb and others are arrested and jailed for protesting production of missile engines at Williams International in Walled Lake, Michigan.
1983	The sanctuary is renovated.
1984–88	Marchiene Rienstra serves as senior pastor.
1985–89	Dennis L. TeBeest serves as associate pastor.
1987	Children in Worship programming begins.
1987–99	Member John H. Jacobson serves as president of Hope College.
1989–97	Dennis L. TeBeest serves as senior pastor.
1989–90	Toni L. Macon serves as associate pastor.
1990	Holland Peacemakers organization donates peace pole to Hope Church.
1991	Hope Church becomes a registered Michigan Historical Site, and an official marker is installed.

1991	Mary T. Van Andel serves as interim associate pastor.
1991–96	Ruth Zwald Staal serves as associate pastor.
1993–98	Delbert Vander Haar serves as assistant minister for pastoral care.
1995	Elsie Lamb and Jo Anne Brooks travel to Okinawa and Hiroshima, Japan, to study issues of war and peace.
1987–89	Member Philip A. Tanis serves as mayor of Holland (though a member of Third Reformed Church while mayor, he later joins Hope Church).
1994–95	Hope Church engages in year of discernment and dialog about issues of homosexuality.
1995	Lost volume one of *Consistorial Minutes* 1862–1896 is found and purchased at a local auction.
1997–98	Arthur Van Eck serves as interim pastor.
1997–99	Evelyn J. Diephouse serves as interim pastor.
1998–2007	Kathryn Davelaar serves as pastor.
1999–present	Gordon S. Wiersma serves as pastor.
2002	Hearing loop technology is installed in the sanctuary and in Commons I, greatly improving sound transmission to those with hearing loss.
2008	Carol Bechtel is elected president of the General Synod.
2008–present	Jill R. Russell serves as pastor.
2009	The RCA General Synod votes to adopt the Belhar Confession. The vote is ratified by classes in 2010.
2012	Hope Church votes to become a Room for All congregation, welcoming all regardless of sexual orientation and gender identity.

Bibliography

150 Years Celebrating Our Ministry in Holland 1861–2011 First United Methodist Church, 2011.

150th Anniversary First Reformed Church [Holland, Michigan], Grand Rapids: West Michigan Printing, n. d. [1997].

"Academic and Administrative Personnel: 1847–1960." http://www.hope.edu/pr/hopecollegechronology/academicadministrativepersonnel.html.

Acts and Proceedings of the General Synod of the Reformed Church in America, 1869, 1899, 1953, 1959, 1985.

Acts and Proceedings of the General Synod of the Reformed Protestant Dutch Church in America, 1848, 1854.

Allen, Edith H. "A Tribute to Mrs. C. V. R. Gilmore." *Golden Years in Miniature: A History of the Women's Board of Domestic Missions of the Reformed Church in America from the Time of Its Organization in 1882 As the Women's Executive Committee of the Board of Domestic Missions to Its Present Golden Anniversary Year.* New York: Women's Board of Domestic Missions, 1932.

Bacon, Edgar Mayhew. *Chronicles of Tarrytown and Sleepy Hollow.* New York: G. P. Putnam's Sons, 1905.

Bailey, Wm., and J. H. Kershaw. "Holland Academy—New Church Organized." *Christian Intelligencer*, 21 August 1862.

Ballast, Daniel L. *Then Now Always 1840-2004 Jesus Is Lord: The History of Central Reformed Church: 1840-2004.* Grand Rapids, MI, n. d.

Bechtel, Carol. "Interview with Miss Ruth Keppel in Her Home on August 6, 1981." Hope College Living Heritage Oral History Project: 1980. http://www.hope.edu/jointarchives/Oral%20Interviews/1980/Keppel,Ruth.pdf.

Bergen, John Tallmadge. *Evidences of Christianity.* Holland, Mich.: Wm. H. Bingham, Printer, 1902.

———. "Geronimo's Conversion." *Historical Highlights*, no. 40, February 1994: 13–20. Reprinted from a tract, undated, published by the Chicago Tract Society.

Boersma, Lois. "History of Brim Bunch," n. d. W91-1034, box 12, Hope Church, Holland, Michigan, Joint Archives of Holland.

———. "Hope Church History," n. d. W91-1034, box 12, Hope Church, Holland, Michigan, Joint Archives of Holland.

Boersma, Vern. "My Work with Migrants," n. d. W91-1034, box 12, Hope Church, Holland, Michigan, Joint Archives of Holland.

Boonstra, Harry. "The Dutch Equation in the RCA Freemasonry Controversy, 1867–1885," Lecture Series of the Van Raalte Institute Visiting Research Fellows Program, no 6. Holland, MI: The Van Raalte Press, 2008.

Braaksma, Randall. "China: Crisis of Faith" and "A Black Day." *Church Herald*, September 1989:24–28.

Bratt, James D. *Dutch Calvinism: A History of A Conservative Subculture.* Grand Rapids, MI: Wm. B. Eerdmans, 1984.

Brouwer, Arie R. *Reformed Church Roots: Thirty-Five Formative Events.* New York City, NY: Reformed Church Press, 1977.

Bruggink, Donald J. "Extra-Canonical Tests for Church Membership and Ministry." In *A Goodly Heritage: Essays in Honor of the Reverend Dr. Elton J. Bruins at Eighty,* ed. Jacob E. Nyenhuis. Historical Series of the Reformed Church in America, no 56. Grand Rapids, MI: Wm. B. Eerdmans, 2007.

Bruins, Elton J. *The Americanization of a Congregation,* 2nd ed. Historical Series of the Reformed Church in America, no. 26. Grand Rapids, MI: Wm. B. Eerdmans, 1995.

———. "The Holocaust in Holland: 1871." *Michigan History*, 55, no. 4 (Winter 1971): 289–304.

Bruins, Elton J., Karen G. Schakel, Sara Frederickson Simmons, and Marie N. Zingle. *Albertus and Christina: The Van Raalte Family, Home and Roots.* Grand Rapids, MI: Wm. B. Eerdmans, 2004.

Bruins, Elton J., and Karen G. Schakel. *Envisioning Hope College: Letters Written by Albertus C. Van Raalte to Philip Phelps Jr., 1857 to 1875.* Historical Series of the Reformed Church in America in Cooperation with the Van Raalte Institute, no. 71. Grand Rapids, MI: Van Raalte Press and Wm. B. Eerdmans, 2011.

By-laws of the Guild for Christian Service of Hope Church, Classis of Holland, Reformed Church in America. W91-1034, box 5, Hope Church, Holland, Michigan, Joint Archives of Holland.

"Centennial" General Circular of Hope College at Holland, Michigan. Albany: Weed, Parsons and Company Printers, 1872.

"Church Notes." *Christian Intelligencer*, 7, no. 284 (3 May 1940):18.

Classis Holland Minutes 1848–1858, trans. Joint Committee of the Christian Reformed Church and the Reformed Church in America. 2nd ed. Grand Rapids, MI: Wm. B. Eerdmans, 1950.

Coakley, John W. "Women in the History of the Reformed Church in America," in *Patterns and Portraits: Women in the History of the Reformed Church in America*, ed. Renée House and John Coakley. Historical Series of the Reformed Church in America, no. 31. Grand Rapids, MI: Wm. B. Eerdmans, 1999:1–15.

Consistorial Minutes, vol. 1 [1854–96], vol. 2 [1897–1917], vol. 3, [1917–34], vol. 4 [1935–40], vol. 5 [1940–42], vol. 6 [1943–45], vol. 7 [1945–47], vol. 8 [1947–49]. W91-1034, box 1, Hope Church, Holland, Michigan, Joint Archives of Holland. Vols. 9–22 for the years 1950–63 are in box 2. Vols. 23–34 for the years 1964–75 are in box 3. Vols. 35–45 for the years 1976–85 are in box 4. Subsequent volumes by year are at Hope Church. Minutes from 1996 to the present are on computer at Hope Church. *Consistorial Minutes* from 1970 through 2012 also include minutes of the Board of Elders, Board of Deacons, Executive Committee, and various ministries and task forces.

"Constitution of the Ladies' Aid Society of Hope Reformed Church, Holland, Mich.," 1883. W91-1034, box 5, Hope Church, Holland, Michigan, Joint Archives of Holland.

"A Contemporary Account of the Holland Fire," in *Dutch Immigrant Memoirs and Related Writings*, selected and arranged by Henry S. Lucas. 2nd ed. Grand Rapids, MI: Wm. B. Eerdmans, vol. 2: 492–97. [This account, published in Dutch in a joint issue of *De Grondwet*, *De Wachter*, and *De Hollander*, 12 October 1871, was translated by the Reverend Henry De Mots for this Lucas volume.]

Cook, James I. "A Task Force Ministry." *Church Herald*, 15 May 1970:12–13, 23.

Corwin, Edward Tanjore. *A Manual of the Reformed Church in America (Formerly Ref. Prot. Dutch Church), 1628–1902*. 4th ed. New York: Board of Publication of the Reformed Church in America, 1902.

De Bruyn, Maxine. *Holland Rhythmic Choir Archives: Early History and Beginnings* [scrapbook donated to Joint Holland Archives].

De Valois, John James. *Autobiography of John James De Valois Agricultural Missionary, Church of South India*. Zeeland, MI: Ottawa Color Graphics, n. d. W91-1034, box 12, Hope Church, Holland, Michigan, Joint Archives of Holland.

De Vries, Michael, and Harry Boonstra. *Pillar Church in the Van Raalte Era.* Holland, MI: Pillar Christian Reformed Church, 2003.

"Dedicated to Hope: The Renewing Hope Building Project." W91-1034, box 12, Hope Church, Holland, Michigan, Joint Archives of Holland.

Douma, Michael J. *Veneklasen Brick: A Family, a Company, and a Unique Nineteenth-Century Dutch Architectural Movement in Michigan.* Grand Rapids, MI: Wm. B. Eerdmans, 2005.

Dunn, David, Paul N. Cursius, et al. *A History of the Evangelical and Reformed Church.* New York: Pilgrim Press, 1990.

Elders' Minutes of Second Reformed Protestant Dutch Church of Holland, Michigan. W91-1034, box 5, Hope Church, Holland, Michigan, Joint Archives of Holland.

Ester, Peter, Nella Kennedy and Earl Wm. Kennedy. *The American Diary of Jacob Van Hinte: Author of the Classic Immigrant Study* Nederlanders in Amerika. Historical Series of the Reformed Church in America, no. 69. Holland/Grand Rapids, MI: Van Raalte Press/Wm. B. Eerdmans, 2010.

"A Formula of Agreement," https://www.rca.org/sslpage.aspx?pid=432.

Gasero, Russell L. *Historical Directory of the Reformed Church in America 1628–2000.* Historical Series of the Reformed Church in America, no. 37. Grand Rapids, MI: Wm. B. Eerdmans, 2001.

Granberg-Michaelson, Wesley. *Unexpected Destinations: An Evangelical Pilgrimage to World Christianity.* Grand Rapids, MI: Wm. B. Eerdmans, 2011.

Hageman, Howard G. *Lily Among the Thorns*, 30th Anniversary ed. New York: Reformed Church Press, 1983.

Hayden, Jim. "Allegan Co. POW Camp a Reminder of Local History, *Holland Sentinel*, 21 May 2011. http://www.hollandsentinel.com/feature/x157795564/Allegan-Co-POW-camp-a-reminder-of-local-history.

Heideman, Eugene P. *The Practice of Piety: The Theology of the Midwestern Reformed Church in America, 1866–1966.* Historical Series of the Reformed Church in America, no. 64. Grand Rapids, MI: Wm. B. Eerdmans, 2009.

Hinkamp, Paul E. "Dr. John T. Bergen, a Tribute." *Alumni News*, December 1948:27–28.

———. "Hope Church, Reformed Church in America, Holland Michigan: 1862-1942." Booklet issued in commemoration of the Eightieth Anniversary. 3 May 1942.

"Historical Sketch." *First Catalogue and Circular of Hope College, Incorporated A.D. 1866, at Holland, Ottawa County, Michigan; with a Catalogue and Circular of the Holland Academy 1865-6, Published by the Council.* Albany: Weed, Parsons and Company Printers, 1866.

History of Ottawa County, Michigan, with Illustrations and Biographical Sketches of Some of Its Prominent Men and Pioneers. Chicago: H. R. Page & Co., 1882.

Hoekje, Willis G. "The Oldest Hope Graduate." *Intelligencer-Leader,* 11 June 1941:14.

"Holland Town and Township History." Transcriber: Leslie Coulson Created: 26 August 2006. http://ottawa.migenweb.net/holland/history/1882history.html#HOPE_COLLEGE.

Hollenbach, John W. "Paul G. Fried, Apostle for International Understanding." In *Into All the World: Hope College and International Affairs,* ed. Robert J. Donia and John M. Mulder. Holland, MI: Hope College, 1985.

The Hope Church Cook Book: Tested Recipes Compiled by Woman's [sic] *Aid Society of Hope Reformed Church, Holland, Michigan,* 1935. W91-1034, box 5, Hope Church, Holland, Michigan, Joint Archives of Holland.

Hope Church Highlights: An Historical Chronology of Events and Persons 1854 to 1987 Published on the Occasion of the One Hundred Twenty Fifty Anniversary of Hope Church Holland, Michigan, 1987.

The Hope Church Historical Booklet 1982: Our Time for Rededication. 1982.

"Hope Church," *Holland City News,* no. 117, (16 May 1874):1.

"Hope Church Holland, Michigan A Report to the Congregation from the Consistory," 16 October 1995 (Revised 15 April 1996), "Subject: MORAL DISCERNMENT Regarding the issues of homosexuality and ordained leadership in the church." W91-1034, box 12, Hope Church, Holland, Michigan, Joint Archives of Holland.

Hope Church Manual and Membership Directories. 1902, 1917, 1920, 1923, 1926–27, 1928–29. W91-1034, box 8, Hope Church, Holland, Michigan, Joint Archives of Holland.

Hope Church Membership Records 1862-1910. W91-1034, box 11, Hope Church, Holland, Michigan, Joint Archives of Holland.

Hope Church News. 1951–present.

Hope Church Reformed Church in America Holland, Michigan ... Eightieth Anniversary, 1942.

Hope Church (Second Reformed) Holland, Michigan 1902 [Directory]. W91-1034, Hope Church, Holland, Michigan. W91-1034, box 8, Hope Church, Holland, Michigan, Joint Archives of Holland.

Hope College 2002 Alumni Directory, 10th ed. Holland, MI: Hope College, 2002.

The Hope Milestone of 1930. Ed. Willard Wichers. Holland, MI: Hope College, 1930.

Huttar, Charles A. "The History of Grace Episcopal Church of Holland." *The Joint Archives Quarterly,* 12, no. 1 (spring 2002):1–8.

Hyma, Albert. *Albertus C. Van Raalte and His Dutch Settlements in the United States.* Grand Rapids, MI: Wm. B. Eerdmans, 1947.

In Christ's Service: The Classis of Holland, Michigan, and Its Congregations 1847–1997. Holland, MI: Classis of Holland, 1997.

Jacobson, Jeanne M., Elton J. Bruins, and Larry J. Wagenaar. *Albertus C. Van Raalte: Dutch Leader and American Patriot.* Holland, MI: Hope College, 1996.

Japinga, Lynn. "On Second Thought: A Hesitant History of Ecumenism in the Reformed Church in America." In *Concord Makes Strength: Essays in Reformed Ecumenism,* ed John. W. Coakley. Historical Series of the Reformed Church in America, no. 41. Grand Rapids, MI: Wm. B. Eerdmans, 2002.

Journey Inward – Journey Outward: Hope Church, n. d. [est. ca. 1974].

Kansfield, Mary. "Francis Davis Beardslee and the Leading Ladies of Holland, Michigan, 1912-1917." In *Tools for Understanding: Essays in Honor of Donald J. Bruggink,* ed. James Hart Brumm. Historical Series of the Reformed Church in America, no. 60. Grand Rapids, MI: Wm. B. Eerdmans, 2008.

———. *Letters to Hazel: Ministry within the Woman's Board of Foreign Missions of the Reformed Church in America.* Historical Series of the Reformed Church in America, no. 46. Grand Rapids, MI: Wm. B. Eerdmans, 2004.

Kennedy, James C. "Will the Circle Be Unbroken?: An Essay of Hope College's Four Presidential Eras." In *A Goodly Heritage: Essays in Honor of the Reverend Dr. Elton J. Bruins at Eighty.* Ed. Jacob E. Nyenhuis.

Historical Series of the Reformed Church in America, no. 56. Grand Rapids, MI: Wm. B. Eerdmans, 2007.

Keppel, Ruth. *Trees to Tulips: Authentic Tales of the Pioneers of Holland, Michigan*. Holland, MI: R. Keppel, 1947.

Koopman, LeRoy. *Taking the Jesus Road: The Ministry of the Reformed Church in America Among Native Americans*. Historical Series of the Reformed Church in America, no. 50. Grand Rapids, MI: Wm. B. Eerdmans, 1997.

Lassiter, Jonesetta, "New Heights: The Rev. Marchiene Rienstra Breaks New Ground for Women in RCA." *The Muskegon Chronicle*, 28 January 1984.

Lucas, Henry S., ed. *Dutch Immigrant Memoirs and Related Writings*. 2nd ed. Grand Rapids, MI: Wm. B. Eerdmans, 1997.

———. *Netherlanders in America: Dutch Immigration to the United States and Canada, 1789-1950*. Ann Arbor, MI: University of Michigan Press, 1955. Reprint, Grand Rapids, MI: Wm. B. Eerdmans, 1989.

Masselink, E. J. "Holland, Michigan Residents in the Civil War: Dutch Settlers Quickly Signed up in Civil War." *Holland City News*, 30 November 1961.

Membership Records 1910–1970. [Hope Church, Holland, Michigan].

Membership Records of Hope [Reformed] Church [of Holland, Michigan], vols. 1 and 2. W91-1034, box 11, Hope Church, Holland, Michigan, Joint Archives of Holland.

Memorial of the Rev. Abel T. Stewart, D. D., First Pastor of Hope Church, Holland, Michigan. Who died at Watkins, N. Y. May 24th, 1878. Ed. Charles Scott, Thomas E. Annis and Henry Baum. New York: Board of Publications, Reformed Church in America, 1878. W88-1106, box 1, Stewart, Abel T. (1822–1878), Joint Archives of Holland.

Michigan Dept. of Public Instruction. "August F. Bruske, D. D." *Fifty-Ninth Annual Report of the Superintendent of Public Instruction of the State of Michigan*. Detroit, MI: Bagg & Harmon, 1895.

Michigan State Gazetteer and Business Directory. Detroit, MI: R. L. Polk & Co., 1907.

"Migrant Ministry Program Starts Monday in County," *Holland City News*, 17 July 1958:6.

Miles, Fred T. "1861–1961 Historical Sketch First Methodist Church, Holland, Michigan," 1961.

"Minutes," *Classis of Holland, RCA,* 26 March 1985. W96-1217, Classis of Holland, Joint Archives of Holland.

Minutes of the Ninth Street CRC [First Reformed Church] of Holland, Michigan, November 5, 1850–May 24, 1855, trans. William and Althea Buursma, 2000. [Typescript located in Elton J. Bruins's files, Joint Archives of Holland at the Theil Center].

Minutes of the Particular Synod of Chicago; Convened in Chicago, September 3, 1856, and April 22, 1857. Chicago: Democratic Press Book Printing House, 1857.

Minutes of the Particular Synod of Chicago, Convened ... May 13th, 1863. Grand Rapids: Stompoost Office, 1863.

Moerdyk[e], Peter. "Chicago Letter." *Christian Intelligencer,* 28 July 1897.

Mulder, Edwin G. "Full Participation—A Long Time in Coming!" *Reformed Review,* vol. 42, no. 3 (Spring 1989):224–246. Also at https://www.rca.org/sslpage.aspx?pid=1915.

Myers, David. "Do You Hear What I Hear?" *Church Herald,* February 2002:29–31.

———. *A Quiet World: Living with Hearing Loss.* New Haven: Yale Univ. Press, 2000.

Nemeth, Roger J., and Donald A. Luidens. "Fragmentation and Dispersion: Postmodernity Hits the RCA." In *Reformed Encounters with Modernity: Perspectives from Three Continents,* ed. J. Jurgens Hendriks, Donald A. Luidens, Roger J. Nemeth, Corwin E. Schmidt, and Hijme Stoffels. Conference Proceedings of The International Society for the Study of Reformed Communities (ISSRC). Stellenbosch, South Africa, 2001.

Nutt, Rick. *Many Lamps One Light: Louisville Presbyterian Theological Seminary: A 150th Anniversary History.* Grand Rapids, MI: Wm. B. Eerdmans, 2002.

"One Hundredth Anniversary of the Ninth Street Congregation." Holland, Michigan, 1847–1947.

Ottawa County Times.

Otte, Frances F. C. Phelps. "Hope's Japanese Students." *Anchor,* May 1908: 20–26.

———. "Pioneering in Medical Missions." *Intelligencer-Leader,* 5 December 1941:12–15.

Our Cook Book, Holland, MI: Women's Aid Society of Hope Church, [1926]. W91-1034, box 5, Hope Church, Holland, Michigan, Joint Archives of Holland.

Our Cook Book, Receipt Book Published by the Ladies Aid Society of Hope Church, Holland, Mich. Holland, Mich.: Press of John D. Kanters, 1896. W91-1034, Hope Church, Holland, Michigan, box 5, Joint Archives of Holland.

Our Time for Rededication [Festival of Dedication program], 1982.

Palomino, Amanda. "The Leprosy Federation." *Joint Archives Quarterly* 21, no. 4 (winter 2012):4–5.

Parr, Judy Tanis, John de Velder, and Linda Walvoord de Velder, "A Medical Pioneer." *News from Hope College*, vol. 43, no. 1 (August 2011):12–13.

Phelps, Philip, Jr. "Bernardus Ledeboer." *Anchor*, December 1892.

———. *Hope College Remembrancer. First Inauguration and First Commencement.* 1867.

———. "Synodical Sermon." *Christian Intelligencer*, 15 June 1865, vol. 36, no. 24.

Phelps, Philip Tertius. *A Brief Biography of Rev. Philip Phelps, D.D., LL.D....,* 1941, H88-0122, box 1, Phelps, Philip Jr., Joint Archives of Holland.

Pieters, Aleida J. *A Dutch Settlement in Michigan.* Grand Rapids, MI: Reformed Press, 1923.

"Portraits of the Past: Written for the 125th Anniversary of Hope Church." 1987. W91-1034, Hope Church, Holland, Michigan, box 12, Joint Archives of Holland.

Post, Anna Coatsworth, "Anna C. Post's Remembrances." In *Dutch Immigrant Memoirs and Related Writings*, selected and arranged by Henry S. Lucas, 2nd ed. Grand Rapids, MI: Wm. B. Eerdmans, 1997.

———. "Hope Church Past and Present." *Ottawa County Times*, n. d. T88-0160. Post Family. Papers, 1848–1976, "Post, Margaret—Scrapbook 3 (1935–36)" folder. Holland Historical Trust Archives.

Prins, Edward. *Grootenhuis Families of Gelderland Netherlands.* 1971. Herrick Public Library, Holland, Michigan, Genealogy Room.

"A Process for Moral Discernment at Hope Church (Revised 4-25-94)." W91-1034, box 12, Hope Church, Holland, Michigan, Joint Archives of Holland.

Ramirez, Anthony. "Minister Cited for Performing Gay Wedding." *New York Times*, 18 June 2005. http://www.nytimes.com/2005/06/18/nyregion/18priest.html.

———. "Seminary Votes Out Leader Over Daughter's Gay Wedding." *New York Times*, 21 February 2005. http://www.nytimes.com/2005/02/12/nyregion/12seminary.html.

Ratmeyer, Una H. *Hands, Hearts, and Voices: Women Who Followed God's Call*. New York: Reformed Church Press, 1995.

Receipt Book Published by the Ladies Aid Society of Hope Church, Holland, Michigan. Third Edition. Press of John D. Kanters, 1904. W91-1034, box 5, Hope Church, Holland, Michigan, Joint Archives of Holland.

Record of Hope Church Holland Michigan 1862-1916 [alphabetical list of members and membership data]. W91-1034, box 10, Hope Church, Holland, Michigan, Joint Archives of Holland.

Records Hope Reformed Church Holland, Mich. [Membership, Marriages and Baptisms list 1862–1878, during Rev. A. T. Stewart's ministry]. W91-1034, box 10, Hope Church, Holland, Michigan, Joint Archives of Holland.

Reformed Church in America. Minutes of the Particular Synod of Chicago. vol. 3. Constantine, MI: L. T. Hull, 1876-1885.

Rejoicing in Hope...Romans 12:12: Hope Church 1862 1962. 1962. [Hope Church's Centennial booklet.]

"Report of the First Church of Holland meeting on 27 February," *De Grondwet*, 28 February 1882. Trans. Simone Kennedy. Document in "Masonry" folder, Van Raalte Contemporaries collection, Joint Archives of Holland.

"Report of the Holland Classis Dialogue Planning Team," *Holland Classis Stated Session*, May 2006.

Roosevelt, Theodore. *The Foes of Our Own Household*. New York: George H. Doran Company, 1917.

"'Roving Migrants' Is Topic at Meeting," *Holland Sentinel*, 5 May 1932:5.

Sack, Daniel. *Whitebread Protestants: Food and Religion in American Culture*. New York: St. Martin's Press, 2000.

Scholten, George B. "Crosses on Kulangsu." *Intelligencer-Leader*, 8 March 1940.

Scott, Charles. "Sermon." *Memorial of the Rev. Abel T. Stewart, D. D., First Pastor of Hope church, Holland, Michigan. Who died a Watkins, N. Y.*

May 24th, 1878. AET, 55, ed. Charles Scott, Thomas E. Annis, and Henry Baum (New York: Board of Publications, Reformed Church in America, 1878), 26. W88-1106, box 1, Stewart, Abel T. (1822–1878), Joint Archives of Holland.

Second Annual Catalog and Circular of Hope College 1866–7.

Sobania, Neal. "Hope and Japan: Early Ties." *News from Hope College*, December 1998:11.

South Holland (Michigan) Presbyterian Church Family Records, 1849–1867, compiled by Richard H. Harms. Retrieved from http://www.calvin.edu/hh/family_history_resources/soholland_church.htm

Stegenga, Preston J. *Anchor of Hope: The History of an American Denominational Institution, Hope College.* Grand Rapids, MI: Wm. B. Eerdmans, 1954.

Swierenga, Robert. "Disloyal Dutch? Herman Hoeksema and the Flag in Church Controversy during World War I." *Origins.* vol. 25, no. 2 (2007):28–35.

———. "Getting Political in Holland," paper presented to the Holland Historical Society, 11 April 2006. http://www.swierenga.com/PoliticsHHSpaper2006.html.

Swierenga, Robert P., and Elton J. Bruins. *Family Quarrels in the Dutch Reformed Churches of the Nineteenth Century.* Historical Series of the Reformed Church in America, no. 32. Grand Rapids, MI: Wm. B. Eerdmans, 1999.

Tested Recipes: Hope Church 80th Anniversary Cook Book. [Holland, MI: Women's Aid Society of Hope Church, 1942.] W91-1034, box 5, Hope Church, Holland, Michigan, Joint Archives of Holland.

Tierney, John. "A Hearing Aid That Cuts Out All the Clatter." *New York Times,* 23 October 2011. http://www.nytimes.com/2011/10/24/science/24loops.html.

"A Timeline of RCA History (with related American and world history events)," compiled by Russell L. Gasero. http://images.rca.org/docs/archives/rcatimeline.pdf.

The Twenty-Second Annual Report of the Board of Domestic Missions of the Ref. Protestant Dutch Church: Presented to the General Synod at their Annual Meeting in Hudson, N. Y., June 7, 1854 with Reports from Churches and Missionary Stations Aided by the Board and the Standing Rules for the Government of the Board. New York: J. A. Gray, Printer, 1854.

The Twenty-Third Annual Report of the Board of Domestic Missions of the Ref. Protestant Dutch Church: Presented to the General Synod at their

Annual Meeting in New Brunswick, N. J., June 6, 1855 with Reports from Churches and Missionary Stations Aided by the Board. New York: Board of Publication of the Reformed Protestant Dutch Church, 1855.

Van Cleef, P. D. "Abel T. Stewart, D. D." *Christian Intelligencer,* 6 June 1878:4.

Vande Bunte, Matt. "RCA takes strides toward more inclusion of homosexuals." *Grand Rapids Press,* 19 November 2011. http://www.mlive.com/living/grand-rapids/index.ssf/2011/11/rca_takes_strides_toward_more.html

Vande Water, Randall P. *Holland Happenings, Heroes & Hot Shots.* vol. 2. Grand Rapids: Color House Graphics, 1995.

———. "Holland's First Soldier Killed in WW I Remembered." *Holland Sentinel,* 25 July 2010:C6.

Vander Haar, Trudy, ed. *Branches of the Vine: Hope Church 150th Anniversary Special Edition,* January 2012.

———. *Branches of the Vine: Life Stories of the Members of Hope Church.* 2004–2012.

Vander Meulen, Cornelius. "The Excommunication of Tige," n. d. W91-1034, box 12, Hope Church, Holland, Michigan, Joint Archives of Holland.

Van der Veen, Engbertus. "Life Reminiscences." In *Dutch Immigrant Memoirs and Related Writings,* selected and arranged by Henry S. Lucas. 2nd ed. Grand Rapids, MI: Wm. B. Eerdmans, 1997.

Van Heest, Eloise. "Women's Societies in Holland Classis." In *In Christ's Service: The Classis of Holland and Its Congregations 1847–1997* ed. Gordon G. Beld. Holland, MI: Classis of Holland, 1997.

Van Hinte, Jacob. *Netherlanders in America: A Study of Emigration and Settlement in the Nineteenth and Twentieth Centuries in the United States of America.* vols. 1 and 2. Ed. Robert P. Swierenga, trans. Adriaan de Wit. Grand Rapids, MI: Baker Book House, 1985.

Van Lente, Johannes. *The Civil War Letters of Johannes Van Lente,* ed. Janice Van Lente Catlin. Okemos, MI: Yankee Girl Publications, 1992.

Van Olinda, M. S. "Holland Department." *Reports of Department Superintendents: Foreign Work.* National Woman's Christian Temperance Union. Annual Meeting. Chicago, IL: Woman's Temperance Publication Association, 1893. http://asp6new.alexanderstreet.com/wam2/wam2.object.details.aspx?dorpid=1000689037.

Van Raalte, Albertus C. "Commemoration Address, 1872." In *Dutch Immigrant Memoirs and Related Writings*, selected and arranged by Henry S. Lucas. 2nd ed. Grand Rapids, MI: Wm. B. Eerdmans, 1997.

Van Raalte, Arkie. "Church and new pastor: pioneering together." *Holland Sentinel*, 9 February 1984.

Van Reken, Donald L. and Randall P. Vande Water. *Holland Furnace Company 1906–1966*. Holland, MI: Donald L. Van Reken, 1993.

Van Schelven, Gerrit. "The Burning of Holland, October 9, 1871." In *Dutch Immigrant Memoirs and Related Writings*, selected and arranged by Henry S. Lucas. 2nd ed. Grand Rapids, MI: Wm. B. Eerdmans, 1997.

Van Wyk [Clough], Julie. "'Unto the Least of These': Hope Science Graduates Abroad." In *Into All the World: Hope College and International Affairs: Essays in Honor of Paul G. Fried*, ed. Robert J. Donia and John M. Mulder. Holland, MI: Hope College, 1985:41–56.

Vennema, Ame. "Margaret A. Phelps." *Christian Intelligencer*, 1 May 1907.

VerBeek, Todd. "Jim Dressel (Oct. 14, 1943–Mar. 27, 1992)," *Network News*, May 1992. Republished at http://toddverbeek.com/diffangle/JimDressel.html

Verhave, Jan Peter. "Disease and Death among the Early Settlers in Holland, Michigan." Lecture Series, no. 4, Visiting Research Fellows Program. Holland, MI: Van Raalte Institute, 9 November 2006. http://www.hope.edu/vri/JP_Verhave_Disease_and_Health_2007_7_19.pdf.

Visscher, Geesje Vander Haar. *Diary of Mrs. Geesje Vander Haar Visscher 1820-1901*, trans. C. L. Jalving. Holland, Michigan, 1954. [The original diary is in the Holland Historical Trust Archives. A typescript is in the Van Raalte Contemporaries collection, Joint Archives of Holland at the Theil Center.]

Voskuil, Dennis N. "Piety and Patriotism: Reformed Theology and Civil Religion." In *Word and World: Reformed Theology in America*, ed. James W. Van Hoeven. Historical Series of the Reformed Church in America, no. 16. Grand Rapids, MI: Wm. B. Eerdmans, 1986.

Wichers, Wynand. *A Century of Hope: 1866–1966*. Grand Rapids, MI: Wm. B. Eerdmans, 1968.

———. *The Hope Milestone of 1931*.

Weir, Lynne B., and Mary Grace York. *City of Holland Intensive Level Study Areas: Historic Preservation*. Holland, Michigan, 1993.

Zingle, Marie N. *The Story of the Woman's Literary Club: 1898–1989*. Holland, MI: Woman's Literary Club, 1989.

Index

Abell, Douglas, 350, 353, 364, 367, 378, 386
administrators, church, 421
Advent Crismon tree, 334
Albany, NY, First Church, 177, 219, 223, 299
Alcoholics Anonymous, 185n27, 274
Alcott, Gertrude, 105n60, 419
Alcott, Sarah Gertrude, 77
Alcott, Sarah Gilmore, 28
Alder, LeRoy, 195
Aldworth, Anna C., 166
Alexander, David and Char, 454
Aling, John, 59
Allegan, MI, 2–4
Allendale, MI, 4
Alliance for Cultural and Ethnic Harmony, 372
Althuis, Alice V., 451
American flag in church, 156–59, 207–208, 301n138
American Hamilton Reformed Church, MI, 173
Americanization, 12, 41, 44, 93, 98n35, 101n47, 137
Amoy (Xiamen), China, 21, 186, 199, 212–14
Anderson, Ann Piet, 328, 332, 350, 388
Anderson, Ed, 389
Anderson, William, 385
Annis, Dr. Thomas Emerson, 73, 101, 383, 387
Annis, Sarah J. Baum, 101
Anti-Saloon League, 163
apportionments, 141, 152
Appreciative Inquiry, 369–70
Arendshorst, Dr. Tom, 331n59, 386
Arminianism, 50, 154
Armstrong, John, 386
Association of Holland Churches, 279

Athey, Bryan, 384, 387
Audio-Visual Aid Association, Holland, 217
Aull, Jennifer, 365–66, 379

Bade, Nelis, 384
Bailey, Lois, 435
Bailey, Rev. William, 10–11
Baker, Tunis, 435
Bakker, Frederick, 422
Bakker, J. O., 383
Bakker, Kelwin, 385
Ballast, Dwight, 385
Bangs, Alice, 104
Bangs, I. F., 412n4, 419
Bangs, Isaac, 383
Banninga, Mrs. J. J., 423
baptismal font, 340–41
baptisms:
    adult, 37, 179, 395, 407
    first in Hope Church, 16, 34n131, 35, 240
Barber, Dennis, 233
Barber, Judith, 231
Barber, Marilyn, 232
Barber, R. E., 255
Barendreght, Dina, 402–403
Barendreght, Huibert, 400–401, 417
Baron, Laurie, 389
Baron, Mark, 280n81, 386
Barrows, Mrs. Robert, 419
Barry, Carl Gordon, 201
Bassett, Steven, 385
Battjes, Paul, 385
Battle Creek, MI, 10n34, 46, 82, 173
Baughman, Norma, 417, 435
Baum, Henry 383, 387
Beach, Carla, 389, 436
Beach, Chester L., 383, 417
Beach, Evelyn M., 434
Beach, Leslie R., 389, 435

Beardslee, Rev. John Walter Jr., 423, 434
Beardslee, Rev. John Walter, 134–35,137
Beaverdam, MI, Reformed Church, 174
Bechtel, Rev. Carol, 321, 382, 463
Beck, Irene, 105n60, 402–3, 406
Beck, Rev. Theodoric Romeyn, 28, 46, 49, 70, 74, 111, 387, 402–403, 406, 433
Becker, Arthur, 384
Becker, Clarence J., 297–98, 384
Becker, Elizabeth (Betty), 315, 388, 419, 462
Beckman, Gary, 385, 388
Beckman, Ruth, 388
Beebe, Susan, 233
Beebe, William, 231, 385
Beidler, Rev. Fred P., 4n10, 5, 344n92
Belgic Confession, 458
Belhar Confession, 361, 463
bell tower, 296, 298–99, 302n139
bell, 82, 302n139
Bell, John, composer, 327
Beltran, Beth, 386
Beltran, Ric, 370, 373n161, 386
Benzenberg, Diana, 436Benzenberg, Robert, 385
Bergen, Ellen (Ella) Grace Dean, 144, 241
Bergen, Rev. John Tallmadge, 34, 117–21, 129–31, 133, 139–40, 142–45, 153–55, 174, 223, 433, 437, 439, 459
Bernecker, Robert, 384, 419
Berry, Roy, 388
Bethabara spiritual retreat center, 343, 425n17
Bethel Bible Series, 293–94
Bethel Reformed Church, Holland, 331
Betts, Fred, 383
Beyer, John, 351
Beyer, Stephanie, 386
Bible School, week-day, 228

Bible-reading in public schools, 183
Bichler, Beth, 418
Big Brother mentoring for fatherless boys, 278–79
Billips, Sinnia, 435
Birchby, Hubert, 128n111
Birchby, Mrs. W., 445–46
Birchby, Rev. Henry Gough, 34, 123–30, 439, 459
Birchby, William N., 123–24, 419
Birdsall, Fred, 385
Black Lake, 29, 82, 300
Black River, 31, 300
Blanche Cathcart Library, 242, 348
Bliss, Rev. W. C. H., 9
Blodgett, Walter, 419
Bloemendaal, William, 436
Board of Domestic Missions, Reformed Church, 4, 7, 30, 39, 53, 87, 174, 234, 404, 430
Board of Education, Holland, 14
Board of Education, Reformed Church, 4, 7, 39, 62, 72, 430
Board of Missions, Reformed Church, 1.
  See also Board of Domestic Missions, Reformed Church
Bock, Deborah (Debby) Jean Klomparens, 415
Boelkins, Dave, 389
Boelkins, Rev. Dawn, 427
Boer, Barbara, 385
Boers, Henry Jr., 240
Boers, Henry, 127, 144, 147, 149, 240, 383, 387, 433
Boers, Louis Birkhoff 240
Boersma, Dr. Vern, 252–55, 288–89, 350, 384, 387
Boersma, Lois Hinkamp, xv–xvi, 181, 185n27, 195–96, 215, 229n139, 288
Boersma, Mary Pat, 230
Boeve, Gerald, 385
Bolte, Robert, 385
Bombe, Michelle, 436
Boogaart, Judith, 386

Boogaart, Miriam, 386
Boogaart, Peter, 280, 389
Boone, Beca, 124, 419
Boone, Rike, 419
Bos, Bob, 389, 436
Bos, Judy, 386
Bosch, Emma, 242
Bosch, Gerald J., 242
Bosch, Marthena, 187, 252
Bosch, Nicodemus, 14n47, 242, 382n174, 460
Bosch, Nicodemus, memorial Communion window, 234, 242–43, 298, 348
Bosch, Randall C., 242, 384, 387, 419
Bosch, Rev. Randall Bayles, 424
Bosch, Shirley, 265
Bosch, Theodore, 385
Bosworth, George, 195
Boter, Peter, 195
Bouma-Prediger, Steve, 436
Bowerman, Rev. J. F., 159
Boy Scouts, 148n53, 158–59, 191, 217, 229, 460
Boyd, Jane C. Vander Veen, 165, 240
Boyd, Laura Alice, 434
Boyle, Dana, 420
Boys and Girls Club, 331
Braaksma, Carol, 335–36, 389, 454
Braaksma, John, 336n69
Braaksma, Laurie Beyer, 370, 418, 421
Braaksma, Randall, 335–36, 385, 425, 454
Bradfield, Kristine, 334, 385
Bradish, Dorothy, 385, 388
Bradsell, Marcia, 388
Brandt, Rev. Julius and Mrs. Wilma, 454
Breen, Jane, 194, 388, 419
Brewton, AL, 207, 310, 457
Bried, Mary Louise, 435
Brim Bunch, 218, 461.
  See also Mr. and Mrs. Club
Broadmore, Sarah, 11, 36–37, 394–95

Brockmeier, Jon, 436
Broek, Rev. Derk, 94
Brooklyn, First Reformed Church, NY, 63
Brooks, Earnest C., 14n47, 382n174, 434, 460
Brooks, James family, 339
Brooks, James, 233
Brooks, Jo Anne Vander Velde, 180, 262–65, 275, 303, 305–306, 381, 388, 463
Brooks, Rev. Steven Robert, 425
Brooks, Ruth, 194
Brooks, Susan, 231
Brown, Donald F., 435
Brown, James, 384
Brown, Robert S., 435
Browning, Frances, 139
Browning, George W., 383
Brownson, Kathryn, 388
Brownson, Rev. James, 379
Brownson, Rev. Rachel, 429
Bruggink, Rev. Donald J., 99n37
Bruins, Bonnie, 420
Bruins, Rev. Elton J., xvi, 405
Bruins, Rev. William H. 423
Brummer, Irene Sulkers, 195
Brush, Henry R., 383
Bruske, Rev. August F., 131, 150–51, 440, 460
Brusse, Louise M., 434
Brusse, William, 14n47, 127, 382n174, 383, 387, 459
Bryson, William, 385, 389
Buckley, Margaret, 420
Bultman, Judy, 386
Bultman, Thomas L., 436
Buteyn, Donald F., 435
Buteyn, William Edward, 201
Buys, Adrian G., 384, 387
Buys, Art, 386
Buys, Ekdal, 300, 302, 338n75, 351, 388
Buys, Mary, 389
Buys, Mina, 319n24

Calvary Reformed Church, Grand
    Rapids, MI, 181, 182n14
Calvin, John, 235, 458
Calvinism, 100, 154
Camp Geneva, 208, 346
Campbell, Richard, 388
Canons of Dordt, 62, 100, 458
Cappon, Mrs. J. J., 450
Carder, Brian, 334, 418
Carder, Carol, 418
card-playing opposed, 125–26
Caring for Creation, 280
Carley, Mrs. H., 451
Carollers choir, 229–31
Carter, Nelson E., 201
Carter, Theodore H., 384
Castle Park, 151n53
casualties of war, 198, 201. See also
    Leenhouts, Willard G.; Yntema,
    Gordon Douglas
catechism, 133
Cater, Mary Ada, 207, 453
Cathcart, Blanche, 348n99. See also
    Blanche Cathcart Library
Cavanaugh, Robert W., 388, 417, 435
Cecil, Dorothy, 263, 265, 275
Cecil, Robert, 435
Central Avenue Christian Reformed
    Church, 60n58, 80, 173
Central Park Reformed Church,
    Holland, 174
Central Reformed Church, Grand
    Rapids, MI, 173, 229, 236,
    290n108, 316, 379
Central Wesleyan Church, Holland,
    49n31
Chamberlain, Rev. Dr. Jacob, 84
Chambers, Norman, 386
chandelier, 42, 72
chapel-gymnasium, Hope College,
    20n73, 71
Chapman, Herbert E., 201
charter members, 11–38
Cheff, Harriet Walker, 165
Cheff, Rev. Peter Paul, 131, 148, 153–
    54, 156–60, 162, 167–68, 174n125,
    175, 434, 437, 440, 460
Cherubs choir, 229, 232–33
Chiapas, Mexico, 251, 283–84
Child Development Center. See Day
    Care Center, Holland
Child Development Services of
    Ottawa County, 263
Children in Worship, 327–28, 462
Children's Day, 181
Children's Sabbath, 322
children's sermonette, 180
choir directors, 417–18
choirs, 27, 107, 123, 152, 182, 184,
    193–95, 228, 234, 251, 335
chorister, first, 27
Christ Memorial Church, Holland,
    271, 350
Christian Action Commission,
    273–74
Christian Action Committee, 260,
    275, 287
Christian Action task forces, 461
Christian Endeavor Society, 117, 132,
    134, 179, 182
Christian Reformed Church, 9n29,
    58, 98, 171, 325
Christian Unity in Prayer, 331
Christmas celebrations, 59–61,
    112–14, 218
Church Building Committee, 229,
    235
church bulletins, 147, 151
church dedications:
    1864, 41–42
    1874, 74, 76, 459
    1902, 132–33, 137, 139
Church for Victory campaign, 202
Church Herald, 196n50, 207, 266,
    278–79
Church of Holland. See First
    Reformed Church, Holland
Church of the Good News, Chicago,
    IL 338
Church School. See Sunday School
Church Women United, Holland,
    255, 263

Churches United for Social Action (CUSA), 271, 330. *See also* Four-Parish Council. *See also* Inter-Parish Council.
City Mission, Holland, 271, 274
civil disobedience, 304–5
civil rights, 307–8
Civil War, 16, 18, 35, 41, 52, 203n68, 404
Clapper, Michael J., 48–51, 89, 132
Clark, Dillon P., architect, 135, 345
Classis of Holland, 4, 5n14, 7, 9n29, 11n37, 44, 56n50, 58, 93–94, 96n32, 97, 173–74, 185n26, 222, 269, 271, 275–77, 329, 364–65, 367–68, 381, 458
Classis of Michigan, 10, 26n94, 40, 41n9, 59, 61, 89, 173, 381
Classis of Wisconsin, 58, 97
Classis of Zeeland, 222
Clough. Julie, 386
Cobb, Wilbur, 387
Cochran, Donald, 384
Colenbrander, Rev. Harold A., 226, 420
collections, weekly, 107
committees of consistory, 191, 250. *See also* ministries
Commons I and II, 244, 296, 298, 314, 341, 360
Communion table, 209, 234
Communion, 40, 56n50, 72, 101, 140–41, 216, 302, 322, 327, 346, 459
Communion, including children in receiving, 309, 322
Community Action House, 271, 461
Community Kitchen, 271–72
Computerization Feasibility task force, 302–3
congregational care, 249, 327, 370–71
conscientious objectors, 197
consistory, terms of:
    decided by lot, 12
    limits for, 134, 185–86
    See also deacons, elders

Constantine, MI, 5, 10, 41n9, 173
Cook, Carol, 426
Cook, Jean, 317–19, 388
Cook, Marilyn, 334, 421
Cook, Mark, 436
Cook, Rev. James I., 275–78, 293–94, 346, 356, 382, 387, 461–62
Cook, Richard, 355, 385, 388
Cook, Tim, 386
cookbooks, 128, 138, 219, 444–52
Coopersville, MI, 4
Coplin, Rev. William, 54
Covenant Life Curriculum, 261
Cox, John D., 436
Cran-Hill Ranch, 338
Crispell, Rev. Cornelius Eltinge, 61, 70, 74, 402, 433
CROP Hunger Walks, 286
Cropley, William B., 419
Culliver, Mitchell, 207, 453

Daily Vacation Bible School. *See* Vacation Bible School
Daily, Pat, 334, 385
Dalenberg, Helene Wilhelmina Van Raalte, 414
Dalman, Ronald, 260, 275, 385, 388
dance, sacred. *See* Sacred Dance Group of Holland
dancing opposed, 125–26, 266
Daugherty, Betty Timmer 195
Davelaar, Rev. Kathryn, 358–59, 367–69, 443, 463
Davelaar, Tom, 436
Davidson, Rev. Thomas W., 177–80, 182, 184–85, 187–89, 440, 460
Davis, Harvey O., 417, 435
Day Care Center, Holland, 262–64, 274, 298, 461
DeBlock, David, 385, 389
De Bruyn, Maxine H., 264–66, 317n20, 436, 461
de Forest, William, 249
De Haan, John Jr., 388
De Haan, John, 279, 384, 388

De Haan, Peggy Prins, 180, 193, 388, 417
De Haan, Rev. John D., 427
De Haan, Rev. Martin R., 181, 182n14
De Jonge, Bruce and Tamar, 454
De Long, William, 384
De Pree, Edward Ogden, 201
De Pree, John E., 435
De Pree, Edward J., 384
De Pree, Kenneth, 195, 384, 387
De Pree, Magdalene, 434
De Pree, Mrs. Edward, 419
De Pree, Rev and Mrs. Gordon, 214, 454
DeRidder, Ann, 233
DeRidder, Dean, 230
DeRidder, Helen Ripley, 195
DeRidder, Lester J., 384, 387
De Valois, Dr. Bernadine S., 251, 260, 263, 316–17, 388, 462
De Valois, John J., 262–63, 317, 387
de Velder, Anne, 230
de Velder, Edith, 194, 332
de Velder, Rev. Marion (Mert), 177, 183, 191–93, 196, 201–203, 205n72, 209, 217, 220, 223–25, 227–29, 234–37, 247, 256, 267n49, 290, 334, 337, 339, 347, 350, 382, 440, 441, 460–70
de Velder, Rev. Walter, 183
De Vette, Russell B., 435
De Vries, Bernard J., 123, 383, 387, 417
De Vries, Jason, 386
De Vries, Ulke, 383
De Weerd, Helen and Millard, 311, 388
De Weese, Frank E., 384
De Weese, Helen, 194
De Witt, Kathleen, 233
De Witt, Richard, 384
De Wolfe, Ruth, 262, 435
deaconesses, 205n71
deacons, 383–86, 462
Decker, Rev. Henry E., 49
Den Herder, Chris, 384
Den Herder, Jean, 386
Den Herder, Lesley, 231
Den Herder, Ruth, 186
Den Uyl, Simon, 158n82
Denekas, Rev. and Mrs. Raymond, 453
denominational diversity among those joining Hope Church, 41, 204, 381, 404
Derrick, Rev. Keith, 389
Detrich, Rev. Richard, 282
Dickie, Jane R., 349, 385, 389, 436
Dickie, Larry, 388
Diekema, Gerrit J., 14n47, 120, 152, 154, 156, 158–60, 162, 183, 382n174, 419, 459
Diekema, Gerrit John Jr., 158n82
Diekema, Gerry, 297
Diekema, Mary E. Alcott, 147, 241, 432
Diekema, Willis, 417
Diephouse, Rev. Evelyn J., 356, 442, 463
Dimnent, Edward D., 184, 234n141, 382n175, 387, 433, 437, 460
Dimnent Memorial Chapel, 179n9, 212, 269, 273
Dinger, Christine, 233
directors of Christian education, 420
Dirkse, Anne, 389, 420
Dirkse, David, 385
discipline of a church member, 89–91
district school house, Holland, 5, 7, 16n57, 41
Doeden, Dick, 454
Doesburg, Cornelis, 127, 387, 433
Doesburg, J. Marion, 417
Doesburg, Kittie M., 124, 417
Doesburg, Mary, 105n60
Dok, George, 419
Donk, Teunis (Tony), 436
Dooley, James, 310
Dordt, Synod of, and term limits for consistory, 134n10

Dosker, Rev. Henry E., 91
Doty, Elihu, 84
Douglas, MI, 4
Douwstra, Gertrude Flaitz, 195
Dow, William, 419
Downie, Mr., 417
dramas, 215, 217, 286
Dregman, Cornelius J., 179, 183, 190, 383, 387
Dressel, Jim, State Representative, 307–8
Drew, Charles E., 384, 387
Drew, Elizabeth, 166
Dubois, Henry O., 63, 71
Duey, Barbara, 230
Duinkerken, Anne, 371, 420
Duinkerken, Bert, 386
Dunwoody, Mrs. H., 417
Durfee, Winifred, 434
Dutton, Albert H., 383, 419
Dutton, Charles A., 127, 387
Dutton, Charles S., 144, 149, 163, 387
Dutton, Emeline, 105n60
Dutton, Martha, 105n60
Dutton, Mary Post, 16n57, 34
Dutton, Rev. Charles S., 34n134, 36, 422
Dykhuizen, Adelaide, 434
Dykhuizen, Geraldine, 294, 388
Dykhuizen, Nell, 188, 450
Dykstra, Darrell, 231
Dykstra, Rev. D. Ivan, 261n36, 275, 435

Early Learning Center. *See* Day Care Center, Holland
Early Worship services, 285–86, 293, 346, 462
East Church House, 225n126
East Overisel, MI, Reformed Church, 174
Ebenezer Reformed Church, Holland, 9n29, 145
ecumenism, 83, 117–18, 217, 222, 270–73, 285, 324, 327–30, 332, 357, 373

Edgington, Rhonda, 419
Education Committee, 191
education wing, 229–30, 235, 250, 256–58, 262, 292n113, 296, 345, 348, 461
Educational Concerns for Hunger Organization (ECHO), 283
Eidson, Lambert, 434
elders, 387–9, 462
Elenbaas, Judy, xvii
Ellert, Ernest, 435
Elstner, Harriet Drew, 195
Elzinga, Janet Bast, 355, 370, 421
Elzinga, Paul, 282, 384, 389
Employment Policy Guidelines, 364
Endowment Fund Board, 302, 337–38
Engelsman, Phyllis, 421
Engle, Todd, 340–41
English language, 1–9, 42, 45–46, 62, 174, 404–5
Eriks, Rev. Ken, 356
evangelism, 117, 132–33, 142, 145, 224–225, 255
Evans, Virginia, 232
Everett, Ransome, 435
Everts, Janet M., 320–21, 436
Everts, Peter, 388, 436
exercise classes, 266
Exo, Steve, 385

Fadel, Gail Joan Van Raalte, 415
Fairbanks, Isaac, 405
Fairview Reformed Church, IL, 27
Faith-to-Faith, help for handicapped young people, 278
Family-to-Family, help for first-time homeowners, 277–78
Farmer, Caron, 418
Farmer, Floyd, 418
Fast, Willard S., 417
Fauls, Betty Morrell, 194
Federation of Women's Societies, Holland, 168
Feininger, John, 385
Fell, Egbert E., 154, 179n8, 383, 387

Fell, Elizabeth, 166
Ferguson, J. Scott, 418
Ferris, Dennis, 231
Ferris, Dwight, 387, 435
Ferris, Gary, 233
Ferris, Rev. John Mason, 406
Ferrysburg, MI, 4
Fiedler, John, 436
Fiedler, Julie, 436
Fierro, Rev. Andrés, 372
Fike, Deborah, 322
Fike, Francis, 338–39, 388, 436
Fike, Janice, 386
Fike, Joan, 388, 421
Fikse, Rev. Henry and Mrs., 453
Fillmore, MI, 10
finance administrators, 421
fire of 1871, 14, 23, 32, 65–72, 110n71, 459
First Church, Albany, NY. *See* Albany, NY, First Church
First Church, Holland. *See* First Reformed Church, Holland,
First Presbyterian Church, Holland, 247n2, 271
First Reformed Church, Holland, 5, 7, 8n29, 9–11, 30, 41, 49–50, 54–58, 70, 80, 94–99, 156, 173–74, 207, 316
First United Methodist Church, Holland, 271–73, 300, 324, 330, 373. *See also* Methodist Episcopal Church, Holland
Fish Club, junior high group, 281–82
Fisher, George H., 5n14
flags. *See* American flag in church
Fleming, John, 386
Fleming, Joy, 386
Floch, Michael, 385
Flowerday, Carl, 385
Floyd, Anne, 419
Forberg, Wilmer A., 384
Ford, Peter and Patty, 454
foreign missions, 84
Forest Grove, MI, 4
Formula of Agreement, 329, 330n54

Foster, John, 385
Four-Parish Council, 330. *See also* Churches United for Social Action. *See also* Inter-Parish Council.
Fourteenth Street Christian Reformed Church, 156, 331
Fourth Reformed Church, Holland, 174
Francis, Rev. John, 324
Frederickson, Dorothy (Dody) Visscher, 415
Free Masons, Order of, xviii, 54–58, 92–100, 171, 352n107
Freestone, Linda, 233
Fried, Paul G., xvin2, 197–98, 260, 435
Fries, Rev. Paul R., 292–93, 298–99, 424, 440, 462
funding the church. *See* apportionments, collections, pew rental, and pledging

Garfield, President James A., assassination of, 92–93
Garrod, W. J., 147
Geary, Renie, 389
Geerlings, Ardean, 195
Geerlings, Clyde E., 384, 435
Geerlings, Henry, 14n47, 99n39, 382n174, 459–60
General Synod:
  1848, 1
  1854, 6n14
  1856, 10n34
  1864, 40, 108
  1865, 44
  1867, 63
  1868, 58
  1870, 58
  1878, 110
  1882, 97–98
  1883, 106
  1884, 108, 110
  1899, 125
  1916, 152   (continued)

General Synod, continued
   1918, 164, 316n18
   1929, 182
   1957, 234
   1958–59, 177, 235
   1968, 270
   1970, 276
   1973, 322
   1978, 307
   1979, 323
   1985, 329
   1988, 322
   2005, 366–67
Gensemer, Neta, 418
Gensemer, Ron, 353, 386
German Evangelical and Reformed Church, 98n35
Geronimo, Apache leader, 142–43
Gerrie, Michael, 385
Geuder, Barbara, 233
Geuder, Joan, 231
Geuder, Lawrence, 388
Gillespie, M. W., 448
Gillespie, Rev. John H., 433
Gilmore, Dr. Albertus (Raalte) Van Raalte, 28, 133n6, 411, 413, 417
Gilmore, Christina Catharina Van Raalte, 27, 104, 168–69, 393, 409, 410, 412, 419, 433–35
Gilmore, Darius, 417
Gilmore, Rev. William Brokaw, 11, 26–29, 40, 43, 61, 383, 387, 392–93, 406, 417, 419, 422, 430, 431, 433
Godfrey, Almon T., 434
Good Samaritan Ministries, 362, 373
Gosselar, Dave, 386
Gosselink, Mr., 419
Gould, Amy Mulder, 418
Graafschap, MI, 4n13, 9n29
Grace Community Church, Holland, 364
Grace Episcopal Church, Holland 65, 81, 156, 271, 316
Graham, Mary Linda, 436

Granberg-Michaelson, Wesley, 260n33, 269n54
Grand Haven, MI, 4, 68
Grand Rapids, MI, 4, 21, 108,
Grand Rapids, MI, First Reformed Church, 1, 18, 10n34, 19, 49, 173
Grand Rapids, MI, Second Reformed Church, 18, 9n29, 173
Grandville, MI, 4
Grant, Robert, 385
Gray, Kristen, 351, 378, 388, 436
Great Depression, 183
Green, Cathy, 389
Green, Gregory, 231, 386
Green, Jeffrey, 385, 388
Green, Lawrence (Larry), 262, 384, 387, 435
Green, Ruth, 275
Greenpoint Reformed Church, Brooklyn, NY, 379–80
greeters, 218
Groenevelt, Katherine, 253–54
Gronbert, Hester, 229n139
Grotenhuis, Bernardus, 2, 11–12, 17–19, 30, 73, 111, 387, 392–93
Grotenhuis, Janna Hogewind, 17
group foster home project, 287–88
Gruenler, Curtis, 389, 436
Guild for Christian Service, 236, 251, 270
Guy, Frances Jeanette, 400–1, 406

Habitat for Humanity, 283, 331–32
Hadden, Marguerite, 201, 435
Hadden, May, 201
Hadden, Mayo Jr., 201
Hadden, Mrs. J. B., 449
Haddock, Frank D., 127, 383
Hains, John, 202
Hakken, Elda Van Putten, 453
Hakken, Harold, 387
Hakken, Margo, 230
Hakken, Merry, 232
Hakken, Peggy Hadden, 195
Hakken, Rev. Bernard Daniel Jr., 423
Hakken, William, 384

Hall, Craig, 232
Hall, Robert, 275
Hallan, James H., 435
Hallan, Roberta, 231
Hallan, Sally Jo, 232
Hamilton, MI, 4, 10
Hamilton, MI, First Reformed
    Church, 174
Hanchett, Merrick W., 384, 387
Hansen, Libbie Ann, 231
Hansen, Michael, 388
Harderwyk Christian Reformed
    Church, Holland, 287
Harrington, E. J., 58n50
Harrington, Edward J., 14n47,
    382n174, 398–99, 459
Harrington, Lucy, 105n60
Harrington, Matilda, 398–99
Harrington, William, 412n4
Harrington, Wilson, 383, 387
Harrison, Clinton, 194
Harton, Helen L., 435
Harvey, Alonzo, 207, 453
Harvey, James, 261n36
Hastings-on-Hudson, NY, Reformed
    Church, 6, 20, 42n13, 129
Haverkamp, Harold J., 384
Hawes, Carolyn, 434
Hawkinson, Ella, 435
Hawley, David, 370
Hawley-Lowry, Rev. Ruth, 427
Haworth, Dorcas, 348
Haworth, Edna, 331n59, 388
Haworth, Gerrard W., 331n59, 348,
    384, 387
Haworth, Julie, 230
Hayward, Lauralee, 232
Heald, Laura, 77
Heald, Richard, 383
hearing loop technology, 309, 313–
    15, 360, 463
Heasley, Bob, 195
Heasley, June Baker, 194
Hector, J., 244
Hector-Braaksma, Carol, 425
Heeren, Aleida Vennema, 422n

Heeren, Rev. Enne Jansen, 84, 396–
    97, 406, 422
Heeringa, George, 229n139, 256,
    338n75, 384, 387
Heidelberg Catechism, 57–58, 100,
    458
Heine, Werner, 435
Heinen, Charlotte, 268, 420
Heisler, Jacqueline, 436
Heisler, James, 385, 436
Helbing, Edward, 385, 388
Henry, Michael, 386
Heringa, Rev. Donald, 426
Herold, Ernst, 58n50, 383, 387,
    398–99
Herold, Mrs. S., 447
Herold, Sarah Bertsch, 398–99, 451
Herold, Susanna, 104
Herrinton, Charlene, 275
Heuer, August, 383
Heusinkveld, Arthur H., 434
Heyboer, Clare, 385, 389
Hietbrink, Marian De Weerd, 435
High Hopes, senior high group, 281,
    379
Hillegonds, Libby, 262, 264–65
Hillegonds, Rev. William C.,
    227n132, 247–50, 256, 260n33,
    267, 269, 311, 436, 440, 461
Hills, Arthur C., 384, 387, 435
Hills, Craig, 231
Hills, Stephen, 233
Hilmert, Rev. William, 435
Hilsman, Amy Kate, 418
Hinga, Gladys, 236
Hinga, Milton Lage, 216, 226, 384,
    387, 434
Hinga, William, 384
Hinkamp, James B., 195–96, 301–2
Hinkamp, Martha, 186
Hinkamp, Rev. Paul E., xv, 177, 189,
    206, 220, 222, 247, 387, 404, 434
Hinkle, Patricia, 232
Hinkle, Stephen, 232
Hinman, Annie E. Broadmore, 36
Hintz, Peter, 389

Hiroshima, Japan, 306
Hodgson, Gary, 385, 388
Hoekje, Rev. Willis G., 146–47, 152, 186, 196, 198–99, 205, 453, 460
Hoeksema, Rev. Herman, 156–58
Hoeksema, Rev. Robert, 289
Hoekstra, Robert, 388
Hoff, Joanne, 388
Hoffman, Carolyn, 351n104, 388
Hoffman, Rev. Milton J., 434
Holland Academy, 5, 7, 8n28, 9, 14, 28, 35, 39, 46, 108, 344, 404–6, 430
Holland Classis. *See* Classis of Holland
Holland Community Health Center, 254
Holland Is Ready, 376, 379
Holland Peacemakers, 303, 341, 343, 381, 462
Holland Restorative Circles, 371
Holland Rhythmic Choir. *See* Sacred Dance Group of Holland
Hollenbach, John W., 261n36., 351, 387, 435
Hollenbach, Winifred, 332
Holy Relationships conference, 367
homosexuality, 98–99n37, 307–9, 350–53, 365, 367n143, 378–79, 463
Hoogerwerf, Steven D., 351, 378, 436
Hooyman, Phyllis, 385
Hope Academy. *See* Holland Academy
Hope Church News newsletter, 218, 461
Hope College student church. *See* student church, Hope College
Hope College, faculty and staff also members of Hope Church, 430–37
Hope Hi-Lites, World War II newsletter, 200
Hope Is Ready, 375
Hopkins, Clarence, 384, 388
Hopkins, Clifford B., 387
Hopkins, Kurt, 230

Housel, Teresa Heinz, 436
Housing Opportunities Made Equal (HOME), 282–83
Howard, Loren, 232, 384
Howell, Charles, 387
Hoyer, John, 418
Hoyt, Ira, 2
Hubbard, Kay, 372, 388
Hudsonville, MI, 4
Huey, Miss, 419
Huizenga, Rev. Henry, 423
Hunt, Elizabeth Ann, 434
Huyser, Howard, 385
hymn books, 107
hymns, singing of, 11, 28–29

identity, Hope Church:
    described by 1959 self-study, 247
    described by 1963 self-study, 255
    described by Beardslee, J. W., 137
    described by de Velder, 203–4, 335
    described by Hillegonds, 250–51, 256
    described by Mission Statement, 290–91
    described by Phelps, 41, 404
    described by Peterman, 273–74
    described by Rienstra, 337
    described by Van Hinte, 170–71
inclusion for all, 308–23, 367, 378–79, 381
Ingraham, Amy Gould 421
Inner Church Parish of Chicago, 282
Institutional Statement on Homosexuality, 1995, by Hope College, 375–76
insurance, 64, 73, 161, 185n27
Intelligencer-Leader, 193, 196n50
Inter-Parish Council, 330–32. *See also* Churches United for Social Action. *See also* Four-Parish Council.

Iona Abbey, Scotland, 313
Iona, Scotland, music from, 327, 346
Israels, Marvin, 385
Israels, Michael, 386
Israels, Michelle, 386

Jackson, Neva, 385
Jacobson, John H. Jr., 382n175, 436, 437, 462
Jacobson, Jeanne M., 436
Jamestown, MI, 4
Jamestown, MI, First and Second Reformed Churches, 174
Japinga, Rev. Lynn, 317n20, 320–21, 378, 436
Jara, Rev. Roberto, 372
Jarzembowski, Tim, 386
Jenison, MI, 4
Jenks, Florence, 251
Jentz, Arthur H. Jr. 259–60, 388, 435
Jerow, Jon, 380
Johnson, Michelle, 386
Johnston, Dierdre, 436
Jones, Kittie, 105n60
Jones, Rev. Thomas Walker, 28, 91, 107–108, 116, 130, 439, 459
Junior Christian Endeavor Society, 128n110, 134, 179
Junior Church, 205
Junior worship chapel, 196

Kaiser, Christopher, 388
Kaiser, Martha, 295
Kammeraad-Bos, Karla, 370, 421
Kamps, John G., 383
Kandu Industries, 277
Kansfield, Rev. Ann, 365–66, 379
Kansfield, Rev. Norman, 365–67
Karsen, Wendell, 306
Karsten, Harold J., 384, 387, 419
Karsten, Helen Prisman, 434
Karsten, John H., 74
Karsten, Nancy, 232
Kast-Keat, Rev. Jessica, 429
Katpadi Agricultural Institute, 454
Kaylor, Betsy, 386

Kellogg Peace Pact, 181–82
Kennedy, President John F., assassination, 259
Keppel, Albert C., 209, 242, 460
Keppel, Anna Helena Van Raalte, 411, 413
Keppel, Bastian D., 147, 383, 387
Keppel, Kate De Vries, 209, 242, 460
Keppel, Ruth, 171, 209
Keppel, Teunis, 56n50, 92, 94–95, 209n82
Kershaw, Rev. Joseph H., 10–11
Ketchum, Harold, 384
Kids Hope USA, 280
Kids Clubs, 330
Kiefer, Shirley, 249, 265, 420
Kimura, Kumaje, 24, 26, 309
King Jr., Robert A., 388
King, Mrs. Adolphus, 139
King's Daughters Society, 134
kitchen, 348–49
Klay, Robin K., 385, 388, 436
Kleinheksel, Anna Sophia Van Raalte 409, 411, 412
Kleinheksel, Anna Vera, 240, 413
Kleinheksel, Frank De Moen, 229n139, 410, 413
Kleinheksel, H. J., 384
Kleinheksel, J. Harvey, 384, 387, 434
Kleinheksel, John H., 240, 387, 411, 433
Kleinheksel, John Lewis, 158n82, 413
Kleinheksel, Paul Edwin, 413
Kleinjans, Dr. Everett, and Mrs., 454
Kleis, Margret Elizabeth (Toodie) Van Raalte Plowe, 414
Kleyn, J. R., 73
Kliphuis, Trish, 418
Klomparens, Andrea, 233
Klomparens, Deborah, 231
Klomparens, Gerald, 232
Klomparens, Jean Marie Van Raalte, 414
Klomparens, Melissa, 232
Klomparens, Roy D., 384
Klooster, David, 389, 436

Koch, Jacquelin, 436
Koch, John, 373n161, 386
Koch, Pamela, 436
Kolk, Michael, 386
Kollen Park, 180–81n12
Kollen, Estelle Marie, 413
Kollen, George E., 180n12, 241
Kollen, Gerrit J., 34, 36, 45n18, 122, 127, 129, 241, 382n175, 387, 411, 419, 433, 437, 459
Kollen, Lena, 410
Kollen, Maria Van Raalte, 105n60
Kollen, Martha, 180–81, 192, 419, 460
Kollen, Mary Diekema, 165
Kollen, Mary W. Van Raalte, 241
Kooiker, Anthony, 418, 419, 435
Kools, W. C., 384, 387
Kooyers, Duane, 386
Kooyers, Karmen, 351
Korean War, 214, 219
Korstanje, Fruena Dowstra, 195
Kraft, George, 389, 436
Kraft, Roberta, 436
Kramer, Minnie, 419
Kramer, Wayne and Lucie, 287
Kranendonk, Rev. Paul William, 424
Kremers, Alice, 455
Kremers, Dr. Henry, 14n47, 382n174, 455–57, 459
Kremers, Mrs. E. D., 419
Kroll, Jackie, 386
Kuyers, Mark, 386
Kuyper, Rev. Lester Jacob, 382, 435, 462

Ladies' Aid Society, 33, 77, 104–106, 134, 139, 147, 187–88, 459
Ladies' Missionary Society. *See* Women's Missionary Society
Ladies' Society, 77
Lage, George L., 383
Lakeshore Ethnic Diversity Alliance, 372–73
Laman, Char, 271–72, 389
Laman, Earl, 271–72, 389
Laman, Mark, 385

Lamb, Hermina (Mickie). *See* Van Eyl, Hermina (Mickie) Lamb
Lamb, Elsie, 264–65, 303–7, 317n20, 318, 341, 381, 388, 462–71
Lamb, Lawrence W. (Bill) Jr., 14n47, 229n139, 296–97, 338n75, 382n174, 384, 387, 462
Lammers, Alice, 435
Lampen, Tom, 386
Lang, Alois, 209–12, 242, 460
Langdon, Elvira, 3
Langejans, Calvin, 418
Last Supper woodcarving, 209–10, 234, 242, 295, 300, 460
Latin Americans United for Progress (LAUP), 254, 372
Leaske, Fred, 360, 385, 388, 436
lectionary-based worship, 293, 339, 346
Ledeboer, Allida Goetschuis, 11, 13, 15, 17–18, 392–93
Ledeboer, Dr. Bernardus, 11–15, 17–18, 39–40, 70, 73n84, 387, 392–93, 458
Leenhouts, Dr. Abraham, 153–54, 159, 188, 201, 383, 387
Leenhouts, Elizabeth De Kruif, 165
Leenhouts, Willard G., 158n82, 160–62, 460
Levai, Dr. Blaise, and Mrs., 453
library. *See* Blanche Cathcart Library
Lichty, Elizabeth, 434
Lindeman, Marvin C., 384
liturgical dance. *See* Sacred Dance Group of Holland
liturgical seasons, observing, 286, 347
lodge membership. *See* Free Masons, Order of
Lokker, Clarence John, 201
Lokker, Jacob, 387
Lord's Supper woodcarving. *See* Last Supper woodcarving
Lord's Supper. *See* Communion
Loveless, Barbara, 435
Loveless, James, 435

Lubbers, Irwin J. 158n82, 223, 267n49, 382n175, 384, 387, 434, 437, 460
Lubbers, Margaret (Peggy), 232, 426
Luidens, Donald, 388, 436
Luidens, Peg, 389, 436
Lutheran-Reformed dialogues, 329
Luttikhuizen, Henry, 386
Maassen, Lois, 372, 373n161, 386, 389
Mackay, Malcolm, 384
MacKenzie, Kay, 334, 388, 421
MacLaren, John Dyce, 434
MacLean, Brad, 386
MacLean, Clark, 380
MacLoed, Robert, 384
Macon, Rev. Toni L., 339, 442, 462
Maentz, Henry S., 435
Mahaney, Janice, 275
Maodush-Pitzer, Rev. Diane, 426
Maple Avenue Ministries, 331
Marcus, Anne, 420
Marcus, Keith, 386
Marsh, Dr. C. P., 13
Marsilje, Herbert, 261n36, 388
Marsilje, I. Herbert, 384
Marsilje, June, 229n139
Martin, Jean, 388
Martin, Sam, 386, 389
Martiny, Betsy, 278
Martiny, Walter, 278, 387
Masonic Temple, Holland, 172, 212
Masons. *See* Free Masons, Order of
Mass, Peter, 232
Masselink, Mrs. Henry, 419
Mastenbroek, Judy, 385, 388
Masterton, J., 73
May, John R., 435
mayors of Holland, Hope Church members, 14n47, 382
Mazurek, Doris, 317, 385, 388
McCreary, Rev. George B., 434
McFadden, Jean, 386
McGraw, David, 386
McGraw, Kim, 386, 389
McKay, Malcolm, 419

McKnight, Ian, 284
McKnight, Jim, 284, 386
McLean, Mrs. E. P., 449
McLean, Charles M., 147, 183, 387, 419,
McLean, Charles W., 154
McLean, Ida Sears, 139, 241
McLean, Jean, 188
McLean, Rev. Edwin Paul, 174–75, 423, 434
Medema, David, 385
Meek, David, 230
Megow, Gerhard F., 435
membership decline in RCA, 269–70
memorial garden, 361–62, 364
memorial windows, 174, 234, 239–41, 244–45, 295
Men's Bible Class, 152
Men's Club, 201, 218, 251, 270, 460
Men's Forum, 152
men's prayer breakfasts, 461
Menning, Rev. Vicky, 362
Methodist Episcopal Church, Holland, 9–10, 11n37, 53, 60, 65, 70, 81, 85, 101, 114–15, 133n6, 139, 156, 216, 302n139. *See also* First United Methodist Church, Holland
Metz, Ethelyn, 217
Meyer, Harris, 417, 419
Mezeske, Barbara, 436
Mezeske, Richard, 436
Michigan Classis. *See* Classis of Michigan
Michigan Council of Churches, 273
Michigan Historical Site, Hope Church, 343–45, 462
Michigan Migratory Opportunity, Inc. (MMOI), 263
Middle Dutch Church, New York City, NY, 42–43
migrant workers and their families, ministry to, 187, 251–55, 274, 381
Miller, Conn V., 207, 453

Minderhout, Apollonia De Boe, 396–97
Minderhout, John W., 73, 396–97
Misch, George, 76
Mission Statement, 290–92, 352, 382
mission trips, 282–84, 380
missionaries, 422–29
    453-56Missionary Society, 33, 115
Moerdyke, Rev. Peter, 34, 152, 402–3, 406, 422, 430–31, 433
Mokma, Mary, 386
Moody Movement, 132, 255n25
Moody, Lawrence, 194
Moody, Leon N., 191, 384, 387, 419
moral discernment process regarding homosexuality, 351–52, 364–65, 378
Morse, Clarie, 232
Moser, Frank, 388
Mott Haven Reformed Church, the Bronx, NY, 282
Mr. and Mrs. Club, 218, 270, 461. *See also* Brim Bunch
Muiderman, Elly, 331
Muilenburg, Rev. John P. and Virginia, 205–6, 212–14, 453
Mulder, Anne, 385
Mulder, Cornelius, 435
Mulder, Janet, 343n91
Mulder, Jeannette, 166
Mulder, Jeff, 331n59, 386
Mulder, Jeffrey, 322, 385
Mulder, Jeri, 331n59
Mulder, Karen, 280, 284, 294, 331n59, 363, 388
Mulder, Larry, 284, 307, 331n59, 385, 388
Mulder, Rev. Bruce, 429
Mulder, Rev. Michael L., 428
Mulder, Ronald, 389
Mulder-Sheridan, Kathy, 389
multicultural diversity, 372–74
Multi-Racial Journey Initiative, 373
Munger, Alverton G., architect, 135, 345

Muñoa, Phillip B. III, 436
music from around the world, 327
Muste, Rev. Abraham J., 150–51
Myers, Carol, xvi–xvii, 295, 317–18, 357, 388
Myers, Charles, 384, 388
Myers, David, 290, 308, 313–15, 367n143, 388, 436
Myers, Laura, 351

Nakajima, Rev. Andy, 372
Naoum, Abraham, 309
Nappen, Elder, 3
National Council of Churches, 224, 273, 306
Natural Church Development (NCD), 362
Navis, Audrey, 316, 385, 462
Neckers, Suzanne, 275
needlepoint art works, 332–34
Neighborhood Connections ministry, 373
Nelson, Jean, 386
Nguyen family, 287, 289
Nibbelink, Doug, 386
Nieboer, Dave, 351
Nieuwsma, Marilee, 389
Nieuwsma, Milt, 389
Niles, Rev. Edward, 131, 148–50, 439, 460
Ninth Street Christian Reformed Church, 6n18, 96n30, 113–14, 171–73, 209–10n82
nominations process for election of deacons and elders, Hope Church, 364n133
non-discrimination on basis of sexual identity or orientation, 364, 376–78
Noordeloos, MI, 9n29
Nordstrom, Eileen, 388
Nordstrom, John, 388
North Blendon, MI, Reformed Church, 174

North Holland, MI, Reformed Church, 174
Nykerk, John B., 123, 150, 177, 179, 183, 383, 387, 417, 433

O'Connell, Rev. James J. Jr., 426
Oddfellows Lodge, 59
Oggel, Christina Johanna, 413
Oggel, Rev. Melvin Verne, 423
Oggel, Rev. Pieter J., 46, 406
Oghimi, Motoitero, 22–26, 85–86, 198–99, 309, 422
Okinawa, 306
Old First Church. *See* First Reformed Church, Holland
Old Wing Mission, 2, 247n2
Olgers, Gregory S., 436
Olive, Margaret, 166
Olive, William J., 383
Oosterink, William, 435
Oppenhuizen, Greg, 385
Oppenhuizen, Rachelle, 386, 389
organists, 419
organs, 40, 71, 113, 138–39, 183, 209, 234, 294, 300
Osborn, Barbara, 386
Osborn, Jonathan, 436
Ottawa Beach Hotel, 152
Ottawa County Migrant Health Clinic, 255
Ottawa Reformed Church, Holland, 174
Otte, Dr. John A., 20–21, 183, 199–200
Otte, Frances F. C. Phelps, 20–21, 72, 77, 105n60, 183, 186, 198–99, 423, 432, 452
Otte, Margaret, 183
Overisel, MI, Reformed Church, 174
overture from Grace Community Church to Classis of Holland, 364
overture from Hope Church to Classis of Holland, 376–77
overture from Hope Church to General Synod, 329

Paalman, Hazel, 417, 435
Paarlberg, William, 420
Padnos, Barbara, 286, 357
Padnos, Stuart, 357–58
Page, Mrs. R., 419
Page, Tom, 385
Pardo, Jose, Olga and family, 288
Parents, Families and Friends of Lesbians and Gays (PFLAG), 379
parish hall, 135n11, 209, 295–96
Parish Life Center, 244, 296–98, 302, 341, 462
parish nursing program, 332, 361, 369–71
Park, Jane Den Herder, 262, 265
Parr, Judy, 389
parsonages, 63–64, 147–48, 229–30, 292n113, 458–59, 460, 461
Particular Synod of Chicago, 10n34, 89, 90n10
patriotism, 153–58, 162m, 202, 203n68
Payson, Rev., 3n10
peace pole, 341–42, 462
peacemaking, 303–7
Pearson, Karen Nordell, 436
Pearson, Mark, 436
Pelgrim, Estelle Kollen, 409, 411
Pelgrim, Eva, 188, 192, 194, 226–27, 255, 260
Pelgrim, George A., 384, 387, 419
Pelgrim, Jacob (Jay) Carleton, 409, 411
Pelgrim, Willard George, 201
Pellebon-Smith, Fronse, 310, 350, 385, 388
Pellebon-Smith, Germaine, 436
Persinger, Richard, 385
Personnel Committee, 353–56, 358
Peterman, Rev. Glen O., 267–68, 273–74, 277, 284–85, 289, 404, 440, 461
Petit, Mr., 419
pew rental, 47, 88, 92, 107, 412n4, 115, 132, 459

Pfanstiehl families, 444
Pfanstiehl, Bessie, 77
Pfanstiehl, Peter Frederick, 89–91
Pfanstiehl, Rev. Albert Angus, 91n14, 422
Pfeiffer, Carl, 73, 345
Pham family, 288
Phelps, Edward J. H., 20n71
Phelps, Eliza Tephi, 20, 22, 432
Phelps, Frances Few Chrystie. *See* Otte, Frances F. C. Phelps
Phelps, John, 20n71
Phelps, Margaret Anna Jordan, 6, 11–12, 19, 22–25, 104, 130, 240, 392–93, 406, 430
Phelps, Rev. Philip Jr., xvii, 6–12, 16, 19, 28, 34, 36–37, 39, 40–41, 44–48, 51, 61, 63, 73n84, 74, 91, 93–96, 108–11, 127–30, 240, 300, 344n92, 382, 391, 404, 406, 419, 430, 433, 437, 438, 458
Phelps, Rev. Philip III (Tertius), 20–21, 24, 72, 422
Phelps, Theodore Seth, 20, 22
Piers, James, 389, 436
Piet, David, 424, 454
Piet, Rev. John H., 260, 325–26, 388, 436
Piet, Nancy, 424, 454
Pietenpol, W. B., 434
Pieters, Rev. Roelof, 11n37, 94
Pillar Church. *See* First Reformed Church, Holland
Pioneer School, Holland, 35, 344n92
pledging, funding the church by, 8, 39, 60, 77, 88, 106, 115, 132, 141, 183–84, 459
Plewes, Jack, 387
Plewes, John D., 229n139
Poling, Rev. Clark V., 182n15
Poling, Rev. Daniel A., 182
Polkton, MI, 9n29
Poppen, Rev. and Mrs. Alvin J., 454
Port Sheldon Presbyterian Church, West Olive, MI, 323, 325
Port Sheldon, MI, 4

Post, Anna Coatsworth, 3–4, 11, 31–35, 118n89, 130, 392–93
Post, Charles Francis, 11, 35–36, 387, 392–93
Post, Charlotte D. Taylor, 35, 396–97
Post, Henry Denison, 3, 11, 29–35, 73, 101n48, 392–93
Post, Hoyt, 32, 35, 383
Post, Kate Garrod, 35n134, 36, 147, 165
Pott, Terrance, 385, 436
Potter, Edmund P., 417
Powell, David O., 435
pranks, 76, 302n139
prayer chain, 347
Presbyterian Church in the United States, 182
Presbyterian Church of the United States. *See* Southern Presbyterian Church
Presbyterians, uniting with considered, 83, 182, 221–22
presidents of General Synod, Hope Church as church home to, 382
presidents of Hope College, Hope Church as church home to, 382
Price, William E., 385
Price, Amanda, 386
processional cross, 340–41
Progress Council denominational financial campaign, 186
Prohibition, 101n48, 163
Protheroe, Jean, 261n36, 265, 435
public address system, 224

radio broadcast of worship services, 225, 312–13, 461
radio, 201, 312
raising money. *See* apportionments, collections, pew rental, and pledging
Ralph, George, 285, 290, 385, 436
Ralph, Leola, 285
Ramirez, Melissa Ann Klomparens, 415
Ransford, Rev. Paul, 424

Raymond, Bruce M., 384, 434
Raymond, Lynn, 386
RCA Women's Triennials, 318
Reagan, Theresa, 386
Rebhan, Wendy, 420
recipes:
    Balkanbrij, 451
    Calf's Foot Jelly, 445
    Candied Tongue, 449
    Coffee, 449–50
    Doughnuts, 449
    Dutch Soup, 444
    Hutspot, 451
    Jugged Chicken, 450
    Krakaling, 451
    Little Pigs in Blankets, 448
    Noodle Soup, 447
    Omelet, 448
    Roast Goose, 450
    Scripture Cake, 452
Recycling task force, 280n81
Reeverts, Emma, 251
Reformed Protestant Dutch Church in North America, 1–2, 8, 27, 42, 45, 62–63, 300, 458
refugee families, assisting, 287
Reid, Paul E., 435
Reimer, Ted, 386
Reimold, Julia (Lu) Christina Van Raalte, 410, 413
Reimold, Orlando Jr. (Andy), 410, 414
Reimold, Philip Benjamin, 414
Renabai, Merci, 335
Renewing Hope Building Fund, 348
Resthaven Care Community, 206–207, 312
Restorative Circles, 369, 371
revivals, 48–51, 132–33, 255n25, 459
Reyes, Tino and Lupita Cantu, 254
Rhea, Joseph, 383
Rhoades, Mark, 386
Rhythmic Choir, 461. *See also* Sacred Dance Group of Holland
Rich, Mary, 230
Rich, Perma, 435

Richardson, Barrie, 385
Ridder, Rev. Herman J., 267n49, 276
Ridenour, Charles, 233
Ridenour, Debra, 233
Riemersma, John J., 158–59n82, 179n8, 207, 216, 223, 383, 387, 419
Riemersma, Madeline, 216
Rienstra, Rev. Marchiene, 185n27, 323–27, 335–39, 347, 441, 462
Rienstra, Rev. Ron, 427
Rizner, Ellen, 420
Rizner, Gary, 351, 386, 388
Robards, Danita, parish nurse, 371
Robbert, Louis (Bud), 384, 388
Robbins, Martha, 419
Robins, Daina, 436
Robinson, W. G., 73
Rock, Nancy, 287, 350–51, 385, 388
Rock, Rev. Stanley, 296
Rodriguez, Happy, 355
Roe, John, 386
Rogers, Lida, 460
Rogers, Rev. Samuel J., 46
Room for All Affirmation, signed by Hope Church, 379, 381
Room for All, 367, 378–79, 463
Roorda, Andrea, 249, 420
Roorda, Ervin, 249
Roosevelt, President Theodore, 145, 155
Roost, John, 74
rooster weathervane, 299
Rosenau, Kevin, 386
Ross, Metta J., 434
Rottenberg, Rev. John and Mrs. Gloria, 454
Rottschaefer, Bernice Takken, 423
Rottschaefer, Diane, 230
Rottschaefer, Margaret, 453
Rottschaefer, Susan, 233
Rozeboom, Rev. Roger W., 424
Rumpsa, Claire, 386
Russell, Rev. Jill R., 368–71, 373n161, 443, 463

Sabbath observance, 90, 102, 125–26, 169, 184, 274–75n69
Sabbath School. *See* Sunday School
Sacred Dance Group of Holland, 264–67, 461
Sakkers, Johanna Voorlagen, 394–95
Sakkers, Peter, 383, 394–95
salary to pastor:
   Bergen, 117
   Davidson, 177–78, 184–85, 187–90
   de Velder, 191
   Hillegonds, 248–49
   Van Pelt, 88
Sall, Andrew G., 384
Sanford, William, 384
Santamaria, Richard, Mary and family, 288, 385
Saugatuck, MI, 4
Schaddelee, K., 73n84
Schellenberger, Kenneth C., 229, 418
Schmidt, John, 388
Schmidt, Rebecca, 436
Schmidt, Rev. John E., 425
School for Christian Living, 193, 217, 228, 261–62, 460
Schout, David, 418–19
Schouten, John (Jack) H. L. 434
Schouten, Bess, 262
Schouten, F. J., 383
Schregardus, Darell, 388
Schrier, William, 435
Schroeder, Rev. Carl J. and Mrs., 453
Schuelke, Rev. Paul F., 434
Schutter, Rev. William, 328–29, 388
Schuyler, Jane, 389
Scott, James O., 383
Scott, Maria R. Stelle, 103
Scott, Matthew Scott, 383
Scott, Rev. Charles, 28, 36, 61, 70, 73–74, 85, 89, 108, 382, 419, 433, 437, 459
Scudder, John, 84
Scudder, Nancy, 424, 454
Scudder, Rev. Lewis Jr., 424, 454
seal of Hope Church, 47

Seaman, Bill, 388
Seaman, Joyce, 338n75, 389
Season of Reconciliation, 371
secretaries, church, 421
Seder services, 286, 357
Seibert Jr., Arthur, 385
Selover, Carl, 384
Selover, Prudence, 418
Sennett, Fritzi, 319
separation of church and state, 157
service flag. *See* World War I
Sewing Society, 40
sexual orientation, prohibiting discrimination on basis of, 307–308
Shaw Goodrich, Shirley, 195
Sherburne, Frank, 261n36, 302, 350, 387, 435
Shields, William A., 59, 383, 400–1, 406, 430, 431, 433
Shindler, Simon, 63
Sigal, Rabbi Phillip, 324
Sikkink, Ben, 343, 385, 389
Singapore, MI, 4, 31
Singleton, Mildred, 435
Sipp, Elizabeth Welcher, 11, 37, 394–95
Sipp, James, 37, 383, 394–95, 406
Sipp, Jane Elizabeth, 402–403
Sixth Reformed Church, Holland, 174
Slaghuis, Gertrude, 194
Smit, Marcia, 385
Smith, Alfred, 385
Smith, Chester, 388
Smith, Jan, 389
Smith, Loretta, 386, 389, 420
Smith, Rev. Paul, 368, 388
Smith, Rev. C. C., 133, 255n25, 459
Smith, Rev. George N. and Arvilla, 2n6, 247n2
Smith, Richard, 388, 436
smoking, 161, 185
Sneller, Ann, 389
Sneller, Mark, 386, 389
Snow, Bob, 189n39, 192–93, 386

Snow, Esther, 188, 194, 196, 417, 419, 434
Snow, Janet, 189n39
Snow, Jean, 189n39
Snow, Lotus, 435
Snow, Murray, 189n39, 194
Snow, W. Curtis, 184, 417, 188–89, 419, 434
Snyder, Jeff, 386
social evils opposed, 125–27, 274–75n69
Souter, George H., 127, 383
South Blendon, MI, Reformed Church, 174
South Holland, MI, Presbyterian Church, 18n64
Southern Normal (Teachers') School, 207, 310, 453
Southern Presbyterian Church, 83, 270
Sprick, Norma, 421
Spring Lake (Mill Point), MI, 4
St. Francis de Sales Catholic Church, Holland, 156, 270, 273, 324, 330, 373
St. Nicholas Day celebration, 331
Staal, Rev. Ruth Zwald, 336–37, 346, 351, 353–55, 427, 442, 463
Stall, Timothy, 385
Stapert, Rev. John, 367
Steeby, Cory, 386
Steele, Harlan, 202n66
Steele, William Henry, 84
steeple, 191, 299
Steffens, Rev. Cornelius M., 423
Steffens, Rev. Nicholas M., 94–96
Stegeman, Rev. William, 423
Steininger, George, 384
Steininger, Janet, 232
Steininger, Ruth, 385
Steketee, Charles, 289n104, 387, 435
Stempfly, Louis J. Jr., 388
Stempfly, Joyce, 385
Stewart, Eliza Jane, 402–3, 406
Stewart, Jonathan B., 63, 400–1

Stewart, Rev. Abel T., 36, 47, 49, 51–54, 56–57, 61, 63, 69–71, 73n84, 74, 76, 82–86, 111, 130, 391, 402–3, 406, 438, 458
Stewart, Sonja, 306
Stryker, Elsie B., 215, 217, 226, 420, 461
Stryker, Marian Anderson, 435
Stryker, Nancy, 386
Stryker, Tom, 386
student church, Hope College, 260n54, 269, 274
student interns, 293
subscription. *See* pledging
suicide prevention, 277, 279
Summit on Racism, 373
Sunday observance. *See* Sabbath observance.
Sunday School orchestra, 151
Sunday School picnic, 82, 115
Sunday School superintendents, 183, 419
Sunday School teacher training, 228
Sunday School, 3, 5, 39, 43, 60–61, 69, 107, 115–16, 134, 180–81, 209, 215, 217, 224, 251, 257, 270
Sutphen, James, 433
Sutton, Viola L., 207, 453
Swart, Caleb and Joanna, 454
Swartz, Alicia, 233
Swartz, Leonard, 384, 387
Swartz, Suzanne, 232
Sychowski, Barbara, parish nurse, 361
Sytsma, Louis, 454
Sytsma, Marilyn, 386, 454

t-coil. *See* hearing loop technology.
Taize Community music, 327, 346
Tallis, James H., 418, 419
Tallis, Joan, 418
Talmadge, Reverend Goyn, 47
Talmage, John Van Nest, 84
Talmage, Millie, 187
Tanis, Philip A., 14n47, 382n174, 436, 463

Tappan, Mary, 188
Tappan, William, 384, 387
Tarrytown First Reformed Church, NY, 47, 51–53
task forces ministries, 276–77
Taylor, Marjorie, parish nurse, 361, 370
Taylor, Walter T., 35
Taylor-Perry, Rev. Angela, 372
TeBeest, Rev. Dennis L., 306, 323, 326, 331, 336–37, 339, 346–47, 350, 353–55, 442, 462–71
Te Winkle, Rev. John William, 383, 396–97, 406, 422, 430, 431
Telecare daily phone calls to elderly persons, 278
television broadcasting, closed-circuit, 224
Tellman, Mary, 262, 436
Temperance movement, 100–3, 274–75n69
Ten Cate, Lois, 260
Ten Cate, Vernon, 188, 191–92, 384, 434
Ten Haken, Kathleen, 436
Tenebrae services, 346
Tenth Street house, 362
Ter Molen, Edna Hollander, 418
Ter Molen, Larry, 384
Teusink, Joyce, 386
Theological Department of Hope College, 27, 63, 70, 95n25, 110. *See also* Western Theological Seminary
Think Hope silent auctions, 283
Third Reformed Church, Holland, 11n37, 59–60, 65, 70, 81, 94, 99, 156, 173, 183, 206, 216, 263, 271, 330–31, 358, 373
Thomas, Herbert, 384
Thomas, Jean, 230
Thompson, Florence, 421
Thompson, Rev. Abraham, 87
Thompson, Robert, 418
Thoms, May De Pree, 423
Thornhill, Connie, 361

Thornhill, Harold, 384, 387
Thornhill, Thomas, 233
Thurber, Louise Martin, 149
Tiananmen Square student protests of 1989, 335–36
Tillema, John, 434
Timmer, Albert H., 434
Timmer, Blaine, 384
Timmer, John Norman, 385, 388, 436
transitional home for families, 362
Trask, Richard, 385
Trinity Reformed Church, Holland, 173
True Dutch Reformed Church, Holland 9n29, 80, 98, 173
Trueblood, C. R., 384
Tsugawa, Rio Zon, 24, 26, 309
Tulip Time Festival, 460
tutoring, 277, 280
Tysse, John, 385, 388, 436
Tysse, Pat, 385

Unger, James, 435
United Church Women. *See* Church Women United, Holland
United Presbyterian Church of North America, 221–22, 325
Utterwick, Rev. Henry, 11n37, 59, 74, 94
Utzinger, John, 435

Vacation Bible School, 205, 216, 252, 255, 332, 461
Van Andel, Rev. Mary T., 343, 351, 425, 442, 463
Van Bronkhorst, Rev. Steven and Mrs. Susan, 454
Van Cleef, Rev. Paul D., 85
Van Dam, Ed, 389
Van Dokkumburg, Mark, 233
Van Domelen, Louise, 435
Van Domelen, Peter Jr., 211n85, 216, 384, 387
Van Domelen, Peter, 383
Van Dyk, Leanne, 321, 389
Van Dyke, Bill, xvin2, 385

Van Dyke, Lillian, 251
Van Eck, Rev. Arthur (Bud), 356, 442, 463
Van Eenenaam, Isla, 351, 388, 435
Van Es, Jane Vander Haar, 428, 454
Van Es, Rowland, 428, 454
Van Eyl, Hermina (Mickie) Lamb, 285, 316, 322, 388, 462
Van Eyl, Phillip, 335, 388, 435
Van Haitsma, Eleanor DePree, 246
Van Haitsma, Titus, 387
Van Heest, David, 350–51, 353, 361–62, 364, 367, 378, 386, 436
Van Heest, Eloise, 316n20, 318–20, 336–37, 339, 388, 420–21
Van Heest, Jocelyn, 322, 327, 386, 419–20
Van Heest, Rev. Gerard, 319, 436
Van Hinte, Jacob, xviii, 170–72
Van Hoeven, Rev. James, 299–300
Van Houte, Rev. Jacob, 92
Van Landegend, George, 383
Van Lente, Carol, 262
Van Lente, James, 384, 388
Van Lente, Michael, 385
Van Leuwen, Bruce, 194, 384, 387
Van Olinda, Marietta Shuler, 28, 102–4, 105n60, 394–95, 433
Van Otterloo, Evelyn Kramer, 195
Van Pelt, Gertrude F. Scott, 88
Van Pelt, Peter, 338n75
Van Pelt, Piet, 385
Van Pelt, Rev. Daniel, 87–89, 91–93, 97–102, 130, 439, 459
Van Putten, Carol, 226–27, 262
Van Putten, Christina (Chris) Van Raalte, 411, 413
Van Putten, Jacob G., 14n47, 382n174, 459
Van Putten, James Dyke, 219, 435
Van Raalte Hall, Hope College, 72n82, 296
Van Raalte memorial plaque, 172
Van Raalte, Adeline (Addie) Huntley, 410
Van Raalte, Albertus (Allie), 409, 410, 413, 423
Van Raalte, Albertus Christiaan (1811–76). See Van Raalte, Rev. Albertus Christiaan
Van Raalte, Albertus Christiaan (1889–1944), 411, 413
Van Raalte, Benjamin, 409–10, 412
Van Raalte, Christina (Tia) Pfanstiehl, 411
Van Raalte, Christina Johanna De Moen, 18, 409
Van Raalte, Christine Cornelis, 165
Van Raalte, Derk (Dick) B. K. Jr., 414
Van Raalte, Dirk (Dick) Blikman Kikkert Jr., 413
Van Raalte, Dirk Blikman Kikkert (D. B. K.), 16, 127, 383, 387, 409, 412
Van Raalte, Edna Pillsbury, 409, 410
Van Raalte, Gail, 230
Van Raalte, Henry Charles (Carl), 414
Van Raalte, Julia Gilmore, 105n60
Van Raalte, Katharine Goetschuis Ledeboer, 16, 165, 400–1, 410, 412n5, 419
Van Raalte, Maria (Mary) Wilhelmina, 409, 412
Van Raalte, Rev. Albertus Christiaan, xvii, 1–4, 6, 8, 10, 12, 17–18, 27, 29–30, 32, 34, 50–51, 54–56, 58, 73n84, 94, 101n48, 300, 404–405, 409, 458
Van Raalte, Wilhelmina (Minnie), 410, 413
Van Raalte's Church. *See* First Reformed Church, Holland
Van Riper, Joan, 227, 229n139, 420
Van Schaak, Eva, 343n91, 435
Van Schelven, Gerrit, 58n50, 73n84, 93, 165, 170, 383
Van Schelven, Priscilla, 105n60, 448
Van Soest, Bert, 202, 205
Van Verst, George W., 384
Van Verst, Miss, 417

INDEX

Van Vleck Hall, Hope College, 7, 8n28, 20, 22–23, 80, 95n25, 108, 110, 129, 198
Van Vleck, Rev. John, 5–6, 108, 344n92
Van Vyven, Margaret, 418
Van Westenberg, Christine Cornelia Van Raalte, 414
Van Wyck, Rev. A. J., 9
Van Zanten, Rev. Jacob J., 423
Van Zanten, Robert, 384
Van Zetten, Sarah, 418
Van Zoeren, Albert, 190, 384
Van Zoeren, Gerrit, 228n136, 384
Van Zoeren, Irene, 451
Van Zwaluwenburg, James G., 434
Vande Vusse, Barbara, 421
Vande Wall, Rev. Giles, 6–9
Vande Water, Terry, 436
Vande Water, Nancy, 389
Vanden Berg, Jean Wishmeir, 195
Vanden Berg, Rev. Richard, 387
Vanden Bos, Lura, 262
Vanden Brink, Everett, 252–53
Vander Broek, Anna Christine, 416
Vander Broek, Charles Donn, 207, 386, 389, 416
Vander Broek, Charles William, 416
Vander Broek, Gertrude Christine Keppel, 298, 414, 462
Vander Broek, Gertrude: memorial windows 244–45
Vander Broek, Jack [1943–], 385, 415
Vander Broek, John (Jack) Keppel [1922–2008], 244, 298, 384, 387, 387, 415
Vander Broek, Philip John, 416
Vander Broek, Richard George, 416
Vander Haar, Rev. Delbert, 347, 442, 463
Vander Haar, Trudy, 318–19, 347, 389
Vander Heuvel, Claudia, 231
Vander Heuvel, Heidi, 233
Vander Lugt, William, 387, 435
Vander Meulen, Cornelius, 455
Vander Meulen, John H., 236
Vander Meulen, John, 256
Vander Meulen, Rev. Cornelius, 300, 455n1
Van der Meulen, Rev. John M., 119n90, 131, 133, 145–48, 152, 171–72, 434, 437, 439, 460
Vander Veen, Francis M., 434
Vander Velde, Margaret, 194
Vander Velde, Dr. Otto, 384, 387
Vander Werf, Calvin A., 382n175, 435, 437, 461
Vander Wilt, Judy, 280, 287, 436
Vander Wilt, Rev. Marlin, 281, 285–86, 289–90, 292–94, 298–99, 302–303, 323, 346, 378, 440, 462
Vander Woude, AnnaMae, 389
Vander Woude, Jim, 386
Vanderbilt Charter Academy, 280
Vanderbush, Alvin W., 435
Vanderham, Diane, 230
Vanderham, Marian, 332
Vanderham, Robert, 384, 387, 435
Veenhuizen, Rev. Albertus Bernardus, 406–407
Veghte, Henry, 433
Veldheer DeYoung, Rev. Cindi, 318n21, 389, 428
Veneklasen Brick Company, 135, 345
Veneklasen bricks, 296
Vennema, Rev. Ame, 382, 434, 437, 460
Ventura, MI, 10, 82–83, 89
Ver Hulst, Anthony, 423
Ver Hulst, Irene Brusse, 434
Verburg, Rev. James, 423
Veurink, Barbara Borr, 287, 355, 363, 418, 419, 421
Vietnam War, 287
Visscher, Anne G., 434
Visscher, Arthur, 383, 387
Visscher, Geesje Vander Haar, 93, 96–97
Visscher, Helene Gertrude Keppel, 195, 414
Visscher, Robert, 14n47, 382n174, 461

Visscher, William, 96n32
Visser, John E., 435
Vissers, Carla, 436
Vleeschal of Haarlem, the Netherlands, 135–136
Vohlken, Kyle, 373n161, 386
Voogd, Helen, 421
Vos, Mrs., church collector, 141
Vos, Rev. David, 425
Vriesland, MI, 4n13, 174, 300

Wade, Lawrence, 384, 387
Wagenaar, Larry, xv
Walchenbach, Rev. John R., 258–59, 267–68, 440, 461
Wall, Joan DeJonge, 370, 385, 421
War on Afghanistan, 343
Ward, Brian, 384
Ward, Dr. James, 332–33, 384, 387
Ward, Mildred, 194
Wars on Iraq, 342–43
Water Missions International, 283
Waters, MaryJo, 389
Wayer, Rev. James E., 220–21, 223, 247, 249, 434
WCTU. *See* Woman's Christian Temperance Union
Week of Prayer, 132
Welch, Russell H., 384, 387
Wenke, Lee H., 436
Werkman, Barry L., 436
Wesleyan Church, Holland, 65 *See also* Central Wesleyan Church
Wesleyan Church, Ventura, 89
West Church House, 147n53, 229n137
West End Collegiate Church, New York City, NY, 135–36
West Michigan Migrant Authority, 254
Western Theological Seminary, 27, 63, 95n25. *See also* Theological Department, Hope College
Westra, Eugene, 418
Westrate, Jack, 385

Westrate, Millard C., 384
Weymon, Ella, 385
Wheeler, Charles C., 383
White, James, 233
White, Pamela, 230
White, Phyllis Pelgrim, 195, 229n139
Whitenack, Erastus A., 433
Whitenack, Sarah Gertrude Alcott, 432
WHTC radio station, 225, 312–13
Wick, Gertrude, 194
Wick, Martin, 386, 389
Wiers, Christopher, 373–74
Wiersma, Anne Heath, 436
Wiersma, Bethany, 380
Wiersma, Rev. Gordon S., 358–61, 364, 369, 373n161, 443, 463
Wiley, James, 385
Wilkinson, Martha, 232
Wilkinson, Raymond, 384
Williams, Bette, 389
Williams, Cecil, 349, 354–56, 388
Williams, Sister Joan Mary, 324
Wilms, Peter H., 383
Wilson, President Woodrow, 155
Wimmer, Charles R., 435
Winchester, Paul, 229n139, 384, 387
windows in the church, 174. *See also* memorial windows
Wing, Helen, 166
Wing, William, 383, 387
Winter, Alice Kools, 165
Winter, Amelia, 165
Winter, Egbert, 434
Winter, Helena Anne Visscher, 332, 415, 416
Winter, Henry, 190, 383, 387
Winter, John G., 434
Winter, Lynn Anne, 416
Winter, Paul Arthur, 416
Winter, William G., 384, 387
Winter, William Garrett III, 416
Wise, Melodie, 230
Witkowski, Kris, 386
Witty, Cathy, 230

Woman's Christian Temperance Union (WCTU), 33, 101–2, 106, 163, 167
women and men: vote to call pastor and elect deacons and elders, 87, 96n30, 103, 164, 309–10, 459
women, consideration of their holding offices of deacon and elder, 164–65, 222–23, 270, 275–76, 309, 315
women, support for their ministry of Word and Sacrament, 323
Women's Aid Society, 200–2, 218–19, 236. *See also* Ladies' Aid Society
Women's Board of Domestic Missions, 168
Women's Board of Foreign Missions, 104–5, 115
Women's Club, 219, 236
Women's Foreign Missionary Society of Holland, 104
Women's Guild for Christian Service. *See* Guild for Christian Service
Women's Missionary Society, 105–106, 115, 134, 186, 236, 252, 459
Women's Missionary Union, Holland Classis 168, 179n12
Women's Suffrage Movement, 163–67
Wood, C. C., 217
Wood, Helen, 181, 217
woodcarving. *See* Last Supper woodcarving
Woodson, Jethro J., 207, 453
Working, Thomas, 230
Workman, John, 385, 388
World Council of Churches, 273, 305
World War I, 153–63
World War II, 196–201
Wright, Rev. Barbara, 428
Wright, Rev. Frank Hall, 142–43
Wyckoff, Rev. Isaac N., 3, 45, 300
Wyma, Mr. and Mrs. David, 454
Wyman, Scott, 230

Yamaoka, Alan, 310, 385
Yates, Amy, 419
Yates, Oscar, 14n47, 121, 382n174, 383, 459
year of discernment. *See* moral discernment process regarding homosexuality
Yeomans, Edward J., 194, 226–27, 384, 387
Yeomans, Frances, 192
Yeomans, Jack, 195
YMCA. *See* Young Men's Christian Association
Yntema, Clara E., 434
Yntema, Cynthia, 287
Yntema, Dwight B., 287, 434
Yntema, Gordon Douglas, 287
Yonker, Carol, 421
Yost, Brian, 386, 436
Young Ladies' Aid Society, 134, 138–40, 459
Young Men's Christian Association, 118, 121
young people's meeting, 114–16, 134
Young, Martha Harriet Broadmore, 36
Youth Council, 285
youth director, first, 226
youth groups, 281–82
Yurk, Brian, 436

Zeek, Carolyn, 388
Zeeland Classis. *See* Classis of Zeeland
Zeeland, MI, 4n13, 146, 300
Zeeland, MI, First and Second Reformed Churches, 174, 271
Zell, Rev. Beverly, 373n161
Zimmer, Rev. Mark, 308
Zook, Ephraim J., 434
Zuverink, Kenneth, 385